HELL IN THE TRENCHES

Austro-Hungarian Stormtroopers and Italian *Arditi* in the Great War

Paolo Morisi

Helion & Company

Helion & Company Limited
Unit 8 Amherst Business Centre
Budbrooke Road
Warwick
CV34 5WE
England
Tel. 01926 499 619
Fax 0121 711 4075
Email: info@helion.co.uk
Website: www.helion.co.uk
Twitter: @helionbooks
Visit our blog http://blog.helion.co.uk/

Published by Helion & Company 2018
Designed and typeset by Mach 3 Solutions Ltd (www.mach3solutions.co.uk)
Cover designed by Paul Hewitt, Battlefield Design (www.battlefield-design.co.uk)
Printed by Hobbs the Printers, Totton, Hampshire

ISBN 978-1-912174-98-0

British Library Cataloguing-in-Publication Data.
A catalogue record for this book is available from the British Library.

For details of other military history titles published by Helion & Company Limited contact the above address, or visit our website: http://www.helion.co.uk.

We always welcome receiving book proposals from prospective authors.

Contents

Introduction

During the first two years of the First World War the Italian Army fought a war of attrition against the Austro-Hungarians which was made even harsher by the cold climate of the Alps. In addition, its leadership lacked initiative and a clear strategy to win the war.

The eleven Italian massive offensive operations in the Isonzo sector (the so-called Battles of the Isonzo River) proved extremely costly, mainly because they lacked the vital element of surprise. The Italian doctrine of mass frontal infantry attacks in successive waves was both extremely outdated and costly in a war of positional warfare. Nevertheless, it was the only strategy that was tried again and again to break the Austro-Hungarians. The rather lengthy preparatory barrage showed where the infantry was planning to attack, often giving advance warning to the Austro-Hungarians who could shift reserves and equipment to parry the blow. In addition, two other factors inherent with this doctrine contributed to the failure of these offensive operations. First, the Italian artillery was often ineffective due to a lack of large field guns which were necessary in taking down enemy defenses, and once its infantry charged the enemy lines its offensive impetus was stymied by fully functioning barbwire works, blockhouses and machine gun nests. Second, the Italian Army lacked specialized assault troops that were capable of carrying out rapid and overpowering attacks against enemy trenches. In most cases the preparatory artillery fire would pre-warn the enemy of the impeding attack and once the successive waves of densely packed, slow-moving Italian infantry units reached the enemy barbed wire they would be mowed down mercilessly by the machine guns.

The Italians basically adopted the breakthrough tactics of the Western Front whereby with the concentration of artillery fire and infantry against one sector of the enemy's defenses the army would attempt to make a major frontline breach. In most cases however, the Austro-Hungarians would pull back, reorganize their defenses to the rear of the frontline defenses and seal the infantry advance.

In contrast, beginning in 1917, the Austro-Hungarian troops were able to complete a number of surprise attacks and counter-attacks by using new German-inspired infiltration tactics and weapons, which in many cases yielded important results. These actions were often conducted by specialized assault patrols and battalions (*sturmtruppen*) which through daring and unexpected maneuvers would surprise and overwhelm the Italian defensive lines and penetrate deeply into their positions. These swift counter-attacks, preceeded by equally swift, pinpoint barrages, would often take back in one day the positions and territory that the Italian infantry had conquered through massive artillery and infantry deployments and at a great cost. The *sturmtruppen* tactics were based on a brief but very intense pinpoint artillery barrage, which forced the enemy to seek cover within their trenches and tunnels. These highly trained units would then advance under the cover of the artillery barrage in order to reach the first-line enemy trench. As the artillery lengthened its fire, the *sturmtruppen*, armed with hand grenades, knives, flamethrowers and light machine guns, would penetrate the enemy trench and begin neutralizing its major centers of resistance such as the machine gun nests. They would often throw hundreds of hand grenades, which were carried in large bags worn over the shoulders, often fooling the enemy infantry into believing that the artillery barrage was still in progress.

Their attacks relied heavily on the element of surprise, on flawless execution and detailed planning. The objectives were determined ahead of time through extensive surveys of enemy lines, often through the key contribution of aerial surveillance. Every assault patrol was assigned a specific task and each unit coordinated its assault with the other patrols. The *sturmtruppen* operations were so meticulously planned and so well orchestrated with artillery fire that they often succeeded in overcoming the resistance of the Italian infantry units thus allowing the Austro-Hungarians to retake possession of heavily contested positions.

The observation by Italian intelligence officers of the deeds of the *sturmtruppen* together with information on their weapons and training gleaned from interrogations of Austrian prisoners of war allowed the Italian *Comando Supremo* to take into consideration the impact of these stormtroops on the course of the war. Specifically, the Italian High Command remarked on the high degree of integration that had been achieved between artillery and infantry assault enemy units during raids and attacks. In addition, how the combination of innovative use of artillery batteries (rolling and creeping barrages) in conjunction with swift counter-attacks by specialized infantry detachments allowed the Austro-Hungarians to prevail in several major battles beginning in the spring of 1917.

As a result of these enemy tactics and by following the example of the Austro-Hungarian stormtroopers, the Italian High Command would initiate a profound reform of infantry tactics by creating new special assault units (*arditi*) and reorganizing its artillery which would in turn play a vital role in the final outcome of the war.

Thus the purpose of this book is to analyze the evolution of offensive infantry tactics on the Italian Front by focusing upon both the Austro-Hungarian *sturmtruppen* and the special Italian assault unit, the *arditi*. At the onset of the war both the Austro-Hungarian and the Italian Army were unprepared for a continental, long-term war of attrition. As the war progressed and despite several defeats, both armies improved their combat performance by increasing their ability to conduct successful offensive operations, mainly by altering tactics and by increasing artillery and infantry firepower. This book will analyze their military evolution and the changes made to improve battlefield capabilities in the changed environment of trench warfare.

The first chapter will deal with the German *sturmtruppen* on the Western Front since both Austro-Hungarian and Italian special assault units of the First World War took inspiration from the German example. The second chapter will focus upon the origins and evolution of the Austro-Hungarian *sturmtruppen*, while the third chapter will focus upon the capabilities of the Italian Army in 1915. The fourth chapter will detail the *sturmtruppen*'s most important battles during 1917–18. The fifth chapter will focus on the evolution of the Italian *arditi*, while the sixth chapter will center on their major battles. The final chapter will focus upon the major differences between the *arditi* and the *sturmtruppen* as well as providing an overall assessment of their role on the Italian Front.

The evolution and impact of these special assault units will be analyzed specifically from the perspective of the concept of tactical effectiveness.

According to Allen Millett and Williamson Murray one of the main features of military effectiveness is tactical effectiveness. It is defined as:

> The tactical level of military activity refers to the specific techniques used by combat units to fight engagements in order to secure operational objectives. Tactical activity involves the movement of forces on the battlefield against the enemy, the provision of destructive fire upon the enemy forces and targets, and the arrangement of logistical support directly applicable to engagements.[1]

The key components of tactical effectiveness include several factors such as:

1. The army's approach to training,
2. Troop morale,
3. Unit cohesion (especially relations between officers and ordinary soldiers),
4. The supply of proper weapons for offensive operations,
5. The consistency in the application of battle tactics,
6. A high degree of combined arms integration,
7. The degree to which tactical solutions favor the swift, unexpected and over-powering use of offensive force.

The Finnish Army of the Second World War is held up by Millett and Murray has one of the most prominent examples of a very tactically effective instrument of war. During the interwar period Finnish officers dissiminated the German ideas and tactics of the First World War to the bulk of the Finnish Army. Thanks in large part to the stormtrooper tactics of the German infantry, the Finnish infantry was able to take on a much more powerful Russian Army during the Winter War of 1939–40 by using small platoons of machine gunners and riflemen on skis to ambush enemy positions and to slowly degrade their capability to fight.[2]

Against great odds, the Finnish Army stopped a major Russian/Soviet offensive in its tracks and forced the Soviet government to the negotiating table.

1 Allen Millett and Williamson Murray (eds.) *Military Effectiveness Volume I First World War* (Boston: Unwin Hyman Inc., 1988), p. 19.

2 Pasi Tuunainen, *Finnish Military Effectiveness in the Winter War, 1939–1940* (London: Palgrave Macmillan UK, 2016).

Deep mountain trench in the Italian-Austrian front. (Ufficio Storico – official archive, Italian military, Rome)

Ettore Viola, commander of the VI *Reparto d'assalto*. A gold medal awardee for the raid against Austro-Hungarian positions near Mount Grappa in 1918. (Ufficio Storico – official archive, Italian military, Rome)

Badge of the *Reparto d'assalto* (assault battalion) with the dagger and oak leaves. (Ufficio Storico – official archive, Italian military, Rome)

Ardito badge. FERT was the motto of the House of Savoy derived from the latin Fortitudo Eius Rhodum Tenuit. (Ufficio Storico – official archive, Italian military, Rome)

Green Flames *Alpini/Arditi* unit with Stokes mortar. Note the *alpino* cap and badge. The Stokes mortar could fire as many as 22 bombs per minute and had a maximum range of 1,200 yards. (Ufficio Storico – official archive, Italian military, Rome)

Alpini ski patrol unit in the Adamello sector 1916. (Ufficio Storico – official archive, Italian military, Rome)

Alpini at outdoor mass in a high mountain position in the Dolomites 1916. (Ufficio Storico – official archive, Italian military, Rome)

Alpini arditi officers. (Ufficio Storico – official archive, Italian military, Rome)

The First World War's most important characteristic versus prior conflicts was positional warfare which is defined as a "form of warfare in which the mobility of a force is severely restricted in and around positions that are in the immediate proximity of an opposing force."[3]

In a context of entrenched positional warfare it was very difficult for any of the contenders to achieve a significant breakthrough of the enemy lines in order to win the war. Positional warfare, which was so unlike prior conflicts such as the Napoleonic Wars, was determined by three main factors. First, the introduction of heavy weaponry such as precision artillery guns, mortars, and machine guns which when deployed at or near the front line could not be totally eradicated by the attackers' preparatory shelling. Thus, when the attacking infantry attempted to breach the front line, it was systematically shot to pieces by these lethal weapons. This vastly increased firepower, which was the product of the industrial age, gave the defenders an unprecedented advantage favoring a war of position over one of movement. Second, the concentration of entrenched positions consisting of concrete bunkers, pillboxes, and barbed wire works further reduced the ability of the assaulting infantry to penetrate enemy positions by further exposing it to the deadly fire of the defenders. Third, troops could be also be moved more quickly than in the past to shore up threatened defensive positions with the development of modern trains and lorries thus further bolstering the capabilities of the defenders. Thus, the opening battles of the First World War on the Western Front, mainly because of the above factors, yielded poor

3 William R. Griffiths (ed.), *The Great War: Strategy and Tactics of the First World War* (Garden City Park: One Square Publishers, 2003), p. 10.

offensive results for both sides causing huge casualties and soon the stagnation of trench warfare prevailed.

While the Allies pointed primarily to technological innovation such as the development of tanks, aircraft and armored vehicles to achieve success in a context of positional warfare, the German Army focused primarily upon better trained and equipped infantry assault detachments. In order to reach this objective, the German High Command made several reforms that are well summarized in Timothy Lupfer's seminal article.[4]

First and foremost the German Army changed its approach to training by forming highly specialized infantry assault detachments including units of *sturmtruppen*. Second, it attempted to increase troop morale with the Ludendorff doctrine, mainly by safeguarding the physical integrity of its soldiers by avoiding unnecessary mass wave assaults and putting its infantry units mostly on the defensive.[5]

Third, unit cohesion was improved through the creation of the specialized units where handpicked, highly capable junior officers and NCOs led their men by example and shared the same risks during training and offensive operations.[6]

Fourth, the German Army also focused on developing the proper weapons for unlocking entrenched enemy positions by arming the stormtroopers with light machine guns, small artillery units, mortars, hand grenades and especially flamethrowers. The new weapons provided the necessary direct fire support when it was most needed, mainly when the troops had already crossed no man's land and were face to face with entrenched enemy defenses. Fifth, the *sturmtruppen* consistently applied winning battle tactics mainly by developing 'Hutier tactics' whereby attackers bypassed frontline enemy strongpoints in order to push through and capture the enemy's vital rear defenses, command and communication centers. The German Army stuck to such doctrine and conducted all of its operations in a methodical fashion by spending large periods of time in conducting proper reconnaissance and in assembling in secrecy the artillery batteries necessary to break through enemy defenses. Sixth, the German Army also achieved a very high degree of combined arms integration by increasing the production of artillery pieces and by using its artillery in ways in which it could favor the *sturmtruppen* 'Hutier tactics.' This included artillery barrages that were short but intense (creeping barrages) and that often used explosive and gas shells raining down on a single sector of the enemy front line to disrupt and disorient the enemy. Moreover, artillery preparation observation was also improved markedly with several reforms including the massive reliance on aerial reconnaissance. Seventh, the German Army also became much more adept at implementing swift and unexpected attacks. This was achieved by the use of deception such as amassing the *sturmtruppen* on the front lines covertly during the night, by improving

4 Timothy Lupfer, 'The Dynamics of Doctrine: The Changes in German Tactical Doctrine During the First World War', *Leavenworth Papers*, 1981.

5 Robert Asprey, *The German High Command at War: Hindenburg and Ludendorff and the First World War* (New York: W. Morrow, 1991).

6 Ernst Jünger, *Storm of Steel* (New York, Penguin, 2014).

the timing between the lifting of the artillery barrage and the launch of the infantry charge and lastly by increasing the physical prowess of the troops comprising the assault detachments.

Both the Austro-Hungarian *sturmtruppen* and the Italian *arditi* will be evaluated based upon how well their respective armies approximated the German model of offensive warfare and/or whether they introduced significant variants which ultimately improved upon the German example. Both armies improved their performance in the battlefield by adaptation which is defined as a process focused on changes to tactics, techniques and procedures that were made in the field of battle and as the war progressed.[7] It is a process originated by mid level officers that floats at the top and then travels down through directives and training manuals. In most cases, however, it also travels from the bottom to the top and the military leadership then disseminates it to the whole army.

7 Theo Farrell, 'Improving in War', *Journal of Strategic Studies*, 33/4, 2010, pp. 567–594.

1

The German Stormtrooper Example

For the German High Command, whose basic principle of war was predicated on offensive operations, the impasse on the Western Front that developed in 1914–15 represented a huge problem. On the Western Front both the Germans and the French initially attacked each other in dense infantry formations and suffered tremendous losses from enemy machine gun fire and artillery. In essence, after the first major battles, which essentially led to a standstill, the German High Command faced a tactical dilemma. It could either accept a long-term war of attrition, which most likely favored the more industrially resourceful Allies, or attempt to overcome trench warfare and stalemate with new tactics to win the war. While the Allies, especially the British, sought to overcome positional warfare by opting primarily for a long term strategy based upon technological innovation (i.e., tanks, armored vehicles and artillery), the Germans focused primarily upon infantry specialization.

But in order to change tactics and to better train its infantry for a long term conflict the German Army had to first jettison many of its pre-war doctrines.

The German Army in 1914 was permeated with the offensive spirit. The German Field Regulations Manual of 1906 stated that:

> Infantry is the primary weapon. In tandem with artillery, its fire will batter the enemy. It alone breaks his last resistance. It carries the brunt of combat and it makes the greatest sacrifices. Consequently, it garners the greatest glory. Infantry must nurture its intrinsic drive to attack aggressively. Its actions must be dominated by one thought: Forward against the enemy, cost what it may.[1]

The manual stressed that enemy positions should be attacked with a combination of fire from the artillery and the infantry. As Stephen Bull aptly puts it:

1 Militargeschichtliches Forschungsamt, *Handbuch zur Deutschen Militärgeschichte 1648–1939* (Munich: Bernard & Graefe, 1979), vol. 3, p. 159.

> In common with Entente expectations, the assumption of the 1906 drill regulations was that to win the infantry had to attack, and that to attack it had to advance, deploy into linear formation to allow maximum use of weapons, and finally, charge home. The impact of war had modified ideas considerably by mid 1916, with close formations, for example, having been found catastrophic in 1914.[2]

The Battle of the Somme in 1916 represented a turning point for the German Army in terms of its general strategy and tactics. The first consequence of the huge losses sustained particularly during this battle was the introduction of a new defensive posture, which relied upon the redeployment of the infantry into two or more trenchlines. Rather than a rigid front line in defense of territory at all costs the Germans first opted for a thinly held outpost zone to retain a preliminary line of defense but most importantly to shield the bulk of the infantry from the enemy's artillery barrage. The bulk of the defending infantry was moved back in deep dugouts that could better withstand heavy barrages and thus better protect the troops from enemy shells. Second, the Germans adopted a second line of defense called a battle zone which was often two to three miles deep. This line consisted of the bulk of German defenses which included such obstacles as concrete pillboxes, barbed wire entanglements, and steel cages as well as enfilading machine gun posts, infantry strongpoints often situated on reverse slopes, mortar emplacements and specialized sharpshooter outposts. This second line was followed by another defensive line which consisted primarily of artillery emplacements and dugouts where counter-attacking units were shielded from the enemy's barrage in order to be launched in the battlefield as the enemy infantry advanced. The purpose of this new defensive structure was to minimize casualties and force the enemy into a killing ground, where the machine guns would systematically mow down opponents which where then subsequently finished off by artillery batteries placed beyond the range of the enemy's mid to large field guns.

The counter-attack by fresh, specially trained units was an essential element of this new defense in depth approach utilized by the Germans. In fact, the second consequence of this new defense posture was the development of better trained, better equipped and more specialized infantry assault units which could be deployed for counter-attacks, small raids beyond enemy lines, as well as for playing the role of vanguard forces during large-scale offensive operations.

Historian Stephen Biddle has argued that the First World War differed from prior wars given that modern weapons of mass destruction such as artillery guns, machine guns and poison gas had become by 1914 so lethal that the infantry was unable to function according to the pre-war tactics and maneuvers. In other words, Biddle argues that the infantry could only carry out successful offensive and defensive operations if it adopted what he called the modern system of warfare. "This consisted in the use of cover, concealment, dispersion, suppression, small unit independent

2 Stephen Bull, *British Infantryman Versus German Infantryman* (Oxford: Osprey, 2014), p. 19.

maneuver, and combined arms at the tactical level, and depth and reserves and differential concentration of the operational level of war."[3]

The German Army had some of the most progressive-thinking officers and junior officers during the war who sought to adapt to the changed, modern system of warfare by increasing the specialization of its infantry forces. Another major reform within the German Army (similar to the French Army) was the bolstering of the artillery with the increase of the size and the number of batteries.

As Lupfer asserts:

> Although artillery support of the attack was not well developed in anyone's prewar tactical doctrine, the experiences of the first months of war indicated that artillery fire was essential in support of an infantry attack. The destruction of enemy machine guns, enemy batteries and dug in enemy positions, in turn, required vast quantities of munitions. Heavy guns became particularly useful to accomplish this. Unfortunately, to sustain the infantry advance beyond the initial range was extremely difficult, because such heavy guns could not displace quickly.[4]

The Germans also perfected innovative, less costly, artillery tactics in the hope of facilitating the offensive potential of its infantry. Under the guidance of Colonel Georg Bruchmüller new tactical methods were implemented. The first major change was the overall redefinition of the artillery's role during offensive operations. The artillery was seen as the combat arm that could facilitate the infantry advance and breakthrough with neutralization and suppressive fire. Unlike the Allies, who continued with the tactic of multiple days' destructive rolling barrages, the Germans opted for swift but extremely violent artillery barrages, which often lasted just a few hours, the aim of which was to stun and paralyze the enemy. This facilitated the infantry advance as it allowed it to cross no man's land with little or no opposition from Allied troops seeking shelter in their trenches and dugouts from the enemy's batteries.

Another change was to make the artillery more mobile thus allowing it to move forward providing fire support as the infantry advanced. This was achieved with the creation of small units of horse-drawn artillery batteries which were attached to *sturmtruppen* units and infantry regiments.

In addition, the German Army experimented with small artillery pieces (first with the *Krupp Sturmkannone* and then with the heavier captured Russian 76.2 mm fortress guns) which unlike heavy artillery guns, could be carried across no man's land during an assault in order to focus upon unexpected pockets of enemy resistance. This solution enabled the infantry units to receive prompt artillery support as they moved through the enemy trenches rather than having to wait for the more cumbersome field artillery to move up the line.

3 Stephen Biddle, *Military Power: Explaining Victory and Defeat in Modern Battle* (Princeton: Princeton University Press, 2004), pp. 2–3.

4 Timothy Lupfer, 'The Dynamics of Doctrine: The Changes in German Tactical Doctrine During the First World War', *Leavenworth Papers*, 1981, p. 2.

Finally, the Germans perfected artillery preparations by subdividing them is specific stages. The first stage pitted German guns upon the enemy's central command and communication centers. The second stage consisted of counter-battery fire aimed at paralyzing the enemy's artillery. While the final stage consisted in swift but intensive barrages over the enemy's front line in order to facilitate assault infantry penetration.[5]

Although there is an ongoing debate amongst military historians regarding which army of the First World War developed the first specialized assault units, the German Army is generally credited with the creation of these highly trained units as early as 1915.[6]

The first German special assault unit was constituted in March 1915 under the command of Major Calsow. Its soldiers were capable of conducting raids and patrols and they also possessed pioneer/engineering skills, mainly making gaps in the enemy's defenses. The first battle experiences of the so-called *Sturmabteilung Calsow* were rather unsuccessful mainly because field commanders used it as an ordinary infantry unit. But things began to change when in August 1915 Captain Willy Rohr assumed command of the unit. Rohr differed from his predecessor mainly because he placed a renewed emphasis on training and on the development of new weapons which were suited for clearing obstacles and occupying enemy trenches in close combat situations. Training focused on three elements: increasing physical fitness, coordinating unit assaults with the artillery, and task specialization. Each battle action was preceded by extensive reconnaissance of the objective, which included a detailed survey of the enemy's deployment as well as detailed maps and plastic models of the enemy defenses. The unit was often ordered to conduct multiple rehearsals and trained extensively to fight at night. It used conventional infantry weapons such as rifles, machine guns, trench mortars and hand grenades as well as less conventional weapons such as flamethrowers and light artillery pieces.

Initially the unit consisted of two sapper companies, a 37 mm gun section, a mortar unit (four small mortars) a machine gun platoon (with six 1908 Maxim guns) and a flamethrower section (six small portable *kleine* flamethrowers). By the end of the year the unit had expanded into a battalion with the incorporation of two additional assault companies and was renamed *Sturmabteilung Rohr* (Assault Battalion Rohr).

Training took place in the town of Beuville and typically lasted from two to three weeks. "What distinguished Rohr's techniques from the pre-war German tactical doctrine was the organization of attack forces in small groups deployed in depth, instead of advancing in a broad firing line, and the arming of individual infantry soldiers with various types of weapons, instead of the standard issue rifle."[7]

5 David T. Zabecki (ed.), *Germany at War: 400 Years of Military History* (Santa Barbara: ABC-CLIO, 2014), p. 78.

6 William Philpott, *Three Armies on the Somme: The First Battle of the Twentieth Century* (New York: Random House, 2009). Paddy Griffiths, *Battle Tactics of the Western Front: The British Army's Art of Attack, 1916–18* (New Haven: Yale University Press, 1994).

7 Timothy Lupfer, 'The Dynamics of Doctrine', p. 28.

Italian grenade launching unit in gun pit. (Ufficio Storico – official archive, Italian military, Rome)

Italian *arditi* with Stokes mortar unit during training. Note the *ardito* badge on the left arm of the soldier that is depositing the missile into the weapon. (Ufficio Storico – official archive, Italian military, Rome)

Italian infantry field artillery unit in 1916. (Ufficio Storico – official archive, Italian military, Rome)

Ardito officer being awarded a gold medal. (Ufficio Storico – official archive, Italian military, Rome)

Sante Dorigo, an officer of the XXIX *Reparto d'assalto* and a gold medal awardee. (Ufficio Storico – official archive, Italian military, Rome)

Arditi alpini of III *Reparto d'assalto* marching along a mountain ridge during the White Battle in May 1918. (Ufficio Storico – official archive, Italian military, Rome)

Alpini ski patrol unit attacking enemy position. (Ufficio Storico – official archive, Italian military, Rome)

Arditi flamethrower training. (Ufficio Storico – official archive, Italian military, Rome)

Arditi flamethrower unit. (Ufficio Storico – official archive, Italian military, Rome)

Similarly Gudmundsson has argued that Rohr's tactics consisted of three essential elements:

1. The replacement of the advance in skirmish lines with the surprise assault of squad sized stormtroops (*Sturmtrupps* or *Stosstrupps*),
2. The use of supporting arms (machine guns, infantry guns, trench mortars, indirect artillery, flamethrowers) coordinated at the lowest possible level to suppress the enemy during the attack, and,
3. The clearing of trenches by rolling them up with troops armed with hand grenades.[8]

Thus small assault infantry and sapper units supported by tremendous artillery fire and armed with new weapons such as flamethrowers would advance under the cover of darkness to assail enemy positions. Their offensive purpose was to deeply infiltrate enemy positions by bypassing the frontline strongpoints and reaching the enemy's rear. This allowed the *sturmtruppen* to attack the enemy's command centers and artillery batteries and prevent enemy reserve units from reaching the front lines. Often these rear positions were cleared by saturating them with hundreds of hand grenades, while the fortified bunkers were overwhelmed with flamethrowers and light artillery units. Then once the rear positions had been occupied, special pioneer units would arrive on the scene and reorganize its defenses against a likely enemy counter. Thus, the *sturmtruppen* would not only paralyze the enemy's defenses by capturing its rear communication and command posts but would also open up the way for a broad infantry advance.

The reformed unit was deployed for the first time in major combat on 10 January 1916 in the Alsace Vosges Mountains sector. *Sturmabteilung Rohr* was tasked with springing a surprise attack and opening the way for the infantry to advance upon the French position on the Hartmansweilerkopf ridge. The operation began with a detailed artillery preparation. Field howitzers and large mortars were used to rain down tremendous fire and soften up the French infantry positions. A box barrage invested the rear of the French defenses blocking any enemy attempt to come to the aid of the besieged position. Then a brief preparatory barrage ensured that the French forces could not put up any resistance while the *sturmtruppen* followed closely by two infantry regiments crossed no man's land. When the preparatory barrage was halted, flamethrower, small artillery, mortar and hand grenade squads in close collaboration invested the French positions with heavy fire. The flamethrower units were particularly instrumental in snuffing out French machine gun nests allowing the German infantry to reach the objective and occupy the positions.

One of the new *sturmtruppen* weapons, the flamethrower, was a vital element in their tactics for opening up enemy defenses. It was not their most powerful weapon, but it had a vast psychological impact on opponents. In January of 1915 Major

8 Bruce I. Gudmundsson, *Stormtroop Tactics: Innovation in the German Army, 1914–1918* (New York: Praeger, 1998), p. 49.

Hermann Reddemann had created a special unit called *Flammenwerfen Abteilung* which specialized in handling flamethrowers of different sizes. The most easy to use was the smaller, back-pack *kleine* flamethrower which was not only lighter, hence lending itself to be carried during the battle, but also because it could be operated by only two men. One man carried the flamethrower, while his partner carried the tube and operated the flamethrower against the enemy. The weapon consisted of a tank of oil and a steel tube. The oil was then lit and fired at high pressure. The flamethrower proved useful for the special assault units because it was not only feared by enemy troops but also it could be used effectively to overcome impenetrable defenses such as a fortified bunker which would be engulfed in flames forcing the enemy into a horrible death or any equally quick surrender.

Reddemann's flamethrowers unit first saw action during a small infantry assault against French infantry at the village of Malancourt in February 1915. During this assault both large and small flamethrowers were utilized to overcome French resistance. Large flamethrowers were positioned at approximately 30 feet from the French positions and were used as an alternative to the artillery. Then the smaller flamethrower units advanced into the French positions engulfing them with fire and paving the way for the infantry to advance.

> The fiery serpents which, rising out of the earth, fell roaring and hissing on the enemy's trenches and drove him to precipitate flight, leaving behind their weapons and equipment. Even in the rear positions and in the adjacent positions to the right and left the enemy fled from the trenches and left important material in our hands. The first flame attack showed that the use of flame projectors could be very successful, if the apparatus was correctly used as regards tactics and technique and if the flame projector were properly fitted into the general plan of attack and into the duties and formation of the assault infantry.[9]

The operation was an overwhelming success as the French positions were occupied and the Germans suffered few casualties. In their first deployment, the flamethrowers proved to be a nightmare for the French soldiers, who in most cases, when faced by smoke and flames, ran for their lives.

The success at Malancourt brought about an expansion of the flamethrower units. In addition, special flamethrower detachments were formed and attached to the first *sturmtruppen* units. The units would then be deployed at the Battle of Verdun to sweep up the French infantry passageways and forts. A member of one of these units recalled: "The air was suffocating. A mixture of the horribly sweet smell of putrefaction, of phenol and iodoform, the stench of human excrement, explosive gases and dust took our breath away."[10]

Another key weapon of the *sturmtruppen* was the light artillery unit, the 37 mm gun. The weapon was light enough to be carried by the assault units as they were

9 Charles Theune, *Flammenwerfer und Sturmtruppen* (Berlin: Landes Verlag, 1921), p. 3.
10 Hermann Wendt, *Verdun 1916* (Berlin: E.S. Mittler & Sohn, 1941), p. 202.

advancing in no man's land against the enemy. In this way the assault units could deploy artillery fire at close range against stubborn defenses during attacks rather than having to rely on the more cumbersome and less mobile field artillery.

Lastly, the stormtroopers were also armed later in 1917 with Maxim automatic machine guns that could be used during infantry attacks giving them much increased firepower.

The combination of new weapons and artillery that could be used deep into enemy positions during the offensive along with the physical stamina of these handpicked soldiers made the stormtroopers particularly effective units.

After the battles of Verdun, Riga, Caporetto and Cambrai, in which the stormtroopers played a vital role, the German High Command decided to expand their role within the army. Now Assault Battalion Rohr was tasked with training the entire German infantry in stormtroop tactics. In conjunction with revamped infantry training, the German High Command distributed the pamphlet "The Attack in Trench Warfare" written by Captain Greyer as an outline of the new infantry tactics. The key to unlock enemy defenses, according to the pamphlet, lay in the decentralization of command at the platoon level. Small units of stormtroopers armed with light machine guns, hand grenades, trench mortars and flamethrowers were tasked with infiltrating as much as possible enemy defenses in order to destroy the command centers. The line infantry then would follow the stormtroopers to mop up and take control of captured positions, while the stormtroopers would continue to advance against the next enemy fortified line.

By 1918 the German *sturmtruppen* underwent six weeks of intensive training and the typical 800–1,000 men strong battalion was equipped with the following:

24 light machine guns
8 trench mortars
8 flamethrowers
4 artillery pieces
several heavy machine guns
hand grenades
A signal horn.

Thus, the outcome of the 1916 fighting on the Somme led to a turning point in terms of the development of new infantry tactics. While the British and the French sought vast increases of firepower for both artillery, air units and the preliminary experimentation with tanks, the Germans assembled a number of combat arms for offensive operations that foreshadowed the combined arms offensives of the Second World War. Stormtroop training became more relevant for standard infantry units as the goal became to familiarize the bulk of the troops to the new tactics. Existing doctrines for the attack were further refined with the massive use of artillery guns, trench mortars, portable small artillery pieces and even air units. The Germans were also the first to deploy a defense in depth approach that was later adopted by the French,

Austro-Hungarian and Italian armies. This new approach used the stormtroopers in a counter-attacking mode.

As will later be detailed, the German example was of vital importance to both the Austro-Hungarian and the Italian Army as both entities adapted to the new tactics by a combination of internal innovation and adaptation of the German *sturmtruppen* model.

The Austro-Hungarians initially learned about the new stormtrooper tactics by having some of their officers participate in German training exercises conducted in the rear of the Western Front. They then implemented these tactics on the Eastern Front where combined German/Austrian combat units attacked Russian positions by using stormtrooper tactics. The Italians first learned about the stormtroopers from detailed intelligence reports written by French officers. Beginning in 1917 the Italians would experience first hand the new stormtrooper tactics when Austro-Hungarian special units stormed Italian positions in the Asiago Altopiano and Dolomites sectors. The Austro-Hungarian stormtroopers served as a stimulus to the development of the Italian special assault infantry detachments.

German Stormtrooper Diary

Ernst Jünger (29 March 1895–17 February 1999) served in the German Army during the First World War where he received multiple decorations. As the leader of a stormtroop unit he published after the war *Storm of Steel*, which recounts his actions during the conflict.

> Trench fighting is the bloodiest, wildest, most brutal, of all. ... Of all the war's exciting moments none is so powerful as the meeting of two stormtroop leaders between narrow trench walls. There's no mercy there, no going back, the blood speaks from a shrill cry of recognition that tears itself from one's breast like a nightmare.

2

The Austro-Hungarian Army

In 1914 the Austro-Hungarian military was comprised of four units: a common Army (*K.u.K.*), the Austrian *Landwehr*, the Hungarian *Honvéd* and the *Landsturm* reserve army. The tripartite setup reflected the federated nature of the Dual Monarchy and military historians have argued that the multinational character of the Austro-Hungarian Army was its key weakness. But despite the fact that the Austro-Hungarian Army was very heterogeneous, being comprised of soldiers belonging to 12 ethnic/national groups, it can be argued that it remained a cohesive fighting unit throughout the duration of the war. The Emperor, Francis Joseph I, for instance, was a strong charismatic figure and a symbol of unity and continuity for the various national groups of the Dual Monarchy. Many non-Austrian soldiers, for instance, were very loyal to the cause because of the Emperor's charisma and leadership. Another charismatic figure that unified and rallied the soldiers to the Habsburg cause was the Army's supreme commander, Field Marshal Franz Conrad von Hötzendorf. Conrad retained a strong influence over the army even when in 1917 he was demoted by Francis Joseph's successor, Emperor Karl. Prior to 1917 Conrad had not only penned the army's instruction manuals but he had also refined the army's tactics and had played a key role in the military's overall procurement process. Thus, despite nationalist political pressures from within the Dual Monarchy combined with the anti-Habsburg propaganda of the Allies, and despite the food shortages that plagued Austria-Hungary during the last years of the war, its Army kept on fighting until the end. Even in October of 1918, when it faced a massive Italian offensive while its supply of weapons, shells and most importantly food were quickly being depleted as a result of the weaknesses of the Habsburg economy, the soldiers fought on. This should be considered quite an achievement given the growth of centrifugal, nationalist tendencies especially during 1918 and also because approximately 70 percent of the officers during the war were Austrian.

Although many historians have argued that the Austro-Hungarian Army possessed well trained and strong infantry divisions and a particularly efficient and well-organized artillery branch, they have also asserted that in 1914 it was not prepared for a long war of attrition due to the limitations of the economy.[1] In addition, they have also argued that overall the Austro-Hungarian Army, given its ethnic heterogeneity and its relatively weaker supply base "could never come close to an effective emulation of the spirit and efficiency found in the German system."[2] That may be correct, but however, even though the Austro-Hungarian Army never reached the degree of combat efficiency of its German ally, it did greatly recover in 1916. Thus, despite the earlier huge reversals of fortune in 1914–15 on the Eastern Front, by 1917 it became a much more viable fighting force capable of holding its own in both Eastern Europe and on the Italian front. It played an important contribution in knocking Russia out of the war and later inflicted a grave defeat on the Italians at Caporetto. Thus, it can be argued that by 1917 the Austro-Hungarian Army had reached its peak level of combat efficiency of the First World War and it had largely recovered from its major blunders in 1914–15.

Supreme Command

The Army Supreme Command (*Armeeoberkommando* or AOK) had control over the four armies and over common navy and air forces. Its leader for most of the war was Field Marshal Conrad, a close associate of Archduke Franz Ferdinand, who held the position of commander in chief of the armed forces between 1906 until 1917 and was responsible for the overall conduct of military operations. The Field Marshal was a first rate military tactician who had had a strong imprint on the Habsburg Army pre-war training and tactical procedures. According to military historian Liddell Hart, 'Conrad had a sense of mobility and an aptitude for bold maneuver." But according to the same author he was also "the man that juggled with his armies, and broke them."[3]

Conrad, for example, displayed this aptitude for bold maneuver with the unexpected launch of the *Asiago* Offensive (also known as the *Strafexpedition* 'Punitive Expedition') against Italy in May 1916. Despite German objections, Conrad ordered a surprise attack supported by 2,000 artillery guns and involving up to 300 infantry battalions to advance through the mountain passes of the Trentino and then outflank and trap the bulk of the Italian Army deployed on the Isonzo. Since Conrad's blow came down unexpectedly from the mountains it initially achieved the desired tactical surprise resulting in a deep, 15-mile long penetration of the Asiago Altopiano with the capture of the towns of Asiago and Arsiero. Ultimately, a combination of Italian resistance and the start of Brusilov's Offensive on the Eastern Front forced Conrad to halt the *Asiago* Offensive in June 1916. By then, however, the Austro-Hungarian

1 C.R.M.F. Cruttwell, *A History of the Great War, 1914–18* (Oxford, Oxford University Press, 1936), p. 48.
2 William R. Griffiths, *The Great War: Strategies and Tactics of the First World War* (Garden City Park, Square One Publishers, 2003), p. 13.
3 B.H. Liddell Hart, *History of the First World War* (London: Pan Books, 1972), p. 147.

Army had shown that it could move troops and artillery expeditiously through rough terrain and that especially its mountain infantry units were well trained and equipped to carry out offensive operations in the most difficult mountain regions.

Most recently Conrad's record has been re-evaluated. One Austrian historian, for instance, has argued that the Field Marshal excelled in grand strategy but ultimately failed to understand the limitations of his army.[4] To prove the point, historians point to one of Conrad's major offensives on the Eastern front, that ended up in disaster when Austro-Hungarian units attacked strong Russian positions in the dead of winter 1914–15. This offensive, the Carpathian Winter Offensive, is often given as an example of Conrad's tendency to punch above his weight and overestimate the offensive potential of his army. The offensive against the Russians lacked detailed planning, viable logistic support and was poorly timed ultimately consigning Austro-Hungarian troops to defeat. As Graydon Tunstall asserts the first attack against entrenched Russian troops soon turned into a disaster given the lack of planning:

> Separated attack groups often lost their bearing in the blinding snowstorms. The soldiers suffered from frostbite; their weapons jammed from the bitter cold. Nevertheless, Conrad's soldiers continued their attacks. Troops were expected to undertake exhausting marches through meter-deep snow to reach the battlefield, only to find no shelter awaiting them. In a cruel twist of fate, frigid conditions interspersed with sudden periods of rising temperatures and thaw. Steady rain and melting snow turned the valley terrain into a pit of mud as troops, artillery, ammunition, animals, and supply wagons sank into the mire. Rising floodwaters swept away bridges, and soldiers were forced to lie in their waterlogged positions.[5]

Without adequate artillery support and with the Austro-Hungarian infantry units lacking proper winter clothing and equipment, the Russians began to launch massive counter-attacks inflicting grave losses on their enemy. The Carpathian Winter Offensive, consisting of a hasty and poorly planned assault, gravely weakened the Austro-Hungarian war effort and Conrad's gamble of a quick victory demonstrated the downside of his high stakes, bold maneuvering. As historian John Schindler asserts "Conrad's Carpathian offensives of early 1915 achieved nothing save the destruction of dozens of Habsburg divisions."[6]

Similarly, Tunstall has argued that the offensive was strategically and tactically flawed. "From a tactical standpoint, the Habsburg military leaders failed to

4 Manfried Rauchensteiner, *The First World War and the End of the Habsburg Monarchy, 1914–1918* (Vienna: Boehlau Verlag GmbH & Co., 2014).

5 Graydon A. Tunstall, *Blood on the Snow: The Carpathian Winter War of 1915* (Lawrence: Univ. Press of Kansas, 2010), p. 69.

6 John Richard Schindler, *A Hopeless Struggle: The Austro-Hungarian Army and Total War 1914–18*, Unpublished Thesis, McMaster University, 1995, p. 265.

incorporate the lessons of modern warfare and instead continued launching sacrificial uncoordinated infantry attacks without sufficient artillery support."[7]

Like all pre-First World War European military leaders, Conrad believed that the infantry was the branch that would win battles. Infantry units were to be comprised of fit, highly motivated and well-armed soldiers that would charge at the enemy and overwhelm him with rifle fire and bayonets. Since in any attack against a fortified enemy position the casualty count was likely to be high, Conrad maintained that if a unit had high morale, it could continue fighting in the face of strong opposition even if it lost up to 50 percent of its ranks. Therefore, Conrad's pre-war training exercises were largely centered on drills that included accurate rifle shooting and, most importantly, bayonet training. According to Conrad the latter type of drills, in particular, which largely centered on attacking tactics, increased a soldier's physical stamina, aggressiveness and determination.

In one of his most important books Conrad provided an analysis of the Franco-Prussian War of 1870–71 asserting that offensive infantry tactics, rather than artillery support, had determined the outcome of that war. In his view, Prussian infantry's offensive spirit, in particular, had been the catalyst for major battlefield successes, while the artillery had played a much more secondary role.[8] The downplaying of the role of the artillery arm, that was inherent in his tactical approach, along with the Austro-Hungarian government cutbacks in military spending prior to the war, would later have a detrimental impact upon the Habsburg military effort in 1914–15. During the third offensive of the Carpathian Winter Campaign, for example, the 11th *Jäger* Battalion moved against the Russian positions with no artillery support and as a result suffered over 50 percent losses.[9]

Conrad was not only an offensive minded enthusiast but he was also a visionary, as he believed that future combat would be dominated by the most advanced technology such as the combustion engine and especially by air power. "Conrad's pre-war vision of the future military campaign had included large masses of rapidly moving infantry seeking encounter battles with enemy forces, masses supported overhead by hundreds of aircraft."[10] Although Conrad was a forward thinker and his tactical methods were ahead of the time, the heavy equipment (i.e., trucks, aircraft and tanks) required to implement his offensive combined arms vision were in their infancy from a technological standpoint when the Great War erupted. Hence, these weapons could not be fully exploited and the Austro-Hungarian Army did not have the financial resources to fully develop them during the course of the war anyway. Moreover, Conrad, and in general the AOK, in 1914 initially failed to realize the importance of artillery support for the completion of successful offensive operations.[11] Austrian military historian Peter Jung correctly argues that:

7 Graydon A. Tunstall, *Blood on the Snow*, p. 10.

8 Franz Conrad, *Gefechtsausbildung der Infanterie* (Vienna: L.W. Seidel and Sons, 1900).

9 Graydon A. Tunstall, *Blood on the Snow*, p. 189.

10 Lawrence Sondhaus, *Franz Conrad Von Hötzendorf: Architect of the Apocalypse* (Boston: Humanities Press, 2000), p. 241.

11 Ibid., p. 41.

> Before 1914 the importance of the artillery was underestimated in contrast to that of the cavalry which was overvalued by the general staff. As a consequence, in the summer of 1914 the Austro-Hungarian divisions were mostly under provided with artillery: a regular infantry division normally had only 46 pieces, in contrast to the German norm of 60, the Russians 50 and the French army's scale of 72 guns.[12]

Of the major combatants only the Italian Army in 1915, for instance, had less artillery pieces per infantry division than Austria-Hungary. As Tunstall asserts: "A serious and perpetual shortcoming of Habsburg artillery, particularly heavy guns, during the three Carpathian Mountain campaigns resulted in the inability to counter effective Russian heavy artillery."[13]

Conrad's tactical principles, which focused almost exclusively on the offensive, did not fully prepare his army for the type of industrial trench warfare that characterized all major phases of the war. His lack of attention to defense principles, for instance, resulted in Austro-Hungarian troops suffering high casualties during the first year of the war due to their lack of experience with excavating trenches, building barbed wire and other steel obstacles, and digging deep dugouts able to withstand the enemy's barrages. Moreover, the infantry, in particular, lacked training on defending with trench mortars, machine guns and other essential weapons of trench warfare. In fact, his army initially lacked the high angle fire weapons which were essential in the mountainous terrain allowing fire to be directed over the hills and the mountain tops. Conrad initially also failed to see the need for infantry specialization since his emphasis was on well-trained standard infantry units that could be deployed in large scale tactical offensives. As a result, the Habsburg Army entered the war with a large field army that had few special mountain, mortar and hand grenade assault units.

For the most part, Austro-Hungarian officers and NCOs were generally less effective during the war than their German counterparts. During the early stages of the war, for example, they followed to the letter Conrad's offensive tactics. "Since 1914, tens of thousands of officers had attempted to lead their troops and spur them on through their personal example and tireless commitment. The result was that the loss of officers was proportionally considerably higher than the losses of enlisted men, and that tens of thousands had fallen or were no longer fit for the front."[14] As a result, in 1916 due to several reverses on the Eastern front, the Germans had to step in and provide greater support to their faltering ally. Beginning in 1916, for example, the most critical decisions of the Eastern campaign were made by German officers. German power, tactics, weapons and leadership were also primarily responsible for the success of the Central Powers during the battles of Riga and Caporetto in 1917.

12 Peter Jung, *The Austro-Hungarian Forces in World War I (1): 1914–16* (Oxford: Osprey, 2003), p. 35.

13 Graydon A. Tunstall, *Blood on the Snow*, p. 192.

14 Manfried Rauchensteiner, *The First World War and the End of the Habsburg Monarchy, 1914–1918* (Vienna: Boehlau Verlag GmbH & Co., 2014), p. 535.

The Germans themselves admired the standard Austro-Hungarian infantry soldier, but had disdain for the upper echelons of the army, which they often accused of being lazy and unprepared.

The German General Hans von Seeckt, for instance, furnished an assessment of the Austro-Hungarian Army that was critical of some of its tactics. Habsburg soldiers "were physically strong and humble as well as accustomed to work and subordination." While the officers were "clumsy and too schematic." This resulted in an army that was well equipped but "was not well organized and frequently fails."[15]

Despite increased dependence on German power, the quality of the Austrian junior officers and NCOs markedly improved in 1917. This was the result of their participation to joint training camps with the Germans on the Western Front and also because of fighting highly specialized Russian Commando units on the Eastern front. The Germans, in particular, would be instrumental in training their ally to the new stormtrooper tactics as well as to the use of new weapons such as poison gas shells and flamethrowers. In addition, through the German Army, the AOK was able to introduce new artillery tactics as well as the defense in depth principles that were first experimented with on the Western front. As a result, by mid 1916 a revitalized and stronger Austrian-Hungarian Army would first help to stem the losses on the Eastern Front and later contribute to force Russia out of the war.

The Army

In 1914 the Austro-Hungarian Army could count upon over 2,000,000 soldiers organized within 48 infantry and 11 cavalry divisions. Each infantry division had an approximate total strength of 450 officers and 18,000 soldiers subdivided into four regiments, while cavalry divisions had approximately 5,500 soldiers. Each infantry regiment was also comprised of eight-unit machine gun companies, specialist mountain warfare units, a light infantry battalion and an artillery unit. In addition, the Austro-Hungarian Army had four regiments of alpine units, the *Kaiserjägers*, 30 rifle battalions of sharpshooters (*Feldjäger*) and four Bosnian regiments.[16] The alpine units, in particular, had a long history of service within the Habsburg Army and specialized in high altitude warfare with their own dedicated mountain guide, small artillery and machine gun units. The Bosnian units were comprised by fierce fighters specialized in close combat techniques and well trained in using knives, brass knuckles and steel clubs. Their units were reputed to be the most ruthless of the Habsburg Army and were feared by the enemy especially because they were extremely capable of springing surprise attacks and raids against enemy strongpoints.

15 Ibid., p. 511.

16 On the Bosnian troops see: Christoph Neumayer, and Erwin A. Schmidl (eds.), *Des Kaisers Bosniaken. Die bosnisch-herzegowinischen Truppen in der K.u.K. Armee* (Vienna: Verlag, 2008).

Standard infantry soldiers were armed with the 8 mm M 1895 *Mannlichen* rifle, while the *Kaiserjäger* units and other technical units were armed with the smaller *Strutzen* rifle. The standard rifle fired 8 mm bullets from a five round magazine with an exceptionally high rate of fire of 35 rounds per minute, while the *Strutzen* rifle performed similarly, but being less bulky and more versatile, was more suited for assault or mountain units fighting in close combat conditions. At the beginning of the war the Austro-Hungarian Army was equipped with several types of hand grenades. Some of the earlier Austrian manufactured models, however, were very unreliable resulting in frequent injuries to the hand grenade throwers. In 1915–16 the army was re-equipped with German made weapons such as the 'egg' and the 'stick' hand grenades which were much more effective and safer to operate than Austrian grenades. The German model 24 stick grenade, for example, had a powerful blast effect and could be thrown to a distance of 30–40 feet. It was easy to handle and to throw representing a vast improvement over earlier Austro-Hungarian explosive devices. This type of grenade was also extremely useful for assault stormtroopers that could throw it even while in motion or while in the speedy process of rolling up entrenched infantry positions. Assault units also used it very effectively to make gaps in the enemy wire by creating bundles of several grenades. The standard machine gun was the 8 mm *Schwarzlose* M07/12. It had an impressive rate of fire of 500 rounds per minute making it one the most reliable machine guns of the First World War. It was tripod mounted and most models came with a protective shield for the troops. In 1915, but particularly in 1916, the army was also furnished with trench mortars such as the 90 mm M15 and M16 *Minenwerfer* which were particularly suited for close combat in the trenches and high altitude fighting environments. These weapons were instrumental in eliminating particularly stubborn enemy strongpoints such as machine gun nests and small artillery emplacements. They were also extremely useful in mountain warfare as they could be deployed in close proximity of enemy positions and performed well in rugged terrain given their curved trajectory. The weapon fired an explosive shell weighing 35 pounds and had a range of fire of over 3,000 feet. At the end of 1916 the light trench mortars were at the front in large numbers, alongside 83 platoons of 120 mm and 100 platoons of 220 mm trench mortars.

Artillery

In the summer of 1914 the artillery arm was subdivided into three components: field, mountain, and fortress artillery consisting of 483 batteries and 3,000 artillery pieces. Although it enjoyed a formidable reputation grounded upon a long and glorious tradition of excellent service, the artillery arm entered the war underfunded and as a result up to one third of its artillery pieces were older models that by the end of 1914 were in need of replacement. The artillery's most popular gun was the M99 howitzer (104 mm) that had a range of 2,000 feet and could fire mainly explosive shells. This howitzer is a good example of the limitations imposed on the Austro-Hungarian artillery due to pre-war budget cuts and delays in the manufacturing process. During the first year of the war, for instance, many of these howitzers were damaged due to wear and tear and had to be sent into the interior for repairs, while new pieces were not available for frontline troops due to insufficient numbers.[17]

Another weapon that was widely used by the Austro-Hungarian artillery was the M8 70 mm mountain gun, which was also a fairly antiquated gun by 1914–15 standards. Both mainstream guns had a bronze barrel, lacked an advanced recoil system and used an ineffective spring-mounted spade brake. Nonetheless, they remained the standard field howitzer and mountain gun for the Austrian Army at the outbreak of the war due to the budget limitations. While the fortress artillery was the backbone of an impressive frontier defense system, the mountain artillery was the most versatile artillery component of the Habsburg Army. Its guns could be disassembled into four or five components and could be transported by pack mules in support of infantry assaults in the Carpathians and later in the Alps. Moreover, mountain artillery units could easily shift their range of fire with little or no registration and within just a few hours. As the war progressed, the mountain units were re-equipped with the *Skoda* mountain gun, which was probably one the most effective guns in its range. It was so effective that it was one of the few Austrian weapons supplied to the German Army and preferred by the Germans even against domestic similarly manufactured guns. The *Skoda* M15 (75 mm) gun had a range of over four miles (7,000 meters) and could fire explosive, shrapnel and gas shells. Standard shrapnel shell weight was 6.5 kg. Like most mountain guns the M15 could be broken down into six components for pack mule carriage. The gun also had a defensive shield which was much appreciated by the artillery crews.

Fortress artillery was initially responsible for manning the Dual Monarchy's fixed defenses such as Conrad's concrete forts and fortifications surrounding Trento. But as some of the fixed defenses became obsolete, some of its units were transferred to support line infantry operations and as a result were required to be much more versatile and mobile. The fortress artillery arm had excellent guns. For example, the 30.5 cm M11/16 *Skoda* heavy howitzer was by far the most effective heavy weapon of the Austro-Hungarian Army. It was one of the few weapons that could breach Italian concrete defenses along the Trentino and the Isonzo front with its 380 kg (840 pound) high explosive shell and a firing range of up to 12,000 meters (7.4 miles). This crew served weapon was operated by a 15-soldier unit and was towed by a 15-tonne tractor. Fortress artillery also had heavier pieces such as 35 cm and 42 cm howitzer guns. In addition, during the course of the war the artillery would also be equipped with excellent mid size guns such as the M14 (149 mm) howitzer which proved to be very effective on the Italian front to break up enemy attacks. It fired a 42 kg high explosive shell at a maximum distance of 8,000 meters (five miles).

The problem in 1914 was that the army did not have enough of these heavy pieces for what would become a prolonged campaign of entrenched warfare where these

17 Gunther E. Rothenberg, *The Army of Francis Joseph* (West Lafayette: Purdue University Press, 1998), p. 150.

units were necessary to destroy fortified bunkers, concrete pillboxes and extensive barbed wire defenses. In the beginning, the army also lacked an adequate number of shells for a prolonged campaign of trench warfare. The shell shortage, especially for the heavy weapons, continued into 1915 and it would take the Austro-Hungarian economy a year to fully rectify the situation.[18]

Thus, while the Habsburg Army had many strengths, its major deficiencies in 1914 were due to the lack of infantry specialization, of adequate numbers of large field guns and trench warfare equipment such as small mortars. In 1914 the standard infantry division also had fewer machine guns than its rivals such as the Russians and the mountain units lacked the necessary quantities of high angle mortar fire units.

Austro-Hungarian Tactics

The 1911 Austro-Hungarian training manual affirmed that the infantry is the main arm and decides the outcome of battle. At the time offensive operations were conducted in two stages: destruction and decisive. The destruction stage involved the infantry shooting their rifles at enemy defenses, while the decisive stage consisted in the infantry bayonet charge. The typical infantry company was composed of four platoons, three would charge the enemy lines, while the fourth would initially be held in reserve.[19] Like with most other European military manuals, the pre-war Austrian tactical manual failed to give the artillery, the indirect fire and machine gun sections the proper central role that they would assume during the course of the First World War. In fact, in 1914 the infantry was believed to have enough elan and firepower to overtake fortified enemy positions even without the support of the artillery. Infantry morale, speed and superior numbers were thought to be the key elements to a successful attack. The 1911 manual, for instance, did not give the artillery a primary role during the preparation of offensive operations or during the defensive phase with counter-battery fire. In one instance it states that "it is seldom possible to mount a successful artillery attack upon a well entrenched enemy in the field until they are forced by the infantry to send their troops out to meet artillery fire."[20]

Such tactical infancy is recognized by the Austro-Hungarian official history, which, for instance, states that prior to the war "doubtless too little attention was paid to the cooperation of infantry and artillery."[21]

This major tactical flaw of the manual and the adherence of Austro-Hungarian infantry commanders to pre-First World War strategies would lead to high casualties during 1914–15 for Austro-Hungarian infantry. The Austro-Hungarian military commanders, however, were not alone in following these obsolete tactics since all

18 Ibid., p. 184.
19 *Exerzierreglement fur die K.U.K. Fubtruppen* (Vienna: Seidel and Sons, 1911), p. 3.
20 Ibid., p. 188.
21 Edmund Glaise-Horstenau (ed.), *Österreich-Ungarns letzter Krieg 1914–1918* (Vienna: Verlag der Militärwissenschaftlichen Mitteilungen, 1936), Vol. 1, p. 34.

armies, including the German, suffered huge losses during 1914. In fact, it would take almost a year for all combatants to recognize that an adequate artillery preparation to soften up enemy positions prior to the infantry assault was a necessary precondition of any infantry operation of any scale and for any army.

The manual also did not call for widespread collaboration between the various tactical arms of the military including the artillery and the infantry. The former was to operate largely autonomously from the infantry and there were few provisions for inter-arm collaboration. Moreover, the standard infantry company of 1914 was a fairly hierarchical structure highly dependent during combat operations on the decisions of its commander. The latter, in fact, directed infantry fire, gave orders to fix bayonets and to charge against the enemy line and his span of control was very wide. Although the infantry commander was powerful, he could not command the artillery to intervene as the latter was considered a standalone military branch. During the first year of the war, for instance, the artillery could also do little after the preparatory barrage to further an infantry attack given its lack of indirect fire weapons such as small field mortars and grenade launchers and due to its lack of mobility. As a result, often the infantry would be caught in no man's land with few options once it had charged against enemy lines and had found that the barbed wire and the machine guns had not been destroyed by artillery fire.

The fighting in the mountainous terrain of the Carpathian Mountains proved especially challenging for the Austrian artillery which was not accustomed to operating in such treacherous conditions. With regard to the mountainous terrain an Austrian artillery officer wrote: 'As for the artillery, we had to learn new shooting techniques because this is the first time in the mountains. … It was difficult to observe the effectiveness of the artillery fire because of distance, snow and wooded areas, bushes and steep ridges all prevented observation. The snow cover, in particular, proved to be a major deterrent."[22]

During the first year of the war the Austro-Hungarian Army would suffer huge losses while adhering to obsolete pre-war offensive tactics against the Russians and the Serbs. In the first campaign against the much smaller Serbian Army during the Battle of Cer, the Austro-Hungarians lost 600 officers and 22,000 soldiers. By attacking without an adequate artillery preparation against enemy positions situated on hilly terrain, the Austro-Hungarian infantry assault waves were systematically mowed down by accurate machine gun fire.

Similarly, in a series of major battles in August and September 1914 in East Galicia the Habsburg Army suffered a tremendous reversal of fortune losing entire battalions to the Russians. The defeat was staggering as the Austro-Hungarians were ultimately pushed back all the way to the Carpathian Mountains losing 350,000 soldiers between the dead, wounded or captured. By the end of 1915 the Habsburg Army had lost over 1,000,000 soldiers as a result of its campaigns against Russia and Serbia. Moreover, infantry losses were compounded by the fact that Austro-Hungarian soldiers were not well equipped for trench warfare as they were often required to

22 Cited in: Graydon A. Tunstall, *Blood on the Snow*, p. 179.

Austro-Hungarian 75 mm *Skoda* mountain gun deployed in the high mountain environment of the Dolomites in 1916. Note the shield which was very effective in protecting the crew from enemy bullets and other dangers. The gun was the result of successive attempts by the Austro-Hungarian Army from 1899 to 1915 to design a mountain gun that could be broken down quickly for carriage by mules. After lengthy tests the gun entered service with the Austro-Hungarian army in April 1915, and proved to be a very good weapon. The Germans also used it extensively during the First World War. (Kriegsarchiv Vienna)

Field Marshal Conrad at work at his desk. Conrad remained the Austro-Hungarian Army Supreme Commander for much of the war (1914–17). (Kriegsarchiv Vienna)

(Lieutenant General) Ludwig Goinger. One of the most able Austro-Hungarian commanders who led the Austro-Hungarian troops during the counter-attack against the Italians that had captured Mount Ortigara in 1917. (Kriegsarchiv Vienna)

Austro-Hungarian stormtroopers training with hand grenades. The stormtroopers worked enemy trenches by attacking them from the flanks and by tying down the enemy by launching countless hand grenades. (Kriegsarchiv Vienna)

Austro-Hungarian stormtroopers with machine gun. The *Schwarzlose* machine gun was a tripod mounted, infantry weapon served by a crew of three soldiers, one of whom was the commander, usually an NCO, a gunner who fired the weapon, and a third soldier who served as an ammunition carrier and loader. (Kriegsarchiv Vienna)

Austro-Hungarian stormtroopers in the barracks. The stormtroops kept their rifles and hand grenades at the exit of the dugouts so that they could be quickly picked up when conducting counter-attacks after the enemy's barrage had moved forward. (Kriegsarchiv Vienna)

Austro-Hungarian stormtroopers with machine gun in anti-aircraft mode. (Kriegsarchiv Vienna)

Stormtroopers in a propaganda photo showing their gear and equipment. Clearly visible are the German stick grenades, the steel helmet and the gas masks. (Kriegsarchiv Vienna)

Austrian stormtroopers training with stick hand grenades. Note the Austro-Hungarian stormtroopers wearing German helmets. The special assault units were some of the first units within the Austro-Hungarian Army to be equipped with German helmets. Many Austro-Hungarian troops in 1915 and 1916 did not have helmets and were at the mercy of explosions, rock and debris flying everywhere and splinters from hand grenades. (Kriegsarchiv Vienna)

Captured Italian troops being escorted by German soldiers after the Central Powers breakthrough at Caporetto in October 1917. (Kriegsarchiv Vienna)

Stormtrooper company commander Otto Gallian. (Kriegsarchiv Vienna)

Austro-Hungarian steel club. This Austrian trench club consisted of a simple wooden haft, fitted with a cast iron head. The shape of the head with the spikes made the club a deadly weapon in close combat situations. Bosnian soldiers were especially well adept in using this weapon during raids and other offensive operations. (Kriegsarchiv Vienna)

charge against entrenched machine guns emplacements without steel helmets and camouflaged uniforms.

As a result of this terrible loss of manpower, the German Army was forced to come to the aid and prop up its ally in the Eastern Front.

The Austrian official history underlines that by then the German influence over the Dual Monarchy Army became overwhelming:

> Many times German military writings and training methods, especially for the new actions involving gas and stormtroops, were accepted as standards. In other areas, however, Austro-Hungarian and German methods were contradictory; moreover, many Austro-Hungarian headquarter issued further instructions on their own initiative for their own units. To restore uniformity amid this flood of instructions that was inundating the front, at the start of 1917 the AOK had a whole series of new regulations published to codify the lessons, courses and alterations to date. Reflecting the military situation of the Danube Monarchy and the course of the war, the emphasis was on trench fighting and defensive battles. The regulations deliberately relied heavily on German examples.[23]

Not only did the Germans influence Central Powers infantry tactics but German officers also took control of combined frontline operations. Rauchensteiner has argued that by 1916 on the Eastern front the German troops were acting as "corset strings" for the Austrian Army.[24] In addition, the Austro-Hungarian Army for most of 1915 was placed for the most part on the defensive since it could not afford to lose any more men.

The new, mostly defensive posture gave the army the breathing space to reorganize and re-equip its infantry units for a prolonged campaign of trench warfare. As a result, the Austro-Hungarian Army was able to recover from the major crisis of early 1915. During 1915 a limited Central Powers offensive forced the Russian Army out of Austrian Galicia, while Serbian forces had also been driven back and forced to concede territory. The 2 May 1915 offensive of the Central Powers, in particular, achieved a major victory for the combined German/Austrian infantry deployment. The Gorlice-Tarnow campaign not only stabilized the Austro-Hungarian positions on the Eastern Front, but also dealt a serious blow to the Russian Army. Thus, beginning in 1916 the Austro-Hungarian Army, no longer facing a major crisis, was able to implement a series of far reaching reforms that would significantly improve the fighting quality of its soldiers.

The first major change initially implemented in Eastern Europe and in Italy during the *Asiago* Offensive in the Trentino sector, involved infantry tactics. No longer was the infantry instructed to make frontal attacks with successive mass waves of

23 Edmund Glaise-Horstenau (ed.), *Österreich-Ungarns letzter Krieg 1914–1918* (Vienna: Verlag der Militärwissenschaftlichen Mitteilungen, 1936), Vol. 6, p. 44.

24 Manfried Rauchensteiner, *Der Tod des Doppeladlers: Österreich-Ungarn und der Erste Weltkrieg* (Graz: Styria Verlag, 1993), p. 372.

soldiers but it was to advance in small groups directed primarily against the flanks of the enemy line. These small groups were to infiltrate the Italian lines by coming down from the mountain passes and leaping forward a few miles at the time often by seeking cover within forests and hilly terrain. The new German-inspired tactics required close coordination with the artillery that was required to open up the way for the assault units. The infantry was to advance under the cover of the artillery bombardment that would be lifted only when the troops had arrived at approximately the range of 300 feet of the enemy positions. In order to safely cross no man's land, the infantry was instructed to utilize a myriad of new offensive weapons including mortars, machine guns, small artillery, hand grenades and rifles to overcome enemy machine gun posts. The artillery fire was not to be slowed down but had to continue to pound the rear enemy lines as the infantry approached the wire. The emphasis was placed on how small groups of well trained and armed assault detachments could more quickly take possession of enemy trenches than large, more static line infantry battalions. These new units, led by special hand grenade squads, would shoot and bomb their way through an enemy position by leveraging the element of surprise as well as new offensive weapons.

What follows is an accurate description of the meticulous Austro-Hungarian attack on Asiago during the *Asiago* Offensive by Italian General Giuseppe Pennella. His observations are an indication of the change of tactics by the Austrian-Hungarians:

> The fighting was intense. The enemy thrust was particularly ferocious against the left flank of our deployment. The artillery barrage never relented as it continued to smash our fragile defenses from morning to night. The enemy pounded us not only with the large and medium field guns but also with infantry fire from dedicated machine gun squads. Small groups with light machine guns infiltrated our lines by attacking from the flanks while our strongpoints were threatened by infantry battalions attacking resolutely in different waves. These large assault waves tried multiple times to achieve a breakthrough and take possession of our main communication hubs such as the train station of Val Canaglia. The infantry assault was well coordinated with the artillery preparation. Special communication units advanced hand-in-hand with the infantry and as the latter moved up the front line the artillery fire was lengthened accordingly. With its artillery fire rectified, the enemy began pounding our lines with every gun at his disposal. It massacred our troops as bloodied bodies together with steel debris, large rocks, tree trunks and branches were thrown violently in the air.[25]

Although this major operation in the Trentino ultimately failed mainly because of the strong resistance encountered by the Austro-Hungarian forces and the lack of mobile support which slowed down the infantry advance, the new infantry tactics would become a central feature of future operations.

25 Enrico Acerbi, *Strafexpedition* (Valdagno: Edizioni Rossato, 2003), p. 276.

The change in tactics became apparent by the end of 1916. By then the Austro-Hungarian Army had moved away tactically from the breakthrough battle whereby strong artillery fire preceded determined infantry assaults. As the Austro-Hungarian official history states the first key to success was in the increased cooperation between artillery and infantry: "The lessons of the first ten months of the war were used to apply the theory to practice; the concepts which achieved a fixed form involved the importance of artillery preparation, of coordination between the two principal arms, and of a well-planned, systematic advance. It was recognized that nothing should be left to chance, and that success had to be organized."[26]

The second factor was that the infantry was to advance against the enemy positions while the artillery preparation was still unfolding and so that the attacking units would typically be within three to two hundred meters from the enemy trenches when the fire was moved forward. Another factor was the reliance by the attacking troops on a whole host of new weapons such as trench mortars, flamethrowers and light machine guns to overtake entrenched defenses.

Finally the vital fourth factor was the speed with which the stormtroopers would advance on the flanks in order to maintain the momentum of the attack by quickly overrunning the second and third enemy lines to suppress their artillery as quickly as possible.

Second, new tactics also provoked changes in infantry organization. Infantry specialization was pushed forward as the army created new units such as dedicated assault units specialized in the throwing of hand grenades against fortified enemy positions. In 1916 a pioneer company with communication, sapper, mortar and flamethrower sections was added to the standard infantry regiment. These units were created with the purpose of supporting the infantry against fortified positions especially in eliminating the wire and other obstacles that stood in the way of a troop advance. In order to achieve this objective they were furnished with new weapons, such as trench mortars, grenade launchers, land mines and flamethrowers and they were often deployed at the forefront of an infantry attack. In the high mountain sectors they were also furnished with pneumatic boring machines that were used to dig tunnels through rock or ice to facilitate surprise attacks by the stormtroopers. A number of close combat weapons platoons were formed and during offensive operations its members were split up in various squads to aid the advance of the stormtroopers and the infantry.

The standard regiment's firepower was also increased as each machine gun unit doubled the number of machine guns at its disposal from eight to 16. Two years later industrial capacity ensured that the number of machine guns per regiment was brought to 72, evenly split between the unit's three infantry battalions. Each battalion by then had a standard machine gun company as well as a light machine gun company with four guns. By then every army was in need of automatic weapons that could be carried in forward positions to aid the assaulting infantry and to deal with particularly stubborn positions of enemy resistance. Initially the Austro-Hungarian Army

26 Edmund Glaise-Horstenau (ed.), *Österreich-Ungarns letzter Krieg 1914–1918* , Vol. 4, p. 47.

experimented with the standard *Schwarzlose* gun, but found that it was too bulky to use as a light machine gun. It later received shipments of German Maxim guns, which was truly a light automatic weapon. Specialization of the standard line infantry units began to be the buzzword of the new, revitalized Austro-Hungarian Army, which split up each battalion into four highly specialized infantry assault companies. The increased specialization of its troops also went hand-in-hand with the growth of the army, which by the end of 1916 had five million soldiers. Training was also expanded considerably. Initially the standard training of the Austro-Hungarian infantryman lasted just eight weeks and it was focused almost exclusively on marksmanship. In the fall of 1915, after several complaints put forth from frontline commanders, the standard infantry training was extended to three months and it was also brought near the front were sessions were led by experienced NCOs. By 1916 a new uniform for the standard soldier was also introduced. The old "pike-gray" uniform was replaced by a new versatile field gray version with a shade of green for purposes of camouflage.

The third major reform involved an increase in artillery firepower that was necessary to face the new realities of trench warfare and where the battlefield was dominated by guns, barbed wire and machine guns. According to Christian Ortner, in 1916 the Austro-Hungarian Army greatly modernized its artillery arsenal by replacing obsolete artillery units with modern artillery guns.[27] By 1916 infantry divisions had on average 60 guns, with 24 field guns, 30 howitzers and four or six heavy artillery guns.[28]

By then not only did the standard infantry division had more guns but it also had more efficient, modern units. Large numbers of M14 (149 mm) and M15 (150 mm) guns were shipped to the battlefield to replace the obsolete M99 gun. These modern guns had a mechanically advanced recoil system and an excellent range of fire that exceeded 3.5 miles. Mortar units were also greatly expanded. Each division could in fact count upon four (120 mm), four (220 mm), six (90 mm) *Minenwerfer* and six portable *granatwerfer* which provided direct fire support to infantry.[29]

By 1916 the artillery had grown to 804 batteries and 48 detachments with a total of 4,175 guns and howitzers. Fortress artillery, especially along the Italian front, also saw large improvements with several new large sized 30.5 cm, 35 cm, 38 cm, and 42 cm turreted and non-turreted guns being introduced into service. By 1916 the Habsburg Army had a total of 420 fortress artillery units, a 44 percent increase versus the number of units the army had at the beginning of the war. Its most important artillery weapon remained the 30.5 cm M16 howitzer of which by 1916 there were 21 batteries mostly deployed on the Italian front.[30] One other key weapon was the

27 Christian Ortner, *Die Österreichisch-ungariche Artillerie von 1867–1918* (Vienna: Verlag Militaria, 2007), p. 551.

28 Ibid., p. 381.

29 Kriegsarchiv: K.u.K., AOK, Op. Nr. 30662, 25 September 1916.

30 Filippo Cappellano, *L'artiglieria austro-ungarica nella Grande Guerra* (Novale: Rossato, 2001), p. 221.

M15 150 mm long range gun which was widely used in large quantities by the army in late 1916.

Overall by the end of 1916 Austro-Hungarian artillery experienced tremendous growth, with a 54 percent increase in the number of artillery guns since the beginning of the war. In addition, by 1916 the gap with the other armies in terms of the ratio of artillery pieces per division had been drastically narrowed. By then there were 60 pieces per Austro-Hungarian infantry division rather than 46 per division during 1914.

It is important to note that by this time the Austro-Hungarian artillery arm had several major advantages against the new Italian enemy. In 1916 it was well versed and equipped in the tactics of modern warfare, while the Italians were still in a trial and experimental phase. It was beginning to provide effective support to infantry with counter-battery fire as well as in the attack thanks to more precise fire furnished by expanded teams of forward observers and by more experienced gunners.[31] Finally, it was very well integrated with the rest of the army. Especially after the 1917 reform of the army, each infantry division had its own standalone artillery brigade spearheaded by two 30.5 cm howitzers, with expanded teams of observers and with its own air squadron to provide advanced reconnaissance.

Mostly importantly, the army began to also receive large quantities of 75 mm *Skoda* mountain guns, one of the most effective guns of the war within its range. The Austro-Hungarians were also re-equipped with German trench mortars with ranges up to 1,300 yards replacing the obsolete Austrian-made 9 cm mortar. The Germans also furnished the army with large quantities of egg and stick hand grenades replacing the unreliable Austrian made 'corn cob' grenades. The Germans were also instrumental in furnishing the Austrians with modern gas masks. Again as a result of collaboration with the German Army, the Habsburg Army also experimented with new lethal weapons such as mustard gas which was used for the first time during the assault of Monte San Michele on 29 June 1916.[32]

The Austrian Army also began to constitute the first flamethrower platoons in 1916 as support units for infantry. In 1917 flamethrower platoons were also attached to stormtrooper units. Initially two or three flamethrower squads were attached to stormtrooper assault patrol units. But beginning in February 1917 large flamethrower units were also attached to the newly formed stormtrooper assault battalions and first saw action in the Isonzo in the spring of 1917. In 1917 the Austro-Hungarian Army had also constituted Special Sapper Battalion 61 that included four companies, each with four flamethrower platoons, in addition to a number of support troops. The standard platoon had four assault detachments each armed with three *kleine*-type portable flamethrowers. Each company had 48 *kleine* flamethrowers of 15 liter fuel capacity and 20 large of 50 liter fuel capacity. By then each stormtrooper battalion typically was comprised of a flamethrower unit consisting of 30 soldiers and six *kleine*-type flamethrowers and two large flamethrowers. While early Austrian

31 Kriegsarchiv: K.u.K., 12. FABrigade Kommando, Op. Nr. 26/833, 7 July 1916.
32 Holger H. Herwig, *The First World War*, p. 237.

flamethrower platoons were often ineffective due to the poor quality of the Austrian-manufactured flamethrowers, their performance improved markedly as a result of the adoption of the German *kleine*-type flamethrower. Another problem that affected the early performance of these specialized platoons was that at times they were not used appropriately. In some sectors of the front line, for example, they were used to carry out sapper or engineering tasks such as building bridges.[33] However, these units were to prove their worth initially in the Battle of Mount Ortigara where in essence special flamethrower sections aligned with the stormtroopers at the forefront of the fighting, tearing huge gaps in the Italian defensive lines. Later in the year the special flamethrower battalion fought extremely well at Caporetto and during the Solstice Offensive of 1918.

Thus given greater German assistance and increased output by Austrian-Hungarian defense industries the army was able to make significant progress in re-equipping for a long-term war of attrition with modern artillery and machine guns. Progress was achieved in almost all departments including the areas of weakness that plagued Austria-Hungary when it entered the war. These were mainly an efficient but not large artillery arm and a lack of new weapons for positional warfare such as large quantities of trench mortars, grenade launchers, small artillery guns and hand grenades. The only two areas of weakness that persisted in 1916 were within the Air Force and the logistics/transportation sectors. Both were due to low production rates within Austria-Hungary domestic industry. Such areas would continue to be a cause for concern until the end of the war since the Dual Monarchy could only produce roughly 3,000 vehicles and 500 planes per year, a rate insufficient to keep pace with the number of units being destroyed or under repair.[34] The Austro-Hungarian defense industry would also lag the Allies in the race to develop and build modern tanks. As a result, its army was one of the few armies of the First World War that failed to field armored tank squads in late 1917 and 1918.

The Birth of the Storm Troopers

A major reform was the adoption of new and innovative infantry tactics. The adoption of German *sturmtruppen* training and tactics was an outgrowth of the infantry specialization process that characterized the Austro-Hungarian Army of 1916. But it can be argued that the stormtrooper idea also drew heavily from the experiences of German infantry units on the Western front and from that army's creation of elite assault infantry detachments.

The Austrian military historian Ernst Wisshaupt has argued that: "The decision to constitute special assault battalions was determined by the impasse on the front line that was caused by the adoption on both sides of highly fortified defensive positions

33 Chris McNabb, *The Flamethrower* (Oxford: Osprey, 2015).
34 Holger H. Herwig, *The First World War,* p. 237.

in combination with the diminished capacity for firepower and movement on the part of the average soldier."[35]

Wisshaupt's interpretation to explain the rise of the stormtrooper units is accurate in that he identifies the two major reasons that prompted the AOK to change course during 1916. Although none of the AOK archive documents reveal the reasons why the stormtroopers were formed in late 1916, we do know that the Austro-Hungarian Army at the time faced a singular predicament. Their origin in fact was the result of a situation of distress within the army felt especially by the infantry and caused by the offensive-minded tactics adopted by AOK during 1914–15. First, like all major fronts during the First World War, the Italo-Austrian sector by 1916 had reached an impasse as both armies had vastly increased the defensive structures such as the machine gun and artillery strongpoints coupled with the barbed wire works that made major offensive operations risky and costly. As a result of the impasse, the AOK likely sought to constitute the stormtroopers to carry out a dual mission of training the standard infantry in close combat fighting and lead offensive operations as elite units. By further improving the fighting qualities of the standard infantry and by having better trained and armed elite units to lead it, it was envisioned that such a combination offered the best chances of breaking through the enemy's fortified positions. Second, by mid 1916 the Austro-Hungarian Army had reached a major turning point. During 1914–15 it had bled profusely, losing one million soldiers on the Eastern front. Thus by 1916 its infantry consisted of two major groups. A group of mostly older, less physically fit soldiers that had started the war, but that was by 1916 deployed in more defensive-minded tasks such as digging trenches and manning frontline positions. And a more offensive group made up by more physically fit, and generally younger cadres of soldiers on whom the responsibility of carrying out offensive operations ultimately fell upon. Thus by better harnessing the offensive potential of these soldiers with improved training and better equipment, the AOK sought to achieve the much desired breakthrough as well as overcome the problem of limited resources amongst the infantry ranks.

The birth of the Austro-Hungarian special assault units was also influenced by three main external factors. First, it was the result of the growing need for specialized troops in the new combat environment of trench warfare. Conrad's offensive operations of 1914–15 in Serbia and on the Eastern Front had shown the weakness of obsolete tactics with standard infantry units attacking in different linear waves without the proper equipment and adequate artillery support. As a result, by 1916 several Austro-Hungarian infantry units had already constituted special bombing squads for the attack and had increased the strength of the pioneer/sapper units specifically to tackle the wire. These units were the forerunners of the Austro-Hungarian stormtroopers and represented the new reality of the Austro-Hungarian Army of late 1916, and early 1917. Italian intelligence reports from that period, for instance, detailed how the enemy army was divided in roughly two groups of soldiers. On one

35 Ernst Wisshaupt, *Die Tiroler Kaiserjäger im Weltkriege 1914–1918: vol. 2* (Vienna: Simon Franz Goth, 1936), p. 350.

hand, there were the older soldiers, the veterans that had started the war and due to a host of factors such as age, combat fatigue, etc. these soldiers could only be deployed in defensive tasks such as trench excavating, laying barbed wire or manning defensive positions. On the other hand, there were younger, more physically fit soldiers, complemented by a sprinkling of junior officers and more mature soldiers, that could be more readily be deployed for offensive operations. It was this last group that the Austro-Hungarian Army would rely constantly upon to conduct offensive operations during the last two years of the war. Second, the German Army offered a viable model for stormtrooper operations and tactics. In fact, after Rohr's German unit (*Sturmabteilung Rohr*) had completed a number of successful combat operations on the Western front, the AOK began to take notice of the new battle tactics adopted by German infantry. The German Army had just fought the great defensive battle of the Somme where it put in practice new attacking and counter-attacking methods. Small units of assault infantry were used in the battle to counter-attack French units that had infiltrated deep into the German lines. These units relied on advanced placed small artillery, mortar and machine gun units to provide a first anti-infantry screen. After the French units had advanced they were targeted by forward positioned artillery. Softened up by the trench warfare equipment, French infantry would then be attacked by stormtroopers which were often followed by the technical detachments such as flamethrower and light machine gun units.

Some of the Austro-Hungarian troops which fought alongside the Germans on the Eastern front were also familiarized with these new tactics during the storming of the Russian bridgehead at Zarecze in September 1916, in which the Central Powers infantry units successfully counter-attacked under German leadership.

Third, by then Russian Army commando units had also scored important victories against Central Power forces in the East especially during the so-called Brusilov's Offensive in June 1916. Even before that offensive the Russian Army had formed the *Jagdkommandos*, special assault/commando units that frequently raided Austrian positions inflicting casualties and destroying trenches and gun emplacements with increasing regularity. The constant threat posed by the *Jagdkommandos* forced Austro-Hungarian units to form their own special assault patrol units in a bid to stop the enemy raids. These troops would later be integrated in the *sturmtruppen* battalions.

As a result of the external influences/factors outlined above, in the fall of 1916 the AOK asked the German High Command if Austro-Hungarian troops could take part in the training at Beuville, the camp of *Sturmabteilung Rohr*.[36] At first approximately 15 senior Austro-Hungarian officers attended stormtrooper training during October 1916. This first group was then followed by a much larger group composed of 120 officers and 300 NCOs that was trained in three successive waves between November 1916 and January 1917.[37] These soldiers would later constitute the core

36 Helmuth Gruss, *Die deutschen Sturmbataillone im Weltkrieg* (Berlin: Aufbrau und Verwendung, 1939), p. 69.

37 Christian Ortner, *Storm Troops* (Vienna: Verlag Militaria, 2014), pp. 64–65. The original German edition is Christian Ortner, Stefan Rest, (eds.), *Sturmtruppen. Österreichisch-ungarische*

organizers and instructors of the Austrian training camps and would be responsible for the formation of the first stormtrooper units.

In 1916 one of the first Austrian officers to attend the training at Assault Battalion Rohr, General Staff Colonel Alfred Edler von Wittich, issued a report to the AOK on what he had observed at Beuville that would later have important ramifications for the development of the Austrian stormtroopers. In his report, Wittich praised the German unit stating that it demonstrated a mastery of close combat skills. The Austrian officer was particularly impressed with how the German assault soldiers handled heavy weapons such as trench mortars and small cannons during offensive training exercises as well as by the way the troops had mastered the art of handling and throwing hand grenades. He also argued that "the Austro-Hungarian assault battalions should be used as elite formations and function as independent battalions both from a logistic and an administrative point of view. The battalion's training function was to take second place and be confined to periods of recuperation and rest."[38] In his view, the *sturmtruppen* were to be deployed primarily as a fighting force during offensive operations. This was to some extent in contrast with how the German Army deployed *Sturmabteilung Rohr*, which spent most of its time training other infantry units and only saw occasional frontline deployment. German and Austrian perspectives on stormtrooper training and tactics also differed. While the AOK's initial intent was to constitute elite infantry units, the German High Command main objective was ultimately to train all standard infantry units with special assault tactics. This divergence of opinion stemmed mainly from the uneven level of resources available to the German and Austrian Army. In fact, the latter was never able to match the quantity of weapons and the number of physically fit soldiers available to the Germans and was therefore never in a position during the war to train every infantry unit to the newly developed close combat tactics.

On 24 November 1916 the AOK issued a directive instructing the Army to constitute special assault units:

> In connection with the ... close combat instruction ordered, the training of Sturmpatrouillen (sturmtrupps) in all Austro-Hungarian infantry and Jäger units is to be carried out during the coming winter. As a result of this training, every infantry company should have one or, if possible, two assault sections comprising one NCO and eight men, at their disposal by the spring. There should also be one or two officers, fully trained in this form of combat, to every battalion. Guidelines for the instruction and realization of assault attacks, compiled from the German experiences, will be issued shortly.[39]

Thus according to AOK, the Austrian special assault units were initially conceived primarily to take part in exploratory and offensive functions, while training other

Sturmformationen und Jagdkommandos im Ersten Weltkrieg (Vienna: Verlag Militaria, 2005).

38 Ibid., pp. 68–69.

39 Kriegsarchiv: K.u.K. AOK, Op. Nr. 34435, 24 November 1916.

infantry units was not initially seen as a priority. It is clear from the directive that AOK sought to constitute stormtroopers that could, based on their superior training, lead standard infantry units during offensive operations. Moreover, the stormtroopers were also seen as being instrumental in raising the overall fighting qualities of the army. To this end, the initial core of the Austro-Hungarian *sturmtruppen* would be constituted primarily by German-speaking officers and NCOs. And the first *sturmtruppen* units on the Italian front were to be formed within experienced infantry and mountain units. The initial organizational structure chosen by the AOK was for the creation of assault patrols (*Sturmpatrouillen*) whereby by the spring of 1917 every infantry company should have constituted two stormtrooper assault patrols. The AOK also envisioned the creation of assault battalions (*Sturmbaon*) at the army corp level which would have been responsible for carrying out specific planned assaults against obstinate enemy strongholds. Mountain troops were to have their own special assault companies (*Hochgebirgs-kompanien*) which were tasked with reconnaissance and combat in high altitude environments. Each high mountain company had three alpine infantry platoons, one machine gun platoon with two guns and a small mountain guide platoon. Many high mountain enemy posts were hard to reach as they were often located past a deep valley or a glacier and could only be reached after hiking and/or climbing for several miles. Thus, only these small patrols of specialized mountain troops could cross no man's land to reach them unobserved in order to conduct commando-type raids.

Another AOK stormtrooper directive soon followed establishing very generic guidelines for army commanders:

1. To form a particularly skillful unit to be called upon to perform difficult attacks when necessary.
2. To train the whole infantry, for the time being only one or two sturmpatrouillen per infantry company, in the performance of close combat with special weapons.[40]

Thus according to AOK the initial organization and training of the stormtroopers was the responsibility of the army corps commanders who thus enjoyed significant leeway and independence in shaping the organizational structure of their own special assault units. It was the army corps commanders, for instance, that were responsible for shifting soldiers and resources from within their own ranks to the specialized infantry assault units. The latter were also responsible for the construction of suitable training camps and shooting ranges. Finally, they were responsible for arming the new units. The assault patrols and battalions were to be designated with the numbers of their respective infantry battalion or regiment. Thus, for example, the stormtrooper battalion of the 11th Army was to be named the *11 Armee Sturmbaon*. The lack of additional resources such as machine guns, mortars, etc. was the specific reason why stormtrooper training was shifted toward the army corps level rather

40 Kriegsarchiv: K.u.K., AOK, Op. Nr. 36342/11, 1 December 1916.

than the AOK. In this directive the AOK, however, did not abandon the long-term inspiration to eventually train as many infantry units as possible to the close combat tactics of the stormtroopers. This aspiration, which approximated the German model, would however never be put into practice since the Austro-Hungarian Army lacked the necessary resources to reach the objective.

Technical Manual

Once the first wave of Austrian trainers had completed their stay at Beuville, in December 1916 the AOK issued an instruction manual titled "*Anleitung für die Ausbildung von Sturmtruppen*," which was the result of a collaborative effort with its German ally. The 50-page manual established standard training and tactics guidelines for the newly formed Austro-Hungarian *sturmtruppen*.

According to the manual the overall aim of the training program was:

> To ensure that each stormtroop unit conssted of handpicked soldiers possessed with considerable drive and courage. Each unit will be trained on how to properly operate its weapons (i.e., hand grenades, etc.) and will be outfitted with steel helmets and protective shields. Moreover, each stormtrooper will wear a special badge that not only will make him easily recognizable by the rest of the armed forces, but also contribute to raise his self-esteem and pride ... The main role of shock troops is the removal of stubborn enemy defenses including blockhouses, machine gun nests, fortified dugouts, and concealed enemy defenses. Moreover, stormtroopers must be deployed to roll up enemy trenches and facilitate the breaching of enemy positions.[41]

Initially army corps commanders were instructed to constitute two types of *sturmtruppen* units; infantry assault battalions (*Sturmbaon*) and infantry assault patrols (*Sturmpatrouillen*) that acted within standard infantry companies.

The recommended basic organization of the assault battalion should include:

1. Four infantry assault companies
2. Two machine gun companies (each with four guns)
3. One mountain battery and one field artillery battery (each with four guns)
4. A mortar unit (with four medium trench mortars and four standard mortars)
5. A flamethrower unit with six small, portable units
6. One sapper/engineer company.[42]

41 Kriegsarchiv: K.u.K. AOK, Op. Nr. 36/300, '*Anleitung für die Ausbildung der Sturmtruppen*', 2 December 1916, pp. 1–2.
42 Ibid., p. 4.

The standard infantry company included approximately 250 soldiers each belonging to one of four platoons.

While the standard stormtrooper assault patrol, the basic unit of the company, included the following:

1. A patrol leader armed primarily with a pistol, a flare gun a few hand grenades
2. Two hand grenade launchers carrying up to twelve hand grenades
3. Three grenade bearers carrying extra hand grenades and armed primarily with rifles
4. One sapper carrying explosives
5. Finally, two soldiers with rifles charged with defending the rest of the platoon from enemy ambushes.[43]

According to Austrian historian Viktor Schemfil the first *Kaiserjäger* high mountain assault patrols, for instance, were armed with the following: six grenades for the throwers, 12 for the bearers, 40 cartridges for the riflemen, and two wire cutters. Special mountain stormtrooper assault patrols were also equipped with heavy boots, skis, ice picks, climbing ropes and snow camouflage smocks.[44]

Similarly to Assault Battalion Rohr or to the Russian commando units, the training course of the *sturmtruppen* was highly specialized. Like German stormtrooper basic training, it lasted 14 days for those in the assault patrols, followed by six weeks of extensive training for those that formed the infantry assault companies/battalions.

The core training was based on throwing hand grenades, sharpshooting from different distances and positions and a heavy focus on physical exercises. The section on hand grenade training (*Ausbildung im Handgranatenwerfer*), for example, was very detailed prescribing 12 different exercises for the proper handle and use of hand grenades. The manual was later expanded with additional training elements such as instructions on the use of daggers, bayonets and steel clubs in close combat in the trenches. It also included a section on how to properly operate captured enemy weapons such as mortars and machine guns.

From a tactical perspective the *sturmtruppen* were to be deployed in two types of operations:

1. planned attacks
2. small scale raids/reconnaissance missions.

With respect to planned attacks the stormtroopers were expected to infiltrate enemy lines within the weakest enemy sectors or those that offered little resistance in order to achieve a deep penetration and with the ultimate aim being the capture of the

43 Ibid., p. 5.

44 Viktor Schemfil, *Das K.u.K. 3. Regiment der Tiroler Kaiserjäger im Weltkritg 1914–1918* (Bregenz: J.N. Teutsch, 1926), p. 445.

enemy's artillery batteries. To surprise the enemy, the *sturmtruppen* were to use extreme caution and secrecy. The tactical manual states that: "Every soldier should observe absolute silence while on the front line before and after having mounted the attack. It is forbidden to discuss *sturmtruppen* assault plans while at the front line or over the phone. The assault units shall move forward at a designated time by looking at their clocks rather than through an alarm given by auditory means such as a shout by their officer."[45]

The troops would then climb over the parapets and exit their trenches before the preparatory barrage was moved forward. As soon as the assault units had passed no man's land, the barrage would be lifted forward. The stormtroopers would then penetrate into the enemy trenchline as the latter was still hiding in the dugouts and caverns to avoid the barrage. At that point, with the barrage already lifted, the *sturmtruppen* would deploy their hand-to-hand combat techniques to breach the enemy line and push forward to deepen the opening. In order to force the *sturmtruppen* to advance deeply into enemy positions and achieve the tactical breakthrough for which they were deployed, these special forces were instructed to always move forward. "It is forbidden," the manual states, "to handle prisoners of war, injured soldiers or enemy weapons until the objective of the operation has been achieved. Even dead comrades have to be left on the battlefield until the task is completed."[46]

As the assault troops moved forward and encountered particularly obstinate resistance they were instructed to put into practice proven German techniques. One of the most popular ones entailed pinning down an enemy strong point with a combination of rifle, machine gun and light artillery fire. This would immobilize the enemy nest so that one of the assault platoons could circumvent it and then reduce it with hand grenades. Another popular tactic instructed small patrol units on how to mop up an enemy trenchline strong point with a combination of hand grenades, grenade sticks and detonation charges. Special crack mountain companies adapted infiltration tactics in high altitude alpine conditions by scaling mountain peaks with daring maneuvers. These units would then overrun enemy positions with hand grenades lobbed from above and from the flanks of an enemy mountain outpost.

The manual then stressed how critical it was to teach both junior officers and standard soldiers on taking the initiative and acting autonomously during planned attacks or raids since the battle field required quick thinking especially when a platoon leader was missing or had been wounded.

> Every soldier must know exactly what to do, how to behave and how the enemy is deployed. Even if all the officers die during the operation, the soldiers must carry on and carry out the operation outlined in the plan of attack.[47]

45 Kriegsarchiv: K.u. K. AOK, Op. Nr. 36/300, '*Anleitung für die Ausbildung der Sturmtruppen*', 2 December 1916, p. 13.
46 Ibid., p. 14.
47 Ibid., p. 15.

Stormtroopers were not to fight as one big unit, but as many small assault patrol units taking enemy positions frontally, by the flanks and by the rear. The high degree of autonomy in decision-making given to stormtrooper platoon commanders enabled them to push forward without having to rely on the orders of an overbearing, distant chain of command. Unlike standard infantry units, the stormtroopers, NCOs, and soldiers alike, were all considered leaders in the battlefield. In the midst of an encounter with the enemy, the stormtroopers were to spread out in the field of battle and attack the objective from multiple directions. This was a radical change in Austro-Hungarian tactics since historically the officer gave directions to his soldiers from the rear and NCOs would be highly dependent upon their commander's instructions during combat operations.

During most major offensive operations the *sturmtruppen* functioned as the lead of the infantry assault, but they never fought together as one unit. The *sturmtruppen* battalion, for instance, was typically split into four units with each of its companies leading the fight in front of one or more standard infantry battalions. For example, during the Battle of Mount Ortigara in June 1917 the *sturmtruppen* of the 11th Army were split into three groups each responsible for breaching one section of enemy defenses. The stormtroopers were heavily armed with hand grenades, flame-throwers and grenade launchers and were used as the battering ram to open up enemy defenses. They were required to identify weak spots in the enemy's defenses and then exploit them, while the infantry was to advance in their wake. The way the *sturmtruppen* were deployed was slightly different from how the Italian *arditi* attacked enemy positions, but ultimately both fought very similarly and often adopted the same tactics.

Once the objective had been taken the *sturmtruppen* were trained on how to 'turn around' the captured positions by deploying sandbags, steel shields and machine guns. In order to defend the position from a likely enemy counter-attack the stormtroopers were also trained on how to use enemy weapons such as Italian mortars and machine guns. Infantry commanders were instructed to relieve the assault units as quickly as possible in order not to wear them down with trenchline duties.

The second role of the *sturmtruppen* was to conduct quick raids against enemy front lines to capture prisoners and weapons or to simply conduct reconnaissance for planned attacks. These were typically conducted when least expected such as during the night or under tough weather conditions such as heavy snow, rain and fog in order to conceal the troop advance beyond no man's land. "The assault patrols are to undertake their mission of penetrating the first enemy position without artillery preparation, unnoticed and unmolested by the enemy, in short taking them by surprise, and maintain this element of surprise for as long as possible."[48]

Reconnaissance was critical to both the preparation of planned attacks and for the execution of successful raids. Thus officers were trained in drawing sketches of enemy positions, in interpreting intelligence material such as aerial photographs, and

48 Kriegsarchiv: 26. Gebrige Brigade, Op. Nr. 217/5, '*Direktiven fur den uberfallsartigen angriff durch Sturmpatrouillen*', 12 June 1917, p. 2.

An Austro-Hungarian mountain soldier saturates an enemy post with hand grenades. (Kriegsarchiv Vienna)

Austro-Hungarian stormtroopers training with wire cutters. (Kriegsarchiv Vienna)

Austro-Hungarian stormtroopers with gas mask, rifle, steel clubs, steel helmets and hand grenade bags slung over the shoulders. The Bosnian *sturmtruppen* in particular were particularly skillful in the use of steel clubs, brass knuckles and other close combat weapons. (Kriegsarchiv Vienna)

Austro-Hungarian stormtroopers training with hand grenades. The Model 24 *Stielhandgranate* (stick grenade) was the standard hand grenade of the Austro-Hungarian army during the First World War. The stick provided a lever, significantly improving the throwing distance. The stick grenade could be thrown up to 40 yards, while the British Mills bomb could only be thrown about 15 yards. (Kriegsarchiv Vienna)

Austro-Hungarian mountain soldiers looking at the *Tre Cime di Lavaredo* (Three Peaks of Lavaredo) probably the most beautiful and spectacular mountains of the Dolomites. (Kriegsarchiv Vienna)

Austro-Hungarian mountain soldiers with, in the background, the Austro-Hungarian position of the *Torre di Toblin*. (Toblin Tower) in the Dolomites. The position was a true eagle's nest with its peak observation points, its artillery and machine guns flanking posts. (Kriegsarchiv Vienna)

Seep Innerfolker, the famous Austro-Hungarian mountain guide surrounded by the members of his 'flying patrol' of expert mountain climbers in 1915.

Austro-Hungarian stormtroopers of 11th Army *Sturmbaon* in the Mount Pasubio rear in 1917. The Tyrolean *Kaiserjäger* regiments were comprised for the most part of German-speaking soldiers from the Tyrol. Many of these soldiers were excellent mountaineers and some were even experienced mountain guides and climbers. By 1917 each infantry regiment consisted of three field battalions and one stormtrooper assault company or battalion. (Kriegsarchiv Vienna)

Austro-Hungarian stormtroopers of 11th Army *Sturmbaon* in 1917. By late 1917 every infantry division was to constitute one divisional stormtrooper assault battalion consisting of four assault companies. The soldiers of the assault companies were from each of the four divisional regiments. Independent brigades had to raise half-battalions. The number-designation of the assault battalions, half-regiments or half-battalions was the same as the parent division/brigade. (Kriegsarchiv Vienna)

Emperor Karl salutes a pluridecorated stormtrooper of the high mountain/alpine company. (Kriegsarchiv Vienna)

Stormtrooper during wire cutting training. Stormtroopers were imbued with the offensive spirit and many assault companies led very successful attacks. By June 1918 the Austro-Hungarian Army had many specialized stormtrooper units at its disposal. (Kriegsarchiv Vienna)

how to carry out proper reconnaissance to identify ways through no man's land to penetrate enemy trenchlines. They were also instructed on how to carefully observe enemy movements and their defensive deployment including the location and span of fire of the machine guns, and locating sentry posts and weak enemy positions where the barbed wire could more easily be probed. Training also instructed officers on how to build models of targeted enemy positions and to train their troops in a physical environment that resembled the physical surroundings of an enemy position.

The following is a detailed intelligence report written by an assault patrol leader. It demonstrates the extent to which these special assault platoons would challenge the mountainous terrain by climbing dangerous peaks and hills to get as close as possible to the Italian positions in order to capture valuable intelligence. Moreover, while on reconnaissance these special troops would likely be posted under inclement weather for hours or for days in barren mountain terrain with little or no communication with their comrades on the front line. Stamina and physical endurance were some of the key attributes of the stormtroopers.

> While conducting reconnaissance to plan the raid against Casa Minoldo, I was able to ascertain the following on the enemy deployment.
>
> 1. On Col dell'Ai I noticed intensive enemy activity by its strong garrison. On Cima Vallone (2,536 meters high) the artillery observation post is fully occupied with smoke bellowing out of the chimney constantly. Numerous sentries were spotted in strategically located posts.
> 2. On the Minola mountains infrequent snow shoveling was noted. The strong point on Hill 1,440 in the Digon valley is thinly held, and at Hill 1,872 a mountain gun was being cleared of snow. Longerin hill at 2,569 meters is not occupied.
> 3. Strong enemy presence observed at Candide and on the main road to San Nicola. At Danta lots of smoke bellowing out of the chimneys. It's cableway system to Campedello was very active. At Hill 1,249 and in the nearby forest intense enemy activity noted (lots of smoke).
> 4. Col Rosson little or no enemy activity. Mount Spina is unoccupied during the winter. On Col Quaterna strong enemy presence was noted.
> 5. Val Digon no enemy activity was noted.[49]

During the raids enemy sentries were often the first victims of the assault patrols as they were dealt primarily with daggers and bayonets. When the assault patrols entered into enemy trenches they deployed a special assault tactic. Two teams of grenade launchers would be in the lead, while the platoon leader followed in their footsteps covering their advance by firing a machine gun pistol against the enemy. The rest of the platoon members included two grenade carriers responsible for replenishing the

49 Kriegsarchiv: K.u.K. Abschnittskommando Karnischer Kamm Nr. 239, '*Wahrnehumgen uber der gagner*', 28 January 1917.

launchers and two riflemen responsible for covering the flanks. "After infiltrating the assault patrol split up and advanced from the right to left (not frontally like an attack) and silently took out observers and sentries. Depending on orders, men found in dugouts were either rendered harmless or captured."[50]

The manual also instructed unit commanders to teach their soldiers various assault tactics by conducting daily drills especially in mountainous, wooded and difficult terrain. In order to carry out successful raids the manual instructed soldiers how to attack enemy positions by crawling, by running, by running with shields and weapons (mainly rifles and hand grenades), by jumping from one spot to the next while opening fire from different positions. Lastly, how to build physical endurance by advancing with full gear against enemy positions while overcoming obstacles such as ditches, hedges, dense forests, trenches, sand pits, rocky, mountainous terrain, walls, and penetrating into blockhouses.

The manual prescribed both individual and crew served weapon training to enhance unit specialization including hand grenades, rifles, light machine guns, mortars, mine and grenade throwers, small artillery guns and flamethrowers. The manual also focused on how to overcome enemy barbed wire works with makeshift devices such as grenade sticks and other detonation charges.

The prescribed six week training program included:

1. General instructions on the purpose and role of the shock troops.
2. Instructions on how to properly conduct field assessments and reconnaissance of enemy positions in order to recognize where the enemy lines and flanks are, where the blockhouses are located, detecting specific areas of enemy weakness and determining the best point of attack.
3. Reading maps.
4. How to view and interpret maps and various types of sketches.
5. Instructions on how to facilitate the interaction between support and assault squads.
6. Lean how to properly use our own as well as the enemy's hand grenades.
7. Learn how to load, shoot and recharge an enemy machine gun.
8. Instructions on how to use small flamethrowers in the attack.
9. Lessons on how to use light grenade launchers.[51]

Additionally, the manual prescribed how soldiers should be dressed, equipped and armed during offensive operations. The stormtrooper was expected to wear a steel helmet, field-grey uniform reinforced with knee and elbow pads, a rucksack, and a special sack across the shoulder to carry six hand grenades. He also carried four rations of tinned food, two water bottles, an electric flashlight, gas mask, and four empty sandbags. If the stormtrooper fought for one of the mountain regiments he also had

50 Christian Ortner, *Storm Troops*, p. 184.

51 Kriegsarchiv: K.u.K. AOK, Op. Nr. 36/300, *'Anleitung für die Ausbildung der Sturmtruppen'*, 2 December 1916.

extensive camouflage equipment such as a white helmet cover and a white over-suit to blend in with the snow-covered terrain. He was armed with a small rifle with bayonet (or automatic pistol for the officers), 40 cartridges, hand grenades, and also had a small shovel, or ice pick and gas mask. The light artillery crews were armed with mortars (M6 90 mm *Minenwerfen*), machine guns (*Schwarzlose* M07/12), grenade launchers, flame-throwers (*kleine* model) and small artillery units (typically two 75 mm *Skoda* guns).

To encourage comradeship, the soldiers of the *Sturmbaon* were authorized by AOK to wear a special stormtrooper steel badge on their collar. In most cases it was the 'deathhead,' a skull with crossed bones with the name of the unit under it. Initially, when the AOK decided to create the assault patrols and battalions it was decided not to give these troops special collar badges, probably because the High Command wanted to conceal the existence of these new units from the enemy. Later in the summer of 1917 the proposal of a special badge was discussed again because many battalions were adopting their own unofficial badges. The issue was finally decided in 1918. It was determined that the badge should be awarded: "To every officer or soldier, who passed the assault course, showed over average skills and had at least three successful missions."[52]

During these missions the soldier was expected to excel in the performance of highly dangerous tasks and produce concrete results such as inflicting enemy casualties, capturing enemy soldiers and destroying enemy defenses.

Since stormtroopers comprised elite units they typically received better and more complex equipment than the standard infantry. The *sturmtruppen*, for example, wore steel helmets since their inception, while many standard infantry soldiers only received them after two years of fighting.

Several stormtrooper officers and NCOs have left us their war memories which furnish relevant information regarding the type of drills executed during assault training.

> "With assault training," argued Captain Ernst von Verdross, "I always placed a strong emphasis amongst my men of taking advantage of the rugged mountain terrain. While advancing against an enemy stronghold, my soldiers were always instructed to lay low close to the ground and to hop into shell holes or on the reverse slopes. I used to shout to them 'Get down. Get your head to the ground.' There were also specific instructions for the machine gun platoons. The weapon was always to be used to surprise the enemy after it had been dug into a concealed position.
>
> There were also specific instructions for the defense such as rehearsing how to speedily exit our dugouts after the enemy artillery barrage had ended or had moved forward.[53]

52 http://www.austro-hungarian-army.co.uk/badges/*sturmtruppen*.html <Accessed 10 October 2016>

53 Ernst von Verdross, '*Kriegserlebnisse eines Österreichischen Sturmzugskommandanten*', Schwizerische Monatschrift für Offiziere aller Waffen, 1929, p. 57.

Some of the most relevant information on stormtrooper training can be gleaned by reading the war memories of a well-known *sturmtruppen* commander named Otto Gallian. Gallian led an assault company belonging to one of the *Kaiserjäger* regiments which participated to numerous operations including the attack of Mount Asolone:

> Prior to the great offensive in the summer of 1918 I took part in daily drills with live fire rounds. I would lead my officers and soldiers into a rehearsed attack against an enemy hilltop position. We advanced under the arc of fire provided by flanking machine guns. Supported by both artillery and machine gun fire, my men grew in confidence and were no longer afraid of running toward the enemy line and advanced all the way to the point where they could throw the hand grenades.[54]

In his work Gallian also discusses how *sturmtruppen* operations were typically prepared in every detail. In a raid to capture enemy soldiers, Gallian recalls how the operation was organized through countless night reconnaissance missions, the careful selection of the team that was to take part in the raid, and the extensive training given to the selected soldiers on how to cut the wire and how to advance quietly and close to the ground.

Storm Trooper Strength Spring 1917

Since initially the *sturmtruppen* units fell under the army corps, the AOK decided to conduct a survey in April 1917 to determine their strength and consistency. It revealed that by then army commanders had constituted several assault battalions and assault patrol units across the Italian front:

1. Boroevic's 5th Army had one assault battalion and an additional 7,700 soldiers trained as stormtroopers.
2. Army Group Conrad had one assault battalion with the 11th Army, one assault patrol in each brigade of the XX Army Corps. And two assault patrols per company of Rayon I and II.
3. 10th Army: had one assault battalion, assault patrols per each infantry battalion, and small assault patrols per each alpine company.[55]

The survey revealed that given the absence of a firm AOK directive instructing how many assault battalions/patrol units each army corp should have, the army commanders had failed to follow uniform patterns. Each had created a myriad of stormtrooper formations depending upon the type of frontline sector (mountains,

54 Otto Gallian, '*Ufgaben des Sturmtruppenfuhers*', Militar, n. 21, June 1921, p. 33.
55 Christian Ortner, *Storm Troops*, p. 77.

mountains and valleys, Carso/Isonzo sector, etc.) in which their units operated and also based on the troops at their disposal.

It revealed, however, that despite the initial broad vision of extending close combat training to many units, the Austro-Hungarian Army on the Italian front had only managed to form a few elite battalions and several hundred stormtrooper assault patrol units. In essence these units comprised highly specialized, elite infantry forces.

Overall, the Austro-Hungarian Army had primarily two types of stormtrooper units: assault battalions and various assault patrol/rapid reaction platoons. The assault battalion was more autonomous and almost always was deployed for special operations, while the *sturmpatrouillen* were engaged within their respective infantry company. The assault battalion typically spent more time in the rear training and from time to time participated in planned attacks. The assault patrol took part in many raids and reconnaissance missions and generally spent less time training in the rear. The assault patrols of 5th Army, for instance, spent the vast majority of their time on the front line being frequently called to action in order to exploit every opportunity. Their situation was somewhat unique since the other armies did not keep their stormtroopers continuously on the frontline to avoid wearing them down and thus risk losing highly trained soldiers.

Consolidation of Storm Trooper Units

In the fall of 1917 after the Austro-Hungarian *sturmtruppen* had completed a number of successful operations thus proving their worth to the Austro-Hungarian High Command, each infantry division was requested to constitute at least one *sturmtruppen* battalion. This AOK directive paved the way for an important expansion of the stormtroopers within the Austro-Hungarian Army that went hand-in-hand with the infantry re-organization. The AOK stressed that "training in assault tactics must become common property of the whole infantry."[56] Each infantry division was now to be based on regiments composed of three rather than four infantry battalions. But as the standard infantry division became smaller, its degree of specialization was increased markedly. According to the reorganization plan each division would not only have its own dedicated sapper battalion, but also a large flamethrower section, a mortar and trench-mortar group, and a grenade launcher group. With regards to the stormtroopers, each division was to constitute one *sturmtruppen* battalion whose task was to lead the infantry into battle but also to train the division's infantry soldiers. To this end, stormtrooper training was to be centralized at the divisional level. Each division was instructed to create a divisional training ground where the infantry units would receive training in close combat tactics. In contrast to the Italian Army, this directive maintained the *sturmtruppen* as elite units within regular infantry divisions, while their Italian counterparts, the *arditi*, formed a separate combat arm from the infantry.

56 Kriegsarchiv: K.u.K. AOK Op. Nr. 29/021, 12 October 1917.

By this time, the typical *sturmtruppen* battalion consisted of four companies, while each company was subdivided into four platoons with 28–30 soldiers. In addition, the battalion also comprised a machine gun company, a small artillery company, a mortar company and a flamethrower company. The total strength of the battalion varied between 800–1,000 soldiers.[57] The trainees were typically very young, not married, or if they were married it was preferable that they be childless. There was a predisposition toward the physically fit and the experienced mountaineers. Soldiers that had been part of special hand grenade or light artillery support units were also preferred over soldiers lacking specialized experience.

The Organization of the Stormtroopers During the Last Year of the War

The end of the Battle of Mount Grappa, which coincided with the start of winter 1918, brought about a prolonged period of stasis on the Italian front that allowed the AOK to further reorganize the stormtroopers. Before Caporetto a directive issued by AOK had approved the formation of *sturmtruppen* battalions at the divisional level. But given the ongoing preparations for the major battle as well as due to ongoing shortages of men and weapons, several infantry divisions could not complete the formation of their assault detachments until the spring of 1918.

For the Supreme Command the time had come for another major expansion of the *sturmtruppen* so that the original goal of training standard infantry in assault tactics could become reality. As a result, the vast majority of the infantry divisions set up training centers for the stormtroopers. The trainers were in essence the members of the prior army corps *sturmtruppen* battalions which were disbanded in favor of the assault battalions at the division level. During the months of February, March and April 1918 several training schools were set up by the infantry divisions with the goal of uniting regimental *sturmkompagnien* into a single *sturmtruppen* battalion. The 11th Army was one of the first armies to constitute stormtrooper battalions (*Sturmbaons*) at the divisional level by issuing the following communiqué: "Now that the frontline has stabilized the time is ripe for systematic stormtrooper training and the constitution of infantry division *sturmtruppen* battalions. The Army Corp is fully supportive of this objective as the formation of the *sturmtruppen* at the divisional level will ensure effective performance on the battlefield together with a high spirit of comradeship."[58] As a result its *Sturmbaon* was dissolved and a new stormtrooper battalion was formed to take its place. It initially had a force of 51 officers and 1,000 soldiers under the command of Captain Oskar Teuber. It was to serve as the *sturmtruppen* battalion for the *Kaiserjäger* Division and the 159th Infantry Brigade.

At the time, one of the factors that allowed for a major expansion of the stormtroopers were the vast amounts of ammunition and weapons that had been captured at Caporetto. By the spring of 1918 the Austrian stormtroopers could count

57 Kriegsarchiv: K.u.K., AOK Op. Nr. 43/785, '*Organization der Sturmtruppen*', 9 September 1917.
58 Kriegsarchiv: K.u.K. 11. Armee aberKommando, Op. Nr. 3678, 11 January 1918.

upon record numbers of Italian machine guns to augment their firepower without taking away much needed guns and ammunition from their divisional infantry forces.

As a result, the Austro-Hungarian official history states that in June 1918 the army had 65 *sturmtruppen* battalions and 10 *sturmtruppen* half-battalions.[59] The *sturmtruppen* battalions were numbered as follows: 1, 2, 3, 4, 5, 6, 7, 8, 9, 10, 11, 12, 13, 14, 15, 16,17, 18, 19, 20, 21, 22, 24, 25, 26, 27, 28, 29, 30, 31, 32, 33, 34, 35, 36, 37, 38, 39, 40, 41, 42, 43, 44, 45, 46, 47, 48, 49, 50, 51, 52, 53, 54, 55, 56, 57, 58, 59, 60, 62, 64, 70, 74, 106, and 155. While the majority belonged to the K.u.K. Army, the following battalions: 13, 21, 22, 26, 43, 44, 45, 46, 54 and 56 belonged to the *Landwehr* and battalions: 20, 37, 38, 39, 40, 41, 51, 64, 70, 74 and 155 to the *Honvéd*. Finally, assault battalions 62 and 106 were *Landsturm* formations while Battalion 23 did not exist because the 23rd Infantry Division had been captured in 1915 almost in its entirety by the Russians and was never reformed.

By mid 1918 each infantry division was comprised of two infantry regiments with a total of 12 standard infantry battalions and an additional stormtrooper battalion and one of field artillery with 16 artillery batteries.

The final organization of the standard divisional *sturmtruppen* battalion was as follows:

1. Four storm assault companies of three platoons plus a light machine gun squad
2. A heavy machine gun company
3. An infantry gun platoon
4. A technical platoon
5. A close combat weapons platoon (equipped with trench mortars and searchlights)
6. A flamethrower platoon,
7. A telephone section.

The final make up of the stormtrooper battalions was modeled on the German units fighting on the Western front in 1918. The main difference with the early battalions of 1917 was the addition to each infantry company of a light machine gun squad. Both on the Western front during the spring 1918 offensives and in Italy with the Solstice Offensive, the light Maxim 08/15 machine gun supplanted the hand grenade as the most important weapon of the stormtroopers.

In the aftermath of the great Solstice Offensive in June 1918 the vast majority of the *sturmtruppen* battalions were placed on reserve in the rear. From July 1918 to the end of the war in November 1918 these troops would see very little action, mostly deployed for small-scale raids and planned attacks to improve the frontline positions of the Austro-Hungarian Army. With the end of the war the *sturmtruppen* units were disbanded.

59 Edmund Glaise-Horstenau (ed.), *Österreich-Ungarns letzter Krieg 1914–1918* (Vienna: Verlag der Militärwissenschaftlichen Mitteilungen, 1936), Vol. 7, p. 58.

Weapons and Equipment

What ultimately distinguished these units from the standard infantry battalions were extensive training and increased firepower both in terms of the amount and size of the equipment. These units combined assault training with engineering/sapper and small artillery skills. They could thus assault enemy positions by covering them with hand grenades, clear the obstacle zone with explosives and destroy stubborn enemy defenses with small cannons and mortars. Like their German ally, the Austrian stormtroops had a great variety of weapons to unlock intricate situations resulting from positional warfare. Each battalion would typically have eight flamethrowers, eight mortars, four small artillery guns, eight machine guns and several light machine guns. The German manufactured Maxim 08/15 light machine gun, introduced in late 1917, became one of the key weapons of the Austro-Hungarian *sturmtruppen*. It was a relatively light weapon that could be moved into a forward position to cover the assault detachments advancing against the enemy or to fight off a potential enemy counter-attack. While the stormtroopers charged against the enemy, surprise fire from a machine gun in a forward position was often enough to force the enemy to the ground and enable the attack. It also allowed the stormtroopers assault patrol units to pin down an enemy strongpoint and allow the assault unit to outflank it and then destroy it. The 1918 tactical manual states that: "During an attack machine guns should be used as frequently as possible. Not so much to achieve a material result, but more to prevent enemy retaliation by combing the enemy trenches."[60] This portable automatic gun was perhaps the most important weapon that complemented all other stormtrooper weapons and tactics since it could be carried into the attack to suppress enemy defensive fire.

The 15-liter *kleine* portable flamethrower was another important weapon for the stormtroopers. Their standard battalion had a flamethrower platoon divided into three teams with eight men and two flamethrowers. The tactical manual outlined that the weapon could be used for both defensive and offensive purposes:

> The flamethrower can be seen as an additional close combat weapon for small scale attacks or defense and will be mainly used to defend positions. It can also be used to set flammable objects alight. A) Close range attack. If it is possible to advance under cover to within working distance to drive the enemy out of field cover or houses with fire. B) Defense. As soon as the enemy is within range.[61]

In 1917–18 the stormtroopers would use the flamethrower platoons primarily as an offensive weapon. The platoon was generally deployed in the second wave of the attack and it was primarily responsible for mopping up enemy trenches and caverns. In some instances the flamethrower units were used in the lead in the *Messertaktic*, the so-called knife attack. With this method of attack, flamethrower squads were deployed at the

60 Die Angriff, *Abschnitte aus der Gefechtslehre* (Vienna: Teil VII, 1918), p. 19.
61 Cited in Christian Ortner, *Storm Troops*, p. 266.

forefront and in the center of the infantry assault, while the machine gun and rifle squads were positioned at the flanks. While the latter were deployed primarily to cover the flanks and protect the infantry attack, the flamethrowers were charged with attacking head on with multiple portable flamethrowers squirting flames into the enemy line. During the attack on Mount Ortigara in 1917, for example, the Austro-Hungarian forces there deployed used this tactic which proved very successful.

Trench mortars were also used as a forward weapon for trench and wire busting. In 1918 the Austro-Hungarian Army received the new 9 cm M17 trench mortar which was widely used during the Solstice Offensive. This mortar was an improvement over earlier versions since it was lighter than previous models but it retained the same projectile weight of 5 kg and the range of 0.6 mile. Since it could be brought forward into no man's land, the trench mortars allowed the stormtroopers to advance under their own preparatory artillery fire. Moreover, it was very effective at short range to destroy enemy strong points that had been left undamaged by artillery fire. In the midst of close combat conditions it allowed stormtrooper commanders to direct their own small artillery fire instead of having to rely on the artillery in the rear which would always react more slowly to the needs of the frontline troops. In 1918 the stormtrooper battalions received their own support mortar platoons comprised of eight 9 cm M17 mortars and eight smaller mortar units (the even lighter M18 small trench mortar).

The tactical instructions for these units were purely offensive:

> At the moment of the attack, on the order of the sector commander and according to the progress of the attack, light and medium trench mortar fire is to be moved in the area behind the enemy line at its greatest range. The mortars will fire on the communication and supply routes to prevent evasion by the troops in the trenches and reinforcements from moving in ... the most important thing at the moment of attack is a secure connection between the trench mortar crews and the assault troops.[62]

As Cornish asserts the combination of new very versatile weapons along with more extensive training allowed for the full execution of small unit tactics in which the *sturmtruppen* excelled: "Small unit tactics changed profoundly as light machine guns and automatic rifles took their place with hand grenades and grenade launchers alongside the traditional rifle and bayonet. Their presence permitted independent action by platoons, facilitating the development of more flexible infantry tactics."[63]

With these heavy weapons the typical *sturmtruppen* battalion could thus advance past no man's land to then dismantle particularly stubborn enemy defenses. Unlike

62 Die Minenwerfer, Abschnitte aus der Gefechtslehre (Vienna: Teil VII, 1918), p. 21.

63 Paul Cornish, 'Machine Gun,' in: *1914–1918-online. International Encyclopedia of the First World War*, ed. by Ute Daniel, Peter Gatrell, Oliver Janz, Heather Jones, Jennifer Keene, Alan Kramer, and Bill Nasson, issued by Freie Universität Berlin, Berlin 2015–12–02. DOI: http://dx.doi.org/10.15463/ie1418.10779. <Accessed 12 December 2015>

the standard infantry unit, these battalions had their own autonomous artillery support and did not have to wait for the field artillery to catch up to them in order to move through successive enemy lines. By mid 1918 the divisions deployed in Italy received greater numbers of lorries, wagons and pack mules to increase their mobility. As a result, it became more feasible to move around the battlefield with these heavier weapons. For instance, during the 1918 Solstice Offensive, the *sturmtruppen* battalions had small horse-drawn wagons to carry grenade launchers, mortars and small artillery guns across no man's land and beyond. The Trentino mountain units, on the other hand, had packed mules to transport their heavier artillery equipment.

In addition, they also possessed the necessary weapons to confront the enemy in the trenches in close quarters combat. Steel clubs, daggers, and hand grenades allowed the stormtroopers to fight in hand-to-hand combat against the enemy.

In close quarters combat hand grenades were the key weapon. The stormtroopers were the masters of the surprise attack against enemy positions. Hand grenades were often used to neutralize an enemy reaction by lobbing them into the enemy trenches as the stormtroopers approached the wire. Once the infantry assault units had reached the enemy trenches and sealed the exits of dugouts or caverns they would proceed to throw hand grenades into the openings to immobilize the enemy. They were also used as detonation charges to rupture the enemy wire or concrete blockhouses. By wiring several grenades into a plank of wood, stormtroopers would create much stronger charges.

Conclusion

The Austrian official history argues that the constituting of stormtrooper battalions in 1917 was one the foremost innovations of the Austro-Hungarian infantry:

> The most important of these units were the storm battalions which now were being raised, one for each division. (Each independent brigade was to have a storm half battalion and each cavalry division a storm half regiment). The original storm battalions which had been maintained by various army-level headquarters now became training cadres. The new stormtroops were selected from the bravest, best-trained and most efficient soldiers. They would serve not only as proponents of and trainers in the newest tactics, but also as an elite force, motivated by an attacking spirit, which could intervene at decisive points on the battlefield. … Thus constituted, a storm battalion was a substantial force, fully capable of undertaking both training and combat assignments.[64]

In the view of historian John Schindler: "The stormtrooper battalion contained the firepower of a line infantry regiment, particularly with respect to indirect fire

64 Edmund Glaise-Horstenau (ed.), *Österreich-Ungarns letzter Krieg 1914–1918*, Vol. 7, p. 59.

systems."[65] In his view, these special units incorporated small artillery, mortars, machine guns and flamethrowers to effectuate their own barrage. Similarly to *Sturmabteilung Rohr*, it can be argued that Austro-Hungarian stormtroopers in contrast to standard infantry possessed the weapons to make gaps in the wire and penetrate deep into enemy defenses.

Lastly, Austrian military historian Christian Ortner highlights the extensive training of the Austro-Hungarian stormtroopers that helped shape them into an elite infantry force: "The quality of the trained men was even better than in the German assault battalions, as the latter were used mainly for training purposes. Although the reduced significance of German assault units as classical fighting troops enabled large sections of the infantry to be familiarized with assault tactics, but course graduates by no means reached the level of training of the Austro-Hungarian sturmpatrouillen."[66]

Increase in firepower, extensive training along with tactical innovation were the main factors that separated the stormtroopers from standard infantry. By early 1917 the Austro-Hungarian Army consisted of two main infantry groups. Younger, physically fit, and better-trained shock troops versus older soldiers, less physically fit and with more years of service that were used primarily for defensive purposes such as for line infantry duties, to man machine gun crews and serve as artillery servers. As the war wore on the divergence between the two groups became even greater and as we will see in the following chapters the major Austro-Hungarian offensives for the most part were constantly carried out by the shock troops such as the 11th Army *Sturmbaon*. The questions that we will seek to provide answers for in the next few chapters are the following: Did the stormtroopers have a growing influence on Austro-Hungarian tactics? Did their influence have a positive impact upon the morale and the fighting qualities of standard infantry? Where they a determining factor in key battles?

Equipment and Weapons of the Austro-Hungarian Storm Troopers

Helmet, knee and elbow pads, rucksack, food provisions for four days, 2 water flasks, anti-gas mask, holster, 2 sacks for hand grenades, 4 empty sandbags, flashlight, shovel, rifle, bayonet, dagger, 40 cartridges, small shovel, egg and stick hand grenades. The soldiers of the assault patrols also have wire cutters, watch, compass, leather gloves, and first aid kit.

Source: Italian Military circular n. 11,000 Fall 1917.

65 John Richard Schindler, *A Hopeless Struggle: The Austro-Hungarian Army and Total War 1914–18*, Unpublished Thesis, McMaster University, 1995, p. 193.

66 Christian Ortner, *Storm Troops*, p. 83.

Table 2.1 Organization of 22nd *Schützen* Division Assault Battalion

Company	Number of soldiers	Where soldiers came from
1st Company	144	1st and 3rd *Schützen* Regiment
2nd Company	144	26th *Schützen* Regiment
3rd Company	144	1st *KaiserSchützen* Regiment
4th Company	144	2nd *KaiserSchützen* Regiment
Machine gun Company	Unknown with six machine guns	Unknown
Close combat Company	Unknown	Unknown
Pioneer Platoon	36 with six flamethrowers	Unknown

Source: Massignani, p. 58.

3

The Italian Army and the War

Introduction

The 370-mile long Italian front, mostly consisting of impervious mountainous terrain, was the only European theatre of operations that was most fundamentally dominated by its geography. It was the only front of the war where most of the fighting took place on rugged mountain terrain. On the left flank the western mountain ranges of the Trentino (the Ortles, Presanella and Adamello Groups) spanned from the Stelvio Pass near the border with Switzerland to Lake Garda. Here a major breakthrough was unlikely given that the frontline passed through Alpine ranges and glaciers that were extremely difficult to cross especially by slow moving infantry troops with hard to transport heavy machine guns and artillery pieces. It then snaked through the lower Trentino where the mountains were not as tall but were equally impervious with their dense forests and their wild and rugged peaks such as Mount Zugna, Mount Corno and Mount Pasubio. In this section of the front line each army held entrenched positions that were often only a few hundred meters from each other. The positions were mainly located on hilltops, mountain passes or peaks that dominated entire valleys. It then passed through the Asiago Altopiano with its deep forest that also impeded any major troop movement toward the Veneto plains. The front then cut through the Dolomities, where the troops could only advance along strategic mountain passes that if even thinly held by a few soldiers with a machine gun could prove impossible to circumvent by a much greater enemy force. The rough terrain was not the only obstacle to an Italian advance since the Trentino, in particular, had been heavily fortified prior to the war (1907–14) by Franz Conrad von Hötzendorf, who had always feared an Italian attack against the Alto Adige. Conrad had sought to achieve two objectives with the construction of these fortifications: block a potential Italian infantry advance by expanding existing forts situated along key mountain passes and build new forts that could support offensive operations aimed at the Veneto plains. The existing fortifications (Tonale, Presanella, Pejo, Carriola, Garda, Tombio, and Ponale) were reinforced with additional layers of concrete cement and were equipped with field artillery units. In addition, a new fort was built to block access to the road leading to Folgaria and Lavarone and a new deep trench, the so-called, *Tiroler Widerstandslinie*, or Tyrol resistance line, and extensive field trenches surrounding Trento were also constructed in anticipation of a defensive campaign against the Italians.

The frontier then passed through the Julian Alps which were just as impregnable as the Dolomites. Finally, it ended along the 30-mile long Isonzo River sector which ran down to the Adriatic Sea. This was the only sector of the front line that was relatively flat but had in turn been heavily fortified along the hills just behind the river by the Austro-Hungarians. In the upper Isonzo area the river ran through a gorge that bordered the Bainsizza plateau and the Julian Alps. The river then passed through the town of Gorizia, which had been transformed by the Austro-Hungarians into a heavily defensive fortress. Moreover, the Austro-Hungarians had also blocked access to Gorizia on both flanks by fortifying all the surrounding mountain tops including Mount Sabotino, Mount Pogdora, Mount Santo, Mount San Gabriele and Mount San Daniele, which during the war became the center stage of all the Isonzo battles. Finally the river flowed into the Adriatic Sea passing by the Carso plateau and over this last tract of the front line the Austro-Hungarians had also a commanding view with the occupation of the heavily fortified Monte San Michele.

The frontline consisted of a series of trenches, gun-pits and deep mountain caverns which had been dug or mined to conceal the artillery and machine gun strongpoints from the Italians and were surrounded by ample barbed wire works. The Austro-Hungarians had used the rugged, mountainous terrain to their advantage by taking control of key peaks and passes which were extremely difficult to conquer. The war on the Italian front, given the rugged terrain, therefore followed a similar pattern battle after battle. At first the artillery effectuated the preliminary bombardment and then switched it to secondary objectives in the rear as the infantry moved forward. As the brave but not particularly innovative Italian infantry pushed ahead, it was targeted by well-concealed, high altitude, enemy machine gun emplacements. Countless assaults were halted by a combination of hand grenades, artillery and machine gun fire. Once the Italians had managed to overrun an Austrian trench, their units were not able to proceed any further, being halted by the next row of machine guns and by reserve units that would spring out for the counter-attack. As historian Giorgio Rochat states: "There was little artillery coordination with the infantry, so that the troops were launched against the Austrian barbed wire and machine guns without adequate support. Once halted, they had to hold onto any terrain gained, however small, from where the offensive was to be re-launched."[1]

The mountainous terrain of the Italian front produced a very different type of war than the confrontations that took place on the Western or Eastern fronts. First, the terrain greatly aided the defenders, in this case the Austro-Hungarians garrisoned in well fortified hills or mountains overlooking the Italian lines. While during the winter of 1917–18 the terrain would in turn facilitate for a brief interlude the

1 Giorgio Rochat, 'The Italian Front', in John Horne (ed.), *A Companion to World War I* (New York: Wiley & Sons, 2012), pp. 82–97.

Italian defensive effort on Mount Grappa and the Asiago Altopiano as the latter were pushed back following the Caporetto debacle. Second, the rough terrain also placed increased pressure upon logistics tasks such as the re-supply of troops in hard to reach high altitude environments. Most key positions were several hours away from the nearest base or village and often there were no mountain paths leading directly to them. Shells and artillery, for instance, in many cases had to be either hand carried or transported by pack mules. Thus, the transportation process was painstakingly slow representing a serious handicap to offensive infantry maneuvers. Equally challenging was the procedure for maintaining proper communications with the advanced mountainous positions. Bad weather or continuous artillery fire impeded or totally disrupted communications with forward position units. Often positions were isolated for several days and were vulnerable to enemy attacks. Third, artillery shells landing on the limestone Carso plateau or on the rocky terrain of the Alps caused great havoc among front line troops. Stone and steel fragments caused very high numbers of head wounds forcing both armies to introduce steel helmets and other defensive equipment such as steel shields. Fourth, contrary to popular depictions it is a well-known fact that bayonet fighting was rare during the Great War. Ernst Jünger, for example, fought as an infantry officer in the German Army during the war and recalls being a participant in only a handful of clashes of hand-to-hand fighting.[2] The Great War was the first modern conflict dominated by artillery firepower like no other war before. But on the Italian front, close combat fighting was more prevalent than on the Western Front given the rugged mountain terrain where the trenches were often dug into the rock and were quite difficult to reach. But once an offensive unit was able to pass the wire and reach the enemy's defenses, hand-to-hand combat was often unavoidable as the defenders could not easily pull back from their high altitude entrenched positions. Both Bosnian troops and the *arditi*, for example, excelled in fighting with close combat weapons such as daggers, knives and clubs. The *arditi* were well known for killing their enemy with a dagger thrust to the heart or by slashing their opponent's neck, while Bosnian soldiers were notorious for killing enemies by hitting them with steel clubs and brass knuckles with spikes. Fifth, the war on the Italian front, largely as a consequence of the rugged mountainous terrain, saw even less troop offensive maneuvering that on the Western Front. Tanks and other heavier armored vehicles of maneuver warfare, for instance, were not suitable in such a difficult terrain and hence were not deployed. Troops and heavy artillery also could not be moved as expeditiously as on the Western Front thus slowing down the pace of offensive operations that resulted even in a small breakthrough of enemy defenses.

Sixth, another factor that impeded offensive maneuvering was the difficulty in transporting and emplacing artillery on the high peaks. The troops had to haul up artillery, mortars, and machine guns and emplacing such weapons was equally challenging. New shooting techniques had to be learned because of the poor visibility in

2 Ernst Jűnger, *The Storm of Steel, From the Diary of a German Storm-Troop Officer on the Western Front*, trans. Basil Creighton (London: Chatto & Windus 1929), p. 257.

the mountains due to dense forests and cold weather with snow and ice and the need for indirect fire weapons.

Supreme Command

When in 1915 Italy declared war on Austria-Hungary its army was largely unprepared for the task at hand. It entered the war with outdated infantry and artillery tactics and with few weapons suited for positional warfare. Head of *Comando Supremo* Luigi Cadorna's tactical instructions were published in the so-called 'Red Book' in 1914. Like his predecessors, Cadorna favored a war of movement based upon frontal infantry attacks while the artillery protected the advancing units attacking in different waves.

Cadorna wrote: "Despite today's extended battle fronts which are – in large part-the ineluctable consequence of the perfecting of firearms and the power of improvised fortifications, when one party feels himself stronger than the other he will unleash the offensive, which alone is capable of achieving decisive results: it will always be maneuver that decides the outcome of wars."[3]

His tactical doctrine had a strong emphasis on infantry mobility, firepower and flexibility as motivated, brave and physically fit infantry units were seen as the key to unlocking fortified enemy defenses.

Cadorna's concepts were then slightly revised a month before Italy's entry into the war when he issued a directive which stressed the importance of artillery and infantry coordination in support of planned attacks. Cadorna argued that field artillery was required to support the attack by conducting the preliminary bombardment and then by supporting the infantry as it moved forward with accompanying fire. This would result in the disruption and destruction of the enemy's defensive system, which would in turn allow the infantry to advance against the enemy line. The basic concepts of his doctrine were not new and they were also similar to pre-war Austro-Hungarian battle tactics. With the primary role being given to the infantry, his strategy neglected the fact that during the first year of war on both the Western and Eastern fronts the artillery had caused the majority of the casualties through both defensive and offensive fire. Both the Italian and the Austro-Hungarian Army based their initial tactics upon pre-First World War experiences such as the Franco-Prussian war of 1870/71. Their officer corps believed at the time that offensive operations unlocked a tactical situation or impasse and that the infantry should deploy all of its force in order to take enemy positions. Infantry was supposed to undertake offensive operations even without the aid of the cavalry or the artillery. This basic tenet would be responsible for the huge losses suffered during the infantry charges of the Austro-Hungarian Army in 1914 in Eastern Europe and of the Italian Army in 1915–16. Historian Giorgio Rochat argues that infantry tactics did not change even when it became clear that

3 Luigi Cadorna, *Attacco frontale ed ammaestramento tattico* (Rome: Ufficio Storico, 1914), p. 84.

offensive operations pitted against barbed wire defenses were costly and yielded few results. He writes: "In 1917, the Italian troops were still attacking as they had in 1915, with better artillery fire but still in compact formations, with successive waves massacred by the Austrian cannons."[4]

As will be shown in the later chapters, tactical improvements were initially developed and introduced mainly by lower level commanders fighting in the trenches rather than by *Comando Supremo*.[5] It was through these junior officers' efforts that the Army began to make changes to the way it attacked enemy positions by way of greater coordination with the artillery and by deploying better trained and equipped troops.

Many senior officers were just as negligent as their supreme commander with their focus on outdated and retrograde tactical approaches. Italian senior officers were generally selected by seniority hence many tended to have little experience in trench warfare and were generally conservative with regards to tactics. Cadorna's leadership style also stifled individual initiative because he was very heavy handed on those that did not toe the line or demonstrated a high degree of independent decision-making. "As chief of staff General Cadorna was notoriously intolerant of those who disagreed with or displeased him, dismissing some 800 senior officers in two and a half years. This regime naturally discouraged initiative; and since there had also been high casualties amongst field commanders, most infantry units were led by inexperienced officers by the time of Caporetto."[6]

One of Cadorna's main weaknesses was the harsh disciplinary system that he enforced during the war that led to the death of many soldiers, but it also backfired against the High Command in October 1917. For this reason alone, the supreme commander was loathed by his troops. In contrast, when General Armando Diaz took his place in late 1917, introducing a more humane approach that took into greater consideration the welfare of the troops, he was welcomed by the vast majority of soldiers. During the war 750 soldiers were executed by firing squads after having been prosecuted by military tribunals. Not even France, with a larger army and much greater level of soldier unrest following the Verdun and Nivelle Operations, had such a high number of summary executions as Italy during the conflict.[7]

Another main weakness was the supreme commander's underestimation for the need to train the troops for a campaign of trench warfare. Throughout the war

4 Giorgio Rochat, 'The Italian Front', in John Horne (ed.), *A Companion to World War I* (New York: Wiley & Sons, 2012), p. 89.

5 On tactical innovation see: Robert Thomas Foley, 'A Case Study in Horizontal Military Innovation: The German Army, 1916–1918', *Journal of Strategic Studies*, vol. 35, n.6, 2012, pp. 1–29. Bruce I. Gudmundsson, for example, has examined the role of mid level infantry officers in the development of German infantry tactics during the First World War. Bruce I. Gudmundsson, *Stormtroop Tactics: Innovation in the German Army, 1914–1918* (New York: Praeger, 1989).

6 David Nicolle, *The Italian Army of World War I* (Oxford: Osprey, 2003), p. 16.

7 Irene Guerrini and Marco Pluviano, *Le fucilazioni sommarie della prima guerra m*ondiale (Udine: LEG, 2004), pp. 9–40.

Cadorna never fully focused on training. Soldiers were sent to fight without the basic skills such as knowing how to properly fire a gun or handle and operate heavier equipment such as mortars and machine guns. Cadorna often resorted to directives issued to frontline commanders to adapt his army to modern trench warfare. These directives were often useful in explaining to commanders how the troops should be deployed defensively, how machine guns should be sited and emplaced, how counter-attacking units should be deployed, etc., but were no proper substitutes for frontline troop training.

His offensive strategy was highly predictable. Since it was extremely difficult to conduct large-scale operations in the mountains, Cadorna resorted time and time again to attack in the only non-mountainous sector, the 35-mile stretch along the Isonzo River where the infantry could deploy in tight formations and charge the enemy. The problem was that this stretch of land was like a funnel surrounded by Austro-Hungarian strong points and sealed off by barbed wire and concrete pill-boxes. It was virtually impossible to advance even for a force that held the numerical advantage. Historian John Gooch has argued that Cadorna's plan, to threaten the Austro-Hungarian Army by attacking along the Isonzo River on the enemy's flank and then march on to Vienna, was a "complete disregard of the realities of trench warfare."[8]

Despite his tactical limitations, Cadorna remained as head of the army until the Caporetto disaster. His successor Diaz would bring long anticipated changes, while some of the infantry tactical deployment changes had already been implemented during Cadorna's tenure but largely as a result of the experimentation and impetus of junior officers, were finally implemented by the whole army.

Infantry Tactics

The First Battle of the Isonzo, fought between June and July 1915, revealed the tactical weakness of the Italian Army in facing entrenched machine gun posts and infantry strongpoints that enjoyed commanding views of the terrain. The post-battle report issued by the Italian 3rd Army points out the factors that led to this defeat. First, the artillery barrage, carried out mostly by light and medium sized artillery pieces, was not effective in destroying the enemy barbed wire. Second, the barrage also was not powerful enough to destroy the infantry dugouts and trenches due to the lack of high trajectory mortars necessary to hit the concealed enemy positions situated on the reserve slopes of the mountains. In fact, the vast majority of Austro-Hungarian infantry units survived the barrage unscathed due to the Italian Army's lack of indirect fire weapons. Third, the long delay that elapsed between the end of the barrage and the start of the infantry assault nullified the element of surprise and allowed the Austro-Hungarians to properly man their defensive positions in a timely manner.

8 John Gooch, *Army, State and Society in Italy, 1870–1915* (New York: St. Martin's Press, 1989), p. 170.

> The artillery barrage had little or no effect upon the enemy's barbed wire which was only damaged in few, very narrow sections of the frontline thus impeding our troops from reaching the enemy trenches. … Repeated attacks by the 22nd Division against the top of Mount San Michele failed because after the artillery barrage had been lifted the enemy was able to reoccupy his positions. As soon as our infantry moved forward the enemy opened up an intensive fire consisting of rifles, several machine guns, artillery pieces and hand grenades. It appears that the enemy has built very entrenched positions on the reverse slope just below the top of the mountain. These deep caverns shield enemy troops from artillery fire and have allowed enemy forces to be quickly dispatched soon after the barrage was lifted.[9]

The first encounter battle on the Isonzo revealed how little the head of the Italian Army had properly and adequately followed developments on the Western Front. There, the artillery had become the most lethal weapon, in fact the only weapon that was capable of destroying entrenched enemy defenses and that was responsible for causing the majority of enemy casualties. During this first battle it was clear that the Italian Army lacked the heavy guns and an adequate amount of shells to properly conduct the artillery preparation. Not only did it lack weapons, but the artillery also deployed flawed tactics. The creeping barrage, for example, was still unknown to artillerymen and the guns switched off to the secondary lines once the infantry had exited the trenches. Thus, the latter had very little support in the most important phase of the operation.

Despite huge losses in men and equipment during this first battle, General Cadorna failed during the first year of the war to reconcile Italy's offensive objectives to the new dynamics of trench warfare. The army in fact insisted with the breakthrough tactics, the concentration of artillery and infantry power against one section of the enemy line, without achieving success.

As historian Filippo Cappellano aptly summarizes:

> The great Italian offensives of 1915–1917 consisted of strong attacks preceded by an artillery preparation lasting days that removed the element of surprise and gave the enemy time to send their reserves to the threatened sector. The lack of tanks and the small size of the air force meant having to rely solely on the combination of infantry and artillery for offensive actions. The attacks were carried out by masses of infantry under the cover of artillery fire and generally directed against the strong points, usually high altitude emplacements, of the enemy line. The Italian offensive norms did not include infiltration techniques or attacks at night, while, as regards to defense, resistance to the bitter end on the first or second lines of trenches was favored.[10]

9 Diario Storico della 3. Armata, vol. 1 (Padova: Museo storico 3. Armata, 1915), p. 4.

10 Filippo Cappellano, 'Warfare Italy 1915–18', can be found at: http://encyclopedia.1914-1918-online.net/article/warfare_1914-1918_italy. <accessed 6 June 2015>

On 9 July 1917 Cadorna issued his long awaited revision of infantry tactics which was called the 'Ammaestramenti Tattici' (Tactical Teachings) directive. In the document he lamented the fact that the Tenth Battle of the Isonzo had not achieved its desired results for two specific reasons: First, the enemy had adopted a new defense in depth disposition that trapped the assaulting units between the first and second line of defense with massive artillery and machine gun fire. Second, "the assaults have failed because too much time was incurred between the lengthening of the artillery fire and the start of the infantry assault."[11] And also because the second assault wave was too disjointed from the first wave and as a result had been the target of intensive enemy artillery fire into no man's land which in effect had stifled its offensive impetus.

For Cadorna it was necessary to adopt the type of infiltration-like tactics (although they are not directly mentioned in his report) used by the Germans to achieve greater success and penetration into the enemy's defenses. Special assault detachments were to begin operations on the heels of the barrage by penetrating or circumventing major centers of enemy resistance. In turn these troops were to be supported by the second wave of the attack, which not only had to be deployed immediately by following closely after the first wave but also had to confront the likely enemy reaction by stifling the counter-attack with machine guns and hand grenades. It was an imperative that this second wave took advantage of the short delay that usually occurred between the end of the Italian preparatory barrage and the start of the Austro-Hungarian interdiction fire, which generally began five minutes after the end of the former. Only much closer coordination between artillery and the successive waves of attacking infantry would ensure the consolidation of the offensive and the deeper penetration into the enemy's positions. The document anticipated in a more general way the strategy and tactics that would later be fully implemented and refined by the *reparti d'assalto* and the revitalized and re-equipped Italian infantry units.

The Italian Army offensive campaign was also hampered by a number of additional factors, that were not necessarily mentioned by Cadorna's report. Most importantly, the army did not conduct adequate training for the troops, which generally lacked the knowledge to operate heavy weapons or how to properly prepare defenses in depth. The lack of training was compounded by the fact that resources were scarce and the soldiers could not conduct practice shooting with live rounds of ammunition. An NCO, for example, stated in 1915 that "we have no machine guns, they are running courses for machine gunners using wooden guns and none of the gunners have ever fired a shot using a real weapon."[12]

As Wilcox correctly argues: "Like other armies, the Italians did not respond rapidly to the realities of industrialized trench warfare, and, unsurprisingly, the development of training mirrored the gradual tactical learning process."[13]

11 Basilio di Martino, *Trincee-Reticolati e colpi di mano* (Valdagno: Rossato, 2000), p. 24.
12 Wanda Wilcox, 'Training, Morale and Battlefield Performance in the Italian Army, 1914–1917', in Jonathan Krause (ed.), *The Greater War* (London: Palgrave, 2002), p. 191.
13 Ibid., p. 191.

Austro-Hungarian stormtroopers. (Kriegsarchiv Vienna)

Austro-Hungarian stormtroopers with flamethrower. The weapon in the photo is the German *kleine* flamethrower. (Kriegsarchiv Vienna)

Guardia Napoleone position from which the *Arditi* of V *Reparto d'assalto* emerged on 22 October 1917 to counter-attack Austro-Hungarian troops. (Unknown)

Trench position with steel shield on Mount Piana. (Walther Schaumann)

Commemorative cross on Mount Piana. (Walther Schaumann)

Change to the training regimen was gradual and slow with the only exceptions being if a unit was under the command of a forward-thinking officer or whether troops belonged to special units such as the *alpini*. These units tended to receive more adequate training early on during the war.

Basic training schools for the infantry were only introduced in 1917, three years into the war and in response to one of Cadorna's reports that lamented the front line troops' inexperience with handling crew-served weapons, hand grenades and explosive devices. Most soldiers were conscripted into the army and had to adapt to the war often by learning how to properly defend or attack from first hand experience.

Officer training was also limited. During 1915, for example, the officers received a one-month long training course which covered several areas such as topography, hygiene, tactical instructions, and drafting reports but that fell short in the way of teaching modern tactics. NCOs and soldiers typically trained for two to four weeks prior to being sent to their unit assignment. Their training was extremely brief and due to the lack of ammunition it was also not very formative. The lack of training was compounded by the overall lack of officers and especially NCOs as during the first year of the war the army lost thousands of junior officers and the ratio of officers to ordinary soldiers was approximately one to 25.[14] The lack of experienced and well trained NCOs was probably the number one factor that hindered the adoption of infiltration tactics by the Italian infantry since at the base of the implementation of such maneuvers was the autonomous leadership and quick decision-making capabilities of frontline officers guiding their men in battle. The army had lost too many of these men during the campaigns of 1915 and the highly hierarchical and agricultural-based Italian society did not produce enough middle level junior officers with the necessary educational prerogatives to act as a link between officers and soldiers.

Infantry

In May 1915 the Italian Army could count upon 23,039 officers and 852,217 soldiers. It entered the war with 35 infantry divisions, one *bersaglieri* division, 52 battalions of *alpini* troops subdivided into four regiments, four cavalry divisions, two regiments of *Granatieri di Sardegna* and fourteen sapper battalions.

While the vast majority of the soldiers were part of the standard infantry divisions and lacked specialized training, *bersaglieri* and *alpini* units were better trained and also more cohesive. The *bersaglieri* were well known for their ability as sharp shooters and for their high degree of mobility in the battlefield given above average physical fitness. In fact, the *arditi* battalions of 1917 would draw heavily from the *bersaglieri*. The *alpini* were special mountain units recruited from the northern regions of Italy who like their Austrian counterparts were able to fight effectively in high altitude

14 John Gooch, 'Italy During the First World War', in Allen Millett and Williamson Murray (eds.), *Military Effectiveness Volume I: First World War* (Boston: Unwin Hyman Inc., 1988), p. 182.

environments due to their physical endurance and their experience with mountaineering. These soldiers could withstand long uphill marches with full pack and weapons and were also effective in shooting with rifles and small cannons in the difficult mountain terrain. The vast majority of the Italian soldiers, however, made up the more numerous, less specialized, standard infantry divisions. Although, there were many more infantry divisions than *alpini* or *bersaglieri* units, these units were not as well trained and their soldiers lacked experience with trench warfare.

The army's basic unit was the regiment, which consisted of three battalions of 1,000 soldiers subdivided into four 250-man companies. The battalion typically had three rifle companies and one special weapons company consisting of machine gun squads, mortar squads and a pioneer platoon. Initially the number of rifles was insufficient forcing a vast number of soldiers to train with wooden sticks. Also, there were only two machine guns per regiment while the Austrians had six per battalion. By 1916 however, the shortage of rifles had been rectified, while by 1917 the firepower of the standard infantry battalion had grown considerably with two light machine guns, eight heavy machine guns, and four mortars.

Initially the army was not very well equipped. The infantry began the war with rifles and some machine guns but no hand grenades, flamethrowers or heavy equipment. The number of Italian machine guns, for example, in 1915 was negligible (just 618 at the start of the war), while the standard Austro-Hungarians regiment had four times as many machine guns as the Italian infantry regiment. The standard rifle was the 6.5 mm *Mannlicher-Carzano* model 1891 with a six-round magazine while the standard machine gun was the tripod mounted with a 50 round magazine *Fiat-Revelli* model 1914. Beginning in 1917 the army received shipments of French and British machine guns including the highly effective Lewis gun. Another British weapon that was supplied to the Italians was the Stokes 76 mm mortar (the 81 mm model was introduced in mid 1918). With a weight of only 104 pounds and a relatively light (10.45 lb) bomb, this weapon was excellent for the type of mountain warfare that the Italian Army was involved in. It could fire at targets within a distance of 1,200 feet. Prior to receiving British shipments the army used the more bulky *Ansaldo* 50 and various French-manufactured mortars.

Hand grenades were not part of the original weaponry available to the Italian Army as they were only introduced in late 1915. By then the most popular were the *SIPE* and the *Thevenot* hand grenade. In 1916 the army also began to receive flamethrowers, especially the French *Schilt 3 bis* with a flame range of 15 meters. Special flamethrower training was then set up in the rear at Montecchio Emilia where the first assault platoons were raised and would later serve in combat as support for standard infantry operations. In 1917 special flamethrower platoons were then attached to the newly formed *arditi* units.

By 1918 the standard Italian infantry battalion had less men (150 versus 250 in 1915) but greater firepower. For instance, the number of machine guns per battalion had gone up to eight, while twelve portable flamethrowers were placed at the disposal of each infantry regiment. The latter could also count upon sections of Stokes mortars (four units) as well as of light (37 mm) artillery guns. Similarly, to the

Austro-Hungarians, the Italian infantry had become much more specialized and by mid 1918 each battalion had constituted an *arditi plotone d'assalto* (assault platoon) well-versed in handling hand grenades and light machine guns.

Artillery

In 1914 the artillery branch had only 467 field artillery batteries with 1,800 guns and howitzers. It was subdivided into three main groups: field, mountain and fortress. In the beginning of the war in 1915 "artillery remained the weakest arm of the Italian Army."[15] Its main gun was the *Ansaldo-Schneider* 149A, which was a medium caliber field gun and its main howitzer was the 280 mm unit. Both lacked a modern recoil mechanism. The 149 mm gun, for instance, could fire a 30.4 kg (67 lbs) high explosive shell at a maximum distance of 9,000 meters (5.6 miles). Two areas of major weakness were the absence of an adequate number of large-sized guns and very few light mountain guns. The artillery had only 112 heavy guns in 1915, mostly 280 mm, 210 mm and 149 mm howitzers and guns that were no match for the heavier 30.5 cm Austro-Hungarian guns. Moreover, there were not enough 65 mm mountain guns that were transported by pack mules and were essential for fighting in the Alps. In fact, the army only had 200 light mountain artillery guns in 1915.[16] The 65 mm mountain gun could fire a 4.3 kg (9.5 lb) shrapnel shell at a maximum distance of 6,800 meters (4.2 miles). Like other typical mountain guns it could be dismantled in six components for carriage by mule.

As Gooch asserts the weakness of the Italian artillery was evident just after a few weeks Italy entered the war:

> The Italian artillery gave the first evidence of endemic shortcomings, the result of a combination of insufficient numbers of medium and heavy guns, inadequate supplies of ammunition, and poor doctrine. Fire support was weak and not concentrated on the attack points, gaps in the enemy wire were insufficient and the troops lacked wire-cutters with which to try to get through the entanglements.[17]

Although the Piedmontese artillery had been one of the most effective branches of that army, the Italian Royal Army artillery suffered from several tactical weaknesses. The main issue during the early stages of the war was the poor coordination that existed between artillery and infantry. During 1915–16 major offensive operations began with mass wave infantry attacks preceded by an artillery preparation that often

15 David Nicolle, *The Italian Army*, p. 36.

16 Filippo Cappellano and Basilio Di Martino, *Un Esercito Forgiato nelle Trincee* (Udine: Gasperi Editore, 2008), p. 51.

17 John Gooch, *The Italian Army and the First World War* (Cambridge: Cambridge University Press, 2014), p. 109.

lasted days and hence removed the element of surprise. Although destructive, its duration gave the Austro-Hungarian defenders the time to send in reinforcements to the under siege sector to parry the infantry attack. At times the artillery preparation appeared to be too dispersive rather than concentrated on a specific narrow target or sector of the frontline. This was often the result of inaccurate or unavailable aerial reconnaissance.[18]

Gunners also lacked experience with extensive counter-battery fire exposing attacking troops to fierce enemy artillery barrages.

Shell production was also a major issue during the first year of the war resulting in artillery barrages that often were not adequate for large-scale offensives.

Since the Italians lacked heavy guns and mortars they often used explosives to blow up the wire but in most cases, as Mark Thompson explains, these makeshift devices were ineffective:

> Even when the gelignite tubes exploded (the fuses easily became damp and refused to ignite), the gaps were so narrow that they formed deadly bottlenecks when the Italians tried to crowd through, a gift to enemy machine gunners. Unless enough cylinders were used, the explosions failed to break the wire. Even then, the Austrians usually had time to patch over the gaps before dawn.[19]

The shortcomings of the Italian artillery were known to *Comando Supremo* and were reiterated in the statements made by captured enemy officers. For instance, an Austrian officer stated that there appeared to be a lack of coordination between the artillery and infantry and that the former used an excessive amount of shrapnel when trying to destroy infantry dugouts and trenches. Moreover, in several instances it was observed that the artillery was not fully effective in destroying trenches and barbed wire works thus exposing the packed infantry columns to deadly enemy machine gun fire.[20]

An English officer, Lieutenant Colonel Charles Buzzard of 144th Heavy Artillery Group, stationed in Italy expressed similar concerns regarding Italian artillery operations:

> Almost entire lack of information supplied to the Heavy Artillery. We were never told which way the infantry would attack, the hours named were never adhered to. Fire was lifted far too soon: infantry had no support in passing over four of five hundred yards of open and difficult ground. We could have kept on firing until the infantry was 200 yards from objectives. Austrian prisoners say

18 Ufficio Storico, Comando Supremo: Ufficio Operazioni, Ufficio Affari Vari e Segreteria 'I nostri metodi di attacco nel giudizio degli ufficiali dell'esercito nemico', n. 14250, Relazione del 31 Luglio 1916.

19 Mark Thompson, *The White War: Life and Death on the Italian Front, 1915–18* (New York: Basic Books, 2008), pp. 125–6.

20 Ufficio Storico: Comando Supremo, Ufficio Operazioni, 'Impressioni di un ufficiale austriaco sull'azione delle truppe italiane,' n. 1973, Relazione del 25 Luglio, 1915.

> that during our bombardment all their men were in caverns, and they hardly lost any. The remarkable is that with such utter lack of co-operation between artillery and infantry, the Italian infantry ever take any of their objectives. The artillery preparation is good, a large number of the infantry are quite heroic; but to advance behind a proper creeping barrage is unheard of.[21]

The artillery would increase in efficiency during the course of the war due to greater experience and firepower.

Two examples stand out as to its increased effectiveness as the war progressed. First, while the Austro-Hungarians where attacking in the Trentino, Cadorna launched a surprise attack on the Isonzo in August 1916. The Austrian defenses were submerged by a record number of mortar shells fired by a vast concentration of Italian batteries. Effective and overwhelming artillery fire enabled the infantry to seize Gorizia resulting in Italy's first major win in the campaign. Second, in June 1918 Italian counter-preparation fire was particularly skillful in stifling the enemy offensive by accurately targeting assault infantry on their start lines. As a result, several Austro-Hungarian infantry battalions were decimated even before the start of the battle. The artillery's contribution was one of the major factors that led to the Italian victory during this important battle.

By mid 1917 the Italian artillery had grown tremendously, while shell production increased as well every year. The Italian artillery saw a remarkable increase in firepower in 1917 with 3,828 small caliber guns, 2,933 medium, 157 heavy caliber guns and 2,402 bombards.[22] During the course of the war a reverse relationship between Italian and Austro-Hungarian war production occurred. The latter was stronger during 1916 and 1917, while Italian war production increased markedly in 1918 and later in the year vastly outpaced Austro-Hungarian production levels. In 1918 Austro-Hungarian artillery production had increased steadily and its Army had been able to take out of service all older guns replacing them with modern units. From an average monthly production of 75 finished guns, it increased markedly in 1917 to 288 pieces per month and ultimately fell back to 128 pieces per month in 1918. In contrast, the Italian average went from a low of 55 guns per month in 1915 to 300 in 1918. Ultimately, Italy's war production outpaced Austria-Hungary.

By 1918 the artillery not only had at its disposal a vast amount of 65 mm light mountain guns, but it also had greater numbers of large guns than the Austrians. In particular, by then the Italian military could boast large quantities of 240 mm mortars but also several batteries of 305 mm guns. The latter, for example, while not as effective as the Austrian *Skoda* 30.5 cm gun, represented a vast improvement versus what the army was equipped with in 1915. Thus, the initial Austro-Hungarian superiority in heavy artillery was eventually challenged by the Italian artillery production

21 Peter Hart, *The Great War: A Combat History of the First World War* (Oxford: Oxford University Press, 2013), p. 384.

22 Spencer C. Tucker, *The European Powers in the First World War: An Encyclopedia* (London: Taylor & Francis, 1999), p. 373.

capacity. By 1918 the Italian artillery had approximately 450, 150 mm *Schneider* field guns which replaced the obsolete 149A guns. The 150 mm was introduced beginning in 1916 and by 1918 it was probably one of the most widely used guns in both counter-battery fire and in gun fire concentrated against enemy infantry assembly centers. It could fire explosive, shrapnel and special chemical liquid shells with an average range of five miles.

Conclusion

Although it had fewer infantry soldiers in the trenches, at the start of the war the Austro-Hungarian Army had more firepower than the Italian Army with more far ranging and larger quantities of medium and heavy artillery guns. Austria-Hungary was overstretched by a three-front war, but by 1916 it had its most effective artillery and machine guns units concentrated on the Italian front. Moreover, when in 1915 Italy entered the war, the Austro-Hungarian Army had already accustomed itself to the First World War trench warfare. Its artillery and infantry units had achieved a higher degree of integration, while its line infantry knew how to properly operate crew-served weapons such as mortars, machine guns and grenade launchers. This represented a major advantage over the less experienced Italian infantry which was forced to attack the enemy that was defending uphill positions. By 1916 its infantry had also done away with the costly offensive tactics utilized during the first years of the war. During Conrad's May 1916 Asiago Offensive, for example, the Austro-Hungarian units had already implemented some of the tactics of the German *sturmtruppen* such as the brief but concentrated artillery barrage and the rapid infiltration of various assault units beyond the Italian lines in the Val d'Astico.

Thus, it was the Italians that were the most challenged during 1915–16 by the problems presented by a long-term war of attrition and thus in need to readily adapt to trench warfare.

4

Austrian-Hungarian Stormtroopers' Major Operations

Introduction

The specially trained assault units dedicated to offensive operations first saw action on the Italian front during January 1917 with a number of small raids against fortified enemy positions. These early raids were implemented primarily for the purpose of testing the combat readiness of the stormtroopers and their aims were to capture enemy soldiers and weapons, destroy their gun pits and emplacements, wire-cutting and intelligence gathering. While the first operations took place in the Isonzo River sector, the vast majority shortly thereafter were carried out in the mountainous areas (Asiago Altopiano, Dolomites and Mount Pasubio). To achieve maximum surprise these actions would typically occur on a day with low visibility due either to rain and heavy fog or snow storm and the stormtroopers would further attempt to confuse the enemy by wearing white camouflage over-suits. Under the new tactical guidelines, that emulated German stormtrooper tactics, in the interest of secrecy the Austro-Hungarian attacks were to be preceded by a short or by no artillery bombardment. Consistent with German practice, the artillery would fire a few probing rounds prior to the bombardment in order to conceal from the enemy the real target of the attack. Then it would concentrate a powerful but brief barrage, consisting of a mix of explosive and gas shells, against the position slated to be attacked. The targets of the barrage would be based on accurate mapping of the enemy positions prior to the start of operations so that complete surprise could be achieved. By using this technique no registration fire was required and the troops were put in a condition of achieving tactical surprise on the enemy defenders. If a small raid was attempted the artillery barrage was eschewed altogether in order to achieve maximum surprise.

According to German-inspired regulations: "As soon as the last rounds struck the enemy positions, the infantry must surge forward; in the advance which follows, they must directly follow our rolling barrage, not giving the enemy time to recover from its effects or to make themselves ready for action."[1]

The key of their success was to time the start of the attack with the moment of the moving forward of the artillery barrage, allowing the infantry to invade the trenches before the enemy could react or even set foot out the dugouts and caverns. A new set of powerful weapons would support the stormtrooper in the attack. While charging over no man's land the stormtroopers were supported by standard (heavy) machine guns, which deployed in depth would pin down enemy infantry with flanking fire. The first attacking wave of stormtroopers was comprised of teams with hand grenades and light machine guns, which would also be utilized to pin down the enemy under a hail of fire and smoke. To further facilitate the infantry's advance, the second assault wave had its own assigned weapons (mainly light trench mortars and flamethrowers) which were used to overcome pockets of stubborn enemy resistance and destroy the wire.

In mid 1917 the *sturmtruppen* were also used to conduct even more large scale operations as their tactics evolved and also began to be adopted by Austro-Hungarian infantry at large. They were used, for instance, for sudden counter-attacks where the combination of creeping and forward moving barrages along with a surprise infantry attack proved deadly for the Italians on several occasions. These counter-attacks were generally preceded by less reconnaissance and surveillance of the enemy lines due to the necessity of hitting back at the enemy in a timely fashion and before he had the chance to organize the defenses. Given the fact that counter-attacks were to be launched quickly and by surprise, the stormtroopers were well suited for these types of operations as they were held in the rear where they spent extensive time training and thus could be readily dispatched to the designated area. They could then be deployed as a tactical reserve and at a particular time during the battle. Historian Ernst Wisshaupt, for instance, states that the 11th Army *Sturmbaon* "became the tactical reserve of the 11th Army as the unit was always ready to go into action, given that it was highly mobile and a very effective war machine."[2] Once the weak spots of the enemy's defense had been identified a plan of attack was developed so that the stormtroopers could find their way into the enemy's defenses. The tactics were similar to those deployed in the raids as the key to success was the use of fast moving *sturmtruppen* to reach the wire once the barrage had moved forward. The major difference with the typical raid was that the stormtroopers were required to initially hold on to the position once it had been conquered. They had to turn it around by carrying machine guns, empty sandbags and steel shields across no man's land and ultimately turn it over to standard infantry whose role was to fight off any enemy counter-attack.

The third use of the *sturmtruppen* was their deployment as shock troops in paving the way for the infantry in the offensives. In this role the *sturmtruppen* fought at the

1 Edmund Glaise-Horstenau (ed.), *Österreich-Ungarns letzter Krieg 1914–1918, vol. 7* (Vienna: Verlag der Militärwissenschaftlichen Mitteilungen, 1936), p. 122.

2 Ernst Wisshaupt, *Die Tiroler Kaiserjäger im Weltkriege 1914–1918, Vol. 2* (Vienna: Amon Franz Goth, 1936), p. 350.

head of the infantry going in first after the barrage had been lifted. Their role was to seek out weak enemy strongpoints, overrun them and then exploit the openings to the fullest by attempting to arrive at the second or third enemy line. Particularly stubborn enemy strong points were left to the second wave of the attack, while the *sturmtruppen* attempted an advance in depth mainly with the aid of hand grenades, machine guns and flamethrowers.

This tactical approach for large-scale offensives is outlined in the AOK's instruction manual:

> In an offensive battle, where the enemy troops in the trenches have been shaken by the preparatory artillery fire, the objective of the assault group is to overrun the first enemy position (be it three or four times) before the enemy troops realize what is afoot. They are unlikely to be surrounded because, if enemy troops attempt to encircle, they will in turn be surrounded by the following waves and reserves. Not only is the clearing of the trenches out of place here, the attack must be carried out in leaps and bounds across open ground and the enemy position including the artillery area must be penetrated. It must also be noted that the extremely narrow and deep Italian communication trenches are veritable mouse traps, and it would be advantageous to remain outside them and cover them with hand grenades.[3]

As will be shown, the Austro-Hungarian stormtroopers while adhering to these tactical guidelines would achieve important tactical successes. Their emergence on the Italian front became a cause for alarm in the enemy ranks almost overnight. In fact, soon after the *sturmtruppen* had carried out their first offensive thrusts, Italian commanders recognized that the enemy was employing new tactics and weapons and that its offensive operations were being carried out by a new breed of specialized assault units. However, it would take the Italian *Comando Supremo* and the army corps senior officer staff some time before they were able to issue the necessary countermeasures to fight off more effectively these spirited attacks.

Their first raid was conducted on 18 January 1917 when stormtroops from the 28th Infantry Division attacked an enemy position on the Fajti Hrib in the Isonzo sector, capturing several Italians. More small-scale raids followed all along the Isonzo River during the last week of January. The success of these early raids alarmed *Comando Supremo* which issued a directive meant to alert infantry commanders of the danger posed by these new enemy assault units comprised of hand-picked volunteers.[4]

3 OSTA/KA *Militarische Impressen* 7611ad, p. 4. Cited in Christian Ortner, *Storm Troops*, pp. 203–04.

4 Ufficio Storico, Raccolta F.1–13: Diari Storici, p. 4.

Dolomites Sector

On 5 February 1917 newly formed Austro-Hungarian assault patrols of the 3rd Regiment/74th Infantry Division sprang a surprise attack on a valley position held by troops of the *Calabria* Brigade at Paneveggio near Rolle Pass and the Colbricon in the Dolomites sector. This was another vital sector for the Austro-Hungarian Army, the possession of which guaranteed that the Italians could not break through in the Fiemme and Adige valleys. Preceded by a brief artillery barrage comprising no more than 300 shells fired mainly from 105 mm and 30.5 cm siege howitzers, a few assault patrols with rifles, hand grenades, white camouflage over-suits, white helmet covers and snow shoes charged the enemy position during the afternoon. Even though the raid was conducted with great speed and decision it ultimately failed, as the assault troops were unable to overcome the wire and circumvent the concentrated resistance of the infantrymen of the 60th Infantry Regiment. As a result, the Austro-Hungarians were forced to retreat under heavy enemy machine gun and rifle fire. According to Captain Spadero of the 60th Regiment: "the Austrians were pushed back by a reserve unit led by NCO Grimaldi, who killed with his rifle an enemy NCO that first had thrown hand grenades and then had attempted to penetrate through the wire."[5]

In the same sector on 9 March 1917 the Austro-Hungarians again went into action with a surprise attack as the assault troops sprang out of a makeshift tunnel dug in the snow and ice to infiltrate the advanced enemy position of Ferro di Cavallo. This time the operation proved to be a success mainly because the Italians did not expect an enemy attack originating from a concealed snow tunnel dug all the way near their trenchline and on a day with such poor weather conditions. The commander of the VII Battalion/216th Infantry Regiment, who was responsible for the troops defending this lone forward post, had prior to the raid asked several times permission to evacuate this isolated and advanced position. But his requests had not been granted. As a result, his troops were the victims of a well-conceived pincer movement that led to the post's devastation and the capture of its small garrison.

According to the testimony of Austrian Lieutenant Leopold Othmar:

> At 0245 under most favorable weather conditions, mainly a thick fog and a very heavy snow blizzard, reserve Lieutenant Meuer attacked the Ferro di Cavallo from the left flank, while Lieutenant Konig and NCO Boczubach and their respective assault patrols attacked from the right flank. Meuer and his men advanced with great speed and captured an advanced position along with its officer and 30 men belonging to the Italian 216th, while four enemy soldiers managed to escape and sound the alarm. By then Lieutenant Konig and his men had emerged from a tunnel dug in the snow that ended within striking distance of the Italian position. By the time that his troops advanced upon the

5 Adone Bettega, *Grande Guerra in Val di Fiemme, Fassa e Biois: Cima Bocche, Passo San Pellegrino, Passo Valles, Pale di San Martino, Passo Rolle, Val Travignolo* (Valdagno: Rossato Editore, 2010), p. 244.

> Italian post, the enemy was already responding with heavy machine gun fire and they could not advance any further. NCO Meuer was shot dead during the pullback.[6]

This strategy was attempted again a month later against the Ferro di Cavallo by the same Austrian assault patrols. Since the beginning of the month the enemy post had been under continuous observation by small assault patrol units. According to the commander of the unit 16 April seemed propitious for a renewed attack as the post was by then "held by a fresh, inexperienced unit that did not know the area well and hence represented an easy target."[7]

As we will see the troops of the 91st Regiment/*Seno* Brigade, at the time of the Austrian strike, were taken completely by surprise thus justifying the commander's decision to attack.

> The Lieutenant fired a few rocket flares with a very pistol and then suddenly from the snow tunnel that had been previously dug the assault patrols led by Lieutenant Konig and Eppinger bypassed the small wall of snow that separated them from the Italians and irrupted into the enemy position. The sentries responded by firing at us but were soon overwhelmed and killed. Eight soldiers comprising a small enemy unit that initially stood in our way were also killed. Then we proceeded to assail the main position with hand grenades and rifle fire. Several more enemy soldiers were killed, while the vast majority were made our prisoners, including five officers and 102 soldiers.[8]

In the aftermath of the attack on the Italian side the raid provoked yet another investigation from the military authorities including a reconnaissance by senior officers on the Ferro di Cavallo position as well as the interrogation of the few soldiers that had managed to escape capture. Despite a thorough investigation the final report failed to determine the direction of the enemy attack or to explain how it had developed. A tunnel in the snow was not even one of the options considered in the report which rather underlined that the enemy attack had most likely been conducted by troops equipped with skis.[9]

In the heart of the Dolomites the front line in 1917 passed through the Three Peaks of Lavaredo, probably the most recognizable and spectacular mountains to be found in the Alps. When Italy declared war in 1915 *alpini* units rivaled the Austrian mountaineer patrols to seize the highest points along the Dolomites front mainly in the Pusteria, Fiscalina and Cadore valleys. As a result of the occupations, the front line

6 Leopold Othmar, *Das III Baon (I.R.74) an der Dolomitenfront auf Bocche-Lusia, Riesengebirgler im Weltkrieg* (Vienna: Reichenberg, 1935), p. 122.
7 Ibid., p. 131.
8 Ibid., p. 134.
9 Ufficio Storico, Carteggio Divisioni di Fanteria, BA 9196–91917: 'Relazione del Ten. Gen. Ruggeri sulla sorpresa nemica in regione Bocche', 30 April 1917.

quickly stabilized running directly through the Three Peaks that along with Mount Paterno were held by the Italians, while Toblin Tower and Cima Undici were firmly in Austrian hands. In this alpine sector, any successful Austrian attack would require the *alpini* outposts atop Mount Paterno (2,746 meters) and on the Sasso di Sesto (which faced directly Toblin Tower) to be eliminated. The Paterno was almost conquered by Sepp Innerkofler and his flying patrol under the cover of darkness on a summer night in 1915. One 4 July 1915 the great mountain guide had almost managed to climb the mountain and was within 30 meters of reaching its peak, when an *alpini* squad atop the Paterno spotted him and quickly responded with heavy grenade, rifle fire and even rocks. Hit by a rock, Innerkofler fell from the cliff and plummeted 50 meters to his death. A few days later he was posthumously awarded the Gold Medal for bravery.[10] Two years later the Austro-Hungarian Army attempted again to breach Italian defenses in the Three Peaks sector this time by attacking the Sasso di Sesto with the aid of a special company of stormtroopers. Given that a frontal assault was extremely risky to the point of being pointless, the Austro-Hungarian command of *Rayon* 5 opted for a surprise attack with the assault troops emerging from the bowels of the mountain. Accordingly, the work was begun in earnest during the winter to excavate a long tunnel in the snow that when completed was approximately 650 meters long and four meters wide so that at least two soldiers could advance at the same time without getting in each others way. In March 1917 the tunnel had been advanced all the way to the enemy's barbed wire which was still submerged deep in snow. The wire was cut and the tunnel was continued further until it reached a distance of no more than 20 meters from the enemy's main cavern. The final project consisted in digging a few exits from which the assault units could burst out of simultaneously and quickly lunge against the enemy's position. While this work was ongoing the stormtrooper assault patrols continued to train in the rear mainly by rehearsing the plan of attack and by familiarizing themselves with the Italian positions by studying aerial photographs and detailed maps.

Although comprising an advanced and isolated position, the Sasso appeared to be unassailable especially during the winter or spring when more than nine feet of snow blanketed the mountain. The Italian position was heavily defended with its garrison being comprised of experienced *alpini* soldiers and its defenses consisting of intricate caverns, deep tunnels and several dugouts, dotted by numerous embrasures for the rifles and the machine guns and surrounded by two rounds of barbed wire. The Sasso di Sesto was the most advanced Italian position in the Three Peaks sector located less than 500 meters away from the main Austro-Hungarian position of Toblin Tower. The latter was also a highly impenetrable position with an artillery observation post on the peak and machine and mountain gun emplacements on each side. On 21 April the troops, consisting of 40 *Standschützen*, and 120 *sturmtruppen* from the 11th Army's *Sturmbaon*, were ready to put their plan in motion. During the early evening the troops, which had originally been stationed at Toblin Tower, began to cross the tunnel and at 2300 they assembled in small groups near the exits ready to

10 Antonio Berti, *Guerra in Ampezzo e Cadore* (Milan: Mursia Editore, 1985).

go into action. A few seconds later the commander waved everyone forward. Without warning they emerged from the snow and camouflaged in snow suits took the sentries by complete surprise with daggers and bayonets. After having overcome this first opposition, the assault units dashed toward the main caverns to block the entrances and disarm the enemies. While many Italians were captured without a fight, several others were shot or killed by hand grenades or during vicious hand-to-hand combat. The stormtroopers then proceeded to mop up the last remaining pockets of resistance by clearing the deepest caverns with the aid of flamethrowers, hand grenades, rifles and steel clubs. By midnight the Sasso di Sesto had fallen into Austro-Hungarian hands with a final tally of 18 enemy soldiers killed and 75 captured.

> "In the deep caverns," recalled *Standschützen* Ausserer, "the Italians fought fiercely being led by their senior officer that bravely fell to his death. Inside the caverns the fighting was extremely dangerous as hand grenade explosions were sending steel splinters and rock debris flying everywhere. Rifle fire was also exchanged and there were many wounded. We also fought with bayonets, daggers and rifle butts. While the fighting intensified we could hear the screams and the moans of the many wounded soldiers lying on the ground. These were horrible and desperate sounds. At midnight the Sasso had fallen in our hands."[11]

Asiago Altopiano

Given the vast amounts of snow on the northern edge of the Asiago Altopiano the Austro-Hungarian assault units experimented here too during the tail end of winter 1917 with surprise attacks against fortified Italian positions. These attacks followed a similar pattern as in the Dolomites and involved digging concealed tunnels in the snow to infiltrate the Italian positions undetected and to then suddenly spring surprise attacks upon them. The Altopiano was particularly suited for these types of attacks because the snow was typically nine feet high until early May. The excavation of these tunnels was usually begun well in advance before the start of the attack by sappers using shovels, picks and modern boring equipment to dig through the rocks, snow and ice. The work was done with the utmost secrecy in order to enable the attacking columns to achieve maximum surprise. When a tunnel was finally completed a light diaphragm of snow and ice was left on the enemy side to conceal it from opposing sentries and patrols. On the day of the attack, the remaining snow and ice would be quietly removed a few minutes prior to the start of the operation. The exits of the tunnel were always strategically positioned close to key enemy positions such as a machine gun stronghold, an artillery emplacement or an enemy dugout. This allowed the stormtroopers to reach the enemy positions within a few minutes and hopefully without suffering casualties. In addition, most of the enemy positions that were assailed by the special assault detachments were not chosen at random but

11 Ibid., p. 184.

were carefully selected as a result of extensive reconnaissance. Often, for example, the timing of the attack coincided with the handing over of the enemy position to an inexperienced or 'green' unit that did not know its new assigned territory well. In other cases, these attacks would target isolated positions that were either located high up in the mountains or on an advanced frontline post that could not easily be reached by reinforcements. In most cases the position was kept under observation for several days and the wire secretly breached with wire cutters ahead of the day of the attack.

One of the first raids of this kind was carried out by the three assault patrols of the 73rd Infantry Regiment whose goals were to "capture enemy soldiers and cause the destruction of their dugouts and trenches."[12] For over a month prior to the scheduled date of the attack, Austro-Hungarian sappers had excavated two tunnels in the snow near Casara Zebio Pastorile. When the work terminated the first tunnel had a length of 80 meters and the second one 60 meters. Both ended in close proximity to the machine gun strong point held by troops of the 130th *Perugia* Infantry Brigade. According to the post-battle report:

> At dawn on 20 February a surprise attack was carried out by three assault patrols which simultaneously emerged from snow tunnels to reach an enemy position. The stormtroopers lobbed hand grenades into the enemy's caverns and trenches. After having destroyed several enemy gun pits and dugouts the assault troops retreated through the tunnels. Upon completion of the operation the tunnels were blown up.[13]

The raid yielded the capture of three officers, 17 soldiers, nine rifles, and four gas masks, at a cost of one NCO severely wounded, one soldier lightly wounded and two soldiers missing in action. It was later determined that the two soldiers had actually been wounded and later captured by the enemy infantry. These soldiers were immediately interrogated and their special gear and uniform gave away the fact that they were not standard infantry soldiers but stormtroopers. Their capture caused considerable concern amongst Italian officers who reckoned that the soldiers belonged to a new breed of enemy assault unit. On the Austrian side the raid was seen as an important success. The commander of the 11th Army issued a bulletin the following day that was full of praise for the stormtroopers. The bulletin was subsequently printed and widely distributed amongst the troops to serve as a stimulus to other units to carry out similar bold operations.[14]

The same tactic was used again on 28 February against outposts held by the *Sassari* Brigade on Mount Zebio. At 0600 the Austro-Hungarians fired a rocket flare near Point 1,476 on Mount Zebio which was followed by a brief artillery barrage that

12 Kriegsarchiv: K.u.K. 73. Infanterieregiment, Op. Nr. 643, 16 February, 1917.

13 Kriegsarchiv: K.u.K. 11. Armee Kommando Op. Nr. 669, 24 February 1917.

14 Maximillian von Hoen, *Geschichte des Salzburgisch-oberösterreichischen K.u.k. Infanterie-Regiments Erzherzog Rainer Nr. 59 für den Zeitraum des Weltkrieges 1914–1918*, (Salzburg, Rainerbund, 1931), pp. 403–407.

killed one soldier, injured 17 soldiers and one officer. The aim of the barrage was to confuse the Italians given that shortly thereafter the *sturmkompagnie* of the 3rd *Schützen* Regiment emerged from two snow tunnels to attack nearby Italian sentry posts.

While special bombing platoons engaged the enemy *alpini* units, a few pioneers advanced through barbed wire entanglements armed with grenade sticks and wire cutters. After a huge hole in the wire was made, the stormtroopers proceeded to enter into the enemy defenses. In the hand-to-hand fighting that ensued, one sentry was killed, one was injured and two were captured.

According to the Austro-Hungarian post battle report:

> A surprise raid was carried out at dawn on 28 February out of sections 56, 57, 58 of I Battalion. On sections 56 and 57, after having dug a tunnel in the snow, the enemy wire was breached. The explosions created enough confusion to allow the troops to advance rapidly against the enemy trenches on section 58. The position was overpowered by a flurry of hand grenades and an Italian NCO was captured. Lieutenant Niemetz, commander of the artillery support unit, should be singled out for the accurate fire provided by his grenade launching unit, while NCO M. Kozyk of 3rd Company should also be recognized as the audacious commander of the assault patrol.[15]

In March more *sturmtruppen* raids were undertaken in the Asiago Altopiano sector. The first one took place on Mount Forno on 15 March by troops of the 27th Infantry Regiment. The operation was fully thought out, meticulously planned and conducted with considerable ingenuity. The targeted position of the attack must have been under considerable surveillance since the operation was executed on the same day the Italian troops of the *Sette Comuni* vacated the position and handed it over to the *Bassano* Battalion. As will be shown later the inexperience of the *alpini* of the *Bassano* in manning the forward position would play a role during the initial phase of the operation. The timing of the assault was also a factor since the Altopiano was still covered by several feet of ice and snow and the troops by wearing white overcoats could well camouflage themselves while advancing toward the Italian positions. As a result of the bad weather and the high snow, the Italians least expected an enemy assault to take place under such poor conditions.

In order to achieve maximum surprise on the enemy, for several weeks Austrian sappers dug two tunnels under the heavy snow and ice in order to secretly get as close as possible to the Italian positions. By the first week of March the work had been completed, while the *sturmtruppen* assault patrols continued to rehearse in the rear mainly by conducting extensive hand grenade training. The assault patrols of the 27th Infantry Regiment had been chosen for this operation since they were comprised of highly experienced soldiers who had been one of the first to complete

15 Hans Strohschneider, *Das Schutzenregiment Graz Nr. 3 und der steirische Landsturm im Weltkrieg 1914–18* (Graz: Verlag, 1932), p. 98.

stormtrooper training at the Levico training ground, run by 11th Army. They were reputed to be ready to undertake the dangerous operation having gone through the challenging training program which was heavily concentrated on gymnastics, hand-to-hand combat, handling grenades and practicing assaults on entrenched positions.

On 14 March the final plan of attack envisioned the deployment of two distinct infantry columns each organized as follows: two assault patrols in the lead, two standard infantry platoons with rifles in the middle, and finally a small sapper unit carrying explosives to destroy enemy positions. The men of the assault patrols were equipped with a steel helmet, field grey uniform covered by a light white camouflage over-suit, a rucksack, two hand grenade bags flung over the shoulder containing 20 grenades, a flashlight, an ice pick, short rifle with bayonet, and a dagger. The troops were supported by two 75 mm mountain guns, 10 machine guns and two grenade throwers. The plan entailed that the two columns would attack simultaneously several bunkers held by the 62nd Company of the *Bassano*. They would then proceed to break through the ice and snow and later irrupt into the enemy trenches.

At dawn on 15 March small teams of stormtroopers broke through the light icy diaphragm that separated them from the enemy and suddenly irrupted from the north tunnel into the Italian positions "emerging like ghosts from the snow" thanks to their white camouflage over-suits[16] and taking the enemy completely by surprise. During the first few minutes of the attack the defenders, who had already come under heavy fire, sought frantically to determine where and from whom they were being fired on as the Austrians plastered their trenches with hand grenades. Having recovered from the initial shock, the *Bassano alpini* reacted vigorously to stem the tide of the enemy raiding party and, led by their officer Santino Calvi, began to fight back. Their resistance was aided by unexpected difficulties experienced by the enemy as the assault troops at the south tunnel initially could not break through the snow and ice. As a result of this initial setback, they emerged from the tunnel when the battle had already begun. As the Austrian commander was the first to emerge from the south tunnel, he was struck almost immediately by a sentry while several other Austro-Hungarian soldiers were also killed or wounded as they attempted to break through the snow. Nonetheless, the stormtroopers, armed primarily with hand grenades, by then had already captured 22 and killed and wounded several other Italians. Facing increasingly strong opposition they then returned to their positions having suffered only seven wounded soldiers and having left their wounded commander and a few other soldiers behind. Due to the enemy's prompt reaction, the pioneer units were not able to go into action as the assault units were forced to expeditiously make their way back to the Austrian trenches supported by the combined fire of mountain cannons and machine guns.

16 Alessandro Massignani, *Le truppe d'assalto austro-ungariche nella grande guerra* (Valdagno: Rossato Editore, 1996), p. 38.

According to the post-battle report of 27th Infantry Regiment the operation had been partially successful and the technique of digging tunnels to aid the infantry assault was reported to be a worthwhile procedure to be repeated in future operations.[17]

On 15 April the assault patrols of the 7th *Feldjäger* Battalion suddenly irrupted into a machine gun strongpoint of the *Val Tanaro alpini* Battalion at Corno della Segala in the Asiago Altopiano. Here too the *sturmtruppen* used a tunnel dug in the snow to approach the enemy positions as described by the *Val Tanaro* unit diary:

> On the night of 15 April while our position was surrounded by heavy fog and under a heavy snow storm a few enemy soldiers dressed with white camouflage over-suits suddenly broke through a sheet of ice and snow near our position and dashed toward our machine gun strongpoint. At the same time our position began to be plastered by flanking enemy rifle and machine gun fire. However, thanks to our vigilant sentries in combination with the prompt reaction of the whole defensive strong point we were able to foil the bold enemy attack. While some of the enemy troops fell to the ground, the vast majority were able to escape after blowing up the snow tunnel.[18]

Raid on Monte Pasubio

The Tenth Battle of the Isonzo began on 12 May 1917 following a prolonged artillery bombardment lasting several days. Prior to the start of operations large numbers of both Italian and Austro-Hungarian troops were transferred to the Isonzo to take part in this major battle. To prevent the Italians from transferring additional troops to the Isonzo, Trentino-based Army Group Conrad was ordered by the AOK to initiate a number of small raids and two medium-sized attacks to pin the enemy down with increased activity. As a result, Conrad launched Operation '*Grenadiermarsch*' in late May 1917 which saw the stormtroopers carry out numerous attacks along different points of the Trentino front to disrupt the Italian 1st Army. While the largest thrust (on the Pasubio) had been planned for a long time, a few smaller raids were executed without extensive planning.

The first thrust was conducted by unspecified Austro-Hungarian stormtroopers against the heavily fortified position of the Trincerone on Mount Zugna defended by the 207th/*Taro* Infantry Brigade. On 19 May the assault unit attempted to overrun Italian defenses by lobbing a number of hand grenades over the steel and concrete barrier. But the unit was repulsed after heavy fire. Despite the failure of the initiative, the stormtroopers, however, managed to kill three and wound 12 Italians.

17 Kriegsarchiv: AOK Op. Nr. 34/61, K.u.K. Abschnittkommando 27. Infanterieregiment, 'Überfall der Sturmpatrouillen', 17 March 1917.

18 Ufficio Storico: Riassunti storici dei corpi e comandi nella guerra 1915–1918: Val Tanaro, p. 5.

The main thrust of this operation was the planned attack against the heavily fortified Italian positions of Mount Pasubio on the night between 20–21 May 1917 which was also the first major large-scale attack conducted by the stormtroopers in the campaign. Along with Mount Grappa, the latter constituted a position of strategic importance for the Italians being the last bastion of defense of the Venetian Plain. The Pasubio was occupied by the Italians shortly after the summer of 1915 but as a result of the *Asiago* Offensive, the Austro-Hungarian Army had seized its northern peak in 1916. This led to an uneasy cohabitation whereby the Italians held the southern peak, known as Dente Italiano (Italian Tooth), which was separated from the Dente Austriaco (Austrian Tooth) by a small slope named Selletta dei Denti. As both sides held highly fortified positions dug deep into the mountain, which were virtually only a few hundred meters from each other, no man's land became a hotly contested area and the focus of countless artillery duels and several pitched infantry engagements. Most of these attacks conducted during the second half of 1916 resulted in huge casualties but yielded little or no territorial gains. This stalemate led both sides to build extensive tunnels under their opponent's positions and to then attempt mining them out of existence. When even this strategy did not produce tangible results Army Group Conrad resorted to the newly formed stormtrooper units.

The raid on an advanced Italian observation post, several machine gun nests and infantry dugouts on the Pasubio massif, was executed by two infantry columns totaling 330 men between officers and soldiers:

> Group 1 consisted of three assault patrols of 11th Army *Sturmbaon*, three assault patrols of II Battalion/1st *Kaiserjäger* Regiment, and a sapper unit led by Lieutenant Heinisch.
>
> Group 2, led by Lieutenant Adolph, included three assault patrols of 11th Army *Sturmbaon*, three assault patrols of I and III Battalions/1st *Kaiserjäger* Regiment, and a sapper unit. A mountain *sturmtrupp kompagnie* was initially kept in reserve.

The goal of both groups was not to occupy the advanced enemy positions but rather to inflict casualties and destroy enemy dugouts and caverns.[19]

Given the fact that this was to be their first large-scale planned attack, the troops of the 11th Army *Sturmbaon* prepared it with much care and no small detail was overlooked. A few days prior to the start of the attack, the Austrian local commander, Major Hogn along with Captain Kratoschwill, the stormtrooper commander, conducted a series of reconnaissance missions of the Italian positions on Mount Pasubio to identify weak points in their defenses. In so doing, they took every conceivable precaution for secrecy. In fact, when the stormtroopers began to move forward on the day of the attack, the Italians were completely caught by surprise.

19 Viktor Schemfil, *Die Pasubio-Kämpfe 1916–1918: Das Ringen um den Eckpfeiler der Tiroler Front* (Bregenz: Z.A. Teutsch, 1937), p. 207.

The 11th Army had established its main assault training ground at Levico, in Trentino. By April of 1917 it had completed the training of its principal assault battalion and several other smaller infantry assault patrols. The soldiers came from battle hardened mountain units. Given their background, the stormtroopers were vastly experienced in fighting in mountainous terrain with hand grenades, daggers and steel clubs. At the camp they had rehearsed various maneuvers to ambush, overwhelm and kill or capture as many opponents as possible barricaded in fortified positions on mountain peaks and passes. The *Sturmbaon*'s soldiers came from the following mountain infantry units:

1. First assault Company constisted of soldiers from the 3rd, 23rd, and 26th *Schützen* Regiments.
2. Second Company was comprised of soldiers from various Bosnian regiments.
3. Third Company was comprised mainly of soldiers from I and II *Kaiserschützen* Regiments.
4. Fourth Company consisted of *Kaiserjägers* (9 officers and 170 soldiers).

In addition, the Battalion had one mountain gun unit, one machine gun company, one trench mortar group (four 90 mm mortars, two 120 mm mortars) and one pioneer/flamethrower platoon (with six 15 liter *kleine* flamethrowers and two 22 liter flamethrowers). In the fall of 1917 a special mountain assault unit (*hochgebirgskompagnie*) was also added to the battalion and was comprised in great part by soldiers that had undergone the rigorous mountain guide training at Levico.[20] This unit was initially comprised of eight officers and 145 soldiers.

For this operation the stormtroopers were grouped in small platoons of nine soldiers: half as grenade throwers, while the other half as grenade carriers and riflemen. The platoon leader was the only one that during the assault would primarily fire a machine pistol or a rifle instead of lobbing or carrying grenades. Their ultimate aim was to spring a surprise attack on Altitude 2,116, called by the Italians 'Panettone Alto,' consisting primarily of high mountain advanced emplacements in the vicinity of the Dente Italiano. If the main objective was seized the troops had been instructed to continue advancing forward toward the Dente position.

At 2245, on 20 May, as the assault units exited their dugouts, Austrian batteries, including a number of heavy 30.5 cm field guns, began to pound with force the Dente Italiano. Other nearby positions such as Cima Palon, Cogolo Alto, Corno di Pasubio, Cosmagnon and Passo dell'Ometto were also targeted in a bid to neutralize enemy artillery. The intent was to lead the Italians into thinking that it was the start of a prolonged preparatory barrage to be followed by a large scale offensive. The barrage was also supported by the fire of numerous machine guns meant to disrupt the activities of enemy sentries forcing them to seek cover inside caverns and dugouts.

20 Alessandro Massignani, *Le truppe d'assalto austro-ungariche*, p. 53. Kriegsarchiv: K.u.K. 11. Armee Kommando, Op. Nr. 317/67, 'Hochalpine Sturmhalbkompagnie', 4 June 1917.

Under a scenario that saw heavy shells and continuous rounds of machine gun fire investing the Italian positions, the *sturmtruppen* were able to advance virtually unopposed toward the enemy positions where they began to throw hand grenades into machine gun pits and sentry posts.

The Austrian historian Robert Skorpil recalls that:

> The assault platoons had reached the enemy wire and were ready to attack. Prior to the start of operations their commander was calm and exuded confidence among his soldiers. Then after a few seconds he commanded the troops to attack. As he waved the soldiers forward, numerous hand grenades were lobbed into the enemy parapet as the assault platoons shouted out loudly: Hurra! A human wave, a grey wave of *Kaiserjägers* then struck the enemy with much force.[21]

When at 2320 most of the initial obstacles had been eliminated and the artillery barrage was lifted, the *sturmtruppen* suddenly irrupted through the advanced Italian defenses on Altitude 2,116 of the Pasubio plastering with machine gun fire the entrances of their dugouts. Without any chance to fight back, the Italians, who were still taking cover from the barrage, were rounded up and captured. As the *Kaiserjägers* were busy disarming the enemy, the stormtroopers continued to advance into the Italian positions by attacking any dugout or fortified position where the men offered any resistance. They hopped from trench to trench in small groups throwing hand grenades and firing their light machine guns and automatic pistols into the entrances of caverns and dugouts. They pushed through these defenses so quickly that the *alpini* trying to stop them with bayonets were overwhelmed. Within less than an hour of fighting the *sturmtruppen* had advanced approximately 500 meters and had swept up entire fortified positions. They were finally pushed back by a determined counter-attack by both *alpini* and infantry units of the *Liguria* Brigade that met the attackers just as they were negotiating a steep gully on their way toward the peak of the Dente Italiano. The *Liguria's* official history recalls that: "On 21 May a firm counter-thrust undertaken by elements of the 157th Infantry, 65th Infantry and *Morbegno alpini* Battalion was able to repulse an enemy assault unit that with a bold maneuver had managed to penetrate into the trenches of the Panettone Alto."[22]

Thus, then just as quickly as they had broken through the enemy lines they retreated with a very impressive war booty consisting of almost 200 soldiers from the 65th Italian infantry.

According to the Italian commander's post battle report the attack appeared to have been supported by several large artillery guns and by numerous waves "of specially trained shock troops."[23] In reality, it had initially saw the coordinated fire of several artillery batteries but the assault platoons that took part in the operation

21 Robert Skorpil, *Pasubio* (Bolzano: Athesia, 1974), p, 214.

22 Ufficio Storico: *Riassunti storici dei corpi e comandi nella guerra 1915–1918 Brigate di Fanteria* (Rome: AUSSME, 1927), p. 275

23 Ufficio Storico, E1, Raccolta 17: XXIX Corpo d'Armata, n. 9655, 22 May 1917.

were not large at all. Their speed, firepower and aggression, however, made up for the small size of their assault platoons. These elements had evidently deceived the Italian commander into thinking that his troops had been attacked by a much larger enemy force. The day after the raid the 11th Army commander praised his brave troops for their successful raid on Mount Pasubio and claimed the following enemy losses: 4 officers and 190 soldiers captured or killed, and 4 machine guns seized, while a large enemy mortar had been destroyed. The post battle report remarked that "the artillery had provided targeted and effective supporting fire, while the assault units fought with vigor and in close coordination with the sappers."[24]

The last thrust of Operation 'Grenadiermarsch' was executed on the night between 24/25 May 1917 against the Italian position on Mount Majo (Hill 1,472), one of the main defensive strong points on the Posina Valley. It was undertaken by the 3rd assault patrol of the 4th Assault Company (IV Battalion/14th Infantry Division) with a surprise night attack without artillery support. Despite low visibility an Italian sentry was able to spot the enemy platoon as it approached the main position and sound the alarm. Suddenly, concentrated mortar and machine gun fire rained down on the exposed stormtroopers while they were in the process of negotiating the ridge leading to the high altitude enemy position. As a result, the assault was repelled with the following losses: one officer (the unit's commander Franz Loberbauer) and four soldiers dead, while six soldiers were wounded.[25]

Even though the last raid of Operation 'Grenadiermarsch' had not succeeded, Army Group Conrad's collective thrusts had successfully pinned down Italian forces in the Trentino. The post-operation report underlined the critical role played by the assault patrols which were recognized for the way they used the bombing squads in the attack in covering the enemy trenches with hand grenades.

Counterattack on the Isonzo: Battle of Flondar

The Flondar battle saw the Austrian *sturmtruppen* employed for the first time in large numbers in a major planned attack. In May 1917 the Italian Army had just completed the Tenth Battle of the Isonzo when the Austro-Hungarians struck back within just a few days with a furious counter-attack aimed at regaining control of lost positions. Their main target was the forward position of the Flondar in the lower Isonzo. During the Tenth Battle the Italians had pushed ahead on this rugged hill that opened up the way toward Mount Hermada, the last remaining Austrian fortress in defense of Trieste. As a result, General Svetozar Boroević von Bojna of the Austro-Hungarian 5th Army, was determined to push them back and re-establish solid defenses to shield the port city. Boroević, named the 'lion of the Isonzo' for the way in which he inspired his troops to yield not at inch of trench to the enemy, knowing full well

24 Kriegsarchiv: K.u.K. 11. Armee Kommando, Op. Nr. 1456, 22 May 1917.
25 Ernst Wisshaupt, *Die Tiroler Kaiserjäger im Weltkriege*, p. 352.

that his decimated infantry divisions could not afford to fight another major battle of attrition, opted for a preventive strike.

By that time his 5th Army was the only unit on the Italian front that had nominated a Training Officer for Assault Operations, which was responsible for *sturmtruppen* training at the highest level. He functioned as the stormtrooper battalion commander and was also tasked with establishing uniform training procedures across the 5th Army. The April 1917 AOK survey revealed that Boroević's army had completed the training of its 900 unit strong *Sturmbaon* that had drawn handpicked soldiers from its three army corps. The soldiers were reputed to having been trained "in close combat with modern weapons and had mastered the art of wielding hand grenades."[26]

The battalion also had fully equipped support units such as one mountain gun unit, two flamethrower sections and two light machine gun groups.

In the lower Isonzo sector the frontline passed through the small town of Kamarje then it cut through the railway line Jamiano-Brestovica then through the Flondar on Hills 135, 145 and 146 and then it descended to Medeazza on Hill 110. The frontline ended near two railway tunnels of the Trieste-Monfalcone line. Since the Italians had only had few days to 'turn around' the Flondar positions, when the Austro-Hungarians struck, their defenses were reputed to be poor at best. By 3 June only rudimentary and preliminary defenses had been established including: a one meter high parapet, a single line of barbed wire and only in a few sectors of the front had trenches been dug. Moreover, the infantry was very vulnerable to an attack based upon infiltration tactics since it was deployed along a single line of defense including the machine gun strongpoints. The only firm defenses were located on the reverse slopes of the Flondar and within the nearby railroad tunnels where the concrete construction shielded the infantry from artillery fire.

The Austrians, prior to the planned attack, conducted extensive aerial reconnaissance to carefully observe the layout of the Flondar positions. From the information gathered it was determined that the two positions, Hills 145 and 146, were generally considered to be the most exposed and therefore the weakest links on this sector of the frontline. Most importantly, with the Italian troops lacking adequate trenches, they were in full view of the Austro-Hungarian artillery. To make matters worse, the night prior to the Habsburg counter-attack the untested and weakly armed III Battalion/71st Regiment had substituted with its 320 soldiers and 10 machine guns on Hill 145 the more battle hardened II Battalion/ 86th Regiment with its 600 men and 21 machine guns. Thus, for the Austrians all the pieces seemed to be coming together into a well thought out plan of attack to be implemented against the weakest enemy sector, held by troops that were poorly armed and lacked fighting experience.

With this counter-attack the Austro-Hungarians had two major objectives: to retake possession of Hills 146 and 145 and Hill 40, located to the rear of the two tunnels. The counter-attack was prepared in every detail with a particular focus upon the number of guns to be deployed that included the majority of 5th Army's heavy gun

26 Kriegsarchiv: K.u.K., 5. Armee Kommando, Op. Nr. 2454/30, 24 April 1917.

and mortar units. According to historian Walther Schaumann the Austrians assembled their largest field guns of 30.5, 35, 38, 42 cm caliber in order to fire powerful shells from several locations onto the Flondar.[27] The Habsburg plan of attack, formulated by General Schneider Edler von Manns-Au who was later awarded the Knight's Cross of the Military Maria Theresia Order, comprised a brief but overpowering artillery preparation using all available guns followed by the infantry assault. The latter was led by 1st, 2nd and 3rd *Sturmkompagnien* of the 5th Army *Sturmbaon*, which were assigned the most difficult task of the operation of crashing through the Italian defenses. They were in turn to be followed by the *sturmtruppen* Battalion's own light artillery and trench mortar units (4th *Sturmkompagnie*) and by six standard infantry battalions, which were given the task of mopping up enemy defenses.

This was the first large scale Austrian operation that would see the participation of several stormtrooper units. The latter were expected to deploy the German tactic of infiltration by punching deep into the enemy's positions to threaten their command and artillery posts. By using proven German tactical principles, the Austro-Hungarian assault units were to probe the Italian lines for weak spots and exploit them with all available firepower.

According to the Italian official history on 4 June 1917 the Austro-Hungarian counter-attack began with a large-scale artillery preparation: "At 0400 hours our adversary began a violent artillery barrage against our frontline positions, hitting also the dugouts in the rear and the exits of the tunnels on Hills 40 and 43. As the barrage intensified causing severe damage to frontline positions and to the improvised reserve dugouts, casualties began to mount."[28]

At 0445 the 600 strong *sturmtruppen* assault unit followed by six infantry battalions (12th Mountain Brigade and the 28th *Prague* Infantry Regiment) struck the railway line along the Jamiano-Brestovica tract and at 0500 they assaulted the tract near the Timavo River. Though pushed back in numerous spots along the Flondar frontline, the *sturmtruppen* were able to breach into and overrun two separate sectors. The first breach took place at Hill 135, where the stormtroopers, by taking advantage of the rugged terrain and by lying in wait during the barrage on the reverse slope that for the Italians was a blind spot, took the enemy by surprise once the barrage was lifted. The *sturmtruppen*, advancing under a thick artillery smokescreen, pushed through the positions held by III Battalion/71st Regiment killing its commander Colonel Mario Costa and many of his subordinates. By penetrating through the wire and into Hill 135 the Austrians created a first bridgehead which was used as a platform to later outflank Hill 145 and finally to surround the entrances of the crammed railway tunnel. At the time of the assault, the tunnel was packed with soldiers from the IV Battalion/86th Division which were waiting for the signal to counter-attack. Most of the Italian soldiers had assembled near the northern exit of the tunnel and

27 Walther Schaumann & Peter Schubert, *Isonzo, 1915–1917: Krieg ohne Wiederkehr* (Bassano del Grappa: Ghedina & Tassotti, 1993), p. 177.

28 Ufficio Storico, *L'esercito Italiano nella grande guerra, vol. 4* (Rome: Ufficio Storico, 1954), p. 39.

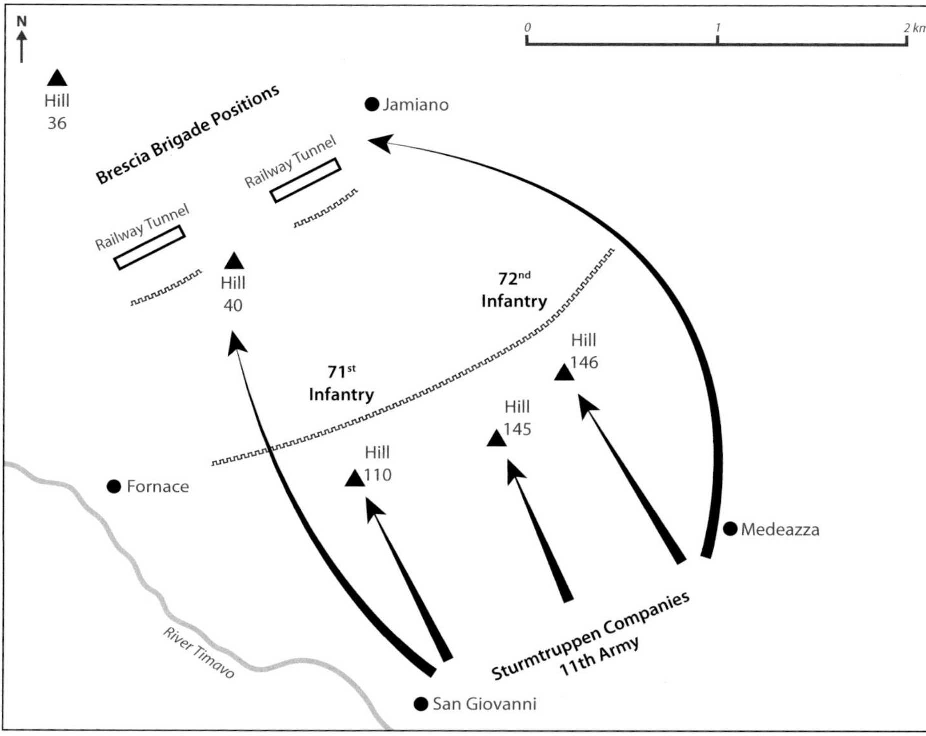

Map 1 The map shows the main assault columns of Austro-Hungarian stormtroopers and infantry as they attacked the Italian defenses on the Flondar. The positions had been seized by the Italians only a few days earlier. But on 4 June 1917 the Austro-Hungarians struck back with a very fast paced counter-attack which caught the Italians by complete surprise.

the Austro-Hungarians took advantage of their poor and crammed positioning by blocking the exits and trapping them inside. They positioned a number of machine guns against the northern end of the tunnel, while the unguarded southern entrance was attacked by *sturmtruppen* armed with flamethrowers. The latter pinned down enemy troops within the tunnel eventually forcing them to rush toward the northern exit to avoid the flames. By this time the vast majority of the Italian infantry had been trapped by the audacious maneuver of the Austrian assault detachments and as it exited the tunnel was forced to surrender.

At the same time the Austrians had also outmaneuvered two other enemy infantry companies defending Hills 38 and 58, which were situated behind walls on the reverse slope of the railway tunnel. Here the Austrians by gaining a foothold over the hill that overlooked the two Italian positions began to barrage their posts with grenades and machine gun fire.

Again according to the Italian official history: "The infantry was hit from above by hand grenades and intense machine gun fire. The infantry defended itself for as long as it could but was ultimately forced to surrender."[29]

Only a few Italian nuclei were able to avoid capture by pulling back along with remnants of the III Battalion/71st Regiment to Hill 36 where a new defensive line was formed halting the enemy advance.

In the meantime, the Austrians had also taken possession of Hill 110 blocking the southern exit of the second railway tunnel and surrounding the units of the II Battalion/86th Regiment. The latter had barricaded itself inside the tunnel blocking the entrance with sandbags. Armed with one small cannon and several machine guns, the Italian unit would only surrender at 2130 hours after putting up a determined resistance and after having run out of ammunition. Despite several attempts by the *sturmtruppen* to force their way into the tunnel, the Italians held out most of the day in the hope of being relieved by an infantry counter-attack. Since most of the field commanders had been killed and communications between the Flondar and the rear had been interrupted, the counter-attack was carried out only on 5 June. But by then, it was too late as the Austrians had already taken possession of the railway tunnel and were entrenched in their positions.

The second main breach occurred on Hill 146 held by the I and III Battalions/246th Infantry Regiment. Here the Austrians had broken through both frontally and on the flanks. The *coup de grace* was administered by the flanking units which after placing several machine guns on the Flondar-Medeazza road began submerging the Italian infantry with heavy fire. The following is the description of the infantry assault provided by the 3rd *Sturmkompagnie* against Hill 146:

> Covered by an intense artillery and machine gun barrage, the assault patrols advanced toward the enemy positions. Some of the *sturmtruppen* units made a frontal assault on Hill 146 while others assaulted its flanks as the enemy put up strong resistance. Violent hand-to-hand combat ensued leading to the wounding of NCO Gass who up to that point had been at the forefront of the frontal assault wave. His wounding encouraged the assault units to attack with even greater intensity and the enemy's resistance was finally breached. Numerous hand grenades were thrown at the entrances of the caverns that shielded the Italian infantry, allowing our men to penetrate line 1c which was heavily defended. Three platoons led by NCO Achzet bypassed hill Hill from the North and then penetrated within line 1c. NCO Achzet led two platoons that attacked the flanks of Hill 146 and within a few minutes the peak fell in our hands. NCO Achzet then bravely fell as he was mortally wounded in hand-to-hand combat and his body was ultimately shredded to pieces by a grenade. The assault units penetrated deeply into Hill 146 and mopped up all the enemy caverns and dugouts. The booty was represented by the capture of 17 machine guns, many prisoners, including the regiment's lieutenant and his staff. Our

29 Ibid., p. 40.

> losses included NCO Achzet and 4 dead soldiers, while NCO Gass and 4 other soldiers were severely wounded and 11 of our men were missing.[30]

As highlighted in the after-battle memorandum above the success of the operation was staggering given the large number of casualties inflicted and the comparatively moderate loss of life sustained by the Austro-Hungarians. The latter had prevailed primarily because the precise and timely artillery barrage had not only caused many victims amongst Italian frontline defenders but also because it forced the Italian infantry to seek cover in tunnels and trenches. Once it was lifted, the assault units were already upon the Italian trenches and could engage an enemy that was still largely disoriented by the tremendous artillery barrage. Without any respite, the Italian units were subjugated mainly by the speed with which the stormtroopers put forth their assault and also by their use of new weapons such as flamethrowers and hand grenade sticks. The crowding in the galleries and near the exits by the Italian infantry allowed the Habsburg assault units to immobilize their enemy under a steady stream of fire.

For the Austro-Hungarian official history the "the artillery preparation fire lasted only 40 minutes, but it was so fierce that it stunned and annihilated the enemy. Then the infantry put forth its attack taking the enemy by surprise, but it also suffered casualties due to artillery fire."[31]

While the official history attributes the success primarily to the fine work carried out by the artillery, it also underlines that the Austrian assault detachments had surprised and overrun their enemy with their tremendous speed and their firepower. The Austrian losses referred to in the official history apparently were the result of friendly fire caused evidently by the fact that the artillery had not fully perfected the art of the creeping barrage. As the infantry moved forward, the artillery was expected to lengthen its fire in response. Apparently, the artillery units and its command structure were still operating under the tactical principles used in earlier offensives when the barrage was controlled not by the assault units but by the artillery commanders. The infantry had used Very pistols to signal to the artillery to shift the creeping barrage forward, but apparently the artillery command post and their field observers had not been able to heed the warning. There were other failures in the execution of the operation not mentioned in the official history but outlined in the after-battle reports of units of 5th Army. One such problem encountered was the incorrect deployment by local commanders of some of the *sturmtruppen* assault patrols that arrived late onto the battlefield and could not take part in the planned attack. The following is the battle report of a *sturmtruppen* assault patrol leader which is indicative of some of the deployment problems:

> I arrived at regimental headquarters at 1145 on 3 June after a 14-hour march. My men were totally exhausted as they each had to carry 32 hand grenades … I

30 Kriegsarchiv: AOK, K.u.K. Abschnittkommando III, 'Tatigkeit der *Sturmkompagnien* vom 28. 5', Op. Nr. 24/50, 6 May 1917.

31 Edmund Glaise-Horstenau (ed.), *Österreich-Ungarns letzter Krieg, vol. 6*, p. 179.

> received the order to move out with the battalion Sturmpatrouillen immediately from the battalion commander. When I asked where the enemy position was, he pointed out at the front line in general. After receiving this order, I moved out with my patrol unit and the battalion patrols. We took two lines. The Sturmpatrouillen had to stop before the next one because the enemy obstacle field was completely intact and the infantry wave did not follow on as they had got lost in the undergrowth … When I withdrew, the regiment's patrols were also withdrawing. The infantry waves were nowhere to be seen. When I gathered my patrol together, the men were quickly given infantry ammunition and were ordered into position as ordinary infantrymen by the battalion commander. I was not able to take my men out until morning. There were only 10 men left.[32]

The battle report by the stormtroop patrol leader is most interesting from an historical perspective because it demonstrates that many senior infantry officers at the time did not know how to properly deploy the special units. First and foremost, his assault patrol arrived late and exhausted onto the battlefield after a prolonged march. The standard practice, which was outlined in the manual, was that the *sturmtruppen* were to be furnished with truck transport in order to reach the battlefield in good condition as fresh troops were considered to be much more effective when expected to go into action. Moreover, once the stormtroopers had completed their task they typically did not serve in the trenches as standard line infantry units. The commander of the Flondar counter-attack apparently flouted or was not aware of any of these guidelines. His first tactical error was to wear some of these special units down by not providing transport. Some of the troops arrived late and were not able to go into action as planned. Second, another major tactical error was to further wear down the manpower of these precious units by keeping them on the battlefield as line infantry following the completion of the counter-attack.

A few days after the battle the 5th Army published its own post-battle report that was based on the summary of the reports provided by the smaller units. It praised the assault stormtroopers for having fought well during the counter-attack and for having achieved all of their objectives. The report also made a set of recommendations in order to improve their battlefield performance. The main recommendation was to arm the stormtroopers with 12 rather than six hand grenades for future operations. It was noted that during the Flondar counter-attack the stormtroopers stocks of ammunition were not nearly enough for the task at hand and that many soldiers were forced to continue fighting only with rifles for a large part of the operation. The second issue was the overall lack of coordination between the infantry assault units and supporting groups armed with heavier weapons. Hence, the second recommendation was for an improvement in communications between the two units through greater reliance on signaling and flares.

A third observation outlined the need to further instruct infantry unit commanders on how to properly deploy the stormtroopers. As a result of these observations, the

32 Cited in Christian Ortner, *Storm Troops*, p.174.

5th Army would shortly thereafter issue an instruction manual that would detail when and when not to deploy these special assault units.

Despite the problems outlined above, the report concluded that the attack had been a success and had achieved the goal of pushing the Italians back and away from Trieste and Mount Hermada.[33]

The operation demonstrated that the Austrian Army had successfully incorporated many of the German *sturmtruppen* tactics. The attack was launched under the concealment of pre-dawn darkness. A large concentration of fire was reversed upon the Italian positions which were hammered by a brief but most violent barrage. Shortly after the infantry assault units had already reached the forward edges of the enemy's defenses as the preparatory bombardment was still unfolding. As the *sturmtruppen* invested the Italian positions, the barrage, albeit with some delay, was moved forward. The *sturmtruppen* then used their close combat skills and weapons to gain the upper hand on the already shaken Italian defense strongholds. Particularly successful was the use of new weapons such as the flamethrowers that were used to trap the enemy inside the railway tunnels.

According to the Austrians they had been able to capture 3,000 prisoners and 50 machine guns as well as recapture three artillery pieces that had been lost to the Italians during the 10th Battle of the Isonzo. Total Austrian losses were reported at eight officers and 300 men killed, 21 officers and 870 men wounded.

The Italian command, unjustifiably so, reacted with much astonishment to the rout of its troops. Once the *Comando Supremo* received information of the loss of the Flondar its leader was quick to blame the infantry troops involved in the battle, pointing out their ineffectiveness, while overlooking some of its own shortcomings such as poor instructions given to the troops while the battle was unfolding and the failure to deploy a zonal rather than linear defense. In fact, several units were captured inside their dugouts on the heels of the strong barrage as no provision had been made for holding reserve units in the immediate rear to be deployed in the counter-attack thus giving enough time to the frontline troops to organize themselves. In the aftermath, both General Cadorna and the 3rd Army commander were furious with the men of the III Battalion/71st Regiment, which in their view, had refused to fight. In his report, the 3rd Army commander, for example, stated that "most troops behaved courageously, the only exception was the soldiers of the 70th Regiment who lacked resoluteness and unit cohesion."[34]

In the same document the following losses were also reported: 18 dead, 75 wounded, nine missing amongst the officers and 460 dead, 2,044 wounded and 1,348 missing amongst the soldiers. What both Cadorna and his subordinate had obviously overlooked was that the new enemy tactics were not easily opposed by poorly deployed line infantry. Moreover, that in the same situation even less war weary, fresh troops, would likely have succumbed to such a fast and overpowering infantry attack. More ample and deeper dugouts and scattered trenches should have been prepared to

33 Kriegsarchiv: K.u.K., 5. Armee Kommando, Op. Nr. 24/52, June 10, 1917.

34 Ufficio Storico: Diario storico della 3a Armata, vol. 4, Museo storico della 3a Armata, Padova.

withstand the withering barrage and a greater number of defiladed machine guns could possibly have contributed to foiling the infantry assault. Moreover, the artillery was taken by complete surprise and unable to implement aggressive counter-battery fire or to harass the stormtroopers as they advanced.

Battle of Monte Ortigara

The counter-attack led by Austro-Hungarian *sturmtruppen* units that put an end to the bloody Battle of Mount Ortigara is particularly noteworthy for understanding the effectiveness of assault patrol and stormtrooper battalion tactics given the huge disparity of forces deployed on the battlefield. From a comparison of the opposing forces the battle favored the Italians due to their superiority in men and equipment. However, with the Austro-Hungarian Army, displaying superior tactics and better timed, more precise artillery fire, the battle ended in a complete and costly rout for the Italians. This operation in fact has all the hallmarks of a well prepared and executed surprise assault on a fortified position carried out by specialized infantry assault detachments. The timing of the infantry attack, coming on the heels of a most powerful barrage, was of crucial importance in allowing the stormtroopers to achieve tactical surprise. Well supported by accurate artillery fire, the *sturmtruppen* and the special mountain units were able to successfully carry out their second major planned attack of the campaign.

On 10 June 1917 the Italian 6th Army began offensive operations on the northern flank of the Asiago Altopiano. The first aim of this vast mountain operation was to conquer Mount Ortigara and Mount Portule, two strongpoints that allowed the Austro-Hungarians to control the northern edge of the Asiago Altopiano. Second, their capture would allow the Italian Army to gain a jumping off platform from which to attack the strategically vital Val Sugana and ultimately threaten Trento. The Ortigara, in particular, comprised by the highest, most barren peaks of the Asiago plateau, represented one of the main hinges of the intricate Austro-Hungarian defenses nested between the Italian bastions of Mount Grappa to the east and Mount Pasubio to the west. In this sector of the front line the Italian Army held a distinctive numerical advantage. Its 6th Army could count on 52 battalions of both *alpini* and infantry and 428 artillery pieces and 220 mortars, while the Austro-Hungarians could only counter with 24 infantry battalions, 150 pieces of artillery and 75 mortars. But the Austro-Hungarians made up for their lack of men and equipment by controlling naturally strong positions most of which were situated along a range of impregnable, 2,000 meters or higher mountain peaks. Moreover these positions were all well entrenched having been fortified throughout the winter of 1916–1917 with several machine gun and mountain artillery bunkers dug in deep caverns. The Austrians also had a great concentration of 30.5 cm *Skoda* heavy howitzers in this sector that outmatched most Italian heavy guns. In addition, the Austro-Hungarians could call on fresh reserves located in the immediate vicinity of the front line. These consisted of well-trained, specialized mountain infantry units and by the *sturmtruppen* Battalion of the 11th Army.

Initially, the Italian plan envisioned a concentrated assault against Mount Ortigara, but subsequently General Ettore Mambretti of 6th Army had opted for a drastic change of plans and ended up with a series of planned frontal assaults against five main enemy positions. This decision would ultimately have very negative consequences on the outcome of the operation because it not only resulted in an unnecessary dispersion of infantry assault troops over a wide section of the frontline, but it also ensured an inadequate artillery preparatory barrage. A troop deployment of such scale in a high mountain environment had never before been attempted by the Italian Army. Needless to say it presented numerous logistics challenges that were not fully dealt with during the preparatory phase of the battle. As a result, the dispersal of forces and artillery power on such a vast and difficult high mountain landscape contributed to a major Italian defeat.

On the afternoon of 10 June 1917 Italian *alpini* units of the 52nd Division attacked in waves the enemy positions on the Ortigara following a prolonged artillery barrage. In order to carry out the attack on the treacherous mountain terrain the *alpini* had to advance uphill for several miles. Initially they were not targeted by enemy fire while advancing under the cover of a thick fog. However, once they arrived at the enemy wire, the fog began to thin out leaving them exposed to horrendous machine gun fire. As a result, thousands were gunned down on the first day of fighting. With the exception of Peak 2,071 (the smaller of the two peaks) of Mount Ortigara, on that day the *alpini* failed to take all of their objectives. Moreover, the latter was taken only because a small unit from *Bassano* Battalion, with a true mountaineering feat, scaled a steep cliff and sprang a surprise assault from the rear of the Austro-Hungarian positions. Italian *alpini* units attempted over and over again on that day to take the main peak of the Ortigara but all attacks failed as the troops were blocked by fully functioning barbed wire defenses.

The Austro-Hungarians, determined to re-take possession of Peak 2,071, launched a counter-thrust at 0230 on 15 June 1917. At first, they concentrated artillery fire on the Ortigara and soon after launched the attack undertaken by three infantry battalions of III Army Corps and led by several assault patrols of 11th Army *Sturmbaon*. At first, the *sturmtruppen* and the first wave of infantry units were able to penetrate the enemy lines on Peak 2,071 and capture several machine guns. But once they had managed to gain a foothold on the mountain they were counter-attacked by *alpini* battalions and thrown back to their starting point with heavy losses. According to the Austro-Hungarian official history their defeat was determined by several factors. First and foremost, the artillery preparation had been insufficient. Second, the assault troops deployed were too few to have any chance of overwhelming the Italian defenders. Third, the operation had been rushed through and had not been fully thought out. "The time allotted for preparation was too short to allow the commanders and troops of the attacking group (a total of three and a half battalions) to gain sufficient knowledge of the terrain, which to most of them was unknown, and to carefully plan their cooperation with the artillery."[35]

35 Edmund Glaise-Horstenau (ed.), *Österreich-Ungarns letzter Krieg, vol. 6*, p. 203.

On 19 June 1917 the Italians renewed the attempt to take Peak 2,105, the highest position on the Ortigara. This time the operation was successful with the artillery blasting the Austrian defenses into submission and the infantry charging up the mountain and capturing an entire *Kaiserjäger* Battalion with a strength of 944 soldiers and 74 officers.

As a result, at the end of the offensive, Mount Ortigara was occupied by the following Italian units: the northern sector, between Peak 2,003 and Peak 2,101, by two battalions of the 9th *bersaglieri* regiment. The central sector, Peak 2,105, by the 2nd Battalion/10th Infantry Regiment on the right and *alpini* from the *Bassano* on the summit. The southern sector (Costone dei Ponari) was defended by two *alpini* Battalions: *Val Arroscia* and *Bicocca*. In addition, three light mountain artillery pieces were positioned on the peak in defense of the central sector. Knowing full well that a counter-attack was likely, the troops (3,000 in total) began to strengthen their defenses. But most of their efforts would be in vain since the Austrians would strike with great speed only a few days later.

It is reported in the Austro-Hungarian official history that upon learning of the Italian advance, Field Marshal Conrad stated to his subordinates that: "The Lepozze/Ortigara position must be retaken; otherwise the whole front is no longer tenable."[36] As a result, on 21 June Conrad ordered that an immediate counter-attack be carried out by the 11th Army to reoccupy the Ortigara. The objective of the planned attack was to retake it before the Italians had the opportunity to consolidate their hold on the position and fully reorganize their defenses. On 22 June Conrad communicated to his subordinates that General Ludwig Goiginger would assume overall command of the operation and that General Romer would organize artillery operations. The former was one of the most capable Austrian generals and probably the most trusted subordinate of the Field Marshal while the latter was an artillery specialist. The fact that Conrad pulled these able commanders from other frontline sectors in order to dislodge the Italians from Mount Ortigara demonstrates how central this position was to the Austro-Hungarian overall frontline deployment.

While General Goiginger was in charge of the operation, the outline of a plan of attack was the responsibility of the sector commander, the leader of the 98th *Kaiserschützen* Brigade. In order to achieve the objective, the Austro-Hungarian sector commander, Lieutenant Adolf Sloninka von Holodow, opted for a brief artillery barrage followed by an infantry assault led by *sturmtruppen* and special mountain infantry units. After a meticulous preparation, entailing several days of reconnaissance near Mount Ortigara, Sloninka determined that the offensive operation, given the rough, uphill, exposed terrain, could only succeed as a frontal attack. Moreover, since it would consist of a frontal attack, the operation had to be preceded by an extremely violent and brief barrage. The overpowering barrage would neutralize any enemy reaction allowing the infantry assault units to reach their destination with few losses. The assault units were to be assembled on the battlefield during the night prior to the attack (24 June) so that their movements and their presence on the Ortigara

36 Ibid., p. 204.

would be concealed for as long as possible from the Italians. Sloninka also maintained that the planned attack was to take place during the early hours of 25 June thus giving the assault units the chance to reach the enemy's barbed wire under the cover of darkness. It was hoped that by fighting during the night the units would lose as few casualties as possible while running through no man's land. Moreover, Sloninka posited that strong cooperation between artillery and infantry during the multiple stages of the assault would ensure that the troops reached their destination with little or no opposition.

On the 23 June the final attack plan was presented by Sloninka to General Goiginger and the latter approved it without any modifications. It envisioned the subtle deployment of artillery power with the intent to disorient the defenders of Ortigara. Solonika had in fact ordered brief five minute barrages to be executed immediately and every hour, including at night, against the peak position. This would not only serve to wear down the Italian defenses but also to keep the enemy guessing as to the precise date and time of the counter-attack. At first, the Italians responded to these mini-barrages with fierce counter-battery fire, but then after several hours their response became more subdued. Eventually they stopped replying altogether to enemy fire. The well-crafted plan entailed that on the night of the attack the artillery barrage would be started in earnest with several medium and large artillery units. The barrage was set to last only 20 minutes but it was expected to reverse upon the Italian positions a record number of shells. The aims of the artillery barrage were twofold: inflict casualties and soften up the Italian positions, and seal off the Ortigara with a box barrage comprised of gas grenades and shrapnel from other nearby Italian positions. The first objective was to be achieved with a creeping barrage that would allow the Austro-Hungarian assault troops to reach the Italian lines unencumbered. While the second, aimed at preventing Italian reserves from the nearby Vallone dell'Agnelizza from coming to the aid of the besieged positions, consisted of a poison gas attack.

For the infantry counter-attack the Austro-Hungarians deployed the following forces: 800 *sturmtruppen* from the highly experienced 11th Army *Strurmbaon* and 4,500 infantry soldiers aided by several flamethrower and machine gun units. In addition, various support units were expected to work in conjunction with the infantry: one sapper company, the artillery units of the 6th and 18th Divisions, including 60 light artillery guns, 31 medium and heavy guns, and 12 mortars.

The attack was articulated as follows:

On the left flank, the unit led by Lieutenant Colonel Forbelsky was to put forth an attack against the Italian defenses of Peak 2,101. Six *sturmtruppen* platoons of 11th Army, together with the *sturmtruppen* platoon of the I/1st *Kaiserschützen* Battalion and two flamethrower sections comprised the first assault wave. The second wave comprised four infantry companies of the I/1st *Kaiserschützen* Battalion, two companies of the III/57th Battalion with two machine gun sections and support units. The latter were responsible primarily for carrying the ammunition and the hand grenades to replenish the soldiers of the first and second wave.

A central column, led by Major von Buol was comprised of a first assault wave consisting of three *sturmtruppen* platoons of 11th Army, one *sturmtruppen* assault platoon of the III/57th Battalion and one flamethrower section. This wave had to advance on and breach the central positions of Peak 2,105. This first assault wave was supported by four infantry companies of III/2nd *Kaiserschützen* Battalion, two companies of the III/57th Battalion, two companies of the II/57th Battalion and two machine gun sections.

While a third column led by Lieutenant Weiss and comprising two *sturmtruppen* platoons of 11th Army and one *sturmtruppen* platoon of III/2nd *Kaiserschützen* Battalion was responsible for attacking Peak 2,105 from the flank through Costone dei Ponari.

To ensure that the operation would succeed in dislodging the Italians, the soldiers were heavily armed. Each soldier's ammunition consisted of 150 bullets, and six hand grenades, while by then all soldiers wore a steel helmet. Each column had also plenty of flamethrowers and various other units in support. Each soldier of the third wave, consisting primarily of support units, was responsible for carrying 300 bullets and 10 hand grenades.

According to the Austrian plan of attack the assault waves were to advance simultaneously with the start of the artillery barrage. This would have ensured that the brief but intense artillery preparation would not inflict casualties on Austrian troops.

The document went on to state that the smashing of the enemy frontline was primarily the responsibility of the 11 *sturmtruppen* platoons. These units, assisted by the assault detachments of the infantry battalions and by the flamethrower units, had to rupture the enemy positions and pave the way for the infantry advance.

At 0230 on 25 June the Austrian artillery laid down a concentrated fire on the enemy positions on Mount Ortigara. Over 90 tonnes of artillery shells and mortar rounds fell on the Italian positions within 20 minutes. Then it was the turn of the rolling barrage aimed at neutralizing rear command centers, artillery positions and reserve dugouts. Finally, the high explosive shells and mortar rounds were followed by a poison gas attack, the second attack of its kind on the Italo-Austrian front.

According to the Italian official history: "The artillery barrage submerged Monte Ortigara under tremendous fire. Within a few minutes its defenses were severely damaged and the infantry suffered many casualties. … The enemy also used large amounts of gas projectiles, which proved deadly. Our entire defensive system was shaken and paralyzed."[37]

The Austrian artillery strategy of shelling the Italian positions during the days prior to the start of the operation had its desired effect since on 25 June the Italian artillery did not retaliate immediately with counter-battery fire. This ensured that the Austrian artillery could carry out its destructive bombardment almost unencumbered and that the assault troops, for the most part, could cross no man's land with few casualties.

Although the barrage for the most part had its desired effects, along the left flank of the Italian deployment the fierce fight for control of Peak 2,101 was made particularly gruesome by the Austrian guns' failure to silence all enemy machine guns. As a result,

37 Ufficio Storico, *L'Esercito Italiano nella Grande Guerra, 1915–1918, Vol. 4*, p. 138.

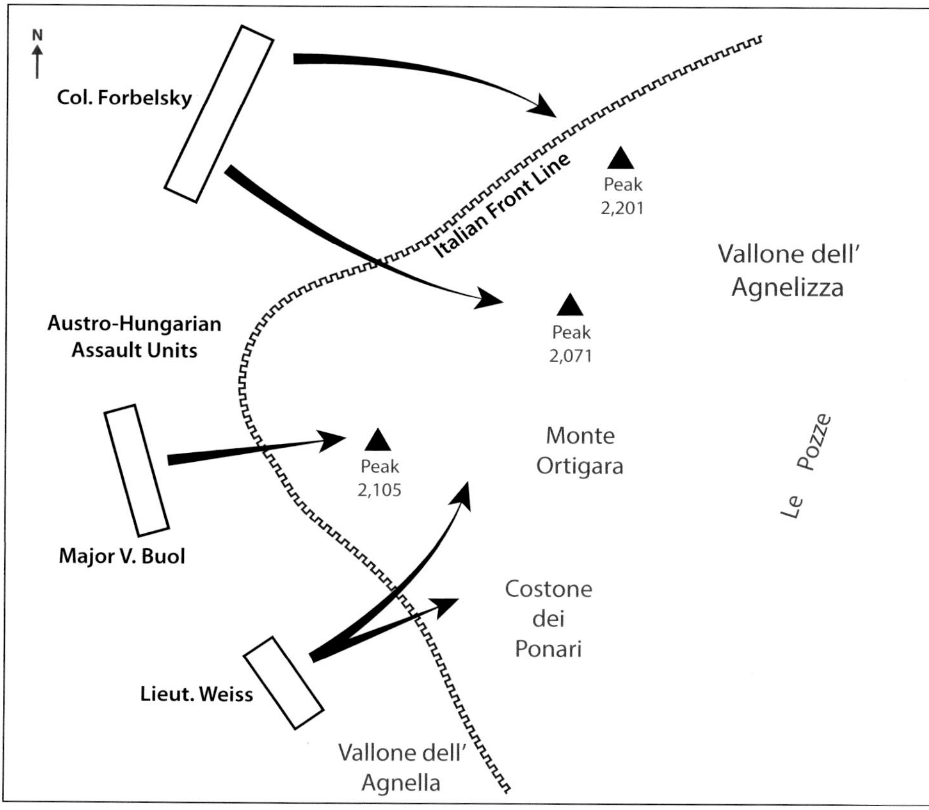

Map 2 At 0230 on 25 June 1917 the Austrian artillery laid down a concentrated fire on the enemy positions on Mount Ortigara. Over 90 tonnes of artillery shells and mortar rounds fell on the Italian positions within 20 minutes. The Italian positions were then attacked by Austro-Hungarian units of stormtroopers and infantry. The Ortigara Battle is also known as 'the Calvary of the *alpini*' for the exceedingly high numbers of *alpini* troops that died.

the machine guns systematically mowed down the first Austro-Hungarian waves. Despite tremendous fire and at a great cost, the second wave managed to unlock the precarious situation by bringing up to the wire a number of explosive tubes which were placed under the enemy's defenses and were then detonated. The explosions wrecked various sections of the front line producing huge tangles of barbed wire. In a timely manner, and taking full advantage of the confusion caused by the explosions, the flamethrower units bypassed the Italian wire from these openings and began to spit huge flames of fire into the passageways and trenches. As a result, huge flames lit up the pre-dawn sky while the smoke penetrated into the enemy trenches and passageways. They were followed by hand grenade assault units, which slowly given the enemy's reaction and at great cost, cleared the enemy trenches and caverns. Once all the guns and other centers of resistance were silenced, the Austro-Hungarians finally prevailed.

In contrast, the central positions on Peak 2,105 were overcome in only 45 minutes largely as a result of the violent barrage which shook the foundations of the Italian defenses destroying parapets, trenches and infantry strongpoints. The defenders were also surprised by the speed with which the Austrian stormtroopers reached their positions. So well timed was the attack of the assault units, that when the Italians exited their dugouts they had no chance to recover from the barrage and were overrun by *sturmtruppen* wielding bayonets, knives, steel clubs, brass knuckles and hand grenades. The infantry assault was also aided by several grenade launchers, which fired their explosive shells at a close distance into the enemy positions. This led the Italians into believing that the barrage was still being executed when in fact it was only a dozen or so grenade units which had been advanced into no man's land and were lobbying up to 25 grenades per minute into the Italian trenches. The Italian official history states that "the hand-to-hand combat in defense of Peak 2,105 was brief but extremely violent. After all of the officers had fallen, the soldiers were overwhelmed."[38] The survivors of the infantry assault were forced to retreat and shortly thereafter were reorganized by their officers under the peak of Mount Ortigara where they waited for reinforcements.

According to an Austrian officer:

> The Italian defense units on the northern edge of the mountain offered little resistance since they were totally overwhelmed. In fact the last artillery shells were still raining down on them when we invaded their outposts. Hundreds of prisoners were rounded up and sent into captivity. … Once we overcame the first outposts our objective was to retake possession of our old positions on the eastern slope of the mountain. An enemy machine gun on Peak 2,101 was making it impossible for us to cross the hill and reach the objective. Moreover, the machine gun nest was impenetrable protected by ample barbed wire works. Here sergeant Draslar's unit was instrumental in outflanking the nest and putting it out of action. The position was destroyed but at a high cost to our company.
>
> Our old positions were occupied by many enemy soldiers. We were able to dislodge them mainly with hand grenades. Anyone that failed to escape to the valley below was captured. Soldier that sought refuge within caverns were eliminated by lobbing hand grenades into the entrances of their defenses. …
>
> Those enemy forces that had initially escaped the onslaught and had retreated C. Caldiera were pursued by machine gun and artillery fire. The Vallone dell'Agnelizza was full of poison gas fired by our artillery. This forced many Italian soldiers to come back and give themselves up.[39]

38 Ibid., p. 138.

39 Adolf Sloninka von Holodow, *Die Kampfe um die Ortigara-Lepozze Stellung im Juni 1917* (Hall: Verlag Der Kaiserschützen Regimenter, 1927), p. 4.

The third column also dashed toward the enemy lines but they too were forced to the ground when an Italian machine gun mowed down the flamethrower unit that was leading the charge. As a soldier manning one of the flamethrowers was hit and fell to the ground, he unintentionally reversed on the packed Austrian assault column bursts of flames. Many soldiers shocked by the fire began to run back toward their lines and the officers had a very difficult time in reorganizing them.

These troops were eventually united to the second assault wave which ultimately reached the objective. Accordingly, "the enemy's machine guns were silenced with several hand grenades. Then the assault units routed the Italian first line of defense with their rifle butts, steel clubs and flamethrowers."[40]

Thus, after an hour of intense fighting the Austro-Hungarians had also conquered the right flank of the Italian deployment.

At 0430, having subdued all opposition, the Austrians on Mount Ortigara launched a white rocket flare thus indicating to General Goiginger that the entire position had been conquered.

The counter was conducted with extreme speed and decision. This is confirmed by 11th Army's post-battle report:

> The artillery barrage began at 02:20 hours and lasted approximately 20 minutes. As soon as it began the assault units ran toward the Italian positions. At first the enemy barbed wire was probed with several tubes of nitroglycerine/nitrocellulose mix. After several openings were made, the *sturmtruppen*, armed primarily with flamethrowers and hand grenades, began to open up gaps in the Italian lines. Several flamethrowers were used to eliminate the major machine gun nests. The interval between the time the artillery lengthened its fire and the start of the infantry assault was extremely brief and within minutes our troops were penetrating the Italian positions in force.[41]

The same version of events is found in a memorandum written by Field Marshal Conrad a few days after the battle: "Following a brief twenty minute barrage at 0300 hours on 25 June the assault units charged the enemy positions. The mountain posts were conquered in 45 minutes. The defenders of Peak 2,003 held out the longest, but they too eventually succumbed after seven hours of fighting."[42]

The Austro-Hungarians claimed the following losses: eight dead, 80 wounded, one missing amongst the officers; 373 dead, 2,414 wounded, and 1,367 missing amongst the soldiers.

In turn, the Austrians had captured 55 machine guns, 5 grenade launchers, 5 heavy guns, 3,000 rifles, and 18 artillery pieces. The Italians suffered countless casualties and 1,800 of its soldiers were captured by the enemy.

40 Ibid., p. 5.
41 Kriegsarchiv: K.u.K. 11. Armee Kommando, Op. Nr. 256/2345, 30 June, 1917.
42 Kriegsarchiv: Franz Conrad von Hoetzendorf, 'Juni-Schlacht auf der Hochflache der Sieben Gemeinden', 29 June 1917, p. 2.

The outcome of the battle was determined by the novel use of artillery as well as by the well-timed counter-attack. The overpowering artillery barrage, which had never before been so short but also so intense, stunned the Italian infantry.

What appeared to matter most in this battle was the adoption by the Austro-Hungarian artillery of German Lieutenant-Colonel Georg Bruchmüller the notion of the creeping barrage which replaced the customary prolonged preparation fire with an extremely brief barrage against known enemy positions. Unlike standard preparation fire, the creeping barrage did not deny the attacker the element of surprise using pinpoint fire against enemy fortifications. As Herwig asserts the "key to the creeping barrage was the closeness with which infantry followed it."[43] As a result of the severity and accuracy of the barrage, the stormtroopers were able to advance approximately 600 meters for the most part unencumbered by enemy fire. With their speed and impetus the assault units then smashed the enemy lines.

The Austro-Hungarian units also used for the first time 12 small and medium grenade launchers, (six 120 mm and six 140 mm units) in forward positions to support the assault units. They were used primarily to open up the enemy's defenses by taking out of action machine gun nests that stood in the way of the assault units. This novel use of light artillery, which the Austro-Hungarians had until then used primarily for defensive purposes, reflected the adoption of proven German *sturmtruppen* tactics developed on the Western Front. According to a 1917 Austrian artillery tactical deployment manual the army had established new offensive procedures for grenade-launching artillery units. It stated: "During attacks grenade launchers become means with which to destroy stubborn enemy positions. … Large grenade launchers are deployed to breach entrenched enemy positions while medium units are used in similar situations. Small grenade launchers are used to counteract and to force the enemy to retreat."[44]

These units would be used again in mass to good effect during the Isonzo/Caporetto battles in October-November 1917.

Finally, the infantry units fought in unison with the stormtroopers by keeping pace with them and not allowing the enemy artillery to split it apart. "*Kaiserschützen* infantry followed very closely the lead of the *sturmtruppen* that were able to quickly open up enemy defenses before the enemy artillery had a chance to intervene."[45] It appears from the battle reports issued by numerous commanders that this time the Austro-Hungarian assault units did not suffer extensively from friendly fire or from an improper use of the stormtroopers deployed as line infantry units. Thus, unlike the Flondar battle there was a marked improvement both in terms of artillery-infantry coordination and in the line infantry promptly coming to the aid of the stormtroopers after the latter had completed their task. Finally, the Austrian official history summarized the impact upon the Battle of the Ortigara of the newly established assault

43 Holger H. Herwig, *The First World War: Germany and Austria-Hungary 1914–1918* (London: Arnold, 1997), p. 208.

44 Kriegsarchiv: K.u.K. 11. Armee Kommando, Op. Nr. 256/2345, 30 June, 1917.

45 Ernest Wisshaupt, *Die Tiroler Kaiserjäger im Weltkriege*, p. 354.

units. "Here for the first time small Austrian-Hungarian storm patrols won a major success over much larger opposing forces. This was proof that specially selected troops, trained for a particular mission and then carefully but gallantly led, could defeat an enemy much stronger in numbers and equipment. They only needed to use the proper tactics and have the will to conquer."[46]

The losses on Ortigara devastated the Italian alpine corps. The 52nd *Alpini* Division suffered 12,633 casualties to their 15,000 men. Total Italian casualties were 2,865 killed in action or died of wounds, 16,734 seriously wounded, 2,600 captured and 3,000 missing in action, totaling 25,199. In this narrow area consisting of three mountain peaks along a two mile stretch the Austrian Third Corps lost 992 killed, 6,321 wounded and 1,515 missing or captured, totaling 8,828.

The outcome of the Battle of Mount Ortigara epitomizes the new versus the old way of conducting large-scale infantry assaults, or at least as developments in infantry tactics had been received from the Western Front and had been then integrated into the mountainous environment of the Italian Front. There is no doubt that during the battle, the Austro-Hungarian Army clearly showed that it was more forward thinking and deployed superior tactics than the Italians. The overall Italian plan of attack was flawed from the beginning. Its hard-to-achieve goal was to occupy high mountain positions by adopting the same tactics used in the Isonzo sector and without having fully thought through the implications from a logistical and defensive perspective of occupying and defending such isolated mountain crests from likely enemy counter-attacks and especially from close quarter artillery fire.

The Italians began operations with a long preparatory barrage lasting several hours to soften up enemy positions. They then put forth the assault which was conducted by packed wave after wave of infantry and *alpini* units pitted against fully functioning barbed wire defenses and machine guns. In addition, it appears that the Italian front-line infantry units did not possess heavier weapons such as flamethrowers, small artillery and grenade launchers to breach the wire when they reached the targeted positions. In contrast, the Austro-Hungarian stormtroopers and infantry not only possessed the necessary heavier equipment to breach the wire, but they also advanced in small groups deploying more sophisticated infiltration tactics. They came up on the heels of a short but very violent pinpoint barrage, which took both the Italian artillery and infantry by surprise. The former was in fact fooled by the enemy artillery as to the day of the attack. The Austrians kept firing upon the Ortigara for five minutes 24 times a day for several days prior to the scheduled attack. As a result of this tactic, when on 25 June the attack proceeded as planned, the Italian artillery failed to open interdiction fire immediately.[47]

Moreover, after the crest positions had fallen the Italian artillery failed to effectuate repressive fire on the Ortigara's peaks. It did however shell the Austro-Hungarian starting positions in a bid to halt the infantry advance. But it only started to fire when it was already too late and it continued to needlessly pounce upon these positions with

46 Edmund Glaise-Horstenau (ed.), *Österreich-Ungarns letzter Krieg, vol. 6*, p. 205.
47 Alessandro Massignani, *Le Truppe d'assalto Austro-Ungariche*, p. 84.

no effect on the final outcome until 0500 the next morning. As the Italian historian Alessandro Massignani has stated the key question is "why the more numerous Italian artillery was not able to neutralize Austro-Hungarian guns in a timely fashion"?[48] Likely, because the Italian artillery had not fully mastered the art of counter-battery fire. Also because the Austrian preparatory power had to a large extent neutralized its adversary especially with the poison gas shells.

Successful Raids

A notable example of a highly successful *sturmtruppen* raid was the operation against Malga di Londo in the Dolomites sector on the night of 18–19 August 1917. Here the objective was to "raid the enemy post, take prisoners and torch the Malga's defenses."[49] The Malga was an ammunition and supply depot serving the main Italian position on Cima Palombino and a host of nearby posts. It was the belief of the commander of the 21st Mountain Brigade that with the Malga position eliminated the Italians would be forced to reduce their presence on Cima Palombino. Given the relevance of the raid, the task was assigned to highly specialized troops consisting of two officers and 18 soldiers from 21st Brigade *Sturmbaon*. Each soldier had 12 hand grenades, two water flasks and food for two days, eight incendiary devices and five liters of gasoline. The plan was for the mountain artillery to fire 20 to 30 shells (with 75 mm guns) against the main Italian post on Cima Palombino to feint a diversionary attack, while the two assault patrols attacked the Malga. The post-combat report states that:

> A twenty man commando unit marched up from the valley to the Malga and then encircled the enemy position by surprise, attacking it with hand grenades. Several prisoners were brought back to the Austro-Hungarian line. The enemy post was torched to the ground. As the two patrols retreated they were fired upon by the enemy's artillery with shrapnel. No one was injured.[50]

Flawlessly executed, the operation yielded five prisoners and the destruction of the enemy position at no cost to the Austrians. Although not a major operation, the raid against the Malga is a demonstration of the great strides made by the special assault detachments in conducting high mountain operations autonomously. A small group of specially trained mountain stormtroopers was able to inflict much damage upon the enemy with the destruction of this advanced position including its store of wood, water and ammunition. As a result of the raid, the post was permanently destroyed and it remained unoccupied for the duration of the war. Reacting to the post-battle report, 1st Army commander Guglielmo Pecori Giraldi warned his commanders that

48 Ibid., p. 88.
49 Kriegsarchiv: K.u.K. 21. Gebrige Brigade Kommando Op. Nr. 526, 18 August 1917.
50 Kriegsarchiv: K.u.K. Sturmabteilung d. 21. Gebrige Brigade Kommando 'Malga di Londo', 20 August 1917.

it was "the lack of proper vigilance by some of our units that had facilitated surprise raids and attacks of this kind by the Austro-Hungarians."[51]

Another fairly successful operation was conducted a few days later against Italian troops in defense of Mount Majo. During the night on 21 August 1917 several assault patrols of the 2nd *Kaiserjäger* Regiment in combination with standard infantry platoons from the III and IV Battalions stormed the Italian positions on Post 1,472 of Mount Majo taking them completely by surprise. After the stormtroopers had left behind a trail of loss and destruction, they retreated toward their positions after having captured four officers, and 160 soldiers, three machine guns and three grenade launchers. The units involved suffered only four casualties, four missing and 36 injured.

The vast majority of operations involving the stormtroopers between January 1917 to September 1917 had been successful. However, in some cases even the fit and highly trained *sturmtruppen* units had stumbled at times demonstrating that success was not always assured. In order to avoid in the future the improper deployment of the stormtroopers the 11th Army in September 1917 published a series of reports detailing the execution of several failed raids and assaults. The reasons that were given for the lack of success were lack of proper reconnaissance and preparation of the operation, lack of proper training and insufficient artillery preparation.[52]

On 18 September 1917 the stormtroopers were deployed along with infantry to repel a dangerous surprise Italian attack in the Sugana Valley. At 0100 five infantry battalions with the 72nd *Bersaglieri* Battalion/20th Regiment in the lead overran several forward posts held by the 18th Infantry Division, destroyed several machine gun emplacements, and pushed deep into Carzano. The surprise assault had been aided by several treacherous members of an Austro-Hungarian battalion and especially by a first lieutenant of Slovenian nationality, that guided the enemy soldiers through the Austrian defenses. The prompt response of some reserve units, including several *sturmtruppen* assault patrols of IV/4th *Kaiserjäger* Regiment,[53] however, helped to seal the breach and ultimately push back the Italians. According to the Austro-Hungarian official history:

> On their own initiative, some small reserve forces hastened to the scene from all sides before dawn. They carried out a concentric counter-attack against the Italians, who intended to thrust to Borgo and were already approaching our batteries. The enemy were soon driven back, suffering heavy casualties. Before the morning ended, and also before the divisional and Army reserves could hasten forward, the original situation had been restored.[54]

51 Ufficio Storico: E-1, Raccolta 17, Comando 1. Armata, 'Contegno delle truppe', n. 49917, 4 September 1917.

52 Kriegsarchiv: K.u.K. 11. Amree Kommando, Op. Nr. 2046, 'Eingehende Vorbereitung von *sturmtruppen*-unternehmungen', 6 October 1917.

53 Ernst Wisshaupt, *Die Tiroler Kaiserjäger im Weltkriege*, p. 357.

54 Edmund Glaise-Horstenau (ed.), *Österreich-Ungarns letzter Krieg, vol. 6*, p. 217.

The Italian casualties included 17 officers and 896 soldiers either killed or captured. The Austro-Hungarians suffered 10 officers and 306 soldiers (dead or wounded).

A few days later the AOK recognized a new potential tactical role for the stormtroopers. According to AOK the *sturmtruppen* were deployed in Carzano as a rapid reaction force and their new role as tactical reserve units to be deployed to stiffen up defensive positions could be leveraged in the future to successfully fight off enemy surprise attacks.

Pre-Caporetto Operations

Prior to the major battle of Caporetto the Austro-Hungarian stormtroopers were used in a number of diversionary attacks in the mountainous sector of the frontline to distract the Italians from the build-up that was taking place in the lower Isonzo in preparation of the major offensive. In total the Austro-Hungarian Army launched three diversionary operations conducted in the Dolomites and the southern Trentino sectors between 18 and 22 October. The first operation took place against Italian positions located on Mount Majo on the night of 18 October, while the second operation took place on the same night on the Sogli Bianchi, one of the advanced posts held by the Italian X Army Corps in the Posina Valley. The third operation took place in the heart of the Dolomites sector on Mount Piana, a key position in the Three Peaks of Lavaredo frontline and only 10 miles away from the Pusteria Valley, where the Austro-Hungarian Army ran its main railroad line to bring in troops and supplies from the Tyrol. The Pusteria Valley with the towns of Dobbiaco, San Candido and Sesto was not only a major transportation hub, but was also strategically important because it was where the bulk of the troops of the 5th *Rayon* trained. Therefore, all attempts to loosen the pressure from the Italian infantry were particularly welcomed.

These operations were meant to not only divert the Italians' attention away from the lower Isonzo but also to capture key jumping off platforms for future offensives in the mountainous sector. In addition to the three operations, German radio stations set up in Trentino were broadcasting false orders after mid October. And it was hoped that Emperor Charles' presence at Bolzano between 15 and 23 October might also deceive the enemy.

Mount Majo

On the night of 18 October the assault patrols of the 2nd *Kaiserjäger* Regiment sprang another surprise attack against Post 1,472 of Mount Majo capturing a few Italians that were performing sentry duty. The Austro-Hungarian units were able to return to their lines with no losses.

Battle of Sogli Bianchi

The Italian positions on Mount Sogli Bianchi comprised one of the most advanced outposts of the X Army Corps on the left flank of the Posina Valley in the Trentino sector. In this valley the Italians held an advanced line, which served as an observation point as well as a first line of resistance against enemy attacks, centered on the peaks of Mount Majo, Mount Gamonda, Mount dei Calgari and Mount Sogli Bianchi. These outposts, which consisted of deep trenches covered by ample barbed wire works and supported by flanking machine gun posts, were connected to each other through a deep walkway. On the reverse slope of the mountains, Italian sappers had dug deep caverns into the rocks, which served as living quarters as well as protective dugouts for the troops during enemy artillery operations. The Sogli Bianchi position also served with its cableway as a logistics hub receiving food supplies and equipment that were in turn distributed by pack mules to the other positions.

Despite its intricate system of defense the Sogli Bianchi position had one major weakness being far too advanced and completely dominated by the nearby higher peak of Mount Seluggio held by the enemy. The enemy positions where in fact only 400 feet away and the Sogli Bianchi could easily be reached via a mountain path that passed through the small village of Casoni di Viosa. From their high mountain emplacements Austrian soldiers could not only keep an eye on enemy movements on the Sogli Bianchi but also continuously torment its defenders with rifle and artillery fire.

Then, unexpectedly on 18 October 1917 the Austro-Hungarian troops sprang a surprise raid on the Italian positions by coming down from the mountain with a unit comprised of one stormtrooper company and one infantry company belonging to 2nd *Kaiserjäger* Regiment. The goals of the 500 strong unit were to inflict casualties, destroy dugouts and trenches and ultimately to keep enemy units from being drawn from this front.

At 1700 on 17 October the Austrian artillery began to target all Italian posts in the Posina Valley including Mount Majo, Mount Sogli Bianchi, Mount Gamonda and Mount dei Calgari which were hit repeatedly by explosive shells. At 2100 the artillery bombardment concentrated fire on the nearby Passo della Lazza where a small diversionary attack was then executed. At 0400 the artillery switched its focus once again as it targeted the peak of Mount Majo exclusively. At 0500 it ceased firing altogether, then all of a sudden 30 minutes later it targeted first Mount dei Calgari and then soon after the Sogli Bianchi positions. At 0545 the full force of the barrage interrupted all communications between the Sogli Bianchi and Italian headquarters by knocking out its telephone line. Once the position had been isolated, the artillery switched once again to suppressive fire forcing the defenders to keep their heads down as the Austro-Hungarian infantry attacked.

The infantry operation began when the stormtroopers overran the Italian outpost on Casoni di Viosa and captured its small unit as it was in the process of being relieved of sentry duty. Split up in small squads of infantrymen that were adept in using shellholes and irregularities in the terrain to shelter them from enemy fire, the *sturmtruppen* then advanced to the wire. Soon after grenade throwing parties attacked the already shaken Italian main defenses with both smoke and explosive and penetrated through a breach in the wire into the enemy's positions. While some of the *sturmtruppen* assailed the rear defenses, others continued to pound fire on the front-line trenches throwing hundreds of hand grenades into them. The speed and agility of the attackers caught the Italians completely by surprise and yielded the capture of two enemy infantry platoons manning the forward trenches. At this point, the Italians could have still managed to halt the enemy advance by activating their two defiladed machine guns, but the post commander initially held these weapons in check since the trenches were still covered by the smoke clouds of the barrage. While the enemy was hesitating, the stormtroopers sought to exploit the confused state of affairs in the enemy camp by firmly maintaining the initiative. With the advantage of poor visibility and with great speed the *sturmtruppen* proceeded to advance, capturing the two idle machine guns and reaching the entrances of the caverns situated on the reverse slope of the mountain where they captured the vast majority of enemy soldiers still barricaded inside. Subsequently, during mop-up operations, a small enemy platoon that was getting ready for a counter-attack was also targeted when the stormtroopers swooped behind it by surprise capturing it in its entirety.

Flamethrowers and detonation charges were then used to destroy trenches and dugouts and to damage the cableway system. After having caused widespread destruction, the two assault companies then retreated to their trenchlines just as quickly as they had attacked the enemy positions. They made their way back to their line having killed five and wounded 14 enemy soldiers and captured 258 prisoners.

The surprise raid proved to be well prepared by the artillery that after repeated and prolonged concentrations of fire on several targets had suddenly turned all of its attention on Mount Sogli Bianchi with a swift and brief barrage. The full force of the barrage stunned the Italian defenders impeding their reaction. Completely cut off by the barrage from the other Italian positions, the troops of the *Volturno* Brigade were powerless and completely unable to react due to the huge smoke clouds that invested their position. Moreover, as communications with other nearby units and from their Brigade's headquarters had also been cut off, the troops were unable to call on their own artillery to implement counter-battery fire. As a result, for the vast duration of the battle the Italian artillery was powerless being unaware that the raid was taking place. It finally intervened at 0630, but by then the Austrian assault units were already retreating. If only during the early stages of the battle the Italian sector commander had given greater prominence to the counter-preparation barrage in defense the final outcome of the operation might have been different. In addition, as mentioned in the post-battle report, despite noticing unusual troop movements half an hour prior to the infantry attack, the commander had failed to take extra security measures merely ordering his troops to be vigilant. Despite the lack of heightened security on the part of the Italians, the operation was equally well executed by the infantry whose rapidity of movement along with the extensive use of explosive devices and smoke bombs disoriented the defenders. Their tactical adroitness was recognized by the post-battle report of the *Volturno* Brigade: "An enemy column amassed north of Casoni

Viosa and then approached the Sogli Bianchi, while at the same time another enemy column outflanked it from the west."[55]

Battle of Monte Piana: The First *Sturmtruppen* to *Arditi* Confrontation

Mount Piana, a 2,325 meter high peak, is an atypical mountain within the Dolomites range since it is not only one of the shortest but also one of the few mountains with a two-mile-long, flat surface delimited by steep cliffs on all sides. Its central location, nested between the Sesto Valley and Auronzo di Cadore, gave its military occupants a 360-degree view of the Dolomites and the alpine valleys. Most importantly, for the Italians Mount Piana's military possession meant control over the 10-mile access road leading to the Austrian base of Dobbiaco, while for the Austrians it represented a jumping-off platform to invade the Veneto plains. As war broke out, given its central position, both armies scurried to occupy Mount Piana's peak. In the race to seize as much territory as possible, the Austro-Hungarians managed to occupy the smaller, northern summit of the mountain (Mount Piana 2,305 meters), while the Italians captured the southern peak (2,325 meters). Both armies then began building extensive fortifications, consisting of deep trenches, caverns, artillery, machine gun and observation posts, and tunnels, in preparation of what would become a long and extenuating campaign of trench warfare. Some of these positions were literally eagle's nests drilled deep into the rock and clinging to precipitous mountain walls. Built on ledges, most infantry and artillery emplacements were not only difficult to reach but were also impenetrable being reinforced by ample barbed wire works, steel shields and high sandbag walls. For two years, these strong entrenchments dotted both halves of the Piana while the Forcella dei Castrati (2,201 meters), comprised of the Italian positions of Trincea della Ghirlanda, Fosso Alpino and Guardia Napoleone constituted the advanced frontline positions fronting no man's land. The former was the most advanced position on the mountain consisting of a deep trench with several machine guns posts. It was connected via a 150-feet long underground tunnel to the Guardia which was situated on the reverse, eastern slope of Mount Piana. The Guardia consisted of an 'offensive' and a 'defensive' cavern drilled deep in the rock with the capacity to hold several infantry companies. The caverns were complemented by machine gun and mortar unit emplacements surrounded by three rounds of barbed wire. Facing these positions almost directly across no man's land were the Austrian fortifications on Mount Piana which consisted of three small concrete forts dug into the mountain and connected to each other by a two-meter deep trench and passageway. Under the forts and along the passageway four caverns had been drilled into the rock and each was large enough to hold an infantry company. On the reverse, northern edge of Mount Piana the Austrians had drilled what equated to

55 Ministero della Guerra, Comando del Corpo di Stato Maggiore – Ufficio Storico *Riassunti storici dei corpi e comandi nella guerra 1915–1918 Brigate di Fanteria, Brigata Volturno* (Rome: Ufficio Storico, 1927), p.103.

a small city into the mountain, including the battalion's headquarters, ammunition and food depots, a kitchen, and several dugouts. Their most important engineering feat, however, was 'the tunnel of the *Kaiserjägers*,' a long passageway inside the mountain connecting all the major positions.

Despite countless attacks and counter-attacks these fortifications removed all possibility of offensive maneuver and relegated both armies to a war of attrition and ultimately to a stalemate. In the fall of 1917, after two years of bloody fighting and countless losses, the Austrian sector commander Franz von Krammer finally received the go ahead for a large-scale offensive to remove the Italians from the southern peak of the mountain. Moreover, for the Austrians, the operation on Mount Piana would also serve a different purpose: divert attention away from the Isonzo sector where two days later on 24 October the massive battle of Caporetto would begin.

In order to expel the Italians and secure a jumping-off platform for the invasion of the Cadore valley, the Austro-Hungarians resorted to a special assault formation. It was comprised of two battle hardened assault companies from the German 3rd *Jäger* Battalion *Brandenburg* and the 4th Company from the Austrian 11th Army *Sturmbaon*, as well as the mountaineers of the VI Battalion/2nd *Kaiserjäger* Regiment. According to the Austrian official history "three German storm battalions arrived from the Western front; one was stationed with XIV Corps on the Pasubio, one with III Corps on the Ortigara, and the third in the Pusteria valley sector (on Mount Piana)."[56]

> This battle thus not only saw the first deployment of German stormtroopers in Italy but it was also the site where the latter first experimented with new light machine guns in the offensive. Most historians erroneously have argued that 08/15 Maxim guns were first used by German infantry units at Caporetto.[57] This is in fact incorrect since it was tested for the first time two days earlier on Mount Piana. Weighing only 43 lbs the Maxim was the first automatic gun of the war. During the battle, the guns were fired by the men of the first assault wave as they ran toward the enemy positions giving them much increased firepower.

Preparations for the planned attack began in earnest at the beginning of October. On 5 October a directive by Austrian XX Army Corps indicated that the German units had arrived near Dobbiaco, the Austro-Hungarian base and logistical hub in the Alto Adige, and that all precautions must be taken to conceal their presence from the enemy. To this end, the directive further indicated that German officers on reconnaissance on the Piana must wear Austrian uniforms to conceal their identity. The document also stated that the German units consisted of: two *sturmtruppen* companies,

56 Edmund Glaise-Horstenau (ed.), *Österreich-Ungarns letzter Krieg, vol 6*, p. 511.

57 Bruce I. Gudmundsson, *Stormtroop Tactics: Innovation in the German Army, 1914–1918* (Westport: Praeger, 1995), p. 130.

one flamethrower unit, one pioneer company, and one light artillery unit.[58] On 10 October further reinforcements, in the form of an Austrian assault company, were also dispatched to Dobbiaco. The directive stated that: "Captain Kratoschwill with one company of the 11th Army *sturmtruppen* battalion is to be transferred temporarily to Villabassa and placed under the command of the 56th Alpine Brigade of General von Krammer. This company will also participate to Operation Herbst."[59] The *sturmtruppen* were to be supported by the infantry companies of the VI Battalion/2nd *Kaiserjäger*, one Austrian dragoon unit, several grenade thrower and machine gun companies, one pioneer company and various other support units.

Another directive indicated that sector artillery firepower would also be augmented in preparation of the attack with the temporary transfer to Mount Piana of an additional mortar battery (240 mm), a battery of field guns (150 mm) and two mountain guns (75 mm).

Following the transfer, the units were held in reserve for several weeks in order to plan and train for mountain warfare in the rear. True to established *sturmtruppen* practices, German reconnaissance of the enemy positions was extensive. According to Austrian historian Viktor Schemfil "the Italian positions were patrolled numerous times in order to identify their weak spots."[60]

During the two weeks that preceded the attack, German officers went so far as to build a model of the Piana fortifications so that the assault units had a clear understanding of their objectives. During this preparatory stage their objective was not only to draft the attack plan but also to drill their Austrian allies into their battlefield tactics perfected on the Western front. Novel artillery tactics based on predicted fire in conjunction with infantry infiltration maneuvers were thus rehearsed successively over a two-week period.

After having completed a final dry run rehearsal of the attack, the units were transported during a heavy snowstorm to Mount Piana during the night of 21 October. In fact throughout the month of October heavy rains and snowfalls had made the terrain extremely treacherous to the point of putting in serious doubt the operation. The weather was not the only problem weighing upon the Austrian commander, since two days earlier and despite having taken every conceivable precaution such as transmitting the attack order by word of mouth, two deserters had handed themselves in to the Italians revealing the plan of attack. Undaunted by the betrayal of two of his officers and rejecting the protests of some of his direct subordinates to cancel the attack, Von Krammer was compelled to action mainly because the German units were to be transferred out of the Piana sector at the end of the October.

58 Kriegsarchiv: K.u.K. XX Korps Kommando, Op. Nr. 3904/24, '*Sturmtruppen* für Monte Piana', 5 October, 1917.

59 Kriegsarchiv: K.u.K. Rayons Kommando V, Op. Nr. 1504/11, 10 October, 1917.

60 Viktor Schemfil, *Die Kämpfe am Monte Piana und im Cristallo-Gebiet. Südtiroler Dolomiten: 1915–1917* (Innsbruck: Universitätsverlag Wagner, 1984), p. 128.

Knowing full well that the Germans were central to the plan of attack, General von Krammer opted to proceed with the operation despite the bad weather and the other setbacks.

His plan, summarized in a directive of the 56th Alpine Brigade, entailed:

1. Seize enemy frontline positions of Mount Piana including Guardia Napoleone, and Trincea della Ghirlanda.
2. Use these positions as a jump-off platform for seizing the Italian main position on the southern edge of Mount Piana.
3. Fend off any potential enemy counter-attack with the use of gas artillery shells.[61]

The Austrians signaled the start of operations when at 0500 on 22 October 1917 a rocket flare was shot from the Landro base. A minute later, Operation *Herbst* formally began when 74 artillery pieces and 18 heavy mortars opened up fire on the Piana positions.

The opening bombardment, directed at the forward positions on Forcella dei Castrati held by a unit from III Battalion/54th Infantry, buried a number of Italian soldiers under piles of rocks and steel. The whole forward sector was severely pounded as the Austro-Hungarian artillery blanket covered the Italian positions with much fury and intensity and without concern for the vast amounts of shells being used. For an Italian officer manning the frontline positions the artillery barrage "was very intense from the start and the enemy also used poisonous gas shells."[62]

Then all of a sudden the artillery halted fire in an attempt to disorient the Italian defenders tempting them to come out of their shelters. Following 10 minutes of relative peace the barrage resumed with equal force pummeling the southern, rear positions of Mount Piana. The Italian headquarters, in particular, were targeted in an effort to isolate the frontline positions and neutralize the Italian artillery from intervening in the battle with counter-battery fire.

At 0525, as the barrage was lifted, the German and Austro-Hungarian assault units attacked in four battle groups.

A) Sturmklotz 1: Comprised of two German *sturmtruppen* platoons and one light machine gun company was instructed to capture the Italian positions on Forcella dei Castrati by clearing up the trenches and passageways leading to the enemy's main underground cavern.
B) Sturmklotz 2: The first wave, consisting of two German *sturmtruppen* platoons, one light machine gun unit, a grenade thrower section and two flamethrower units, was tasked with attacking the Trincea della Ghirlanda

61 Kriegsarchiv: K.u.K. 56. Gebirgs Brigade Kommando, Op. Nr. 367/90, 18 October, 1917.

62 Ministero della Guerra, Comando del Corpo di Stato Maggiore – Ufficio Storico, *Riassunti storici dei corpi e comandi nella guerra 1915–1918 Brigate di Fanteria, Brigata Umbria* (Rome: Ufficio Storico, 1927), p. 51.

and Guardia Napoleone to destroy the well built trenches that snaked in front of no man's land. The second wave consisting of one company of *Kaiserjägers* was instructed to provide support to the first wave by cleaning up enemy outposts located in caverns and deep trenches. The third wave comprised by an additional *Kaiserjäger* company and four *Kaiserjäger* machine gun sections was supposed to set up preliminary defenses on the Ghirlanda by positioning its guns against the Italian positions overlooking the valley below east of Mount Piana (Valle dei Castrati).

C) Sturmklotz 3: The first wave with two German *sturmtruppen* platoons, two light machine gun units, two grenade thrower sections and two flamethrower units was to advance frontally and take the Guardia Napoleone. In its endeavor the unit was instructed to lob several poison gas grenades into the entrances and embrasures of the enemy caverns. The first wave was to be followed by two successive waves of *Kaiserjägers*. The third wave consisting of one company of the Austrian 11th Army *Sturmbaon* and a squadron of dragoons was to attack the flanks of the Italian position. It was expected to do so by advancing on the "via ferrata," (iron road) an exposed mountain route equipped with a pathway of cables and ladders that traversed otherwise inaccessible territory overlooking the steep eastern cliff of Mount Piana.

D) Sturmklotz 4: The first wave was comprised of two German *sturmtruppen* platoons, one light machine gun unit and one grenade thrower section and was tasked to attack the Guardia Napoleone from another flanking position. The second wave consisting of an additional company of Kaiserjäger would contribute to clear the Italian positions.[63]

As the groups moved forward their impact upon the final outcome would diverge depending on the terrain and the type of enemy reaction they encountered. Groups 3 and 4, slowed down by very rough uphill, rocky terrain and heavy snow, were repelled by heavy artillery fire. The Austrian *sturmtruppen* unit and the mountaineers, for example, were the target of intensive interdiction fire and lost many men while attempting to exit the trenches. Once over the top, they were boxed in no man's land by machine and artillery fire and ultimately were unable to reach the enemy positions. Assaults units 1 and 2 were more fortunate as they continued their advance toward the targeted positions by keeping constant pressure on the enemy by firing Maxim guns and throwing hand grenades as they speedily dashed forward. As the barrage accomplished what it was designed to do by keeping the defenders penned into their dugouts, the *sturmtruppen* reached the enemy's forward defenses. At close proximity to the enemy wire, *sturmtruppen* probing parties and flamethrower units pushed their way forward by throwing hand grenades and flames into the Italian trenches. The reliance on the part of the attackers upon numerous flamethrowers was instrumental in clearing the frontline trenches and the machine gun outposts. Several blockhouses

63 Viktor Schemfil, *Die Kämpfe am Monte Piana und im Cristallo-Gebiet*, pp. 135–136.

were thus engulfed in flames forcing the defenders into a quick and horrible death or an equally quick surrender. As one of the defenders recalled "the flames penetrated through the windows and embrasures of the pillboxes filling the trenches with deadly smoke." Once the *sturmtruppen* had overcome the enemy's main weapon posts, the *Kaiserjäger* infantry followed in their steps to mop up and disarm the few pockets left of enemy resistance. Thus a few hours later the Austrians had already 'turned around' these positions (Trincea della Ghirlanda, sections of Guardia Napoleone and Fosso Alpino) by placing several machine guns and two mortars in order to parry the likely enemy counter-attack.

According to the Italian official history:

> The enemy began launching grenades as well as firing several rounds of machine gun fire. Many grenades exploded in our trenches destroying our defenses while jets of flammable liquids prevented our infantry from continuously firing its weapons. Once past the wire, the enemy began to plaster the position with rifle fire and hand grenades. Even though we were surrounded and our ranks were thinning out, we continued to defend ourselves in the hope of receiving reinforcements.[64]

Unfortunately for the defenders the reinforcements were not dispatched in time, and the few survivors of the frontline trenches that had initially parried the onslaught were forced to surrender. The meticulously planned assault was executed flawlessly and within less than an hour the whole advanced frontline sector on Mount Piana had been occupied by German and Austro-Hungarian forces. With its large assault detachment largely still intact, the combined force was by then in a position to move against the southern peak of the Piana in an effort to dislodge the Italians completely from the mountain.

With the Austrian capture of the advanced frontline trenches, the Italian command was forced into speedily taking the necessary countermeasures. Since it had been pre-warned of the enemy operation by the two Austrian deserters, it had called up the V *Reparto d'assalto,* which was to be deployed for the likely counter-attack. The latter had been brought up the prior night and as soon as the enemy had occupied the Trincea della Ghirlanda it was called into action. This unit, created in September 1917 of handpicked volunteers coming from *alpini, bersaglieri* and infantry units, was led by Captain Anchise Pomponi and had an initial force of eight officers, 194 soldiers, four light machine guns, two machine guns, 12 flamethrowers and 10 mules.

Conceived as a crack mountain unit, it trained for a month near Santo Stefano di Cadore where given the mountainous terrain "it was possible to focus upon learning how to fight in rocky and wooded terrain."[65] Suddenly, in late October, and without having completed the standard three-month *arditi* training program, the V was

64 Ufficio Storico, *L'Esercito Italiano nella Grande Guerra,* p. 138.

65 Basilio di Martino Basilio and Filippo Cappellano, *I reparti d'assalto italiani nella grande guerra (1915–1918)* (Rome: Ufficio Storico, 2007), p. 610.

called on to defend this key position in the Dolomites from the combined German/Austro-Hungarian offensive operation. On 22 October the unit would thus find itself fighting against well-drilled and heavily armed German *sturmtruppen* in what would be the first direct confrontation between *arditi* and German/Austrian stormtroops on the Italian-Austrian front line.

At 0900 V *Reparto d'assalto* emerged from a deep cavern on the Guardia Napoleone and proceeded to attack the flanks of the enemy deployment which by then had fully occupied the frontline positions of the Ghirlanda. At first the German reaction was fierce: "Our trenches had been invaded by the Germans and upon our arrival we were greeted by machine gun fire, hand grenades, poison gas and flames from several flamethrowers being activated from above. The trench was covered by steel sheets designed to keep the snow from penetrating inside, but at the time they allowed the enemy to fire on us while we were unable to fire back."[66]

But after parrying the first German counter, the assault unit was able to emerge from the trenches and passageways to engage the enemy in hand-to-hand combat.[67] Armed primarily with pistol machine guns, hand grenades and smoke bombs, the *arditi* had all but cleared the Ghirlanda trenches when they were virulently struck by a second, 200 strong, enemy assault wave. This second contingent, comprised primarily of Austrian stormtroopers, reoccupied the advanced trenches forcing the *arditi* to retreat back to the deep caverns of Guardia Napoleone. When all seemed lost and when it appeared that the Austrians were on the verge of attacking the main Italian positions of Mount Piana, the Italian artillery began intense counter-battery and interdiction fire to dissuade the enemy from advancing any further. The artillery kept on firing for most of the day and night causing widespread casualties amongst the occupiers of the Trincea della Ghirlanda and also wrecking most of its defenses.

It was thanks to this prompt response that the Austrians were prevented from attacking the peak of the mountain and were in fact blocked by the interdiction fire.

Then expecting that the German and Austrian units would be demoralized by being subjected to such constant artillery fire, during the early hours of 23 October the commander of the 54th Infantry ordered V *Reparto d'assalto* to retake possession of the advanced positions. The plan first involved the light and medium artillery guns effectuating a low intensity barrage on the advanced positions. Then all of a sudden at 0500 the tempo of the barrage was to be increased significantly and at 0510 the assault unit was expected to move forward.

The operation was carried out accordingly. At 0500 hours the number of shells raining down on the Ghirlanda quadrupled burying many German and Austrian soldiers under a rubble of rocks, steel and debris and forcing some of the occupiers to a hasty retreat in order to avoid this most destructive barrage. At 0510 the *arditi* lunged forward and upon reaching the wire they broke through the defenses by operating the flamethrowers. Once in the trenches all that stood in their way to the ultimate objective were a number of machine guns that had opened up fire repeatedly

66 Ufficio Storico, Raccolta F. 11, b. 12: Reparti d'assalto, n. 4799.
67 Viktor Schemfil, *Die Kämpfe am Monte Piana und im Cristallo-Gebiet*, p.140.

showering both ends of the deep trench with multiple rounds. After initially suffering some casualties, the *arditi* managed to silence the guns mainly with hand grenades lobbed inside pillboxes and parapets. Within a few minutes, the Ghirlanda and Fosso Alpino trenches had been cleared of enemy troops and a company of *bersaglieri* had arrived to take possession of the recaptured positions.

This final counter-attack had put an end to the hostilities, as both armies in just two days of fighting had spent vast stocks of artillery ammunition and their infantry had suffered great losses.

Field Marshal Conrad's view of the failed operation was rather harsh: "It is my hope that both the troops and their commanders will be more vigorously engaged on the next attempt in order to cancel out this failure."[68]

Austrian historian Viktor Schemfil's concluding remarks on 'Operation *Herbst*', in contrast, appear more balanced outlining a number of complex factors that lead to the failure of the operation:

> The Austrian artillery was outgunned by the Italian which also had advanced knowledge of the time and place of attack. The Italians had greater stocks of ammunition and as a result their artillery kept on firing throughout the night, while the Austrian artillery ceased firing after a few hours due to lack of shells. ... The German assault units equipped for hand-to-hand combat were neutralized by the enemy counter-attack. The attack on Monte Piana was meant to be a large-scale offensive operation to conquer key positions. In reality this objective was not achieved. The attack did however, force the enemy from concentrating upon the Isonzo sector.[69]

As the battle ended and the stretcher bearers began to transport the wounded to nearby hospitals, both forces commenced counting their losses. The Austrians suffered the following: 93 dead, 84 wounded, while the Germans suffered three dead, 11 wounded and several soldiers missing. Italian losses were also severe. The infantry suffered 32 deaths, 99 wounded and 35 missing. V *Reparto* recorded 10 dead, 23 wounded, and 19 missing. The vast majority of the losses amongst the *arditi* were recorded on 22 October, while during the second day of fighting losses were relatively few due to the accuracy of the preparatory barrage that effectively pinned down enemy units and paved the way for the attackers.

According to historians Di Martino and Cappellano the understrength V *Reparto d'assalto* fought well during its baptism of fire. While artillery support had been crucial, the *arditi* nonetheless battled with determination especially on 22 October

68 Kriegsarchiv: K.u.K. 49. InfDionskmdo, Op. Nr. 1600/16, "Monte Piana/Unternehmen," 24 October 1917.

69 Viktor Schemfil, *Die Kämpfe am Monte Piana und im Cristallo-Gebiet*, p. 142.

when enemy forces had flowed over into the Italian positions and all appeared lost. On the 23rd they matched their opponents by deploying some of their tactics.[70]

Subsequently several soldiers of the V *Reparto* were awarded with gold medals of honor. The highest recognition was given to the deceased Lieutenant Ruggero De Simone, whose unit had borne the brunt of the second enemy attack on 22 October. The citation for his gold medal reads as follows:

> As the Commander of an assault platoon rescuing a besieged position, he was first injured in the mouth by a splinter of a grenade. Nevertheless, he continued to lead his troops despite being subjected to heavy enemy fire. He was then injured a second time during the fierce hand-to-hand combat that ensued and ordered to surrender. Refusing to surrender, he shouted out loudly: "Viva L'Italia" and emptied his pistol against the advancing enemy troops. He was wounded a third time and fell to the ground. Ordered once again to surrender he replied once again: "No, Viva L'Italia". He died after receiving a final blow to the heart. A sublime example of courage and deep attachment to the fatherland.[71]

Caporetto

During the Eleventh Battle of the Isonzo (August 1917) the Italians broke through near the Bainsizza plateau and inflicted grave losses on the Austro-Hungarians that the AOK, fearing that its army was unable to withstand a new offensive, was forced to ask for German support. In response, the German High Command entrusted General Konrad Krafft von Dellmensingen, a mountain warfare specialist, to tour the Italian front and develop an attack plan for a preventive strike against the Italians to give the Habsburg Army some time to reorganize. "General Krafft reported to the high command that the Austro-Hungarians could not effectively resist the next Italian offensive. In order to forestall this debacle, the German high command decided to launch an offensive of its own in Italy."[72]

The German High Command together with the AOK developed a plan of attack aimed at pushing the Italians back by several miles. Unlike the standard AOK tactic of attacking the Italians from the mountainous sector of the frontline, the Germans opted for an offensive along the 30-mile lowland stretch of the Isonzo River. The German plan, based on surprise, speed and mobility, could only succeed in trapping the enemy forces with a pincer movement on terrain that was relatively easier to negotiate that the Alps and with the support of large quantities of heavy guns and vast stocks of ammunition. The offensive build up on the front line was done very

70 Basilio di Martino and Filippo Cappellano, *I Reparti d'assalto Italiani nella grande guerra: 1915–1918* (Rome: Ufficio Storico, 2007), p. 612.

71 http://www.frontedolomitico.it/Uomini/protagonisti/DeSimoneRuggero.html <accessed June 25, 2016>

72 Bruce I. Gudmundsson, *Stormtroop Tactics*, p. 126.

slowly in order not to alarm the Italians. Most heavy guns were transported during the night, while the troops were amassed incrementally. Moreover, in order to cause maximum surprise, the Central Powers planned to attack close to the start of winter when normally both Italians and Austrians typically stopped fighting as they traditionally began preparations for surviving the coldest months of the year high up in the mountains.

The German contingent consisting of seven infantry and mountain divisions and several support troops (Alpine Corps, *Jäger* Division, 169th and 200th infantry divisions, *Württemberg* Mountain Division and the Bavarian Regiment) was transferred to Italy during the month of September 1917. Once in Italy these troops trained extensively on how to fight in high altitude conditions by conducting several drills. These included field exercises to transport weapons with pack mules, the rehearsal of attacks against fortified mountain positions and exacting long distance marches in both the mountains and the valleys to accustom the troops to their new environment. In order to support their ally, the Germans not only brought to Italy 536 pieces of artillery but they also instructed the Austro-Hungarian artillery on new battle tactics. For example, the Austrians were taught to perfect brief overpowering creeping barrages focused on neutralizing enemy artillery instead of the traditional prolonged destructive concentration of fire. During the battle, Italian defenses would in fact be subjected to surprise artillery concentrations on a narrow frontline sector typically comprised of 100 shells from large field guns, 50 shells from light guns, 25 shells from medium guns and 10 mortar shells. With little or no artillery fire adjustment, Italian strongpoints were the focus of these lightning, overpowering barrages that paralyzed their defenses and facilitated Austrian and German frontal and flanking attacks.

Moreover, the Germans also drilled the Austrians on how to make their artillery more mobile and 'catch up' with the infantry as it advanced through the enemy's frontline positions. A vast amount of carts, lorries and small wagons were assembled prior to the battle in order to move the guns forward as the battle unfolded. Infantry divisional artillery was also made more mobile by furnishing it with small trench-mortars and grenade launchers that could easily be transported by pack mules. Ultimately the Battle of Caporetto was fought by the Central Powers with a set of artillery and field strategies that were completely new to the Italians. "The heart of these new tactics were surprise and rapid tactical movement designed to pierce and disorganize the enemy defense."[73]

The primary reason the Italian Army was routed at Caporetto was because its 2nd Army had packed most of its infantry on a single line of defense with few mobile reserves. Cadorna after discounting for many weeks that a major offensive was being planned by the enemy, had shifted course only a few days prior to the start of the offensive. But he had mistakenly estimated that the combined German-Austrian blow would primarily involve the frontline positions of the 3rd Army rather than those of the 2nd Army. He therefore shifted all available reserves to the 3rd Army's sector thus seriously depleting the sector held by the 2nd Army. On top of this, the

73 William R. Griffiths, *The Great War*, p. 126.

2nd Army commander General Capello had disobeyed Cadorna's order to place his troops on the defensive. For two years Capello's troops had attacked the Austro-Hungarian positions and had very little experience in fighting a purely defensive battle. For example, the position of the machine guns on the 2nd Army sector was utterly unsuitable as the vast majority of the weapons were not scattered in depth but placed in more exposed forward positions. Once the combined German and Austrian onslaught focused all its might on a small section of the front, where the Central Powers troops held a distinct numerical advantage, the Italian defenses were unable to withstand such a force. In addition to the defensive fallacies of the Italian Army, the outcome of the battle, however, was also determined by additional factors. First, the battle was a demonstration of the effectiveness of short but destructive creeping barrages in conjunction with the use of poison gas. As Holger H. Helwig correctly asserts the new artillery tactic developed by Lieutenant-Colonel Georg Bruchmüller and consisting of the *Feuerwalze* (creeping barrage) had never been executed on such a scale on the Italian Front. "In place of the customary prolonged artillery shelling, which denied the attacker the element of surprise, Bruchmüller surprised the Russians at Lake Narocz with a hurricane-like brief barrage that pitted accurate artillery fire against previously known targets. Bruchmüller used aerial photographs to select the targets and a highly centralized firing command instructed each battery throughout the barrage."[74] Like the Russians, the Italian defenders could not offer any robust opposition to such a combination of deadly fire especially because frontline troops did not have gas masks. In addition the troops had been packed in forward positions exposing them to the deadly preliminary bombardment. Second, it also saw for the first time the mass use of stormtrooper infiltration tactics, for which the Italians did not have many effective defensive countermeasures. Third, the deployment of seven German infantry and mountain divisions, with large quantities of trench mortars, long range artillery and poison gas shells also tilted the balance of power to the Central Powers. As Austrian military historian Christian Ortner asserts, "The Italians could not counter German methods, a short artillery preparation and assault tactics, with anything. In technical terms, German gas warfare agents played a major role, and the Italian had hardly any defensive or protective means."[75] Caporetto was thus primarily a German victory since it was the successful combination of new tactics and innovative weapons that allowed the German units to outflank the Italian defenses in the lower Isonzo causing the collapse of several Italian frontline divisions.

However, by reading the battle reports of the Austro-Hungarian units involved at Caporetto it is clear that although the Austrian stormtroopers were not the determining factor of the Central Powers' victory, they nevertheless played a key role. In many instances they unlocked difficult situations and paved the way for a combined

74 Holger H. Herwig, *The First World War*, p. 207. On the new German artillery tactics see: David T. Zabecki, *Steel Wind: Colonel Bruchmüller and the Birth of the Modern Artillery* (Westport: Praeger Press, 1994).

75 Christian Ortner, *The Austro-Hungarian Artillery from 1867 to 1918: Technology, Organization and Tactics* (Vienna: Verlag Militaria, 2007), p. 631.

Austro-Hungarian stormtroopers. (Kriegsarchiv Vienna)

View of Mount Fratta during October 1917. The Austro-Hungarian mountain top position was stormed by the *arditi* of I *Reparto d'assalto*. This was the first operation of Bassi's *arditi* and their role was to create a bridgehead on the Bainsizza plateau in order to allow the bulk of the infantry to advance.

Austro-Hungarian stormtroopers during the Caporetto offensive October 1917. (Kriegsarchiv Vienna)

Austro-Hungarian stormtroopers training. (Kriegsarchiv Vienna)

Austro-Hungarian stormtroopers training. In a posed propaganda photo three Austrian stormtroopers demonstrate how to properly lob hand grenades over the enemy trench. (Kriegsarchiv Vienna)

Austro-Hungarian stormtroopers. (Kriegsarchiv Vienna)

The photo depicts the main Austro-Hungarian positions in the Isonzo sector including Mount Hermada and the Flondar which was recaptured by the stormtroopers of the 11th Army in a very violent counter-attack in June 1917. (Ufficio Storico – official archive, Italian military, Rome)

Schwarzlose M.7 Machine Gun – With a range up to 2,650 yards. Rate of fire 350–400 rounds per minute. Total weight 40 lbs. (Ufficio Storico – official archive, Italian military, Rome)

Remains of Mount Piana trench system. The mountain's First World War trenches and caverns have been preserved and turned into an open air museum of the Great War. (Walther Schaumann)

Italian observation point on Mount Piana. (Walther Schaumann)

Austro-Hungarian soldier remains, a victim of a flamethrower attack. (Ufficio Storico – official archive, Italian military, Rome)

Austro-Hungarian position on Mount Piana. The position was located on the reverse slope of the mountain and could not be targeted by enemy artillery. (Walther Schaumann)

German/Austrian breakthrough. They were used primarily as the battering ram to overcome particularly stubborn defenses in the northern, more mountainous sector of the Isonzo, mainly Mount Rombon, Mount Caal and Krn, while the German mountain divisions advanced on the valley floors. As General Alfred Krauss asserts the Austrian assault and infantry "mountain groups certainly conquered the first Italian positions, but could not entirely break the line. They could not do so until the columns in the valley bottoms rendered the defense of the elevated positions impossible. Only then did whole brigades fall prisoner."[76]

The Battle of Caporetto (also known as the Twelfth Battle of the Isonzo) began on 24 October 1917 when at 0200 Central Powers artillery launched a hurricane-like bombardment comprised of massive amounts of poison gas shells in a bid to kill frontline defenders and paralyze the Italian artillery. At 0630 the preparatory barrage, consisting primarily of heavy and medium shells, continued to pound the Italian positions with great force. Then, finally at 0700 mortars of all kinds blasted frontline defenses and paved the way for the infantry advance which began at 0900. The rolling barrages, in particular, were aided by extensive aerial reconnaissance by both Austrian and German squadrons which flew countless missions to determine the location of Italian guns. These missions allowed for pinpoint artillery fire resulting in the destruction of several Italian gun batteries on the first day of battle. Facing the combined Austrian and German onslaught were the troops of the Italian 2nd Army consisting of 25 divisions tasked with holding a 30 miles front from Mount Rombon in the north to Gorizia in the south. The defensive positions were strong in certain sectors but poor and inadequate in others. At Tolmino, Krn and Mount Nero, where the main German-Austrian thrusts would occur, the defensive positions were poorly entrenched. In addition, the infantry units were mostly crammed on a single line of defense and thus vulnerable to either a flanking attack or a massive frontal attack against a small section of the front. Most of the machine gun positions also were not staggered in depth but were aligned with the front line troops thereby highly vulnerable to being outflanked by a major breakthrough.

The combined German and Austrian-Hungarian forces attacked in four main *Gruppen* under the command of Otto von Below's 14th Army. North of Caporetto three Austrian divisions and one German division commanded by General Alfred Krauss were to reach Caporetto with a northern flanking maneuver. Likewise, Gruppen von Stein was also to converge on Caporetto with three German Divisions. From the south, three German divisions under General von Berrer were to attack the Italian positions on Mount Tolmino. While further south, Lieutenant Scotti's Gruppen (two Austrian divisions) would also threaten the Tolmino positions.

The overall objective was to attack and envelop enemy forces along the west bank of the Isonzo thus "trapping the Italian forces east of the Isonzo as well as provide a springboard for further penetration through the valleys that led west to the Venetian Plain."[77]

76 Alfred Krauss, *Die Ursachen unserer Niederlage; Erinnerungen und Urteile aus dem Weltkrieg* (Munich: J.F. Lehmann, 1920), p. 120.

77 Bruce I. Gudmundsson, *Stormtroop Tactics*, p. 128.

According to German tactical procedures each group consisted of three main branches: artillery, infantry units and stormtroopers, with the latter in the lead.

Although Caporetto was mainly a German victory, we will focus our attention upon the contribution made by the Austro-Hungarian *sturmtruppen*, acting primarily within Krauss Group, to the final outcome of this battle. Krauss Group consisted of the 3rd *Edelweiss* Division, consisting of four infantry regiments and two brigades, which had one *sturmkompagnie* within its 3rd *Kaiserjäger* Regiment as well as various stormtrooper assault patrols within the 4th *Kaiserjäger* Regiment. The *Edelweiss* Division, led by Major General Wieden von Alpenbach, was one of the most experienced mountain infantry divisions of the Austrian Army. It excelled in both offensive and defensive operations in high altitude environments. Most of its ranks were recruited from Salzburg and the Northern Tyrol and its regiments were full of experienced mountaineers. These regiments had special mountain companies (*Hochgebirgskompagnie*) armed with mountain guns, mortars and with their own logistical support units (mostly pack mules) that allowed them to transport equipment across the mountain ranges. They also had small platoons of experienced mountain guides (*Bergführer*) that excelled in mountain reconnaissance and could pave the way for the rest of the troops as they advanced over difficult terrain.

The division's *Sturmkompagnie*, led by the capable Lieutenant Schäfer, an experienced mountaineer which had served the Habsburg cause since the beginning of the war, at the start of the Caporetto Battle had a force of 210 soldiers. Each soldier began the offensive armed with six hand grenades and 40 bullets. The unit also had at its disposal a flamethrower section with six kleine units, a trench mortar section with four units and a small pioneer group.

The 22nd *Schützen* Division, consisting also of four infantry regiments and two brigades, had *sturmkompagnien* within the 1st, 3rd and 26th *Kaiserschützen* regiments. While the 55th Division, consisting of three infantry Regiments and two brigades had a full stormtrooper battalion (55th) as well as several *sturmkompagnien* within the 4th and 7th Infantry Regiments (Bosnia-Herzegovina). The 55th Division had been recently formed mostly with experienced soldiers coming from both the Galician and the Italian front. Its commander was the able and widely respected Prince Felix zu Schwarzenberg. The unit was comprised primarily by young Bosnian and Charintian volunteers with eight heavy and 12 light machine guns, two 37 mm artillery guns, 12 mortars, six flamethrowers.

On day one of the vast operation, Krauss Group infantry units began to move forward at 0745. Its *Edelweiss* Division, slowed down by snow, sleet and the icy ground, came down from the mountains but was initially blocked from advancing further by the *alpini* of *Borgo San Dalmazzo*, *Durazzo*, and *Saluzzo* defending the fortified positions of Cuklja and Mount Rombon. This stubborn defense was eventually overcome by a flanking maneuver which took the defenders by surprise and allowed the attacking units to overrun their strongpoints. Meanwhile, the 22nd Division faced much less opposition. Its forces, which were advancing below in the valley, reached the Plezzo plateau almost unopposed since the opponents that originally stood in their way, the *Friuli* Brigade, had all been gassed to death by the

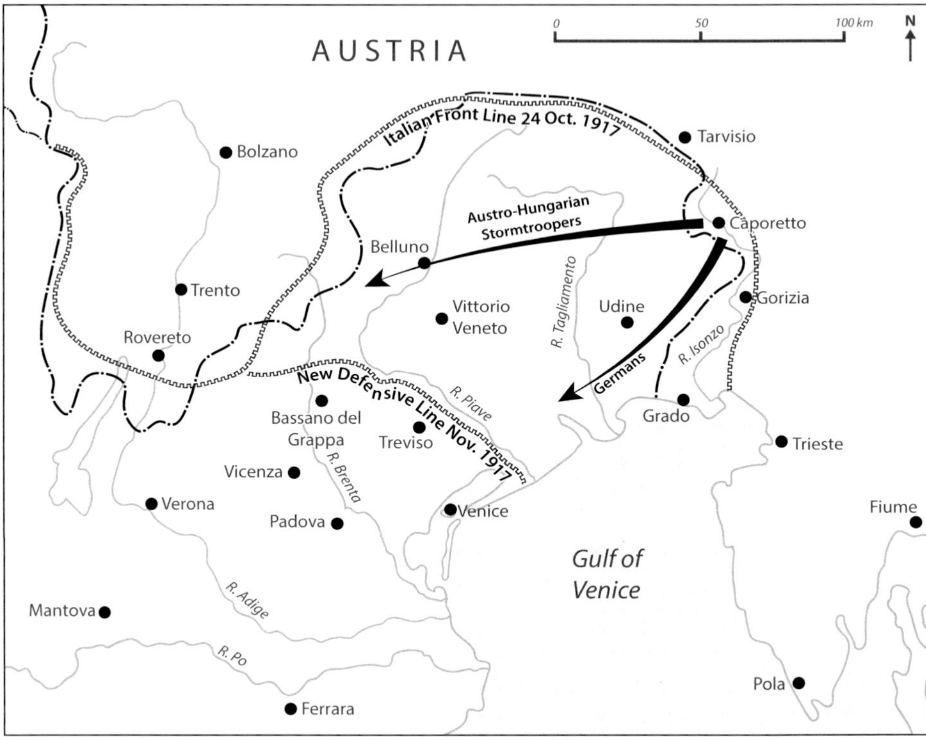

Map 3 The Caporetto offensive began on 24 October 1917 against the forces of the Italian 2nd army. The Austro-Hungarian stormtroopers attacked along the more mountainous left flank, while the Germans struck the right flank. The use of massive artillery shells, poison gas which was then followed by the infiltration tactics of the *sturmtruppen* completely overwhelmed Italian defenses.

artillery barrage. When the Austrians entered their defenses they found the soldiers all dressed in their uniforms lying motionless on the ground as if they were sleeping. As the Austrian historian Fritz Weber asserts "death was assured by poison gas for all those soldiers that had survived the initial barrage."[78] To the south, the 55th Imperial Division advanced over 10 miles notwithstanding a heavy snowstorm that made walking in the mountains extremely treacherous. By day one of the offensive, the 55th had reached Mount Nero virtually unopposed but was unable to move beyond it due to a combination of enemy fire and fatigue. Its units along with the *Edelweiss sturmtruppen* battalion pitted themselves against Italian defenses on Mount Rombon and were pushed back with losses. During this phase of the operation on Mount Rombon the Austrians deployed to good effect their flamethrower platoons with the

78 Fritz Weber, *Tappe della Disfatta* (Milan: Mursia, 1977), p. 159.

stormtroopers. The former played an important role in debilitating the Italians on Rombon, although enemy defenses were not breached.[79]

The following day the snowfall had ceased and the 55th Division, which by then had bypassed Mount Rombon, resumed its advance tasked with capturing Caporetto while the *Edelweiss* with penetrating deeply into the Uccea Valley. The day began with an intensive artillery bombardment aimed at wearing down the defenses of the 43rd Italian Division.

On the morning of 25 October vanguards of the *Edelweiss* Division with the stormtroopers of 3rd *Kaiserjäger* Regiment in the lead engaged the Italian defenses on Mount Caal and Mount Plagne. In the afternoon these mountains were the center of successive Austro-Hungarian attempts aiming at dislodging the Italians from their entrenched positions. The fighting lasted until the night of 26 October when the Austro-Hungarians were able to finally capture Mount Caal even though they were forced to commit some of their best mountain troops and stormtroopers and both had suffered casualties. The Italians fought with extreme decision, but were eventually overrun by the *sturmkompagnie* combination of heavy fire and flamethrowers. The final phase of the battle witnessed the concentration of fire on the peak enemy positions by the mortar and mountain artillery companies of 3rd *Kaiserjäger*. These units had positioned four 75 mm guns and several trench mortars within range of the enemy posts on Mount Caal. The barrage reversed on the exposed enemy peak positions both standard and poison gas shells for more than three hours. After the artillery weakened the enemy with heavy shelling, there was a lull in the battle. During the night, Austrian historian Viktor Schemfil, reveals that:

> The clime to the peak took much time and was exhausting given the steep, rocky and thickly wooded terrain. Only the most experienced mountaineers made it all the way to the top as several of the soldiers fell behind exhausted and unable to proceed any further. Despite losing several men to fatigue, the small unit that managed to reach the peak decided to attack it anyway. After a hand grenade was thrown into the Italian first line, the assault unit stormed ahead.[80]

The unit stormed the first trenchline mainly with the aid of hand grenades. A wild close combat fight ensued and finally the Italians were overrun. After the position had been lost, the Italians mounted three counter-attacks which were also repulsed by machine gun fire and by stormtroopers lobbing hand grenades into the infantry assault waves. At the end of the fighting the Austrians captured 170 soldiers, and four machine guns.

The Austro-Hungarian 7th Regiment (55th Division), led by its *sturmtruppen* units, was given the task of breaking through the enemy defenses at Caporetto. Taking this town would have enabled the Austrians to capture a key logistical hub for the Italian

79 Christian Ortner, *Storm Troops*, p. 268.

80 Viktor Schemfil, *Das K.u.K. 3. Regiment der Tiroler Kaiserjäger im Weltkriege 1914–1918* (Bregenz, Tentic: 1927), p. 472.

Army and fundamentally outflank vast numbers of enemy forces. At 0630 the 55th Division began marching toward Caporetto by coming down from the mountains as the Italians had evacuated most of their frontline positions. By midday the 55th had reached the outskirts of Caporetto where it began to skirmish with more determined Italian troops. "The 55th Division's attack was led by the 7th Regiment which used its *sturmkompagnie* to penetrate the enemy wire. The effective coordination between assault platoons, machine gun flanking fire and divisional artillery encircled and destroyed the Italian forward positions. Immediately after two battalions followed the stormtroopers lead and mopped up the secondary positions."[81] By the afternoon on 25 October the stormtroopers and the infantry had split the enemy infantry forces into two and had taken Caporetto. This together with the taking of Tolmino in the south by the Germans enabled the forces of the Central Powers to outflank the Italians forcing them to retreat. The taking of these two towns that served as main logistic hubs for the enemy was thus the turning point in the Caporetto Battle throwing the whole Italian defensive line in widespread disarray.

By 28 October the Italian 2nd Army was in total shambles. Its troops were retreating as its left flank had been overrun by the combined Austrian and German offensive. As a result of the huge breach at Caporetto and Tolmino, the troops defending the southern flank around Gorizia, mainly from the 3rd Army risked also being encircled and captured by the bold enemy maneuver. They too were forced to retreat as a result of the collapse of the 2nd Army.

As historian John Schindler asserts the Italian 3rd Army, which had not been beaten on the battlefield, had to evacuate frontline positions that had been conquered after two years of heavy fighting: "Objectives that had been bought at such a high cost in Italian blood, Gorizia, Plava, Mt. Santo, Mt. San Michele, Sabotino, Pogdora, Oslavia, were relinquished without a fight."[82]

As the Italian 2nd Army was fast retreating, the race was on to reach the Tagliamento River where the Italians were about to organize their new line of defense.

The 55th Division's stormtroopers, leading an unstoppable charge, were however instrumental in the seizure of a bridgehead on the Tagliamento that would in essence cut off the Italians. As the soldiers of the 2nd Army were hastily retreating in disarray, Cadorna had ordered a general stand along the west–south ridge of the Tagliamento River. The objective of the Austrian unit was to force the crossing of the river and seize the town of Cornino were the Italian forces of the 33rd Regiment had been ordered to hold the front line at all costs.

On 30 October its 4th Bosnian Regiment put forth its first attempt to cross the bridge at Cornino but the enemy forces were able to withstand the blow mainly because the Austro-Hungarian unit lacked adequate artillery support. The following day the bridge was partially blown up by the Italians, and the 55th was unable to advance.

81 John Schindler, *A Hopeless Struggle: The Austro-Hungarian Army and Total War*, Unpublished Dissertation McMaster University, 1995, p. 210.

82 Ibid., p. 257.

However, by 2 November the 55th Division had been able to bring up the frontline its artillery units which began pounding very heavily the Italian defenses at Cornino. Then came the order of Colonel Zedtwitz of the 38th Infantry Brigade directing the 4th Regiment to open up the assault against Cornino: "After the artillery opens up the destructive fire against the enemy, the 4th Regiment shall be the first unit to cross the bridge at 0400. Sometime after 0400 the unit shall form a bridgehead in proximity of Roncis allowing the 38th Brigade to progress into Cornino."[83]

Protected by the artillery fire, which prevented the Italians from firing back, the 55th Division sapper units managed to construct a temporary bridge over the Tagliamento. At 1830, covered by artillery and machine gun fire, two stormtrooper platoons (14th Company of the 4th Regiment) followed by several infantry units (13th Company with two machine guns, 16th, 15th Company and the machine gun company) stormed the Italian defenses at Cormino. In the vanguard, special bombing units broke through by lobbing several hand grenades into the frontline trenches. Despite suffering casualties from machine gun fire, the stormtroopers managed to open up a gap in the defenses from which the infantry passed through to roll up both flanks.

The commander of the 4th Infantry Regiment Eugen Redl recalls that:

> Enemy machine gun fire coming from several homes within Cornino was blocking our advance. Then Italian standard infantry and artillery units also began to fire upon our troops. After having rested a bit, 14th *Sturmkompagnie* together with the 13th Company began to attack the homes occupied by the enemy. Strong assault detachments were dispatched against the enemy's flanks while our machine guns were pinning down the enemy units barricaded into the homes of Cornino and along the road leading to Flagogna and San Rocco.
>
> The mop-up operation lasted approximately an hour. Enemy strong points were cleared painstakingly one by one. The task was made even more difficult by the fact that the enemy positions were scattered and also because it was pitch dark.[84]

This was a tactical victory of primary importance because it forced the Italians to give up more ground and retreat for another 30 miles to the Piave River, the last natural obstacle remaining before the Veneto plains. The Piave, which originates in the Carnic Alps, passes through the Dolomites and ends in the Adriatic Sea, is in most sections over a mile wide. It suited the Italians because it gave the defenders a huge buffer zone to pre-empt enemy attacks.[85]

The 55th Division's speedy maneuvers to cut off the Italians at Cornino was strategically decisive. It forced General Cadorna to abandon any hope of consolidating Italian defenses on the Tagliamento and caused a retreat all the way to the Piave River

83 Kriegsarchiv: K.u.K. 38. Infanterie Brigade Kommando, Op. Nr. 521, 1 November 1917.
84 Eugen Redl, *La Battaglia del Monte Ragogna* (Udine: Gaspari Editore, 2006), p. 71.
85 Edmund Glaise-Horstenau (ed.), *Österreich-Ungarns letzter Krieg, vol 6*, p. 605.

thus approximately yielding another 30 miles of territory to the Austrians/Germans. The breakthrough also allowed the capture of 2,500 enemy soldiers and 50 machine guns. As a result of the Caporetto debacle, on 9 November General Cadorna was sacked and his place was taken by General Armando Diaz. For Italy, Caporetto had been a total catastrophe. Its army had lost approximately 300,000 soldiers between the dead, wounded and missing. Over 3,100 artillery guns, or a third of all artillery inventory, had been captured by the enemy along with 3,000 machine guns.

Mount Grappa/Asiago Altopiano

After the debacle of Caporetto the Central Powers forces continued to pursue the Italians all the way to the Piave River. However, before advancing past the Piave, the attackers had to first take the Asiago Altopiano and especially Mount Grappa since the river was within range of Italian artillery on the mountain. After suffering huge losses at Caporetto in October 1917 the Italians in November could only field 33 infantry and four cavalry divisions against 53 Austrian and German divisions.

The defensive battle, fought in a bitter, windswept and freezing mountain environment, took place in stages. The first stage took place between 10–26 November, while the second between 4–25 December. During both phases of the battle the AOK ordered repetitive attacks to dislodge the Italians from the Asiago Altopiano and Mount Grappa. At the time, Conrad compared the position of the Italian Army to that of a shipwreck victim holding on to a piece of the ship floating in the sea. According to the Field Marshal one final offensive push would be enough to see off the Italians and end the war. However, the Italians were determined to offer prolonged resistance and in late 1917 the tables were turned as they for the first time in the conflict enjoyed the advantage of defending from high altitude entrenchments, while the Austro-Hungarians had to attack from below. As a result, the *sturmtruppen* were once again deployed to overcome particularly stubborn enemy defenses as the AOK sought to promptly end the war.

Conrad's plan was to deploy all of his forces in order to reach the Veneto plains. To reach this objective he wanted to advance south of the Brenta River in the Asiago sector crossing the western flank of Mount Grappa.

Phase 1 November 1917 Asiago Sector

On the Asiago Altopiano sector the main advanced Italian bulwarks were comprised by the Melette massif and the lower Brenta defenses. In order to assail both positions the Austro-Hungarians were first responsible for clearing enemy posts held by rear guard troops. On 11 November the 6th Infantry Division was tasked with occupying Mount Longara and the town of Gallio to secure against flanking assaults before proceeding toward the Melette massif. Infantry units had temporarily captured Mount Longara on two separate occasions, but both attempts had been thwarted by Italian counter-attacks. The battle for control of Mount Longara was finally decided the following day by Lieutenant Morelli's 11th Army/4th *sturmtruppen* Half-Company that had been tasked with breaching the enemy defenses in order to prepare the way for the 75th Infantry Division. "During preparatory fire, Lieutenant Morelli and his men were able to infiltrate the enemy positions by finding an opening in the wire. While the barrage was still in full swing, the unit stormed the Italian position taking the enemy by complete surprise. It captured 40 officers, 1,000 soldiers and 25 machine guns."[86]

On the same night the other half of the unit fought also a guerrilla-like battle within the narrow and winding streets of Gallio. It had originally been moved near Gallio after conducting special training for a mountaintop assault on the Melette massif. However, the mountain operation could not proceed until Gallio and Mount Longara had been seized. As a result, the stormtroopers were tasked with a far more dangerous assignment than what they had originally trained for especially because it required extensive street fighting. The enemy was barricaded inside several homes and dislodging it required bitter, close quarter combat. On that night the stormtroopers put forth four consecutive assaults that were all repelled with great losses as the Italians used poison gas shells with good effect to negate the enemy thrust. However, on the fifth attempt the stormtroopers achieved a breakthrough when they captured a machine gun post and five prisoners. As a result of this initial penetration into Gallio, a much larger standard infantry unit was ultimately able to storm and clear out the remaining enemy outposts. While the Austro-Hungarians finally prevailed, the assault against Gallio had cost the *sturmkompagnie* dearly as it had lost up to half of its original strength.

On 9 November 1917 11th Army/4th *sturmtruppen* Half-Company (Lieutenant Zannini) ruptured several sections of the enemy wire at Camporovere by detonating several explosive charges. This enabled Austro-Hungarian infantry troops to overrun enemy trenches and capture several enemy soldiers. On 13 November 1917 the same unit carried out another surprise attack upon the peak (1,116 meters high) of Mount Sisemol. Despite strong enemy machine and artillery fire, it encircled and then stormed several Italian trenches. The peak of Mount Sisemol was eventually taken after very intense hand-to-hand combat on 6 December by standard infantry units of 21st *Schützen*.[87]

The Austrian tactic of advancing along the flanks of the mountain ridges to then suddenly threaten enemy positions downhill proved successful once again when the *sturmkompagnie* of the 3rd *Kaiserjäger* Regiment outflanked Italian strongholds in the lower Brenta. As winter was fast approaching with the snow and the freezing temperatures that were already considerably slowing down offensive operations in the mountains, Conrad was still determined to breach the enemy positions and reach the plains.

86 Ernst Wisshaupt, *Die Tiroler Kaiserjäger im Weltkriege*, p. 365.
87 Ibid., p. 364.

However, both Conrad and Boroevic's troops faced stiff opposition, which was centered on the new Italian line of defense along the Altopiano di Asiago, Mount Grappa and the Piave River. Ultimately, numerous offensive attempts were repulsed with heavy losses before the winter of 1917–18 set in mainly because they lacked adequate artillery support, Austrian and German troops were fatigued by two months of continuous fighting and also because Italian opposition proved insurmountable. Despite the fact that the first Grappa/Piave battles led to a standstill, the stormtroopers achieved a few final tactical successes in the Trentino sector.

On 22 November five consecutive Austrian attacks were repulsed with heavy casualties while Emperor Carl observed the battle as it unfolded from a post nearby. Despite heavy artillery concentrations, Italian defenses on Mount Tomba and the Meletta di Gallio held the enemy at bay. Conrad, determined to achieve a breakthrough at all costs, ordered another offensive operation to take place along the lower Brenta valley against the *alpini* of the 52nd Division. His objective was to overwhelm Italian defenses on the Asiago Altopiano and then invade the Veneto region. The Italians were deployed on two successive lines of defense. The first, rather thinly held line, was centered on the Colinocello, while the second more robust line was centered on the reinforced stronghold of San Marino (Galleria del Termine).

This time the Austro-Hungarians had greater artillery support consisting of four batteries of mountain guns, four batteries of large field guns and two 30.5 cm howitzers.

In comparison to what had been available in November this represented a 50 percent increase in firepower. Not only did the Austro-Hungarians have a sufficient number of shells but they could also rely on two heavy howitzers to cut the enemy wire and destroy the dugouts. At dawn on the 23rd an intense artillery barrage preceded the infantry assault. Meawhile, Austrian infantry units, with the stormtroopers in the lead (3rd *Kaiserjäger* Regiment *Sturmkompagnie* and *Hochgebirgskompagnie*) began their approach march toward the flanks of the enemy position by negotiating steep mountain ridges. "Shortly after the artillery preparation fire had ceased, a stormtrooper patrol unit advanced to the enemy wire to light an explosive charge. But when the explosion occurred, the enemy blasted the area with artillery and the second patrol unit set to blow up the successive enemy line came under fire and suffered considerable losses."[88]

Coming under heavy fire both units were ordered to pull back. Once the stormtroopers had retreated back to their trenches, the Austrian artillery then went into action again in a bid to further wear down the Italian defenses with explosive and gas shells. By neutralizing the enemy artillery with the gas, Austrian artillery enabled a second attempt by the stormtroopers to bring up to the Italian second line of defense additional explosive charges. After the pioneers ignited the fuses, within seconds the explosion sent pieces of the wire flying everywhere. With the wire breached the stormtroopers began to penetrate the openings while launching several hand grenades and flammable liquid into the Italian positions. The latter were

88 Viktor Schemfil, *Das K.u.K. 3. Regiment der Tiroler Kaiserjäger*, p. 503.

quickly overrun and forced to surrender. A total of 12 officers, 456 men, 20 machine guns, one cannon and 15 mortars were captured.[89]

Phase 2 December 1917 Asiago Sector

After having taken the Galleria del Termine the next major obstacles that stood in the way of Army Group Conrad were the Italian positions on the Melette di Gallio. The Melette are a low but wide mountain range overlooking the Asiago Valley that during the tail end of 1917 comprised the Italian forward line of defense hindering all Austro-Hungarian progress against the Asiago Altopiano and the Brenta Valley. Conrad's objective was to attack on the western flank of the Altopiano, but in order to advance in that direction his 11th Army had to first eliminate these forward enemy positions. The German and Austro-Hungarian armies had already attempted to take the Melette in November but in those frantic days each infantry assault against these positions had been repulsed with heavy losses. In December the Melette system was defended by the Italian 29th Infantry Division. Mount Zomo and the Meletta di Gallio were held by XIX, and XXXVI *bersaglieri* respectively, while the Val Miela was occupied by the 129th Infantry Battalion. Mount Fior was occupied by three *alpini* battalions (*Pasubio*, *Cervino*, *Saccarello*), while three other *alpini* units (*Cuneo*, *V. Dora*, and *Marmolada*) occupied Mount Castelgomberto. Mount Tondarecar and Mount Badenecche were held by troops from the 4th *bersaglieri*. In November the Austro-Hungarians had put forth their first attempt to overtake the Italians on the Melette, but their offensive had stalemated for multiple reasons.

The troops had attacked with haste without conducting preliminary reconnaissance of the targeted area. As a result of faulty and incomplete intelligence, the attacks were badly coordinated. The major deficiency, however, had been insufficient artillery support dictated by the inability of the artillery arm to keep pace with the infantry advance. As the infantry had advanced for several miles into the Italian defenses as a result of the first breakthrough at Caporetto and the subsequent advance on the Tagliamento, the lack of railroads and motor vehicles had slowed down the overall pace of the operation. Only in early December did Conrad decide that his troops had enough artillery support to proceed with a renewed attempt to take the Melette. By then the Austrians had at their disposal 58 light, 18 medium, 13 heavy guns, 16 light and 37 heavy trench mortars for the purpose, while infantry was comprised by units of the 18th Division, including its assault battalion, the 18th *Sturmbaon*. Based upon extensive aerial surveillance the eastern flank of the Melette, comprised of Mount Tondarecar and Mount Badenecche, was identified as the weak point in the enemy system since it had not been previously occupied and its defenses possessed hardly any advanced fortifications. In fact, most positions consisted of shallow dugouts and gun pits and very few sections of trenches had been covered with barbed wire. These organizational deficiencies were due to the hasty Italian retreat that had left little

89 Ibid., pp. 503–04.

time to organize the defenses and to dig deep enough into the ground. This sorry state of affairs was also the result of the determination by the 4th Army commander not to yield any further territory to the Austro-Hungarians even if it meant that his troops were to offer prolonged resistance in advanced, not easily defendable, positions. A further weakness in the Italian flank defenses was the lack of machine gun strong points. It appears that in early December there were only two guns on the Tonderecar, a fact that must not have gone unnoticed when the Austrians conducted the preliminary aerial reconnaissance. It was for the above reasons that the Austro-Hungarian 11th Army would concentrate the majority of its forces on this flank in a bid to overtake the Italians and disjoint their entire forward positioned defensive system. Accordingly, Austro-Hungarian attack plans, that were drawn up largely by Captain Teuber of the 11th Army *Sturmbaon*, involved a first day of operations with concentrated attempts to dislodge the Italians from the eastern flank, and a second day with the main envelopment attack to take the main fortifications on the Meletta di Gallio. Since late November Captain Teuber and his men had begun to scour the Melette sector and had even advanced as far as Mount Lisser and Lambara beyond the first Italian line of defense. Based on the intelligence gathered Captain Teuber had then drawn up the attack plan and later finalized it by discussing it at great length with the commanders of the 9th Infantry Brigade, the 3rd *Kaiserschützen* Regiment and the 22nd Battalion *Feldjäger*. Captain Teuber's deep involvement in the making of the attack plan demonstrates how dependent the Austro-Hungarian standard infantry was upon the *sturmtruppen* while planning offensive operations.

The preparatory barrage, consisting primarily of both regular and gas shells, began on the night between 3–4 December 1917 by investing the entire Melette di Gallio sector. The gas shells, in particular, had a devastating effect as they rained down on several Italian reserve units marching toward the front line. As the shells landed on the ground, the Italian soldiers initially did not realize that these were poison gas shells. But by the time the soldiers had put on their masks it was already too late and the vast majority of them never arrived at their final destination on Mount Tondarecar. In addition to the decimation of the reserve units, as the eastern flanking positions had no elaborate defensive system, the artillery preparation caused widespread destruction amongst overly exposed front line infantry units. After the enemy defenses had been softened up considerably, the Austro-Hungarian assault units accordingly concentrated their main thrusts on the two flanks: Mount Zomo and Meletta di Gallio on the west and the Tondarecar and Badenecche sector in the east.

With the defenders successfully suppressed by the artillery fire, 3rd Company of 11th Army *Sturmbaon* attacked the eastern flank and penetrated deep into the enemy defenses. One of its units outflanked from the right the enemy positions situated on Mount Tondarecar, while a second column attacked Mount Badenecche. The hardest fighting was experienced on the peak of the Tondarecar. Here intense hand-to-hand combat ensued as a result of the Italians initially adopting more advanced defensive tactics aimed at stopping the stormtroopers. In fact, while the vast majority of the Italian defenders were still hiding in their dugouts to shield themselves from the artillery barrage and therefore could easily be captured by the first enemy assault waves, dedicated counter-attacking units had been dispatched in time to fend off the first *sturmtruppen* thrust. As a result, these troops were originally able to parry the blow with a swift counter-attack. The use of dedicated assault detachments to be used for these types of counter-attacks was one of the corrective countermeasures put in place by *Comando Supremo* after the battle of Caporetto. It was a policy intended to shore up threatened defensive positions with reserve units deployed specifically to fight off special enemy assault detachments. The other counter measure was to place machine guns in defiladed positions and rake the enemy from the flanks. The use of these tactics enabled the Italians to initially repulse the enemy with losses. During a lull in the infantry fighting, the Austrian artillery pounded again the Italian defenses on the Tondarecar with considerable force. In full view of the Austro-Hungarian artillery the thinly held positions were the target of almost 40 tonnes of explosive shells. On the heels of this debilitating second barrage the stormtroopers proceeded to tear up enemy defenses with bayonets and hand grenades:

> The *Sturmtruppen* overran enemy trenches at 1000 on 4 December. Cool and collected, the sappers worked very accurately to make breaches in the enemy wire and allow the 3rd Assault Company and the infantry to penetrate and conquer the Italian positions. The first wave, comprised of three assault companies and four infantry battalions, seized Mount Badenecche and later Mount Tondarecar. The enemy then gathered all available soldiers and attempted in vane to conquer Mount Badenecche. Numerous counter-attacks were fought off by our artillery and mortar units. Approximately 3,000 Italian soldiers were captured on Mount Tondarecar.[90]

By 1200 the Tondarecar was completely cleared of any enemy resistance. Mount Badenecche, however, had also been on the verge of being taken by the Austro-Hungarian Army but a timely counter-attack by the *alpini* from the *Monte Berico* was able to push back the enemy infiltration.

On the western flank the 52nd Infantry Division was also unable to proceed to capture Mount Zomo due to strong enemy infantry counter-attacks.

While the Austrians were unable to take Mount Badenecche and Mount Zomo, troops of the II Battalion of the 3rd *Kaiserschützen* Regiment with one assault patrol of the 4th *sturmtruppen* Company led by Lieutenant Morelli captured with a bold stroke Mount Miela. The stormtroopers were instrumental in breaking down Italian defenses by infiltrating their trenchlines on several points and by capturing key machine and artillery gun posts.

As Lieutenant Morelli recalls:

> We quickly positioned a machine gun that began to spew fire against the enemy position. As the enemy was pinned down, and while supported by the flame-throwers unit, all officers, including myself, shouted out 'Hurra' and instructed

90 Ernst Wisshaupt, *Die Tiroler Kaiserjäger im Weltkriege*, p. 368.

> our men to attack. We dashed forward to engage the enemy in close combat as the first teams of Kaiserschützen followed suit. After a confused struggle the enemy relented. We captured the enemy post along with a few officers, 150 soldiers and two artillery pieces."[91]

Once the enemy defenses had been paralyzed by the surprise attacks of the special assault detachment, the battalion's infantry units were able to mop up the remaining centers of Italian resistance and ultimately occupy the contested Mount Miela.

At the same time the Meletta di Gallio, the central Italian position, was also stormed by 22nd *Feldjäger* Battalion with its *sturmkompagnie* in the lead. Strong points were overwhelmed one after the other with hand grenades. Small groups of infantry that had survived the initial enemy attack began a prolonged fighting retreat that held up the Austro-Hungarians for several hours. However, as a result of an enemy pincer movement these units were also forced to surrender leading also to the capture of several machine guns and small artillery pieces. As the Austrian official history states; "unnoticed by the Italian reserves coming up from the south or by the *alpini* stationed to the north (on Mount Castelgomberto and the Malga Lora), they struck the surprised defenders of the trenches on the Meletta from behind and forced them to surrender after a wild fight involving hand grenades."[92]

The Austro-Hungarian official history with regards to the fighting on the Melette di Gallio states that: "In a few hours the attackers had gained ground that had been beyond our reach during the preceding weeks of bloody combat."[93]

While the Italian official history points out that its 29th Division was virtually destroyed by the enemy infiltration tactics whereby small assault detachments acting on the flanks of the Italian positions opened up gaps with hand grenades, bayonets and machine guns.[94]

At the tail end of December 1917 11th Army moved forward with a plan to capture the next objective on the Altopiano, the so-called Three Mountains (Mount Valbella, Col del Rosso and Col d'Ecchele) to eliminate all enemy presence on the southern sector of the Asiago plateau. While the 6th Infantry Division was tasked with occupying Col del Rosso and Col d'Ecchele, the stormtroopers were assigned to conquer Mount Valbella, the lynchpin of the Italian defensive system on the Three Mountains.

The plan of attack was prepared once again with special thoroughness and with key input from Captain Teuber of 11th Army *Sturmbaon*. The latter had previously conducted extensive reconnaissance of the Italian positions from key observation points on Mount Longara and Mount Stenfle and had come to the conclusion that the Valbella could be seized with a two-pronged assault. The stormtroopers would go in first and with the aid of explosive charges would attempt to blow gaps in the wire.

91 Ibid., p. 366.
92 Edmund Glaise-Horstenau (ed.), *Österreich-Ungarns letzter Krieg, vol 6*, p. 686.
93 Ibid., p. 687.
94 Ufficio Storico, E-1, raccolta 17: Relazione del Comando Supremo, 'Difesa della regione Melette', 14 December 1917, n. 74192.

Once that had been achieved, the stormtroopers would penetrate the enemy positions first, closely followed by the standard infantry units. A dry run had also been conducted two days prior to the start of the attack to ensure that the units involved followed to the letter the plan of operations. Accordingly, the plan called for:

> The stormtrooper assault shall begin promptly at 0930 and will coincide with the lengthening of the preparatory barrage. Prior to the infantry assault, various explosive charges will be lighted under the enemy wire. The stormtroopers shall move forward as soon as the smoke clouds from the explosions are visible. The first infantry support wave will then follow the stormtroopers at a distance of approximately 30 steps.[95]

The directive then went on to underline that it was critical for standard infantry to remain in close contact with the stormtroopers whose lead they should follow during the various stages of the battle.

The artillery support assembled for the assault on the Three Mountains was quite formidable including: 440 light, 100 medium and 10 heavy guns. The three infantry groups were equally strong. Each was comprised by assault patrols from the 1st and the 4th Company of 11th *Sturmbaon*, and various flamethrower, sapper, mountain guns, machine guns and grenade thrower platoons from the same unit, and by troops from the 20th *Feldjäger* Battalion, and the 22nd High Mountain Company. In support, mainly as grenade carriers as well as representing the second wave of attack, were two infantry battalions of the 6th Division.

During the night between 22–23 December the artillery first bombarded the Italian batteries and assembly points with a large quantity of mustard gas shells. In the morning it targeted the frontline defenses just a few hours prior to the start of the infantry operation.

The Austro-Hungarian official history reports that weather conditions were quite favorable for the attack: "Twenty centimeters of snow lay on the battlefield. The artillery commanders in their advantageous observation points on the Melette brilliantly directed the destructive fire against targets that were clearly visible in the snow. Under these circumstances the infantry had a relatively easy chore."[96]

The stormtrooper columns then moved forward to attack:

> Italian defenses were particularly strong centered on numerous machine gun strong points, on a system of parallel trenches and deep dugouts. ... Although the sappers had been able to position several explosive charges under the wire, they were forced to use wire cutters in several sections to make gaps in the enemy defensive system. The storming of the enemy trenches was made possible by the following sequence of events. The infantry assault began when the enemy trenches were covered by hand grenades. Machine gun fire from multiple

95 K.u.K., 11. Armee Kommando, Op. Nr. 321/3435, 21 December 1917.
96 Edmund Glaise-Horstenau (ed.), *Österreich-Ungarns letzter Krieg, vol 6*, p. 681.

> flanking directions soon followed. Finally, the flamethrowers went into action. After the fire and smoke had engulfed the enemy trenches, the soldiers then irrupted into them from both flanks forcing the enemy to surrender and/or retreat.[97]

By 1100 Mount Valbella had been seized and large columns of enemy soldiers could be seen being marched into captivity. The operation had yielded the capture of 3,936 soldiers (including one colonel and 200 officers), 30 machine guns and numerous grenade throwers, mortars and light machine guns. At the same time, units from the 6th Infantry Division had also captured the two other peaks of the Three Mountains (Col del Rosso and Col d'Ecchele) where more than 4,000 Italians had been taken prisoner.

Phase 1 November 1917 Grappa Sector

The goal of the Austro-German offensive in the area of the Mount Grappa massif was to overtake its defenses with a combination of flanking assaults. The *sturmkompagnie* of 3rd *Kaiserjäger* Regiment, while advancing in the direction of Mount Grappa together with Erwin Rommel's *Württemberg* Battalion was the first Austrian unit to experience stiff fighting against Italian rearguard troops posted in defense of the Forcella Clautana. These troops, mainly three *alpini* companies (*Val Susa* Battalion), *arditi* from XVIII *Reparto d'assalto*, two *bersaglieri* companies and an artillery section with six mountain guns, were covering the retreat of the Italian 26th Division and had been ordered of holding the enemy for as long as possible.

On 7 November 1917 two German companies under Rommel's command attacked the Italian position on the steep Forcella Clautana, which has an elevation of 500 feet. Despite suffering losses from machine guns positioned on the flanking Col Cavasso, the Italians managed to hold on to their positions.

Then during the night of 7–8 November Rommel's unit, reinforced by the *sturmkompagnie* of 3rd *Kaiserjäger*, attacked again the Forcella. This time with better support from the machine guns, three columns of assault infantry charged up the mountain peak. While some of the attackers slipped on the fresh snow and fell to their death off the cliff of the mountain, the vast majority managed to get within a few meters from the enemy post but were yet again unable to dislodge the Italians from their positions. To make matters worse for the attackers, as the German and Austrian units were retreating they were counter-attacked by the *arditi* with hand grenades and bayonets that lead to further losses. As Rommel asserts "it was the first attack since the beginning of the war in which I had failed. It failed primarily because the advance of the infantry troops was not synchronized with the fire of the machine gun company."[98]

97 Ernst Wisshaupt, *Die Tiroler Kaiserjäger im Weltkriege*, p. 368.
98 Erwin Rommel, *Infantry Attacks* (London: Greenhill Books, 2006), p. 232.

On the morning of 8 November, it was pitch dark, the snow was falling, and the German and Austrian troops were suffering badly because they had camped out in the freezing cold all night. At 0600 a small platoon was dispatched to the Forcella Clautana to test the reaction of the Italians on the peak. But unexpectedly they encountered no resistance since during the early dawn the position had been evacuated. Shortly thereafter, the position was occupied by the *sturmkompagnie* and by the Germans of the *Württemberg*.

Once the 55th Division had passed over the Tagliamento River its objective was to move forward toward the Veneto plains in order to circumvent the major Italian positions on Mount Grappa. In the meantime the Italians were reorganizing their defenses along the Mount Grappa massif itself where large field guns and several machine guns had been rushed into position to offer prolonged resistance. On 11 November the 55th Division had taken Belluno and was poised to meet Italian resistance on the pre-alps around Mount Grappa. Their first objective was the seizure of Mount Tomatico which stood in between Feltre and Mount Grappa and was manned by the *alpini* of the *Val Cismon* (7th Regiment). The first attempt to take the Tomatico was undertaken on 14 November. The 55th Division's 7th Regiment with its *sturmkompagnie* in the lead charged up the mountain but due to insufficient artillery support and fierce Italian resistance it was not able to take the peak positions at 1,600 meters. As the Bosnian troops were retreating they were counter-attacked by the *alpini* and lost several soldiers to enemy fire. On the same day, two more attempts were made by the same unit to take the peak but on both occasions they were rebuffed with casualties. As the Austrian official history asserts the 55th Division was stopped in front of Mount Tomatico after multiple bloody attempts.[99]

The next day, 15 November, the 55th renewed its attempts to force the Italians off Mount Tomatico but once again the Austro-Hungarian forces were unable to take the mountain due to the former's strong machine gun fire. However, on the night of the 15th the rapidly changing situation in the Piave sector forced the *alpini* of the *Val Cismon* to evacuate the Tomatico. As a result, the next day the 7th Regiment advanced again and was able to finally occupy the position without suffering any losses.

Phase 2 December 1917 Mount Grappa Sector

The Austro-Germans had spent the final weeks of November reinforcing their positions surrounding the Grappa massif in preparation of large-scale attacks. By early December 11th Army had managed to assemble 350 light, 100 medium and 10 heavy guns for the scheduled operation. The Austro-Hungarians would have attacked sooner if it wasn't for the delays experienced with moving the guns, mainly because there wasn't a major road leading up to the Grappa and also because many guns had to be dragged into position by teams of soldiers.

99 Edmund Glaise-Horstenau (ed.), *Österreich-Ungarns letzter Krieg, vol. 6, p.* 661.

Finally on 11 December 1917 the Austro-Hungarians were ready to attack. At 0330 a very intense artillery fire reversed both poison gas and explosive shells on the Italian positions on Mount Asolone, Col della Berretta and Col Caprile, the left flank of the Grappa massif which was held by units of the 57th Infantry Division. Then at 0530 there was a brief interruption in the barrage which was then resumed with even greater intensity until 0900. After five hours of almost non-stop bombardment the infantry attack was undertaken by 88th and 99th Infantry Regiments of the Austro-Hungarian 4th Infantry Division and it was spearheaded by its 4th *Sturmbaon* comprised by the 49th, 8th, 99th and 88th *Sturmkompagnien*. The latter, greatly assisted by the thick fog that hindered the defenders' visibility, sprang a surprise attack on the Italians at 0930. On the Col Caprile the *alpini* of *Monte Matajur* Battalion and troops from the 57th Infantry Battalion repulsed all attempts by the 49th and 88th *Sturmkompagnien* to dislodge them from their positions. On the ridge separating Col della Berretta from Mount Asolone, however, strong assault patrols of the 8th and 99th *Sturmkompagnien* bombed their way through the Italian defenses and overcame several machine gun posts. From this ridge, the Austro-Hungarians were then able to infiltrate enemy defenses on the Col della Berretta. Here the Austro-Hungarians, preceded by small assault patrol units, advanced in small groups and armed primarily with machine guns and flamethrowers cleared out several trenches. Meanwhile, from nearby hills, the machine guns and the light artillery raked and bombed the Italian strong points causing casualties and pinning their infantry down. The main assault then swept in from the flanks with the flamethrower platoons, cooperating closely with the machine gun and hand grenade groups, breaking through the main enemy position. Having taken the Col della Berretta, the Austro-Hungarians were now poised to take the main position of Mount Asolone, which distanced less than two miles from the Grappa massif and was just 1,000 feet below it.

Units of the 99th Infantry Regiment were the first to reach the peak of Mount Asolone but they encountered stiff resistance. The following is the testimony of Otto Gallian, lieutenant of the stormtrooper assault company of the 99th Regiment, who fought on Mount Asolone:

> This is hell, with an avalanche of ashes and debris falling on us. I clinch my teeth and as I cling to the ground my mouth starts to bleed. Since the barrage does not seem to relent our unit has taken cover on the reverse slope of the mountain. I nervously smoke one cigarette after the another, then swallow one piece of chocolate after the other as the barrage shows no sign of relenting. It's freezing and in order to get some relief I rub my half frozen fingers in the snow. Unconsciously I turn my thoughts to my little brother who is still in school in Vienna. My little brother has no idea of the enviable place I find myself in.[100]

100 Otto Gallian, *Monte Asolone 1918* (Graz: Leykam, 1933), p. 118.

The fighting on the Asolone ultimately resulted into a stalemate lasting until Christmas. As the Italians held on, the losses on the Austro-Hungarian side increased every day until January set in and the fighting stopped.

Nevertheless, the Austro-Hungarian official history states that its 4th Infantry Division had gained an unequivocal success with the capture of Col della Berretta and the Casera Spiedon (1,476 meters). "The Division thus secured the edge of the heights overlooking the basin where the Val San Lorenzo, which opens onto the plains to the south, has its source."[101]

Both the Asolone sector and the Melette had been the target of the combined German and Austro-Hungarian offensive in November 1917. Why where these positions not taken in November 1917 and why were the Austro-Hungarians successful in taking them in December? In November, the Austrians had decided to push forward with the offensive even against strong German objections based primarily on a lack of adequate artillery support. German opinions on the attack being premature were vindicated when the assault led by two stormtrooper companies of the 59th Austro-Hungarian Infantry Division against Col della Beretta failed miserably mainly because an insufficient artillery preparation had not destroyed the enemy wire. As a result, over 200 stormtroopers were cut down while trying to probe the wire and the second wave of infantry units was forced into a hasty retreat. In contrast, in December the Austro-Hungarian units had ample time to prepare the operation in detail. The final plan of attack, for example, relied on the detailed study of the enemy positions including the examination of aerial photographs and on reports gathered from on-site surveillance. In addition, by then the artillery had assembled enough heavy guns and shells to properly pave the way for the infantry.

The Austro-Hungarians won a major victory at Caporetto and achieved local successes during the winter battle such as pushing the Italians all the way back on the southern edge of the Asiago Altopiano but could not effectuate the necessary breakthrough to invade the plains. The reasons for the final outcome were protracted Italian resistance centered on entrenched high mountain positions, fatigue and exhaustion on the part of the attackers and the lack of the necessary number of bomber planes and siege artillery to achieve the desired breakthrough.

According to General Erich Ludendorff, who had authorized the German intervention on the Italian front, "The troops continued to gain ground, but they did not succeed in capturing the critical Monte Grappa massif ... General Conrad had insufficient artillery, and his infantry was not strong enough to attack."[102]

At Caporetto the Italian infantry experienced first hand the newly developed German *sturmtruppen* tactics on a large scale as well as the massive artillery barrage that preceded the infantry advance. Following the Caporetto Offensive, the *Comando Supremo* issued a post-battle report that summarized the enemy's novel *sturmtruppen* tactics. It singled out in particular the flamethrower and the automatic machine guns

101 Edmund Glaise-Horstenau (ed.), *Österreich-Ungarns letzter Krieg, vol. 7*, p. 344.

102 Erich Ludendorff, *Ludendorff's own story, Vol. 2* (New York: Harpers and Brothers, 1919), p. 117.

as the enemy's most impressive and deadliest weapons. The former was recognized for its effectiveness in clearing out trenches and fortified bunkers and pillboxes, as well as for its huge psychological impact upon frontline troops. Light machine guns on the other hand were seen as highly effective assault weapons especially when deployed on the flanks of attacking units. Light machine guns manufactured in Germany gave infantry the mobility and firepower that were so instrumental in achieving the much sought-after breakthrough. The success of the *sturmtruppen* tactics, however, resided primarily on accurate, timely and overpowering artillery fire.[103]

The main architect of the Caporetto Offensive appeared to agree with the post-battle assessment of the Italian Army. "Destructive fire", asserted General Krafft von Dellmensingen, "was crucial for the offensive. As the advanced Italian positions had been dealt a heavy blow by gas grenade launchers, their artillery appeared to be paralyzed and unable to change the course of battle."[104]

Solstice Offensive

In April 1918 the AOK, by then firmly under a new but less experienced and powerful Chief of Staff General Arz von Straussnberg, issued new artillery regulations styled on the German reforms of 1917 as a prelude to the march on the Piave. The guidelines were to support the planned offensive that Emperor Karl had committed his army with the German High Command and the operation was to coincide with a major German push on the Western Front. For offensive operations the AOK stressed that divisional artillery, with the addition of the newly formed *minenwerfer* sections, was expected to execute swift rolling and creeping barrages to neutralize enemy artillery. The pinpoint barrage was first aimed against infantry frontline trenches in order to relegate the defenders to their dugouts as the assault units moved forward. Other targets of the barrages, as the artillery slowly moved its fire forward, were the enemy's key command centers to inhibit any enemy reaction. Finally, the last stage of the creeping barrage, in particular, was to be concentrated on arms and munitions depots, observation points and strongpoints in order to paralyze enemy defenses. The main objective of artillery preparation was not to annihilate the opponent's defenses, which was an impossible objective in itself, but to immobilize them in an effort to facilitate deep penetrations of enemy positions by the assault detachments.

These reforms were complemented by the earlier re-organization of the *sturmtruppen* of August 1917, which began to take form only after Caporetto. Up to that point, the latter had developed in a less than uniform fashion and the AOK with its new directive aimed to standardize the number and size of the *sturmtruppen*.[105]

103 Ufficio Storico: 'Cenni descrittivi di alcuni apparecchi lanciafiamme germanici, Comando Supremo Ufficio Tecnico'.

104 Cited in Gianni Pieropan, *Storia della Grande Guerra, 1915–18* (Milan: Mursia, 2004), p. 630.

105 Kriegsarchiv: K.u.K., AOK, Op. Nr. 42/363, 11 January 1918.

By mid 1917 the Austro-Hungarian field armies deployed on the Italian front had two types of *sturmtruppen* units: assault battalions under the command of each army or army corps and two assault patrols to each infantry battalion. With this directive the AOK outlined that the *sturmtruppen* battalions were to be constituted at the infantry division and assault half-battalions at the independent brigade level and they were to serve a dual purpose: training the divisional infantry in close combat tactics and take part in divisional planned attacks. It also laid down for the first time a firm structure for these assault units.

Each stormtrooper battalion was to consist of:

1. Four infantry assault companies
2. One machine gun company
3. One infantry gun platoon
4. One sapper platoon
5. One mortar platoon
6. One flamethrower platoon
7. One telephone section.

While the Austro-Hungarian divisions became smaller as a result of the reorganization, by going down from four to three infantry regiments, their firepower was much increased by doubling the number of machine guns (from four to eight) per battalion and by adding a mortar unit. In addition, each division could now rely upon fully specialized units such as the stormtroopers, the flamethrowers (the number of these weapons was also doubled versus 1917) and special machine gun sections.

The divisional artillery arm was also strengthened considerably. A standard infantry division, for example, had an artillery brigade with up to 100 artillery pieces which was a far cry from the initial amount of guns in 1914. The standard infantry division had many guns of different types:

36 field howitzers
24 field guns
20 heavy field howitzers
8 mountain guns
4 mountain howitzers
4 10.5 cannons
4 anti-aircraft guns.[106]

The brigade was comprised of two field artillery regiments (*Feldartillerieregimenter*), one heavy field artillery regiment (*schweres Feldartillerieregiment*) and one mountain artillery battalion (*Gebirgsartillerie-Abteilung*). Further support was provided by a few field artillery regiments kept as a tactical reserve by army commands in order to reinforce success by being quickly deployed in those sectors of the front where

106 http://www.austro-hungarian-army.co.uk/artyorg.html <accessed 2 January 2017>

the infantry had breached the enemy lines. Some units, such as the 29th Infantry Division had as many as 179 artillery pieces. Its artillery batteries included, amongst other pieces, 66 M14 (100 mm) howitzers, 24 M15 (150 mm) howitzers, 16 M15 (75 mm) mountain guns. These guns were all of the most advanced design and equipped with steel shields and that were manufactured in a way that they could also be broken down into several components so that they could be transported in the mountainous terrain.[107]

Each division also had a full team of artillery observers as well as its own air squadron to further enhance its reconnaissance and intelligence capabilities. The air force could now be fully integrated into the new tactical plans. It could support the attack in advance by providing intelligence services and then by supporting the attack as it unfolded by carrying out the saturation bombing as well as the spraying of the advanced enemy lines with machine gun fire. The artillery arm had by then become the division's most important component providing the groundwork for major offensive operations.

According to historian John Schindler by mid 1918 the Austro-Hungarian Army had reached its highest point of tactical maturity and its most formidable degree of firepower. He writes: "The reorganization ensconced the artillery as the key combat arm, the basis of combat power, reflecting the maturity of Austro-Hungarian gunnery and the lessons of four years of total war. The division was an ideal instrument for positional warfare, designed to achieve tactical breakthroughs by infantry-artillery cooperation, bolstered by assault units and sappers."[108]

The reorganization of the Austro-Hungarian Army along with the Army's overall further increase in artillery firepower and the adoption of German infiltration and artillery tactics boded well for the Habsburg leadership. In the view of the AOK at that juncture of the conflict both the stormtroopers and the infantry had been given all available tools and resources to achieve a major victory. The stormtroopers, in particular, although well known by then, were still feared by the enemy. As late as the spring of 1918 General Diaz was compelled to issue another directive to warn his unit commanders about the tactics used by the Austro-Hungarian stormtroopers. Even though the stormtroopers tactics were by then widely known by their adversary, it appears that they were still lethal when deployed especially against 'green' and inexperienced frontline troops.

> It's a known fact that the enemy undertakes raids and planned attacks on cloudy days when the dense fog and the heavy rain allow the assault units to approach the wire undetected. With the aid of brief but powerful concentrations of artillery and mortar fire, the enemy is able to make breaches in the wire. Then the troops advance in small groups as the artillery lengthens its fire upon the secondary lines of defense. Advancing in the midst of snow, fog or heavy rain,

107 John R. Schindler, 'Austria-Hungary in the First World War', in Sanders Marble (ed.), *King of Battle Artillery in World War I* (Boston: Brill, 2016), p. 154.
108 Ibid., p. 154.

> these small units are frequently able to penetrate and threaten the first defensive line.[109]

The planning for the Piave offensive took into account the re-organization of the Austro-Hungarian Army centered upon the division as the foremost tactical infantry arm. Every infantry division deployed was to go on the offensive as one autonomous unit and to be pitted against one section of the frontline. Each *Sturmbaon* was to lead in the attack the divisional infantry. It was the intent of the AOK that the Piave Offensive was to be a return to a war of movement where, it was hoped, the infantry units would be able to smash through the enemy lines and penetrate deep into the Veneto plains. Given the Allied-imposed embargo and the overall build-up of Allied forces vis-à-vis the Central Powers, the AOK approved an all or nothing offensive aimed at ending the war. *Sturmtruppen* battalions were tasked with supporting their divisional infantry assault groups as each division was to attack as a single unit over a wide section of the frontline. Each *sturmtruppen* company was to lead one divisional infantry assault group (battalion) and each group was assigned to take possession of one row of enemy defensive line.

The Austrian stormtroopers would fight this battle in a similar fashion to how the German assault units fought on the Western front. Preceded by the creeping barrage, the *sturmtruppen* would conduct a frontal assault against infantry strong points with the aim of achieving a deep penetration beyond the Italian third line of defense and seize its artillery. The fact that the battle would be fought, for the most part in non-mountainous terrain, made it akin to the battles fought by the German stormtroopers at Verdun or Cambrai as the infantry was expected to maneuver through the enemy's thick defenses.

In order to achieve a breakthrough the AOK structured the attack upon successive waves of infantry units, each of which was to be led by a company of stormtroopers.

The first assault wave was to consist of the following units:

> The first wave, responsible for breaking through the enemy position to the objective (usually the third line position), must have sufficient stormtroops and plenty of hand grenades. If the enemy position is three to four lines deep, the first wave should comprise: at least two, usually three or more Sturmpatrouillen, two to three sections, one hand grenade section, several assault sappers, a signal patrol, and the artillery observer with the commander of the first wave.[110]

The second wave comprised of one assault patrol and up to two or three standard infantry units would provide the necessary support to deepen the breach and advance beyond the enemy's first line of defense. A third wave would follow to mop up

109 Ufficio Storico, *L'Esercito Italiano nella Grande Guerra, Vol. IV, tomo 2, Le Istruzioni tattiche del capo di stato maggiore dell'esercito* (Rome: Ufficio Storico, 1980), pp. 430–31.

110 OSTA/Ka Militarische Impressen, 7611ad, p. 5f. Cited in Christian Ortner, *Storm Troops*, p. 204.

frontline trenches and advance sideways. The ultimate objective of the *sturmtruppen* was to advance deep enough into the "enemy position including the artillery area must be penetrated."[111]

Therefore in order to achieve the much sought-after breakthrough, after the first enemy lines had been breached the stormtrooper assault patrols and the infantry were to push forward. They were to go on and capture enemy gun batteries and neutralize their counter-attacking forces trapping them in their caverns even before they had a change to move forward.

In the spring of 1918 the Austro-Hungarian troops destined to take part in the Solstice Offensive began to train for an "offensive battle that should lead to a war of movement."[112] To achieve the much sought-after breakthrough, the AOK established that the 44th *Schützen* Division was to conduct tactical exercises for the benefit of the entire army. These tactical instructions were based primarily on German *sturmtruppen* fighting methods used in the battles of Verdun, Riga and Caporetto.

Even if the Solstice Offensive was to be a large-scale operation, it was decided by the AOK that it would not be preceded by an extended preparatory barrage. In the interest of secrecy there would be no artillery registration and the barrage would consist of a short but intensive artillery bombardment to be executed before the infantry attacked. This was consistent with German doctrine that aimed above all to achieve a tactical surprise over the enemy. Such practice would favor a timely and sudden infantry assault. The artillery batteries had been grouped for their various roles (infantry support, suppression of enemy artillery, and long range fire). The batteries that were providing direct support to the advancing troops were provided with means to expeditiously move them forward. For example many of the large guns were pulled by tractors or large vehicles.

The assault infantry was to deploy the tactics of infiltration and the ultimate goal was to advance without pause for at least three days in order to reach the rear defenses and capture the enemy's artillery deployment.

The plan of attack stated that the key objective was to:

> To take maximum advantage of the artillery preparation and fire support. As soon as the last rounds struck the enemy positions, the infantry must surge forward; in the advance which follows, they must directly follow our rolling barrage, not giving the enemy time to recover from its effects or to make themselves ready for action. The maxim of the storm battalions – which has led to great success – is that attacking infantry should surge through their own artillery and trench mortar fire; this maxim must become the property of the entire infantry.[113]

111 Ibid., p. 204.
112 Ibid., p. 204.
113 Edmund Glaise-Horstenau (ed.), *Österreich-Ungarns letzter Krieg, vol. 7*, p. 211.

The assault infantry units were to be equipped with new weapons to enhance their ability to overcome strong pockets of enemy resistance. While heavy machine guns would support the infantry as it advanced through no man's land, the latter was to attack using primarily new light automatic machine guns. Each stormtrooper platoon was required to bring the light guns forward as far as possible. The assault patrols were also to be supported by advanced specialist units with light trench mortars, flamethrowers and several mountain guns to break up pockets of enemy resistance or to fend off counter-attacks. The stormtroopers had been given a special incentive to do well during the offensive in the form of bounty money: 50 Kronen for an Allied prisoner of war, 500 for an Allied aircraft downed by machine gun, rifle or small artillery fire, and 3,000 for forcing an Allied plane to land behind Austrian lines.

As the assault infantry moved against the enemy's positions, the artillery would continue to support it with the rolling barrage. Moreover, the Austro-Hungarian Army would also deploy its air force to bomb enemy positions and facilitate ground operations.

With the exit of Russia from the war, for the Solstice Offensive the AOK was able to deploy the most powerful and the greatest number of troops ever seen on the Italian front since the beginning of the war. The Habsburg Army assembled an impressive array of units including 58 infantry divisions (with no German units) while the Italians deployed 56 divisions (of which one Czech, three British and two French). For the attack the Austro-Hungarian Army would be split into two groups: Army Group Conrad (mainly the 10th and 11th Armies) deployed in the Trentino and Field Marshal Boroevic's Isonzo Army (5th and 6th Armies) situated along the Piave River. Both leaders wanted to attack simultaneously. While Conrad wanted to attack out of the Asiago Altopiano and Mount Grappa, thus once again proposing to outflank the Italians by coming down into the valley floors with a broad sweep from the mountains, Boroevic wanted to carry out a frontal attack on the Piave, whose ultimate objective was to smash the enemy's defenses and seize Treviso and Padova. Although General Arz von Straussenburg had initially refused to implement a two-pronged offensive, he was forced to give in after Emperor Karl had authorized Conrad's operational plan.

In mid 1918 the Austro-Hungarian Army still possessed a very powerful infantry and artillery, but by then the Italians had made powerful strides in re-building a new army capable of waging a total war against the enemy. While the Austro-Hungarian artillery in 1918 still held the lead in the heavy (30.5 cm, 42 cm howitzers and guns) segment, the Italians held the lead in the medium gun battery and mortar segments by being able to deploy several more batteries of 240 mm, 150 mm and 100 mm mortars and guns than their rival. In 1918 for example, the Austrian guns were still generally more effective and longer ranging than comparable Italian guns of the similar size range, but the Italians had more guns. Italian heavy field artillery was totally modernized after the tremendous losses at Caporetto by replacing most obsolete models. Even though the Italians had more artillery weapons, since 1916 the Austro-Hungarians had taken the lead in introducing more indirect fire mortars and howitzers with high trajectory shooting, lobbing shells more effectively over the mountain passes. Italian artillery, although more numerous, was also less effective with regards to the small size units such as the mountain guns. Specifically referring to Italian mountain artillery, historian Filippo Cappellano asserts: "The 65 mm cannon, although lightweight, sturdy and with a good ballistic performance, proved to be inferior to the enemy's 75 mm Skoda M15 howitzer, which allowed high trajectory fire."[114]

The Austro-Hungarians had a total of 6,916 artillery guns in mid 1918 with a great increase of field howitzers and mortars (679 guns), while the Italians had over 7,000 pieces of artillery by that time. The Italians still had more direct fire, conventional weapons but they too were in the process of transitioning their artillery to the requirements of trench warfare.

While the Austro-Hungarian Dual Monarchy could boast of generally having more efficient guns, its economic output began to lag in 1918 with respect to the Italians. In 1918 the economy of the Dual Monarchy was still producing record numbers of shells, but it was slowly losing ground to the Italians. Although the Austro-Hungarian economy in 1918 was losing steam and slowing down, it nevertheless provided the frontline troops with sufficient numbers of shells to continue the war and to ultimately launch the much anticipated offensive. The major shortages were in the area of poison gas shells, especially because the German High Command did not have enough of these shells for their own troops and could only ship large quantities of them in late June. By then the Italian infantry also had comparable, if not greater in certain areas, numbers of weapons such as flamethrowers, mortars and machine guns.

Nevertheless the AOK maintained that its troops could overcome the poison shell shortage by repeating the feat at Caporetto by breaking through on the first day thanks to a strong showing by the artillery. Overall, the AOK was confident of victory and felt that their troops had a psychological and tactical superiority over the Italians.[115]

The main Austrian thrust was to be launched across the Piave River by Boroevic's 5th Army, while a second effort sought to overcome Italian defenses on the mountain ranges of the Adamello/Tonale Pass, Asiago Altopiano and Mount Grappa by Army Group Conrad's 10th and 11th Armies. Thus attack plans for this Solstice Offensive differed from the German plan at Caporetto which had sought primarily to attack with maximum force on a narrow section of the frontline. In contrast, the Austrians planned to launch mass attacks against several sections of the frontline. The main thrust would be on the lower Piave as: "Reconnaissance reports now indicated that it wouldn't be hard to cross the Piave by the northern foot of the Montello and to secure this high ground, since as the infantry advanced they would soon enter an area on the other side of the river which couldn't be hit by the Italian artillery."[116]

114 Filippo Cappellano, 'Italian Artillery during the First World War', in Sanders Marble (ed.), *King of Battle: Artillery in World War One* (Boston: Brill, 2016), p. 215.
115 Kriegsarchiv: Anton Pitreich, 'Piave-front', unpublished manuscript., p. 211.
116 Edmund Glaise-Horstenau (ed.), *Österreich-Ungarns letzter Krieg, vol. 7*, p. 254.

The *Luftfahrtruppen*, the Austro-Hungarian Air Force, was instrumental in the preparation of the attack plans by flying many missions to identify the location of the Italian artillery positions. Despite its inferior number of aircraft, it allowed the infantry commanders to know how many artillery batteries each division would face as well as the disposition of their defensive positions.

Operation Lawine

Operation *Lawine* (avalanche) was the first offensive thrust of the Battle of the Solstice. Its aim was to dislodge the Italians from some of the highest peaks in the western Trentino such as Cima Cady, Monticelli and Corno di Cavento in order to penetrate the Val Camonica/Tonale Pass and threaten to outflank the Italian lines from a north-west direction. For this long-ranging mountain offensive the Austro-Hungarian soldiers were equipped with 10 hand grenades, 200 bullets and enough food rations to sustain them for three days of continued fighting. The operation, taking place in the sector held by the 10th Army, was led by General Hugo Metzger of the 1st Division who also had at his disposal the 22nd *Schützen* Division, and the following stormtroopers: 49th Bosnian *Sturmbaon*, the assault patrols of the 29th *Hochegebirgs-kompagnie*/2nd *Kaiserschützen* Regiment and of the 12th *Bergführer-kompagnie*. These were all special crack mountain troops very experienced and possibly the most formidable alpine troops of the Austro-Hungarian Army. Many of its soldiers had fought in the Adamello and Dolomite sectors and prided themselves in being the most experienced mountain climbers, skiers and most durable mountain hikers of the Habsburg Army.

In total General Metzger could count upon a force comprised of 25 infantry battalions supported by over 300 artillery pieces.

At 0330 on 13 June 1918 the Austrian guns opened fire with an impressive artillery barrage that spanned along the entire mountainous frontline terrain of the western Trentino. Although the barrage blanketed the enemy positions for almost three hours of continuous fire, the Austrian artillery was in some areas unable to paralyze the enemy reaction. As a result, Austro-Hungarian infantry units, which had begun operations at 0600, suffered numerous casualties from Italian counter-preparation fire which at 0545 began with increasing accuracy to pound the infantry columns even before they started to move forward. While on Cima Cady the Austrians were pushed back vigorously by enemy machine gun fire, on the Monticelli the *Ellison* Brigade was able to dislodge the Italians from Peak 2,545 after much hard fighting. This vastly experienced crack mountain unit, with its assault battalion at the forefront, managed to gain a foothold on the contested peak by fighting mainly with hand grenades and flamethrowers. Following the clearing of the enemy position, both the stormtroopers and the infantry units attempted to seize the second peak of the Monticelli but all attempts failed under heavy enemy artillery and machine gun interdiction fire. As a result of the impasse, the alpine offensive stalled and the troops were required to 'turn around' the captured positions.

Two days later the Austro-Hungarians attacked again, this time against the icy peak of the Corno di Cavento, one of the most contested mountains in the northwest which had switched hands several times during the course of the war. The occupation of the Cavento, being one of the highest peaks of the Adamello range (3,402 meters), was of strategic importance since it allowed to control the access routes towards Lombardy and Milan. Unlike the attacks against the Monticelli and Cima Cady, the operation against the Cavento had been more meticulously prepared by experienced mountain warfare commanders. A year prior to the start of the operation, the Austro-Hungarians began preparations by building an underground tunnel in the ice. The quarter-mile long tunnel, which spanned from the Vedretta di Lares to near the peak of the Cavento, was to function as the conduit from which the stormtroopers would reach the Italian front line unencumbered and by the uttermost surprise. The work was done mostly at night as during each session a section of ice and rock was removed and thrown down the cleft of the mountain. The last section of the tunnel branched out into three small tunnels: the main one reaching the 'Trincerone' or big trench, the main advanced Italian position on the Cavento, and the other two its flanks. The plan entailed three assault storm columns breaking the small diaphragm that separated them from the Italian lines simultaneously in order to achieve the maximum tactical surprise. The experienced mountain climbers of the assault patrol of the 12th *Bergführer-kompagnie* would lead the main assault columns in the center and on the right while the stormtroopers of the 29th *Hochgebirgskompagnie* would lead the way for the left flanking column. While the column on the left was to deal with the advanced enemy positions of the Trincerone, the mountaineers/stormtroopers were expected to climb the peak of the mountain and seize the main position.

The approach march toward the Italian positions took place on the night of 14–15 June in a very dangerous high mountain environment full of obstacles and dangers. It was an extremely rough march due to the lack of visibility and the freezing temperatures causing the first casualties as a handful of soldiers slipped on the ice and fell to their death into deep crevices, while others suffered from frostbite. At 0400 the stormtroopers arrived at the entrance of the tunnel while the sappers were conducting last minute preparations. Here they gathered to receive last minute instructions and to cock their weapons.

At approximately 0500 the troops broke the thin diaphragm and dashed toward the enemy trenches located approximately 20 feet away.

According to Captain Alfred Schatz the Italian forward position was quickly overrun. "We threw hand grenades and moved forward to attack the enemy position of the Trincerone. There was no time to waste. We quickly overcame the barbed wire which was almost completely covered by the snow and sprang upon the Italians who were for the most part still sleeping in the dugouts."[117]

The only resistance was offered by a lone sentry who promptly bayoneted to death Sergeant Major Schwarz, the leader of the left flanking column, as he broke through

117 From the diary of Alfred Schatz, captain of the stormtroopers *Bergführer-Kompagnie* n. 12, cited in Luciano Viazzi, *Guerra d'aquile* (Milan: Mursia, 1996), p. 92.

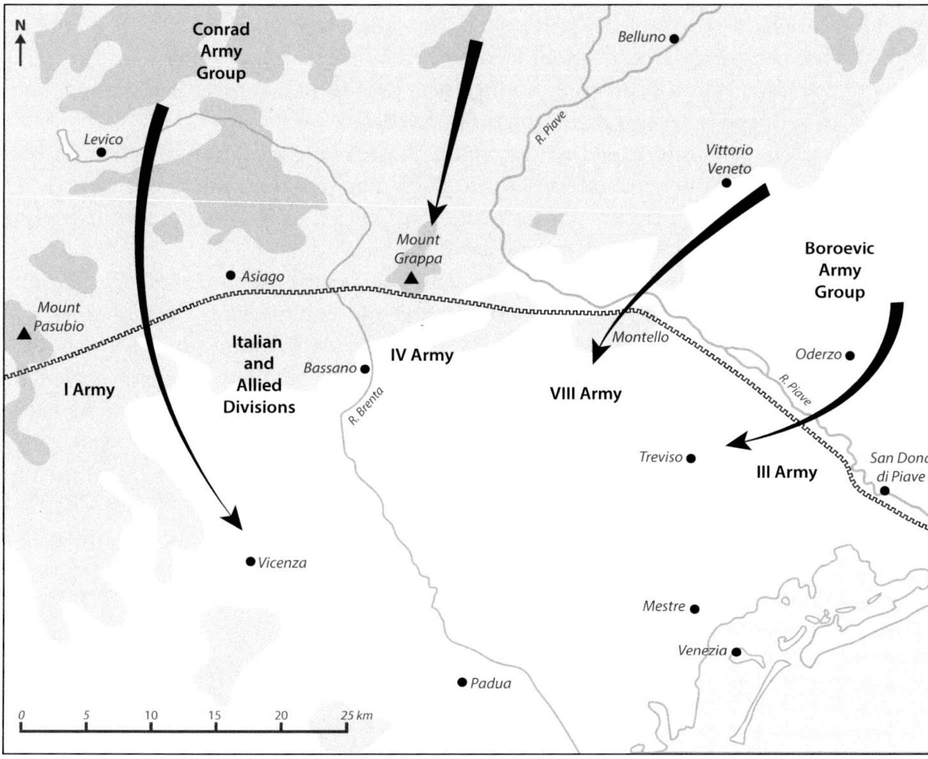

Map 4 The map shows the main points of direction of the pincer movement by the Austro-Hungarian Army during the Solstice Offensive of June 1918. Army Group Conrad and Boroevic's forces along the Piave were to carry out simultaneous attacks against the Italian forces deployed on Mount Grappa and the Piave River. The offensive plan was very different from the plan supporting the Caporetto offensive. In 1917 the Germans attacked along a very narrow sector of the front with a large concentration of infantry and artillery.

the ice. But the sentry was then quickly dealt with and the left flank platoon began to also advance upon the Italians. This platoon, supported by two flamethrowers, began to invest the Trincerone with deadly flames and hand grenades forcing most of the defenders to pull back to avoid being burned to death.

Once the Trincerone had been captured, the Italians defending the peak of the Cavento opened fire against the Austrians from above causing several casualties. Fierce machine gun fire in particular mowed down several men of the 29th *Hochgebirgskompagnie* as they were advancing on the 100-feet long trek that separated the advanced Trincerone position from the mountain peak.

As several men were lost to lively enemy gun fire, the remaining troops of the Austrian assault unit were forced to the ground and were unable to advance. But eventually the special assault detachment regrouped and ultimately turned the tables on the Italians. The Italian units defending the peak were pinned down mainly by grenade launchers shooting explosive shells in quick repetition into their trenches. With the former enemy nest immobilized by several shells raining down on the parapets and the observation posts, the mountaineer assault patrol speedily circumvented it and then reduced it with the aid of hand grenades.

"At this point our unit armed with grenade launchers concentrated its fire against the peak of the Cavento neutralizing the Italian machine guns there positioned. As the pressure was kept on the enemy post, the remaining platoon members outflanked it and finally attacked it from its snowy eastern flank."[118]

As a result of the daring attack on the Cavento positions, three Italian platoons were captured in addition to three machine guns and one mid-sized field gun.

The operation showed how successful specially trained mountain stormtroopers could be in achieving a tactical surprise in extremely difficult terrain. First, the sappers/engineers had been able to put their special knowledge to good use by excavating a tunnel into the ice for almost a year without attracting any attention from the enemy. Second, the stormtroopers promptly reached the assembly point during the night while facing a treacherous high mountain approach march over exposed crevices and steep icy cliffs. Third, by climbing the peak of the mountain under the threat of machine gun fire the experienced mountaineers showed what they were capable of in an extremely dangerous situation.

Therefore despite the lack of success of Operation *Lawine* across the north-western Trentino mountain range of the Adamello, the Austrians had nevertheless captured two important jumping-off platforms (Monticelli and Corno di Cavento) for future offensive operations.

Asiago Altopiano

On 15 June the Austrian artillery began to pound Italian positions along the whole front line from the mountains of the Trentino, to Mount Grappa and the Piave River. This was the start of the largest offensive on the Italian front since the beginning of the war.

The preparatory fire began at 0300 when the enemy's artillery emplacements, the assembly areas for the reserves and the command and observation posts were all targeted by poison gas shells. From 0400 to 0500 the frontline trenches to be assaulted were targeted by the destructive fire. At 0500 the Austro-Hungarian activity once again began to pound enemy artillery and key enemy defensive strong points. From 0600 to 0730 standard explosive shells were fired at the trenchline areas where the infantry would advance, culminating in the creation of a destructive wall of fire. At the same time, more gas shells were fired to pin down the enemy's batteries, command centers and observation points. Then at 0730 the artillery enacted the last phase of the preparatory fire by implementing a rolling barrage to aid the infantry advance. The rolling barrage was moved forward every five minutes by approximately 200 to 250 yards.

118 Ibid., p. 92.

The artillery operation was aided by several squadrons of the Austro-Hungarian Air Force which implemented saturation bombing of the Italian frontline positions. It is estimated that the Austro-Hungarian *Luftfahrtruppen* deployed 18 fighter squadrons and a total of 450 airplanes to bomb the enemy positions on the first day of the battle.

From the start of operations, however, things began to favor the Italians who knew of the enemy's attack plans from the outset as a result of detailed reports received from Austro-Hungarian deserters and from information gathered by the Italian intelligence services. Since the attack plans were known in several sectors of the front, the Italian artillery opened up counter-battery fire concentrated upon the assembly points of the Austrian infantry. Especially along the Asiago Altopiano and Mount Grappa, Austro-Hungarian forces lost many men, even before the assault units had had the chance to move forward.

Given the number of guns deployed and the fact that each medium or light gun could fire on average 30 to 40 rounds per hour, it is estimated that both the Italian and Austro-Hungarian artillery each fired more than a half million rounds from guns and trench mortars during the 10-hour long confrontation.

Despite the heavy blocking fire on the Asiago Altopiano, Austro-Hungarian infantry of VI and XIII Army Corps still managed to overrun the enemy first line of defense and then advance into the Italian lines for more than two miles. The first Austro-Hungarian objective was to take the Three Mountains (which had been seized by the Italians in January 1918) and then outflank the Altopiano and occupy its southern salient. To this end Austrian artillery pounded with great force the hotly contested mountains of Col del Rosso, Mount Valbella and Col d'Echele to pave the way for the stormtroopers of VI Army Corps. The latter, despite huge losses at the hand of enemy counter-battery and interdiction fire, stormed forward with considerable elan to reach their objective. The forces of the 18th Division stormed and occupied Mount Valbella and then pushed forward toward the vital position of Costalunga, the central pillar of the Italian 14th Division second line of defense. As the Austrian assault units inched closer, the Italian units were subjected to greater enemy barrages as the fire from advanced placed machine guns and mortars began to increase considerably. Pinned down by this great fire, the Costalunga position was first attacked from three sides and ultimately overrun by a bold maneuver from the rear. The Col Eckar, the Italian third line of defense, was now threatened and strong fighting opened up for its control. According to the Austrian official history the stormtroopers:

> Thrust through the second Italian line (about half a mile south of the mountain), then with an envelopment attack conquered the forward works on the Costalunga. Here also they took prisoner almost the entire garrison before advancing into the trenches on the Col Eckar. It cannot be determined whether they did in fact capture (or even reach) the hotly-contested summit itself, as was claimed by Division head quarters.[119]

119 Edmund Glaise-Horstenau (ed.), *Österreich-Ungarns letzter Krieg, vol. 7,* p. 301.

On the eastern flank of the Austrian attack, *Edelweiss* stormtrooper assault patrols charged and then occupied the Italian positions on Col del Rosso. But ultimately, infantry was not able to consolidate the attack because "the following waves of troops weren't able to follow the leading detachments because of the onset of a new round of shells from the enemy guns. As the battle groups sprang forward they were simply shot to pieces."[120]

Undaunted by the lack of reinforcements and by Italian counter-battery fire, the *Edelweiss* stormtroopers pushed forward and attacked Mount Melago with the few weapons and ammunition left at their disposal, mainly bayonets and hand grenades, and reached the enemy's second line of defense. "Finally after several hours the destructive enemy fire diminished somewhat and the main bodies of the regiments – already reduced by losses – resumed their advance; they nearly reached the above-mentioned second line, but were unable to overcome stubborn Italian resistance."[121] At that point Italian infantry counter-attacked the *Edelweiss*, and the valiant Tyrolean soldiers were stopped on their tracks. On 17 June Austrians troops at Costalunga were also counter-attacked by the Italians, LII *Reparto d'assalto* with support from *bersaglieri* units, that were able to clear the vast majority of the trenches that had been seized by the enemy.

Despite being halted across the Altopiano, the Austro-Hungarians attempted a surprise coup against an advanced Italian strong point in the lower Trentino. On the night of 15 June 1918 at 0245 the Austrian artillery began to shell the Doss Alto di Zurez, a fortified mountain position held by the 9th Company of the *Pistoia* Infantry Division. A while later the rear Italian defenses, such as the trenches, walkways and the command centers were also targeted by heavy artillery and mortar fire. At 0500 Austrian artillery fire began to weaken and at 0630 it tapered off completely.

In the meantime at 0500 Austro-Hungarian assault troops had begun to advance toward the Italian positions. An hour and a half later the first *sturmtruppen* platoons passed through the damaged sections of the wire and assailed the sentries with daggers and hand grenades. Then they continued advancing in the deep walkways as the enemy troops had retreated into their dugouts to avoid the artillery fire.

One column circumvented the main position by heading east, while a second column scaled the peak of the mountain from its northern flank. At 0600 as the artillery moved the fire forward both columns entered into the mountain and headed directly toward the entrances of the caverns where the enemy was still barricaded inside to avoid the heavy shelling. Bombing squads and flamethrowers mopped up the Italian positions as the enemy was for the most part trapped inside the dugouts and could not oppose the daring assault. The operation yielded the capture of 150 soldiers and seven officers, the vast majority of whom had failed to fire one shot.

120 Ibid., p. 302.
121 Ibid., p. 303.

Monte Grappa

During the tail end of the Caporetto offensive the Austro-Hungarians vainly attempted to capture the Italian defensive bastion of Mount Grappa with a series of frontal assaults. Since these initial attempts had not yielded results, the Austrian 11th Army chose to attack its flanks and attempt to envelop the massif during the Solstice Offensive in the so-called *Radetsky* Operation. Specifically, it sought to outflank the main position by attacking with its best troops its western flank, mainly Col Moschin and Mount Asolone, the weakest and least defended sector. General Ernst Von Horsetzky had at his disposal the 27th Division, which was set to take Col Moschin, the 32nd Division, which was first to take Mount Coston and then the Asolone and finally on the left flank the 55th Division set to take possession of Col dell'Orso. Once these three infantry groups had taken their objectives the 6th Division was to envelop the frontline position on the Grappa and capture the enemy's machine gun emplacements. General Horsetzky had reserved a special role to his stormtroopers since once the infantry had breached the frontline, the special units were to push through in order to speedily reach the rear of the Italians including their main artillery posts. In this endeavor the stormtroopers were instructed not to bother with helping the infantry in subjugating the frontline strongholds so that they could more quickly reach the rear.

On the Mount Grappa sector the Austro-Hungarians were deploying 1,400 artillery pieces and 140 battalions while the Italians 120 battalions and 1,200 guns. The Italian defensive deployment was organized on four successive lines of resistance, each of which was approximately half a mile deep. The Italian 18th Division occupied positions between the Rocce Anzini and the hilltop of Mount Asolone. VI Army Corps occupied all positions from Mount Asolone to Croce dei Lebi, including the main peak of Mount Grappa while the XVIII Army Corps occupied the salient of Col dell'Orso-Solaroli.

At 0300 on 15 June the Austrian artillery began to shell the Italian 4th Army's positions. At 0400 the Italian artillery countered the enemy fire by targeting with little or no respite the trenches and the assembly points of the Austrian infantry. As a result, the latter was targeted by a fierce counter-preparation barrage in the defense. During the exchange of artillery fire some Austrian assault formations lost up to 20 percent of their strength even before they set forth against the Italian positions. Losses were particularly severe amongst the stormtroopers. As Otto Gallian, an Austrian stormtrooper commander asserted, the losses were tremendous and the barrage's impact upon the morale of the troops was devastating. "We suffered much adversity. The company was in tatters even before the start of the infantry advance. The same company that I had trained for several weeks for this operation had been dealt a massive blow."[122]

The Austrians even though weakened by the losses amongst the stormtroopers and the first infantry waves began to advance enabled by the thick fog that covered

122 Otto Gallian, *Monte Asolone 1918* (Graz: Leykam-Verlag, 1933), p. 69.

the mountains. The 27th Division was the quickest to leap forward and to reach the enemy wire and put out of action a number of machine guns posts which were circumvented and taken from the rear at Canale del Brenta. Its 85th and 67th Infantry Regiments then were able to penetrate deeply into the enemy deployment reaching the first enemy strong points of Casera d'Anna and Valle di San Lorenzo respectively. The Austrian official history states that:

> In ten minutes the 85th captured the Casera d'Anna strongpoint along with most of its garrison, then pushed on. The rolling barrage moved ahead of them, but because of poor visibility the artillery commanders could only stick to the pre-arranged schedule as the guns extended their range. The troops broke through the Italians' well-developed network of positions; they suffered casualties while capturing numerous machine gun nests which had survived the destructive artillery fire.[123]

By 0900 hours the stormtroopers, although still targeted by considerable artillery fire, were ready to attack the Col Fenilon and Col Fagheron, the bulwarks of the Italian third line of defense. The assault units of the 85th Regiment first conquered Italian strong points on Col Fenilon and Col Fagheron utilizing new tactics largely dictated by the new weapons at their disposal.

> The first wave, comprised by small platoons of five soldiers and one junior officer, were armed with light machine guns and were responsible for probing enemy lines seeking weak spots and gaps in the wire. This wave was then followed by more numerous hand grenade assault groups. These were charged with widening the breach and pushing the enemy back. They in turn were followed by assault platoons that advanced approximately 300 meters behind the second wave and then by the bulk of the infantry forces. The *Sturmtruppen* had penetrated with great speed the Italian lines and had achieved a tactical surprise over Italian frontline commanders.[124]

By taking advantage of the huge firepower offered by the new Maxim guns, the stormtroopers tore open Italian defenses in several spots allowing the bulk of its infantry to flood enemy trenches. After a brief respite "they stormed the important Col Moschin position itself, on which they captured many machine guns plus two mountain batteries."[125]

In essence, thanks to the dense fog and their exceedingly fast pace, the stormtroopers had advanced in just a few hours past the enemy's third line of defense. The real

123 Edmund Glaise-Horstenau (ed.), *Österreich-Ungarns letzter Krieg, vol. 7*, p. 254.

124 Ufficio Storico, Raccolta E5–34: Comando 17. Divisione, Generale Leoncini, 'Relazione sulle operazioni svolte dalla 17. Divisione di fanteria nei giorni 15–16–17 giugno 1918', 28 June, 1918.

125 Edmund Glaise-Horstenau (ed.), *Österreich-Ungarns letzter Krieg, vol. 7*, p. 256.

danger for the Italians was that the Austro-Hungarians could now outflank the fourth defensive line (Col del Gallo) and threaten to descend towards the valley and ultimately reach Vicenza.

Once the Austro-Hungarian troops reached the Col Moschin they awaited for reinforcements and ammunition in order to continue the advance. In the meanwhile the Italian artillery began counter-battery fire. While the Italian artillery opened fire on the enemy infantry units to dissuade them from advancing further, the commander of the Italian 18th Division called up the IX *Reparto d'assalto* for a counter-attack.

In this critical phase of the battle the Italian artillery effectuated a fierce barrage concentrated upon the hilltops of Col Moschin and Col Fagheron in a bid to halt the enemy advance and gain valuable time in order for the infantry to reorganize sturdier defensive lines and launch local counter-attacks. The Austro-Hungarian 27th Division battle report states that its infantry assault was finally halted by counter-battery fire:

> The troops carried out the assault with great courage. After the commanders shouted: Eljen! The troops moved forward under strong enemy fire and captured all of the objectives within four hours. ... The attack could have progressed even further but the enemy artillery began to fire upon the rear and the flanks of the eastern column which was virtually annihilated. The overbearing fire from unidentified enemy guns halted the assault on its tracks.[126]

IX *Reparto d'Assalto* then in quick succession retook possession of Col Fenilon and Col Fagheron. The next morning the same unit charged up the hill on Col Moschin and wiped out all the gains made by the Austrian stormtroopers.

By midday on the first day of operations even the troops of the Italian VI Army Corps on the other flank of the Grappa massif had lost considerable ground from the concentrated attack of the Austro-Hungarian 32nd Division. Initially, the 32nd Division's units where targeted heavily on their starting points and lost up to 10 percent of their forces. But at the appointed hour they resolutely moved forward against the positions on the southern end of Mount Asolone that were held by the *Bari* and *Pesaro* Brigades. Deployed on the left of the Asolone the stormtroopers of 123rd Infantry Regiment took in quick succession Peak 1,478 and a strong point on the Italian second line of defense along with 1,000 prisoners. In the afternoon an assault patrol reached the Osteria Cibera, on the so-called Cadorna Road which was a vital logistic way used by the Italians to bring supplies to the peak of Mount Grappa.

Forces of the 23rd Infantry Regiment attacked the right flank of Mount Asolone by storming strong points on Peaks 1,490 and 1,503. They then pushed on to Col delle Farine which was seized in the afternoon after a particularly bitter struggle. On this mountain they captured 1,500 soldiers mainly from the Italian 239th Infantry Regiment and two small gun batteries. The 123rd resumed the attack in the afternoon by pushing on to Mount Coston. The objective was to use Mount Coston as a

126 Kriegsarchiv, K.u.K. 27. Infanterie Kommando, Op. Nr. 3416/92, 19 June, 1918.

jumping-off platform to take Mount Rivon and then reach the highest peak of Mount Grappa from its flank. It is unclear whether the stormtroopers, armed primarily with hand grenades and flamethrowers, breached defenses on Mount Coston. Initially their attack proceeded well with the destruction of three enemy artillery batteries. An Italian counter-attack, by units of the 239th Infantry Regiment and the VI *Reparto d'assalto* supported by one mountain and one field gun, was however able to halt the Austrian advance, and push the stormtroopers off Mount Coston and force them to retreat all the way back to Col delle Farine.

I Army Corps' objective was to attack the main bulwarks on the Grappa's right flank held by the Italian VI and XVIII Army Corps and then threaten the massif itself with a flanking operation. During the early hours of the morning, while a dense fog covered the mountains, elements of the 60th Infantry Division seized Mount Pertica thanks to the lightening speed with which its stormtroopers assailed the enemy position. "Stormtroopers of the 119th Infantry Brigade forced a path through the strong barriers on the Pertica ridge, overwhelmed the enemy despite fierce resistance, and captured many prisoners plus several trench mortars."[127] From the Pertica, the Austro-Hungarian forces attempted to reach the main Italian positions on Mount Grappa. While the bulk of the infantry units attempted to circumvent the Grappa from the west, the stormtroopers scaled the mountain from a north-westerly direction and took Hill 1,581. But ultimately multiple attempts to proceed further were stymied by counter-attacks conducted by units of the *Cremona* infantry.

Meanwhile another assault group attacked the Roccolo di Ca' Tasson and brilliantly stormed its peak position. The remnants of three battalions of the *Modena* Brigade were thrown off from the field of battle and were forced to seek shelter in the higher trenches that ringed the Grappa summit. The assault units even managed to descend from the Ca' Tasson to reach Val dei Lebi and seized the ground behind the Grappa massif. This one mile deep infiltration of the Italian lines was ultimately halted by the prompt artillery intervention that with its powerful mass of fire prevented the Austro-Hungarian troops from overrunning the trenches defended by the *Ravenna* Brigade.

Meanwhile the 55th Infantry Division also penetrated deeply into the Italian's XVIII Army Corps positions. Its 7th Regiment seized Mount Valderoa by infiltrating the enemy lines held by the *Como* Brigade from both flanks of the mountain. The 4th Bosnian Regiment captured Mount Solarolo and Point 1,676 of Col dell'Orso thanks to a brilliant maneuver that saw its stormtroopers assail the enemy line with light machine guns and flamethrowers. These local success allowed the Austro-Hungarian troops to reach the Italian's second line of defense. But they were prevented from moving any further in the afternoon by the enemy reaction comprised primarily of machine gun and mountain gun fire. As the Austrian history states, "the nearby batteries of this principal Italian bulwark were spewing fire and preventing the gallant attackers from advancing any further."[128]

127 Edmund Glaise-Horstenau (ed.), *Österreich-Ungarns letzter Krieg, vol. 7*, p. 258.
128 Ibid., p. 258.

Despite the fact that the Austrian-Hungarian offensive on Mount Grappa had stalled, grave losses had been inflicted on the enemy. The Italian 4th Army had suffered 65 officers dead, 167 wounded and 214 missing in action. Amongst the soldiers the losses were 853 dead, 3,530 wounded and 9,160 missing.

Piave River–Montello Sector

Field Marshal Boroevic's Isonzo Army was tasked with effectuating a frontal attack against the Italian positions in the lower Piave with the so-called Operation *Albrecht*. On the Piave/Montello sector the Austro-Hungarian offensive was to take place along the narrowest section of the river near Falze' defended by the 8th Army. Its *Tevere* and *Lucca* Brigades were deployed in defense of the Montello, the main height overlooking Falze' and the Piave, while the 48th Division, with its *Piacenza* and *Aquila* Brigades, occupied the line between Villa Berti and Palazzon to the south of the Montello.

On 15 June at 0300 the Austrian artillery, comprised in this sector of 1,770 guns, opened fire. Small to medium caliber guns were deployed against the Italian first line of defense while the longer ranging guns aimed their shells at the rear artillery and command centers. After a few hours, the Austrian artillery began to concentrate fire exclusively on the five mile area, with the epicenter being the Montello, where its infantry was scheduled to attack. The Montello was the heaviest fortified Italian position of the lower Piave with numerous machine gun nests in addition to barbed wire barriers reaching all the way down to the edge of the river. According to Italian 8th Army commander Giuseppe Pennella, the Montello, given its extensive fortifications, was an unlikely target for an enemy attack. As a result, prior to the start of operations the general had not bothered to take any additional countermeasures to defend it from attack.

Instead this is where General Goiginger of the XXIV Army Corps planned to make his biggest thrust of the Solstice Offensive. He had at his disposal the 31st (General Lieb), the 13th (General Kind) and the 17th (General Stroher) Infantry Divisions. Each division had its own *Sturmbaon* whose role was to land on the opposite side of the river ahead of time and eliminate the three successive lines of defense. In order to achieve tactical surprise, the Austrians had dispatched a number of boats the night before carrying the stormtroopers. The latter had landed safely on islands on the Italian side of the river and had camouflaged themselves under trees and plants in anticipation of the attack. Each boat had brought across approximately 15–20 soldiers.

One company of the 31st Division, for instance, was organized as follows: The first boat transported two *sturmpatrouillen* (18 men total) and two grenade carriers. The second and third boat each transported two more *sturmpatrouillen*, while the fourth boat transported a machine gun section with 15 men and two guns. The fifth boat carried two more *sturmpatrouillen*, while the sixth boat transported another 15 man machine gun squad with two machine guns. Finally the seventh and eighth boats each transported two additional *sturmpatrouillen*.

Apart from the machine guns, the stormtroopers were heavily armed with hand grenades, flamethrowers, rifles, daggers and bayonets.

The infantry landings began at 0600 while the artillery preparation was still in full swing. These were aided by a thick smokescreen laid by Austrian artillery that together with the fog greatly hampered visibility. Another factor that facilitated the initial surprise was that the stormtroopers had gained a head start by hiding in islands and bushes near the edge of the river. Once the artillery lengthened its fire they immediately entered into action taking by surprise Italian sentries and frontline posts with hand grenades and flamethrowers. The 31st was the first to land onshore and when its stormtroopers reached the southern bank they stormed the Italian outposts along the river, which were completely overrun by 0615.

13th *Schützen* Division crossed the Piave near Soligo and its 24th and 25th *Schützen* Regiments, supported by advanced positioned machine guns on Soligo island, overran Italian positions on the Montello. Lastly, the 17th Infantry Division crossed the Piave near Nervesa. Its first assault wave, consisting of the stormtroopers of the 39th and 46th Infantry regiment, overwhelmed Italian sentries and machine gun posts located on the sandbanks.

Thus, by 0700 the observation posts and the first line of defense had been completely overwhelmed and the Austrian troops with the stormtroopers still in the lead began to advance in small groups against the more durable second line of defense.

An Italian officer, whose unit was located near the bank of the river, reports how the *sturmtruppen* circumvented his machine gun strong point by executing German-like infiltration tactics:

> At 0930 the first 100 strong enemy unit appeared at a distance of 300 meters from our machine gun position. Once we spotted them I ordered the machine gun crew and the riflemen to open fire immediately. The enemy however took full advantage of the wooded terrain and was able to circumvent our strong-point and then put it out of action.[129]

By midday three infantry columns comprised respectively by troops of the 13th, 17th and 31st Divisions had broken through the Italian lines between Nervesa and Casa Serena and advance deeply into the combat zone. The Austro-Hungarian official history reports that the troops used primarily flamethrowers, hand grenades, and bayonets to circumvent up to 200 machine gun and light artillery units and advance approximately five miles into the Italian deployment.[130]

Although several Italian artillery squads fought hard in order to maintain possession of their guns, once the latter were seized they were immediately turned against the retreating Italian forces.

129 Roberto Tessari, *Il Montello nella grande guerra* (Udine: Gaspari Editore, 2004), p. 34.
130 Edmund Glaise-Horstenau (ed.), *Österreich-Ungarns letzter Krieg, vol. 7*, p. 261.

By night-time all divisional units had managed to cross the river and had also begun to transport mid- and large-sized guns across the river in order to pursue the retreating Italian units.

On the second day of the offensive the Austrian forces were able to take possession of the enemy stronghold of Casa Serena but were unable to proceed further due to several factors. The main ones being the lack of reserves and the inability to bring more guns on the right bank of the river due to bad weather and the flooding of the bridges. The second factor was the new defensive deployment used by the Italians, an elastic defense of sorts where the front trenches were lightly held mainly as outposts and behind them a true combat zone where the enemy offensive was met. This zone was defended by numerous machine gun emplacements, lone sniper nests and small artillery positions which exacted heavy casualties amongst the Austro-Hungarian infantry. In addition, strong reserves were held in the rear to counter-attack and restore the line of defense. These units intervened on the third day of fighting in the Piave to forcefully fight off the enemy infiltration. Moreover, the Italian artillery by then was heavily engaged in impeding the crossing of the Piave by the reserves, only a few Austrian artillery pieces were successfully transported onshore to support the infantry assault. Most bridges were blown up by the enemy artillery.

Lower Piave River

The objective of the Isonzo Army was to advance toward Treviso while crossing the Piave at Cimadolmo and San Dona'.

The XVI Corps, comprised of 58th and 33rd Infantry Divisions, was deployed as the northern column of the Isonzo Army and was scheduled to attack Italian positions near Papadopoli Island. These positions were manned by the 31st Infantry Division with its *Veneto* and *Caserta* Brigades.

As the Austrian official history asserts in this sector of the frontline the artillery duel decided the outcome of the offensive from the onset. "When the Austrian artillery fire began the enemy was at first almost silent, but after 0400 the thunder of the Italian batteries quickly mounted and by 0700 was louder than ours."[131] As a result of Italian counter-battery fire when the assault units of the 58th Division advanced, mainly its *Sturmbaon*, and 2nd and 11th *Jäger* Battalions, they not only found that the enemy's machine gun posts had not been neutralized but that the Italian artillery continued to target them. These brave units suffered great casualties from enemy fire and initially could not advance very far from the river. While some units were immobilized by the enemy fire, some strong stormtrooper detachments advanced into the third Italian line, where they held on for five hours. But once the Italian infantry counter-attacked these units were pushed back. The Austrian official history states that "The assault troops on the western bank, fighting with the courage of desperation, finally had to yield to strong counter-attacks. Only small remnants of these

131 Ibid., p. 262.

heroic detachments managed to swim back to Papadopoli Island, taking about two dozen prisoners with them."[132]

The same strong artillery fire impeded progress by the 106th Infantry Regiment (33rd Infantry Division) and storm battalions of the 33rd and 7th Divisions and 10 mountain batteries. Once on shore nearby Salettuol the 106th was shot to pieces losing 1,200 men in just a few hours. The stormtrooper battalions also suffered many casualties.

The IV Corps, comprised mainly by the 64th and 70th Infantry Divisions, was to be the spearhead of the Isonzo Army and was supposed to be the first group to reach Treviso. But this group, deployed on four infantry columns, was also heavily targeted at the onset of the offensive by the Italian artillery which decimated its ranks. As the infantry units began to attack, the two flanking columns of both divisions were unsuccessful due to heavy enemy fire. In contrast, the 128th and 207th Infantry Brigades, the two columns acting in the middle of the Austro-Hungarian deployment were much more successful. Once onshore they drove back several units of the enemy's 31st and 45th Divisions, and captured the first defensive line. Immediately after they seized the second line east of Candelu' and Italian trenches near San Bartolomeo.

In the afternoon, however, the Italians counter-attacked and halted the Austro-Hungarian advance near the Treviso fortifications. The assault units were pushed back all the way to the river. "Ceaseless Italian artillery fire and bombing raids by enemy planes hindered the movement of reinforcements to the western bank. The bridges leading to the island were also bombarded."[133]

To the South of VI Army Corps, the VII Corps forces were supposed to break through the enemy positions and reach Punto Sile with the 14th and 24th Infantry Divisions. While the 24th Division was targeted by strong enemy fire, the 14th was able to advance and take numerous enemy strong points. This unit was the most successful of the Isonzo Army with the capture of 58 officers and 2,351 men. Greatly supported by the artillery that paralyzed Italian batteries with gas and high-explosive shelling and laid a thick smokescreen, the attacking stormtroops surged forward.

The latter bypassed and overwhelmed the Italian strongholds on the bank of the river and subsequently attacked the second line of defense. The stormtroopers continued to advance at a very fast pace and by late evening on 15 June, by infiltrating small groups into the enemy lines, had reached the enemy's artillery on the Montello. Several light artillery and mortar positions were overwhelmed by the assault units hurling hand grenades. By that time, nine Italian battalions and 18 machine gun companies of the 58th Division had been put out of action.

Ultimately, however, the Austro-Hungarians were able to advance in several sectors up to the third Italian line of defense, but were then pushed back by a combination of enemy interdiction and counter-battery fire and infantry counter-attacks.

132 Ibid., p. 262.
133 Ibid., p. 263.

The Italian Army with its new zonal defensive in depth system on the Piave was able to repel the last offensive of the Dual Monarchy in the Battle of the Solstice in June 1918. Everywhere, on both river and mountainous fronts, the Austro-Hungarian stormtroopers and infantry were first repulsed by defensive fire and finally counter-attacked by infantry reserve units. The tally of the losses showing 118,000 Austro-Hungarians either killed, injured or missing versus 86,000 Italians clearly indicated that the Habsburg Monarchy had sustained a major defeat. "For negligible gain, the offensive flower of the army had been lost."[134]

The AOK's report that followed the Piave Offensive asserted that the failure to breach the Italian defenses was due to a number of factors during the attacks. One of them was the lack of coordination between stormtrooper and infantry units. Moreover, because commanders improperly deployed the former in concentrated rather than in small assault formations, the stormtroopers were unable generally to penetrate beyond the Italian third line of defense.[135]

Another factor identified both by the post-battle report and by historian Peter Fiala was the lack of strong reserve units. In general at the end of day two of the offensive the Austro-Hungarian troops were no longer capable of any substantial movement toward the plains. They were exhausted after 48 hours of continued fighting and the AOK did not have substantial reserves to throw into the battle and further press the Italian defenses. Moreover, the AOK could not supply an adequate number of lorries or horses to move the troops and most importantly the artillery forward.[136]

A third factor was the lack of viable equipment that stymied the offensive. "A very depressing surprise was the ineffectiveness of our poison gas. Its chemical composition was short-lived, and so on 15 June the contents of many rounds had already broken down and acted only as irritants. Most of the Italians, on the other hand, were now equipped with excellent English gas masks."[137]

The final factor that lead to the failure of the offensive was the inadequate artillery preparation for the result desired. For example, up to a third of the ammunition did not explode. Also, "rigidly timed rolling barrages did not work either while fighting in the mountainous terrain of the Tyrol or while fording a major river in Venetia."[138] Therefore while the barrage lasted longer than at Caporetto it was grossly ineffective due to its rigidity and the below average quality of some of the ammunition.

From the unbiased long term perspective of the historian, it also appears clear that the AOK by deploying the stormtroopers as the vanguard of the infantry assault committed these troops too early as the former had to fight their way through the four enemy defensive lines and especially the vast combat zone between the second and third line. By the second day of fighting the stormtroopers, debilitated by thinning ranks

134 William R. Griffiths, *The Great War*, p. 151

135 Sammelheft Erfahrungen Heft 5 Vienna 1918. Cited in Christian Ortner, *Storm Troops*, p. 271.

136 Peter Fiala, *Die letzte Offensive Altösterreichs. Führungsprobleme und Führerverantwortlichkeit bei der öst.-ung. Offensive in Venetien, Juni 1918* (Boppard a. Rh.: Boldt, 1967), p. 91.

137 Edmund Glaise-Horstenau (ed.), *Österreich-Ungarns letzter Krieg, vol. 7*, p. 423.

138 Holger H. Herwig, *The First World War*, p. 372.

and little ammunition, were no longer capable of breaking through the fourth line of defense. To maximize their effectiveness, these special units should probably have been deployed once infantry had overtaken the first and second line of defense. The other major tactical mistake, as Austrian historian Christian Ortner has pointed out, was the lack of proper extensive reconnaissance prior to the offensive preventing the Austro-Hungarian Army from determining that the enemy had moved from a linear to a zonal defensive strategy on the Piave. More detailed prior knowledge of the new defensive system would have most likely led the AOK to favor much more concentrated attacks.

The authoritative "The Great War" book issued by the United States' West Point Military Academy focuses on the divisions within the Austro-Hungarian military elite to explain the lack of success of the Solstice Offensive:

> Boroevic and Conrad each insisted on conducting the major offensive against the Italian line in his own sector. The resulting dispersion of forces denied both of the attacks the combat power necessary for decisive results. On the tactical level, the operations were designed to follow the successful infiltration tactics of the German army. However they were of inferior quality, suffering from poor coordination, lack of surprise, and the selection of unrealistic objectives. The Austrian version of breakthrough tactics also lacked the highly trained stormtroopers and the strong reserves that had insured German success in the spring.[139]

Although from a strategic perspective the above conclusion is correct, its judgment on the stormtroopers and in general on Austro-Hungarian infantry tactics appears to be too harsh. The Austro-Hungarian stormtroopers were not of an inferior quality to the German infantry assault units since their training was as exhaustive and their weapons were of similar quality. Moreover, the major defect of the Solstice Offensive was not with its execution, but with its initial planning and its unrealistic objectives. Due to squabbles between the major army commanders, the offensive, instead of focusing upon a narrow section of the frontline with maximum force, dispersed infantry units over extremely vast sections of the frontline. Even the most resolute and elite German stormtrooper units could not have overcome the initial mistakes in the planning phase of the offensive.

Even though the offensive proved to be a failure for the Austro-Hungarian Army, the stormtroopers fought well and resulted as one of the most effective branches involved in this massive operation. Three local successes in particular demonstrated what these special assault units were capable of. First and foremost, the 27th Infantry Division's *Sturmbaon* breaching three consecutive Italian defensive lines and capturing in rapid succession Col Fenilon, Col Fagheron and most importantly Col Moschin. Their very successful advance into the Italian defense was ultimately halted not because the stormtroopers did not push hard enough but because the AOK was unable to support them at the most critical time. Lack of reinforcements and ammunition finally halted their most promising advance in the Mount Grappa sector. Second, the mountain

139 William R. Griffiths, *The Great War*, p. 150.

assault unit of the 1st Division was able to capture the Monticelli and the Corno di Cavento under the most difficult conditions. This unit courageously disregarding enemy artillery and machine gun fire that rained upon the men captured one of the highest mountain peaks of the Trentino frontline with an audacious alpine maneuver. Third, stormtroopers of the 31st, 13th and 17th Divisions advanced for more than five miles into Italian defenses on the Montello capturing along the way an exceedingly high number of enemy machine guns and artillery pieces. These troops were also forced to halt their advance as a result of the lack of reinforcements and were eventually cut-off from their divisional infantry and ultimately forced to retreat. Had they not lacked the manpower to exploit their early gains, the stormtroopers might have been able to advance much further. As historian Christian Ortner asserts: "Despite the large number of available combat patrols, they were simply not enough to take all the objectives in the combat zone. This was one of the causes, why the offensive on the Piave River in June 1918 failed."[140] Despite the failure of the massive operation, the official AOK report on the Solstice Offensive justifiably recognized their efforts by stating that the stormtroopers "proved themselves excellently."[141] Rather, General Arz von Straussenburg argued that the failure of the offensive had been the result of gas shells that had proved ineffective because the Italians had been equipped with British manufactured gas masks, of the heavy rains that preceded the offensive that slowed down the troops, and because Czech officers from the 56th Infantry Regiment had deserted and had pre-warned the Italians of the impending attack. He defended the operation by stating that by tying down Allied troops the Austro-Hungarian Army had been spared "an equally bloody, sacrificial defensive battle."[142]

Thus, the causes of the defeat of the Austro-Hungarian Army during the Battle of the Solstice cannot be attributed to the lack of vigor on the part of the attacking infantry units but mainly to broader unresolved strategic issues in connection to the implementation of the operation. First, unlike the German led Caporetto Offensive both Conrad and Boroevic insisted on attacking on both the Piave and the mountainous sector of the frontline leading to a huge and unnecessary dispersal of forces that ultimately led to the weakening of the assaulting thrust. Second, the assault plan was unlikely to succeed because it envisioned a breakthrough in Conrad's mountainous sector where it was very difficult to punch through the Italian lines given the rough terrain and the formidable defenses. While on Mount Grappa the Italian positions consisted primarily of entrenched high-altitude bastions, on the Asiago Altopiano they were centered on a network of trenches, studded with machine-gun nests, situated within a forest. The Austro-Hungarian official history post-battle report states that Conrad failed to consider the difficulties associated with the rugged terrain of the Altopiano: "There is hardly any example in military history where an army has conducted an attack against a forest in closed formations according to plan."[143]

140 www.austro-hungarian-army.co.uk <Accessed 7 October 2016>
141 Kriegsarchiv: AOK, MKSN 69–6–14, 'Junischlacht in Venetien', 14 July 1918.
142 Ibid.
143 Edmund Glaise-Horstenau (ed.), *Österreich-Ungarns letzter Krieg, vol. 7*, p. 353.

At the same time Field Marshal Boroevic is faulted in the same document for pressing ahead a frontal attack against defenders that had superior weapons and were dug in in well-fortified positions.

The official document failed to point out, however, that throughout the frontline the Italians had transitioned from linear toward zonal defenses with four consecutive parallel trenchlines. Each of which had to be painstakingly conquered. Moreover, the Italian main forces and artillery, with their in depth positions, where beyond the reach of the Austro-Hungarian gunners. The dispersal of forces between Conrad and Boroveic's simultaneous offensives did not allow the AOK to send in reinforcements and ammunition in the sectors of the front line where the assault infantry advance had resulted in local breakthroughs.

Last Raids and Planned Attacks

The Zugna mountain chain spreads from Rovereto to the Vallarsa Valley forming a huge natural barrier in the Trentino. Given its strategic position most of its peaks were occupied by the Austro-Hungarians during the major offensive in the spring of 1916. Accordingly, the latter held Mount Zugna and the Zugna Torta, while the Italians held the positions in the valley below, the so-called Trincerone. The opposing trenches where separated by a very thin area of no man's land that was only 40 feet long and given the closeness of the positions both sides proceeded to bomb and machine gun the opponent from close range on a daily basis.

According to Austrian historian von Lichem conditions on the Zugna were appalling for both armies: "The enemy kept Austrian trenches under heavy gun and mortar fire day and night. The dugouts were infested by rats. Several corpses laid in no man's land along with the unburied head of an NCO of the Kaiserschützen."[144] The Zugna strongpoint was held by one company of *alpini* from *Monte Suello* Battalion, a machine gun and a grenade launching section. It was surrounded by five rounds of barbed wire and fortified by a concrete cement wall called Trincerone.

On 23 August 1918 the position was attacked by one *sturmkompagnie* and one infantry company of the IV Battalion/2nd *Kaiserschützen* Regiment whose objective was to seize and hold the Trincerone. At 0523 Austro-Hungarian artillery began concentrated fire against the Zugna from multiple positions including the nearest post on Zugna Torta and also with one battery of 30.5 cm and 28 cm howitzers. Brief artillery barrages were daily occurrences in this sector of the frontline and as a result the Italian defenders initially failed to take any heightened precautions. At 0545 an Austro-Hungarian assault platoon attempted to force its way past the wire but was repulsed by the *alpini* with hand grenades. Soon after the artillery bombardment resumed with more brute force comprised of a greater percentage of heavy mortar shells. The focus by then was exclusively upon the Trincerone, the trenches and the passageways leading to the local Italian command center and the artillery

144 Heinz von Lichem, *La Guerra in Montagna, Vol. 2* (Bolzano: Athesia, 2007), p. 146.

emplacements. At 0600 the fire was moved forward and soon after the stormtroopers attacked with the support of several flanking machine gun units. Though pushed back in several sectors on the right flank, the stormtroopers overwhelmed the enemy's advanced left flank position. Despite disruptive counter-battery fire, the two Austro-Hungarian companies managed to cut through the Italian forward defenses and were involved in fierce hand-to-hand fighting with the *alpini*.

Ultimately, after both sides had suffered casualties, the Austro-Hungarians were pushed back by a prompt enemy counter-attack witnessed by the fact that the dead Austrian commander's body along with those of several of his men remained tangled in the wire.

Despite the courageous charge of the stormtroopers and infantrymen against considerable concentrated enemy fire, the operation failed for a number of reasons. The main one being the lack of effectiveness and precision of the artillery fire. Approximately a third of the medium shells failed to explode, while several heavy shells were fired too high and missed the target altogether. The faltering of the artillery fire demonstrated a lack of proper preparation of the attack and the poor state of supplies and ammunition of the Austro-Hungarian Army during the latter stage of the war. With its industrial complex in decline and lacking primary resources, the soldiers in the frontline no longer had adequate equipment to conduct the war.

The second reason for the failure of the operation was the lack of surprise and the failure to breach the wire.

Counter-attack on Mount Majo

Mount Majo, the strategic 1,499 meter high mountain peak overlooking the Posina Valley, had been seized by the Austro-Hungarians in May 1916. In 1918 the position, consisting of several high altitude machine gun emplacements and deep caverns and trenches drilled into the rock, had been turned into a true mountain fortress by its 350 soldier strong 3rd *Kaiserjäger* Regiment garrison. Given its key position blocking the main route to Rovereto, the Italians had set their eyes on capturing Mount Majo for some time and its V Army Corps finally planned for a surprise attack to take place in late August 1918. At 0545 on 30 August several field and mountain guns began to pound upon Mount Majo's defenses and an hour later three infantry columns (two of *bersaglieri* and one led by XXXI *Reparto d'assalto*) charged against the Austro-Hungarian positions. At first the *arditi* unit, by advancing swiftly and as close as possible to the advancing barrage, was able to storm an enemy unit and capture it almost in its entirety. Its sally was executed so quickly, that the 30-man strong enemy advanced garrison "was caught as breakfast and coffee was still being distributed to the ranks."[145] Soon after the *arditi* unit continued to advance by entering into the labyrinth-like main positions in order to mop them up one by one with the aid

145 Ufficio Storico, Rep. E-2, Racc. 88 1. Armata: Comando V Corpo d'armata, 'Fatto d'arme del 30 Agosto 1918 su M. Majo', n. 7143, 5 September 1918.

of hand grenades, rifle butts, bayonets and flamethrowers. Here they engaged the Austrian alpine units for almost the whole day in protracted struggles to clear and occupy the enemy positions. The fighting was extremely intense as a result of the intricate defensive system that allowed the *Kaiserjägers* to wage a guerrilla type battle. As the Austrians weaned in and out of their positions to then suddenly and unexpectedly attack the enemy and vanish at will into the various tunnels of their cavern system, the *arditi* suffered several losses. Despite the fierce opposition encountered, however, the *arditi* by the evening had been able to irrupt by force into the enemy's main positions and had eliminated several opponents concealed behind the mountain cliff and the caverns with the help of grenades and flamethrowers and had also silenced several machine guns. But while the *arditi* had been able to penetrate deeply into the enemy deployment and were fighting to gain a major foothold into the rear positions, the two *bersaglieri* columns had not been as fortunate. The third column, in particular, acting on the right flank had been counter-attacked in force and this swift strike by a very determined *Kaiserjäger* unit had thwarted its offensive momentum on its tracks. As a result, it was forced to pull back leaving the two other columns exposed to a potential enemy envelopment. Eventually these two flanking columns, were also forced to retreat in order to avoid being cut off and captured by the enemy counter-thrust. The latter, undertaken mainly by *Kaiserjägers* and stormtroopers, demonstrated that the special units were used once again very effectively by the Austro-Hungarian Army as a strategic tactical reserve.

According to the Austro-Hungarian official history:

> The continuing battle-readiness of our units from the alpine lands was also demonstrated in a defensive action at the end of August involving troops of the *Kaiserjäger* Division. In the morning of 30 August, after several hours of destructive artillery fire, an Italian assault battalion attacked the summit of Mount Majo, which was held by two companies of 3rd *Kaiserjäger*. The enemy were able to conquer this strong point only after the majority of the garrison had been killed, wounded or buried alive in their shot-up positions. Other *Kaiserjägers* from the 3rd Regiment, supported by parts of the *Kaiserjäger* storm battalion, counter-attacked twice and took back the mountain summit. The Italians fell back to their starting-points, having suffered extraordinarily high casualties under our effective artillery fire during their defeat.[146]

In the post battle report the commander of the V Army Corps lamented the fact that the *arditi* and the *bersaglieri* had opened themselves up to the enemy counter-thrust by not moving forward in a more cohesive and uniform fashion: "Initially we did not take into proper consideration the distances that the right and left flank columns had to thread. … when XXXI *Reparto* stormed the position causing widespread alarm, the second column (Vicini) was still half way to the objective and the enemy was

146 Edmund Glaise-Horstenau (ed.), *Österreich-Ungarns letzter Krieg, vol. 7*, p. 461.

quick to fire upon it."[147] The Austro-Hungarian casualties were reported as 100 dead, 25 wounded and 29 prisoners, while the Italians suffered 106 dead, 210 wounded and 60 missing.

In another raid the stormtroopers combined their special assault training with their experienced mountaineering skills which, has the Austrian official history reports, led to the conquer of one of the tallest peaks in the Tonale/Adamello sector. The Battle of Mount San Matteo was the last astonishing victory of the Austro-Hungarian stormtroopers and its mountain units. Its objective was to retake possession of the 3,678 meter high mountain resulting in a confrontation that raged on the highest altitude of the Italian Front. The battle took place on 3 September 1918 under the code name Operation *Gemse* and saw the participation of the following units: 3rd *sturmkompagnie*/22nd *Schützen* Division, 21st and 30th *Hochgebirgskompagnie*, 2nd *Bergführer-kompagnie* and 150 soldiers of 1st *Kaiserschützen* Regiment with 10 machine guns while the artillery support was provided by 28 medium and light guns and by one 30.5 cm howitzer. All batteries involved were brought up by hand, along with 22,700 shells, to the nearby Monte Valley prior to the start of operations.[148]

The artillery bombardment began promptly at 1830 and lasted approximately 20 minutes with the shells from the 30.5 cm howitzer inflicting horrendous damage upon the enemy defenses. Soon after the mountain units and the stormtroopers moved forward:

> The storm groups were able to climb the cliffs undetected by the enemy and to reach the ice caverns of the Punta San Matteo. Despite the Italian artillery fire, from this point they continued to climb in a bold maneuver over walls of ice and granite, and recovered both of the summits (Punta San Matteo and Monte Mantello) overlooking the glaciers. In mopping up the enemy trenches they also took a substantial number of prisoners plus many machine guns and trench mortars.[149]

The Austro-Hungarians lost 17 soldiers (two officers and 15 soldiers), while the Italians lost 10 and several others were captured. Stormtrooper First Lieutenant Wilhelm Licka who led 3rd *sturmkompagnie*/22nd *Schützen* Division received the Knight's Cross of the Military Maria Theresia Order for this successful operation. Most interestingly, the bodies of three of these Austro-Hungarian soldiers killed in the battle were found perfectly preserved in the glacier in 2004, almost 100 years later. This was the last significant offensive victory of the Austro-Hungarian stormtroopers before the end of the war.[150]

147 Ufficio Storico, Rep E-2, Racc. 88 1. Armata: Comando V Corpo d'armata, 'Fatto d'arme del 30 Agosto 1918 su M. Majo', n. 7143, 5 September 1918.

148 Walther Schaumann, 'Der österreichische Gegennagriff auf die Punta San Matteo (3692 m ü. m.) am 3 September 1918', *Allgemeine Schweizerische Militärzeitschrift*, n. 10, 1968, p. 582.

149 Edmund Glaise-Horstenau (ed.), *Österreich-Ungarns letzter Krieg, vol. 7*, p. 515.

150 http://news.bbc.co.uk/2/hi/europe/3592268.stm <Accessed 25 August 2016>

Conclusion

Military historian Paddy Griffith has argued that toward the end of the war the tactics associated with the small-scale raid were in some cases more successful that large scale attacks. These operations were less costly in terms of both human life and equipment spent or lost during battle, and in many instances, they achieved similar goals. "Trench raids were admittedly not always successful, and many were unnecessarily costly; but by the end of the war they had evolved into almost a complete alternative to the set piece attack by a large body of men."[151]

They were useful for inflicting casualties as well as for gaining control of enemy posts and terrain. They were generally less costly and did not place an undue burden on the army's stock of ammunition and weapons. They were also a demonstration of how most armies had transitioned from the deployment of large standard infantry units to smaller but much more highly specialized units. The stormtroopers represented the culmination of this infantry specialization process for the Austro-Hungarian Army. These highly specialized, highly trained and equipped units achieved territorial gains leading to the capture of an exceedingly high number of enemy soldiers and weapons by routinely executing small-scale raids and counter-attacks. Even when deployed in a major offensive these troops achieved important successes by executing infiltration tactics that could probably have been more fully exploited by the bulk of the army. Particularly successful, were the counter-attacks led by the stormtroopers that were often successful in taking back possession of important positions that had been previously captured by the Italians. The stormtroopers combination of flamethrowers, hand grenade and light machine gun units was instrumental in breaking down Italian resistance after surprise attacks. These operations proved particularly successful given the good collaboration between stormtroopers and artillery units and whereby the former excelled in following up their attacks immediately after the artillery had blasted the enemy's position. By adopting German-inspired tactics the stormtroopers often penetrated deeply into enemy territory, in many cases reaching the rear positions and knocking out key infrastructure, so that the bulk of the infantry could advance and consolidate the gains.

A little less successful were the stormtroopers when deployed in large-scale offensive operations. The Caporetto Offensive was primarily a victory of German arms and tactics, but the Austro-Hungarian stormtroopers proved themselves as top rate assault units. During the Solstice Offensive in particular, the Austro-Hungarians were incapable or unwilling to move forward cohesively and in some sectors of the frontline the attacks conducted by both standard infantry and stormtroopers were too disjointed and often did not succeed in the much sought-after penetration of the Italian defenses. Moreover, the lack of proper continuous support provided by the artillery as the infantry advanced and passed the initial range led to the ultimate failure of the infantry assault.

151 Paddy Griffith, *Battle Tactics of the Western Front: The British Army's Art of Attack 1916–18* (New Haven: Yale University Press, 1996), p. 62.

In any case, the stormtrooper tactics, along with the effective use of artillery, developed by the Austro-Hungarian Army were one of the elements responsible for giving Austria-Hungary a tactical lead over the Italians, until at least the beginning of 1918. With fewer infantry forces and artillery weapons, the Austro-Hungarian Army, bolstered by the fact that it was holding very high altitude positions, was able to fight off successfully most Italian advances with the stormtroopers inflicting heavy casualties on their enemy with swift raids and counter-attacks. These operations were usually carried out with the aid of detailed planning and fully supported by pinpoint barrages and in most cases they obtained the desired outcome. The excellent training, the new weapons and the tactics of the stormtroopers were one of the factors that enabled the Austro-Hungarian Army to fight off the advances of the Italians for many months.

The timing of the emergence of the Austro-Hungarian stormtroopers was also of critical importance to the overall defensive cohesiveness of the Habsburg Army. The emergence of these units in early 1917 resulted in an overall improvement in the fighting qualities and in the morale of the army, which without the stormtroopers and other specialist units such as the pioneers would likely have further declined in its overall combat efficiency. Given that the Austro-Hungarian Army was for the most part deployed defensively and was worn down by the many months of fighting on a multi-front war, when the stormtroopers emerged an almost sudden change occurred. The emergence of the specialty trained troops not only was responsible for an increase in effectiveness of the standard infantry units that fought alongside the stormtroopers, but also in the successful execution of several raids and planned attacks that yielded significant numbers of casualties and prisoners. Both factors also had positive repercussions on troop morale.

Austro-Hungarian stormtrooper operational tactical deployment as outlined in their training manual can be summarized as follows:

1. Extensive intelligence gathering of the enemy's defenses with the aid of aerial reconnaissance.
2. The execution of several operational rehearsals thus leaving nothing to improvisation.
3. A swift but intense artillery preparation barrage using, large and medium batteries.
4. Close coordination between the lengthening of the artillery barrage and the start of the infantry charge.
5. Infantry attack to be concentrated over a narrow section of the enemy's defensive line.
6. Widespread recourse to hand grenades, machine guns, flamethrowers and mortars during the attack.
7. The infiltration of small, highly autonomous, *Sturmtruppen* platoons beyond the enemy's first defensive line with the task of taking out key enemy defensive posts.
8. The consolidation of the attack with the regular infantry battalions closely following the lead of the *Sturmtruppen* units.

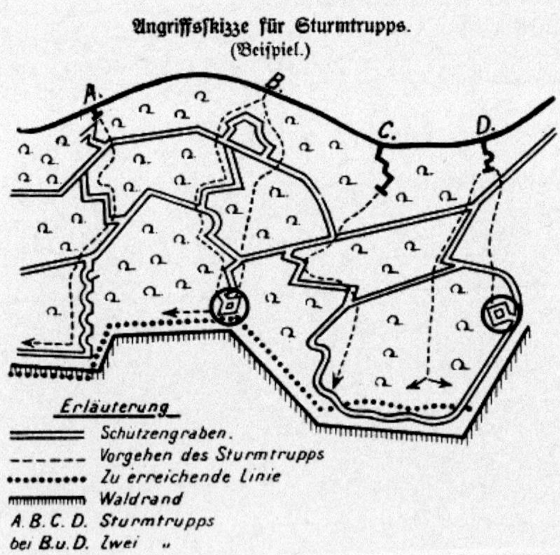

This sketch is taken from the *sturmtruppen* instruction manual and it shows how the special bomb launching squads were to invade and take possession of an enemy trenchline of defense by penetrating from different directions and by maintaining the initiative at all times with the launching of several hand grenades.

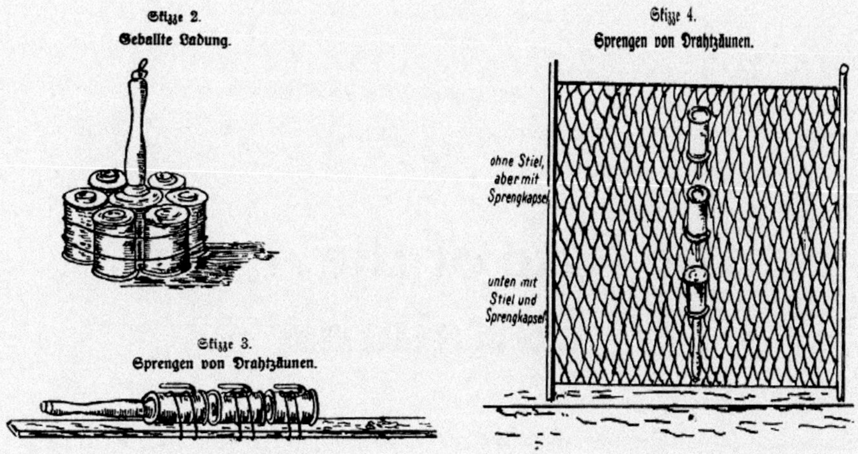

The sketches from the *sturmtruppen* instruction manual show different ways in which hand grenades could be used as detonating devices to destroy the enemy wire. The stormtroopers combined an attacking element with an engineering/trench-busting element.

5

The Rise of the *Arditi* Battalions

By the spring of 1917 the Italian *Comando Supremo* had recognized the threat posed by the newly formed Austro-Hungarian stormtrooper units along the Isonzo and the Trentino front lines. By then these special units had carried out a number of successful operations such as the costly raid on Mount Pasubio and especially the counter-attack on the Flondar which had led to the capture of several thousands of Italian infantrymen. These Austrian successes, which had been widely reported by Italian intelligence reports, led *Comando Supremo* to face the uncomfortable truth that Italian infantry units were facing better trained, more heavily armed and more forceful assault units than before and that these units were also using novel tactics.

An Italian intelligence report published in January 1917, after the stormtroops had already been deployed in a few successful raids aimed at capturing prisoners and weapons, warned that:

> According to several statements made by Austrian prisoners of war, the Austro-Hungarian Army has recently formed special assault units, the so-called Sturm abteilung. These units, typically consisting of thirty men squads, are comprised of handpicked soldiers from standard infantry battalions. They are tasked with being the vanguards of infantry assaults to breach enemy lines and overcome any resistance by throwing hundreds of hand grenades. The *Sturmtruppen* have been created for the specific purpose of carrying out swift and daring offensive operations based on the element of surprise that aim to destroy enemy units and positions, capture prisoners, and generally cause panic within enemy ranks. Moreover, these units have also been used as vanguards of major offensive operations. Their tactical role appears to be the breaching of enemy positions and the destruction of key strong points in order to prepare the way for a broad infantry advance. From time to time, they have also been deployed in raids against trenches in order to assess enemy strength, locate key positions such as machine gun nests and artillery emplacements as well as seek out the most expedient route to breach them. In order to carry out these difficult and dangerous tasks, the *Sturmtruppen* are carefully handpicked often by selecting the bravest

> infantry soldiers from each regiment. Most recruits are volunteers while some are designated by their superiors. Once selected, the recruits attend a four week training course focused upon mastering the art of throwing hand grenades from a host of different positions, the destruction of key enemy posts and trenches, etc. … The *Sturmtruppen* have helmets and wire cutters and are armed with knives and several hand grenades. They enjoy special privileges such as being exempt from standard line infantry duties and are better fed.[1]

A week later the *Comando Supremo* warned frontline commanders in the Carnic Alps sector of the new enemy offensive/raiding tactics that had resulted in the capture of prisoners and machine guns undertaken by small enemy raiding parties that had attacked by surprise and without the aid of the artillery. The enemy troops had hurled themselves against Italian frontline defenses by lobbing hand grenades and firing their weapons in the dead of night. The report stated that the raids had been very effectively executed and had inflicted casualties against the Italian frontline troops. The same report stated that frontline commanders should train their troops by emulating the raiding techniques of the Austro-Hungarian stormtroopers.[2]

Another intelligence report provided a detailed breakdown of how the Austrian stormtrooper units were organized:

> This report is based on the statements given by a Czech prisoner of war belonging to the Jagdkommando of the 21st Infantry who was captured on the night of 11 March 1917 near our trench positions on Hill 144. The unit (Streifkorps) is under the command of the 21st Infantry and is comprised by an assault group (Jagdkommando), a hand grenade launching group (Handgranatenwer ferabteilung), a mortar unit (Minenwerferabteilung), a grenade launching group (Granatenwerferabteilung) and a flamethrower unit (Flammenwerferabteilung). The Jagdkommando has a force of approximately 250 soldiers which is based on two Jagdzuge (each with 50 soldiers) led by a lieutenant and two Sturmpatrouillen (assault patrols) each of which has approximately 75 soldiers and is led by a Offizierstellvertreter.[3]

Yet another intelligence report issued by *Comando Supremo* further elaborated on the assault tactics adopted by the Austro-Hungarian *sturmtruppen*:

1 Ufficio Storico: Promemoria del Reparto Operazioni del Comando Supremo alla segreteria del capo di stato maggiore dell'esercito, 'Reparti d'assalto nell'esercito Austro-ungarico', 23 January 1917.

2 Ufficio Storico: Comando Supremo, foglio n. 1975, Ufficio Situazione ed Operazioni di Guerra, 31 January, 1917.

3 Ufficio Storico: Promemoria di servizio n.9 del Centro Informazioni del comando XX corpo d'armata, 'Corso d'istruzione per truppe d'assalto (da due prigionieri austriaci del 73. reggimento di fanteria'), 23 February 1917.

> Their operations are generally supported by a massive concentration of fire by the artillery upon the targeted enemy positions. Then the *Sturmtruppen* erupt into the enemy trenches armed primarily with hand grenades and knives along with the proper equipment to make gaps in the barbed wire. Usually small infantry support units act as the second wave of the attack. The principal characteristic of *Sturmtruppen* assaults is the element of surprise. These units take advantage of the state of confusion within the enemy's defenses created by the massive barrage to assail the enemy's first line of defense.[4]

These reports were meant to inform frontline commanders of one of the major innovations introduced into the conflict by the enemy as well as to familiarize them with the new tactics deployed by the stormtroopers. To familiarize with these tactics also meant that local commanders could better deploy their troops defensively in order to properly confront the stormtroopers. Ultimately, these intelligence reports also contributed to a general re-evaluation of Italian infantry tactics.

Although the Italian Army had first experimented with special assault detachments as early as 1915, the major push forward was undertaken only in 1917, in part as a consequence of the spread of the *sturmtruppen* within the Austro-Hungarian divisions deployed along the Italian front. As General Luigi Capello grudgingly admitted Austrian offensive successes of 1917 were due to "minute and exact preparation, in which the enemy has unfortunately hitherto been our master."[5]

Reforms to instruct and equip the Italian Army to fight more effectively in an environment of positional warfare were introduced slowly and gradually and some of the defensive tactics were only implemented after the jarring Caporetto debacle. As Gooch asserts "the first step toward a new tactical system came in 1917 with the creation of small assault units of picked men, the *Arditi*."[6]

The *arditi* were hence the first Italian response to overcome the impasse of trench warfare and in part they were constituted to emulate the Austrian example.

But before the constitution of the *arditi*, the Italian high command had already initiated some long term reforms aimed at creating more technically specialized standard infantry troops to complement the formation of special assault detachments. One such reform aimed at increasing the army's firepower and was centered on re-equipping frontline units for a long-term campaign of trench warfare. During 1917, the army continued to grow in strength with a total of two million men under arms but it also made vast improvements in firepower with the introduction of new, more effective weapons. Prior to the disaster at Caporetto, it is estimated that the Italian Army had approximately 7,000 pieces of artillery and 12,000 automatic weapons. By then vis-à-vis the beginning of the war it had made several technological advancements

4 Ufficio Storico, *Le Istruzioni tattiche del capo di stato maggiore dell'esercito negli anni 1917–18* (Rome: Ufficio Storico, 1980), p. 84.

5 Cited in John Gooch, *Italian Army*, p. 201.

6 John Gooch, 'Italy During the First World War', in Allan R. Millet and Williamson Murray (eds.), *Military Effectiveness* (Cambridge: Cambridge University Press, 2010), p. 180.

with the introduction of large-sized field guns as well as a greater number of machine guns and mortars. One of the foremost innovations made by the artillery branch was to introduce in 1916 several short- and mid-range mortar batteries to destroy the barbed wire, forts and pillboxes. The new 50 mm and 58 mm mortars proved to be an important asset to the Italian infantry giving it an edge over its adversary which did not have large stocks of mortars in this size range. Later in 1916 the Italian Army also introduced the more powerful 240 mm mortar which was deployed to destroy large-scale fortifications. This weapon greatly supported the advance of assault troops as stated in a directive issued by the *Comando Supremo*: "Mortars are very effective in destroying the wire and the trenches and to terrorize frontline enemy troops. They therefore constitute a means to support offensive operations and to greatly assist the assaulting infantry."[7]

The Austro-Hungarian official history, for example, states that the trench mortars were one of the distinctive advantages of the Italian Army: "Because of the course of the war, in which the Italian Army was on the offensive against stubborn defenders, and the new nature of positional fighting, it was necessary to create trench mortar formations. Italy had entered the war with 200 improvised mortars. The high command initiated a far-reaching expansion of their "Bombardier Corps" in winter 1915–16; by the end of 1916 there were 2,062 trench mortars (of 58 to 240 mm caliber), which were organized as sections and mixed groups."[8]

Trench mortars proved instrumental, for example, in the 1916 siege of Gorizia as their destructive fire paved the way for the advance of the assaulting infantry which took the town after its defenses had been obliterated by these powerful new weapons.

Large-sized mortars were also used to counteract what the Italian Army lacked in terms of heavy howitzers that were comparable to the Austro-Hungarian M16 30.5 cm *Skoda* large-sized gun. The Italian Army did introduce a 305 mm unit but it was found to be less effective than the Austrian counterpart. To counteract its disadvantage in the large artillery gun and howitzer segment, the Italian artillery often utilized large numbers of the 240 mm mortar batteries to prepare infantry assaults. Although the weapon was not as effective in destroying military infrastructure located in the second and third enemy defensive lines as its Austrian counterpart (the 240C version which was the short range mortar could achieve a maximum distance of 1,000 meters), the Army circumvented the problem by using several mortar batteries during each assault and by moving them forward after the first line had been taken. Mortars could be manufactured more quickly than field guns and were also cheaper to maintain in the field therefore they represented more than a stopgap solution to the lack of comparable large field howitzers.

The Air Force also had made several improvements mainly by fielding more aircraft for both reconnaissance and for strategic bombing missions. This was another sector in which the Italian Army vastly surpassed the productive capacity of its opponent

7 The circular is cited in: Basilio di Martino, *Trincee, Reticolati, e Colpi di Mano* (Valdagno: Rossato, 2000), p. 53.

8 Edmund Glaise-Horstenau (ed.), *Österreich-Ungarns letzter Krieg 1914–1918* , Vol. 4, p. 49.

and by 1918 Italian air superiority was keenly felt, especially in the preparation of large-scale infantry attacks. In the Battle of the Solstice, for example, the Italians deployed 600 airplanes to inflict casualties upon the retreating Austro-Hungarians.

Improvements were also made with crew-served weapons. Throughout 1916, and despite the fact that the army by then had been better equipped, there was still a widespread tendency on the part of infantry soldiers of not properly operating crew-served weapons and hand grenades. A directive issued by Cadorna, for instance, lamented the fact that while small teams of Austro-Hungarian soldiers armed with machine gun could break up enemy attacks, the Italian soldiers often deployed numerous machine guns in forward positions that were easily captured by the enemy. In the same document Cadorna also outlined that frontline inspections had revealed that hand grenades were found scattered over the trenches and were not utilized because the soldiers had not been trained on how to handle them and were apprehensive about injuries.

According to Cadorna these deficiencies were to be addressed by instituting training courses for specialist units such as the mortar and machine gun teams. These courses were held in February 1917 and slowly began to better familiarize the frontline troops with the positioning and handling of crew-served weapons.[9] By then the number of crew-served weapons such as machine guns and mortars of the standard infantry division had been considerably augmented vis-à-vis the beginning of the war. In addition, several commanders had instituted training centers for the troops so that attacking units learned how to properly handle and throw hand grenades. The newly trained specialist units were to be complemented by deeper and much more intricate trench systems and by newly formed, specially trained sentry platoons that patrolled no man's land during the night to pre-empt enemy stormtrooper raiding parties.

The last major reform centered on defensive deployment. As historian Liddell Hart asserts the Italian Army shared many of the tactical defensive deficiencies of the French Army, especially during the first two years of the war. French generals prior to Petain's ascendancy "insisted on the adoption of the long-exposed and wasteful system of massing the infantry of the defense in the forward positions. Besides giving the enemy guns a crowded and helpless target. This method ensured that, once the German guns had made a bloated meal of this luckless cannon-fodder, the German infantry would find practically no local reserves to oppose their progress through the rear zones."[10] Similarly, the Italians in Trentino in 1916 and at Caporetto in 1917 had maintained the bulk of their defenses on a forward line, with few tactical reserves in the rear to plug holes. The defensive posture had been disastrous and was one of the main factors leading to the Austro-Hungarian/German success during the 1917 offensive. After the Austro-Hungarian offensive of 1916 Cadorna had issued a directive titled "Criteri d'impiego della fanteria nella Guerra di trincea" in which he insisted that frontline troops should be deployed in a staggered system of defense rather than on a forward line and that the machine gun emplacements should be well concealed and strategically sited. The move

9 Ufficio Storico, Comando Supremo: Riparto Operazioni, n. 2456, Ufficio Affari Vari e Segreteria, 'Specializzazione dei compiti della fanteria,' 31 January, 1917.

10 Basil Henry Liddell Hart, *The Real War* (Boston: Little, Brown and Company, 1930), p. 413.

toward a zonal system of defense was only undertaken by certain frontline units, while the 2nd Army of General Capello did not effectively implement the guidelines of the directive prior to the Caporetto Battle. But as Gooch asserts "after the retreat from the Piave, Diaz revised defensive doctrine, locating artillery according to the range rather than simply positioning it forward, holding front lines more thinly and extending the defense to cover three separate zones rather than one."[11]

In essence, the Italian Army in 1918 finally transitioned from linear to zonal tactics of defense with the end result being a staggered defense in-depth system centered on a number of well-concealed, defiladed machine gun strong points. The artillery units were also moved much further to the rear being shielded as much as possible from enemy artillery shelling and positioned out of the range of forward enemy mortars or small mountain cannons. In addition, each infantry division by then had created special counter-attacking units that could be quickly dispatched to face an enemy infiltration while the bulk of the defensive forces were still in their dugouts taking coverage from the enemy barrage. With this type of defensive system the Italian Army, for example, assumed many of the defensive tactics and dispositions used by the Germans and the French, in the Western front.

These reforms also corrected one of the main tactical deficiencies of the Italian Army, the lack of counter-attacking reserves to be deployed against stormtroopers attacking on the heels of a destructive creeping barrage and seeking to seal the dugouts. Often the stormtroopers had been successful in capturing entire standard infantry units while facing little or no opposition given the absence of these special reserve units. Infantry units were in many cases captured or rendered obsolete by the speed and the deep infiltrations achieved by the stormtroopers which arrived at their defensive positions virtually unopposed. By late 1916 the Army had created special counter-attacking units that were specifically deployed against enemy attacks and that could be positioned close to the trench area that the enemy was about to invade.[12]

Some of these reforms had already been introduced by Cadorna in response to the Austrian counter-attack on Mount Ortigara in June 1917, but many field commanders had openly disregarded them at Caporetto. For instance, in 1917 *Comando Supremo* had issued instructions on how to counteract raids and attacks of enemy stormtroopers. These special units were to be thwarted mainly by the constant upkeep of the barbed wire defenses, by keeping a constant watch over enemy movements, by better camouflaging defiladed machine gun nests and by creating special infantry units to be held in reserve in order to be deployed in swift counter-attacks. "Determined counter-attacks, promptly supported by artillery interdiction fire, will result in the capture and destruction of enemy troops that have penetrated our first line of defense."[13]

11 John Gooch, 'Italy During the First World War', p.179.

12 Ufficio Storico, E1, Raccolta 17: 'Difesa della regione Melette', Relazione al Comando Supremo, 14 December, 1917, n. 74192.

13 Ufficio Storico, Circolare n. 3024: Comando Supremo, Ufficio Segreteria del Capo di Stato Maggiore, 'Ammaestramenti tattici', 9 July 1917.

One of the first instances in which the special counter-attacking units had been deployed effectively was during the Austro-Hungarian siege of the Melette di Gallio in late 1917. Here Italian troops had been dispatched ahead of the enemy attack and went into action as soon as the artillery barrage was lifted to parry the offensive blow and while the bulk of the troops were still hiding in the dugouts. Their effort was instrumental in thwarting some of the Austro-Hungarian attacks.

As historians Filippo Cappellano and Basilio di Martino have argued these reforms overturned several tactical and troop deployment mainstays of the Italian Army of 1915–16. The changes forged a more professional, less vulnerable and casualty-prone army thanks to better tactics that were more reflective of the dynamics of trench warfare, to increased training and firepower.[14]

The Birth of the *Arditi*

As previously stated the formation of *arditi* battalions represented a profound change in infantry tactics. The Italian Army began to experiment with special assault units (*esploratori*) during the first year of the war as one of the many efforts to overcome the impasse of trench warfare. The soldiers belonging to these units, like medieval knights, wore protective shields and cuirass and were armed with machine guns, hand grenades and wire cutters. Their goal was to probe enemy defenses in order to create gaps in the barbed wire and facilitate an infantry advance. The most famous of these units was led by Captain Cristoforo Baseggio and it was called *Compagnia della Morte* (Death Squad) since it carried out very dangerous assignments. The biggest difference between the *arditi* and the *esploratori* was that the former would become highly trained, fully armed, assault units, while the latter were primarily used in reconnaissance and enemy wire rupture missions.

One of the first proponents of special infantry assault units was General Luigi Capello, commander of the VI Army Corps, which was deployed against the Austro-Hungarian fortress of Gorizia in 1916.

Capello was the supreme architect of the Battle of Gorizia, the first major battle won by the Italian Army in the war. As Conrad's punitive expedition, the *Strafexpedition*, had wound down in the Trentino, General Cadorna went on the offensive on the more exposed, lightly protected Isonzo sector. The Italian Army with a massive concentration of 1,200 artillery units (a third of which were medium or large guns) and 800 trench mortars opened up a tremendous barrage on 6 August 1916 against the impregnable Gorizia bridgehead. For once the preparatory fire had been carefully planned receiving crucial support from the airforce which conducted extensive aerial reconnaissance to locate key enemy strong points. As a result, the Gorizia fortress was blasted into submission and its defenses were vastly debilitated opening up the way for the Italian VI Army Corps that entered victorious into the city. The Italians

14 Basilio Di Martino and Filippo Cappellano, *Un esercito forgiato nelle trincee. L'evoluzione tattica dell'esercito italiano nella grande guerra* (Rome: Ufficio Storico, 2008).

suffered 51,000 casualties while the Austrians lost 37,000 men, but the former had gained their first major breakthrough.

After the capture of Gorizia and the return to positional warfare on the new ossified frontline, Capello began to argue that the stalemate of trench warfare undermined the Italian Army's ability to conduct successful operations by diminishing the soldiers' aggression and fighting spirit as they were fossilized on the trenches. To counteract the stasis of everyday line infantry duties, Capello called on his officers to create special detachments made up of hand-picked soldiers destined to be deployed in offensive maneuvers and dangerous raids against enemy positions. Capello ordered that these special units be fitted with protective steel shields while attempting to open gaps on the enemy wire.[15]

Ultimately the shields were abandoned because they were found to be too cumbersome by frontline troops and could be ruptured by machine gun fire, but Capello's special detachments continued to train and carry out offensive actions.

Another officer that was an early proponent of the *arditi* was Colonel-Brigadier Francesco Saverio Grazioli, the commander of the *Lambro* Brigade in 1916.

Grazioli was an acute observer of the new tactics being developed on the Western Front. He not only followed very closely the growth and consolidation of German *sturmtruppen* units mainly through French intelligence reports, but would later become a proponent of British-style infantry tactics utilizing tanks to smash through enemy infantry lines. Apart from being a keen intellectual, Grazioli sought continuous feedback from his officers. In May 1916 his unit had parried the blow of the Austro-Hungarian *Strafexpedition* Offensive along the Asiago Altopiano. During this major offensive operation the Austro-Hungarians units had used some of the novel tactics of the German *sturmtruppen*, mainly the infiltration of heavily armed assault detachments and hand grenade units well beyond the first objectives of the offensive. Grazioli's officers had briefed him on the actions of the Austro-Hungarian assault detachments during this offensive and the senior officer had collected their observations in a report summarizing key findings.

In this document Grazioli called on the officers of his Brigade to constitute special assault detachments. Similarly to German stormtroopers, the Italian assault units were to be armed with light machine guns and hand grenades and trained to infiltrate enemy positions by attacking them from the rear and the flanks. The goal was to constitute in the short term "special assault units for large scale offensive operations, and for other offensive actions such as immediate counter-attacks, raids, and surprise coups."[16]

In Grazioli's intent was that these units would no longer just carry out reconnaissance but would be involved in the breach and deep infiltration of enemy positions.

15 Ufficio Storico, Raccolta E-5,17, IV Corpo d'Armata: Comando 11. Divisione Fanteria, 'Squadre per operazioni offensive e per ricognizioni ardite', n. 6367, 17 May 1916.

16 Ufficio Storico, Rep. B-1, Raccolta 137D, 1407d: Comando Brigata Lambro, 'Constituzione nuclei speciali nella Brigata', n. 1277, 7 March 1917, Diario storico 206 Reggimento Fanteria, 1–15 March 1917.

Finally in March 1917 the first special *Lambro* assault units were constituted, drawing volunteers from each battalion of the Brigade.

Their training program included such unit exercises as:

1. Flushing out enemy positions by launching hand grenades followed by hand-to-hand combat.
2. Attack enemy machine guns positioned on the flanks of the enemy deployment.
3. Carry out raids by launching hand grenades into enemy posts.
4. Clear out and take control of enemy trenches with hand grenades.[17]

In order to train these special units Grazioli had set up a fully functioning shooting range and training ground. The latter was modeled on an Austro-Hungarian strongpoint with actual trenches to make the training experience more realistic. Training exercises were conducted under simulated battle conditions with the use of live fire. The trainees were familiarized with handling dangerous weapons through long drawn out exercises and the instructors frequently taunted them by testing their mental strength. One of the most common tests consisted of throwing hand grenades in the direction or near the recruits to test their reaction and response to danger. Another was to lock new recruits into a bunker and then lob hand grenades against its roof. Both exercises tested the stamina of the soldiers. Those who lost their nerves under these trying conditions were usually sent back to their unit of origin.

After having completed the training program, Grazioli's *Lambro* Brigade would deploy these special units first in a series of small, successful raids against Austrian strongpoints and then during the Tenth Battle of the Isonzo but obtaining mixed results. In fact on 12 May 1917 the special assault units broke the enemy frontline and penetrated the defenses but were quickly overwhelmed by the lack of infantry support and also because they were lightly armed. As a result, large losses were sustained. Even though these special assault units had experienced some setbacks during their first major test of fire, Grazioli was determined to continue experimenting with them. As a result, after the battle training was resumed and new recruits were selected to replenish the debilitated ranks.

Grazioli's ideas reflected in large part those of Major Giuseppe Bassi who had worked closely with Grazioli and had authored a memorandum urging the Italian Army to use special assault units armed with machine gun pistols to facilitate a deep penetration of enemy defenses.

In a widely circulated memorandum published on 8 November 1916 Bassi had advocated for the employment of light machine gun pistols in the attack by asserting:

> In close quarter combat, the most likely scenario for the deployment of the *Arditi*, hand grenades and knives will be more useful than rifles in fending off enemy counters. … In my view, the first assault units, mainly composed of hand

17 Ibid.

> grenade launchers, should be equipped with light machine pistols which can serve multiple purposes:
> 1. protect assault waves as they attack enemy lines
> 2. surprise and overwhelm the enemy with a steady rate of fire
> 3. facilitate hand-to-hand combat in the trenches, the dugouts and caverns where the enemy usually assembles in order to shield himself from the artillery barrage.
>
> Once the enemy has been dissuaded from putting up resistance especially by hitting him from the flanks, the soldiers armed with these pistols can, together with the hand grenade launchers, fight off the likely enemy counter-attack. By resisting an enemy counter, these units can buy time and allow the infantry with its heavy machine guns to arrive on the frontline and consolidate the hold on the captured enemy position.[18]

Bassi's novel idea was that the *arditi* had to advance with speed and decision in order to arrive into the enemy's trenches as soon as possible after the barrage had relented or had been moved forward. Well-planned surprise attacks in fact allowed the *arditi* to suffer as few casualties as possible due to enemy interdiction fire and they also allowed these special units to overwhelm enemy trenches. The artillery, as well as the *arditi*'s light mountain gun, machine gun and mortar units, played a special accompanying role during these assaults. Their role was to pin down the enemy under a hail of fire in order to relegate opponents to their dugouts preventing them from coming out of shelters to prepare for the assault. Meanwhile, the *arditi* would push forward throwing hand grenades into the enemy trenches while the artillery would slowly move the barrage forward. Bassi also maintained that the *arditi* necessitated new weapons to quickly bypass no man's land and confront enemy blockhouses or bunkers. The full-length infantry rifle, for instance, was too cumbersome to carry across no man's land and to use in close combat trench conditions. The new assault units were therefore to be armed with a smaller, more versatile rifle with a bayonet. In addition to light machine guns, rifles and hand grenades, Bassi argued that the *arditi* should also be armed with other weapons more suited for hand-to-hand combat such as daggers and smoke bombs. The *arditi,* for instance, were taught how to fight with daggers in order to prevail against the enemy in close combat situations, while smoke bombs were necessary to conceal their advance into enemy trenches leading the Austro-Hungarian defenders into thinking that the artillery barrage was still in full swing. The smoke also simulated "a gas attack, which would unsettle the defenders further."[19]

Another innovation introduced by Major Bassi was the introduction of the two-man team. Each platoon was comprised of five two-man teams. Each team was to train

18 Ufficio Storico: Comando 48. Divisione, Ufficio Stato Maggiore, "Memoria del capitano Bassi Sig. Giuseppe sulle pistole mitragliatrici", n. 1949, op. 6 April, 1917.

19 Angelo Pirocchi, *Italian Arditi: Elite Assault Troops, 1917–20* (Oxford: Osprey, 2007), p. 22.

and fight together at all times and this was thought to reinforce the bond between soldiers. Two man teams were formed voluntarily, often by pairing two soldiers from the same town or region, or from the same combat unit. Each soldier would complement the other. One soldier, for instance, would throw hand grenades while the other would carry them, or one would fire the machine gun while the other would provide coverage and support with his rifle. This concept was to instill individual responsibility amongst the soldiers thus allowing the two-man teams to fight autonomously rather than depending for their movements upon the orders of the NCO.

Finally on 12 June 1917 Capello and Bassi constituted the first experimental *arditi* unit within the Italian 2nd Army, the I *Reparto d'Assalto*, which drew heavily from the assault detachments of the *Lambro* Brigade. Such an important development was shortly followed by a circular from *Comando Supremo* ordering all army commanders to constitute *arditi* units. In fact, circular n. 111660 committed all army corps to establish at least one *reparto d'assalto* that should be formed primarily by *bersaglieri* and with the initial force of a standard infantry company.

On 4 July 1917 *Comando Supremo* issued a directive establishing a special badge for the *arditi*, which was to be worn on the sleeve. The badge was created to distinghish the elite units from the standard infantry. On 21 September another circular published by *Comando Supremo* outlined the type of weapons, uniform and the organic composition of the *arditi* battalions. This document also instructed frontline commanders that the *arditi* were to be deployed in two types of operational roles: "small scale raids to capture prisoners, to gain valuable information on the enemy's deployment or to destroy/degrade and/or occupy enemy defenses" and "take part in planned attacks to pave the way for a broad infantry advance."[20]

In addition, the prescribed training for the *arditi* was to be intense and continuous and to be carried out in dedicated shooting ranges and training grounds where the soldiers could harness their offensive spirit. It was forbidden for section commanders to utilize the *arditi* as trench defenses or to transport equipment or food to the frontline.

Therefore the impetus for the creation of the elite assault units came primarily from these three men: Capello, Grazioli and Bassi, with the latter being the main driving force. All three men had experienced command of infantry units in the most entrenched frontline sector of the Isonzo where the Austro-Hungarians had yielded very little territory. On the Isonzo they had experienced both victory and defeat. All, however, had faced the same conundrum of how to initiate a prolonged campaign of movement and continuous advance in the most heavily defended sector of the frontline. Grazioli, in particular, and his *Lambro* Brigade had faced a huge reversal of fortune. Throughout 1916 the Brigade had trained extensively and had undertaken several successful offensive operations. However, the following year, during the Tenth Battle of the Isonzo, Grazioli's assault units suffered many casualties after initially successfully breaching enemy trenchlines and after being surrounded by

20 The circular is cited in: Basilio di Martino, *Trincee, Reticolati, e Colpi di Mano* (Valdagno: Rossato, 2000), p. 57.

the Austro-Hungarians. Despite the huge setback, both Grazioli and Bassi, with Capello's backing, continued to experiment with the special assault units. Without their persistence, the *arditi* might never have been born.

Training

The special assault units began to train at Sdricca di Manzano, the training camp that became the cradle of the *arditi*. Here the troops underwent a comprehensive training regimen including individual and group exercises in gymnastics, hand-to-hand combat, rifle shooting, hand grenade throwing, heavy weapon training and live fire exercises. What was different about *arditi* training was its intensity, as each *Reparto* trained for up to three months, as well as its professionalism. Prior to the *arditi*, standard infantry forces had received very little training, the most fortunate spent a few weeks in the rear learning how to shoot with the rifle and how to march in tight formations. Some also were taught basic assault maneuver tactics. The *arditi*, on the other hand, enjoyed vast amounts of ammunition for training purposes, trained in camps that were well equipped and had replicas of enemy trenches and the trainees were afforded the time to learn new combat tactics. Each *Reparto*, for example, had at its disposal vast amounts of ammunition and weapons for practical, live fire, exercises that the Italian Army had never before made available to standard infantry units. Italian historian Salvatore Farina asserts that "Each training session consumed an average of 12,000 to 15,000 explosive charges, 30,000 to 40,000 rounds of ammunition and 5,000 to 6,000 hand grenades."[21]

The camp, equipped with a number of mock enemy positions, enabled the soldiers to hone their skills by maneuvering against them under live fire conditions. Each *Reparto*'s training course in fact culminated in a large-scale simulated attack on an enemy trenchline.

Finally, each *Reparto* underwent a uniform training process that stressed repeating drills time and time again and familiarizing each soldier with a host of weapons. By having soldiers repeat the same drills several times, Bassi maintained that the *arditi* would develop strong antidotes to danger and fear on the battlefield and develop such attributes as constancy, determination and mental endurance. As Farina correctly asserts, "The repetition of training exercises that were conducted under live fire conditions amidst the deafening explosions of countless hand grenades and the constant whizzing of machine gun fire not only served to deaden any emotions but it also built an indifference to danger."[22] The *arditi* were trained to charge the enemy while the friendly fire of the artillery was still in full swing which was not only difficult to do but it also required soldiers willing to learn and practice very risky tactics. Although very dangerous, the tactic, if well executed, could lead to success on the battlefield. In fact, while the Italian artillery pounded the enemy trenches, the enemy was unable

21 Salvatore Farina, *Le Truppe d'Assalto Italiane* (Milan: Libreria Militare, 2007), p. 147.
22 Ibid., p. 162.

to oppose the infantry advance. Once the *arditi* had reached the wire, the artillery would lengthen its fire beyond the first line. In addition, it was well known that it took some time for the Austro-Hungarian artillery to reply with counter-preparatory fire as soon as the Italian gun fire was moved forward. It was this small window of opportunity that needed to be exploited at the fullest by the *arditi* by reaching the wire at the proper time and as soon as the artillery battaries began the creeping barrage. Entering the trenches before the Austro-Hungarian artillery could intervene meant that the assault units had greater leeway to successfully penetrate the enemy's deployment.

Another major innovation made at Sdricca was the rigorous selection process that volunteers had to undergo. Rejection rates were high, usually 50 percent of all volunteers were rejected. According to Captain Maggiorino Radicati of I *Reparto d'assalto* recruits came from all units of 2nd Army. "*Bersaglieri* soldiers were the most numerous comprising up to one quarter of all trainees admitted to I *Reparto d'assalto*. The remaining three quarters of the ranks where comprised by soldiers from *alpini*, infantry and sapper units. While the officer ranks were comprised primarily by experienced soldiers, most of which had been in charge of frontline units since the beginning of the war."[23]

The training aimed at specialization, at making each soldier a specialist in the handling of one weapon. The specific instructions for the flamethrower squads, for instance, were as follows:

> Flamethrower personnel shall complete a special training program. This will consist in several drills aimed at developing a thorough knowledge of the weapon and how to operate it. Moreover, the soldier will be trained on how to carry the weapon on the shoulders across no man's land, by advancing through shell holes and along mountain ridges. The soldier will then be trained on how to work in close cooperation with hand grenade squads in order to roll up the enemy trenches and caverns. Finally the soldier will be trained on how to promptly substitute in the combat zone a fallen comrade and how to fix flamethrower equipment failures and other operating issues.

In turn, the special hand grenade squads training entailed that:

> The soldier will receive training in the proper functioning and handling of all types of hand grenades (both Italian and enemy grenades).
>
> The soldier will learn how to launch the grenade from both a standing up and kneeling down position and while running.
>
> This training will also serve to deselect those soldiers that demonstrate no drive and little willingness to master the proper handling of hand grenades.

23 Maggiorino Radicati, *I Reparti d'assalto nella Guerra 1915–18* (Turin: Sezione *Bersaglieri* A. Lamarmora, 1957), p. 28.

> Special care shall be taken to master the proper handling and launching of the 'offensive petard', which constitutes the most potent weapon of the *ardito*.[24]

The specialization process was very similar to the training of the Austro-Hungarian stormtroopers has they had been the first to develop special hand grenade/bombing squads, flamethrower platoons and light machine gun teams dedicated to the attack.

Organization and Weapons

After two months of training the first assault units, I and II *Reparto d'assalto*, were constituted within Capello's 2nd Army in the summer of 1917.

Bassi's standard *Reparto d'assalto* was comprised of three infantry and one specialist company with a total of 750 soldiers. Each company was subdivided into four platoons, three of infantry riflemen and one of specialists (pioneers or signal, etc.). The *reparto* also had a light mountain gun section with two 65 mm guns. The gun was highly versatile because by being relatively light it could be disassembled in different components and carried by pack mules. It could fire both standard and shrapnel rounds and was a highly reliable weapon allowing for precision shooting. A machine gun section was also attached to each *Reparto* with eight machine guns (6.5 mm *Fiat-Revelli* model 1914 with a rate of fire of 200 rounds per minute) and 24 light machine guns (*Fiat-Revelli* model 1915 with a rate of fire of 25 rounds per second). Albeit the machine gun was central to Bassi's offensive vision for the *arditi*, it never reached its full potential in the attack. In fact, light machine guns were perhaps the weakest weapon of the *arditi* since they were unreliable and jammed often. And finally *arditi* units were equipped with a flamethrower section. The weapon had originally been introduced in 1916 as a result of the collaboration with French Army engineers. There had been two main impetuses for its introduction. First, it was highly considered as an attacking weapon and specifically used tactically to accompany infantry as it assailed enemy positions and to be used specifically to snuff out stubborn centers of enemy resistance. Second, the flamethrower was also introduced as a response to the first enemy poison gas attack on Monte San Michele on 29 June 1916 that had caused thousands of casualties. The flamethrower was seen as a good defensive weapon to stem the flow of the poison gas clouds.

The weapon had first been deployed on Hill 65 in the Carso on 25–27 April 1916. The war diary of the *Acqui'* Brigade reports that: "The flamethrower section which was lying in wait on the reverse slope of the hill when the enemy attacked, invested with flames the vanguards of the enemy which was approaching Hill 70. The Austro-Hungarians attempted to penetrate our positions, but where pushed back by the flame attack and on the battlefield we later counted numerous bodies of enemy soldiers that had been burned to death."[25]

24 Ufficio Storico, IX *Reparto d'Assalto*: 'Istruzione dei reparti d'assalto', 14 October 1918.
25 Filippo Cappellano and Marco Montagnani, *L' inferno nelle trincee. I Lancia fiamme italiani nella grande Guerra* (Udine: Gaspari, 2015), p. 22.

Soon after this first deployment several platoons were formed both within sapper and infantry units. The flamethrower was small and portable with a 15-litre fuel tank. The weapon that was used in 1916 was the French-made *Schilt* 3 bis model flamethrower, while later on a similar Italian *DLF* model flamethrower was adopted. In 1918 a mortar unit was also attached to each *reparto* armed primarily with four British Stokes mortars. Just like mountain guns, mortars were versatile since they weighed 80 lbs and could be disassembled into three components and transported with pack mules. Moreover, the mortar could fire both explosive and smoke shells and was an excellent weapon for mountain warfare. The soldiers were equipped with the *Moschetto* '91 TS rifle with bayonet that was shorter and less bulky than the standard infantry rifle. Most *arditi* carried hand grenades such as the *Thevenot* and *Olergon* (both weighed 400 grams and had a range of 30–40 feet) and a dagger. Both were *arditi* trademark weapons. Each soldier was taught various throwing techniques and learned when to use incendiary or explosive grenades to achieve maximum effect. Their hand grenades were not very powerful but on impact would create powerful splinters that often proved deadly. The *arditi* also mastered close combat skills such as boxing and judo and most became experts in wielding daggers against the enemy. Both daggers and hand grenades were weapons designed to achieve maximum surprise and instill fear within enemy ranks. The officers carried a machine gun pistol, the *Gilsenti* model 1910.

The standard *ardito* soldier equipment included: rifle, dagger, two wire cutters, hand grenade sack with up to 10 grenades, anti-gas mask, and a small shovel. The *ardito* uniform included: Hadrian helmet, open *bersagliere* tunic with a grey-green turtleneck sweater or a shirt in the summer, knee-length *alpini* trousers and a pair of mountain boots. The *ardito* was not only recognized for his unique uniform which was quite different from that of the standard infantry soldier given its much more sportive look, but also for his sleeve badges. The most common was the Roman *gladium* encircled by oak leaves and with at the bottom the motto 'FERT' from the house of Savoy which was worn on the left arm. In 1918 the *arditi* soldiers were also identified by their battalion's Roman numeral number which appeared on the uniform and on the helmet as well.

The special 'green patches' alpine *arditi* units wore camouflaged uniform which included a white coat with a hood, trousers, helmet, helmet cover, balaclava and gloves. Some were also assigned snow shoes, skis, crampons for boots and white sleeping bags.

Tactics

Once Bassi had constituted the first *arditi* units, General Capello outlined in a memorandum to his subordinates how he envisioned that these units should be deployed.

> No operation shall be successful if it is not planned in detail and thought out with care. The enemy's weakest trenchline positions must be identified and

> targeted. The terrain on which the *Arditi* shall advance and the location of the enemy's guns must also be identified prior to launching an attack.
>
> Combined arms collaboration, especially between artillery and infantry, must be encouraged to the fullest as it is the underlying condition for all successful offensive thrusts.
>
> In order to disorient the enemy, the artillery shall shell both the targeted as well as surrounding rival positions.
>
> In order to overwhelm the enemy trenchline with artillery fire, the barrage must be brief but also intense. It must accompany the *Arditi* as they advance through no man's land.
>
> The assault units shall charge against enemy trenchlines in order to be as close as possible to them when the barrage is lifted. When at the wire, the *Arditi* must push ahead throwing hand grenades against parapets, machine gun nests and enemy shelters. In the trenches, the *Arditi* shall engage the enemy in hand-to-hand combat primarily with hand grenades and daggers. Enemy shelters and caverns shall be cleared out. Enemy passageways shall be blocked with hand grenades and the entrances torched with flamethrowers. Strong pockets of enemy resistance are to dealt with trench mortars, machine guns and small artillery guns. The *Arditi* must be used only in certain types of operations and their numbers should be appropriate for the task. Once the *Arditi* have completed their task, commanders should not wear them down by deploying them as line infantry. The latter shall promptly relieve them by taking possession of captured enemy positions.[26]

Similarly to the Austro-Hungarian *sturmtruppen*, the *reparti d'assalto* were to be deployed to unhinge enemy defenses both during planned attacks and small-scale raids. The novel tactics of the *arditi* was the combination of a well-planned infantry attack put forth by above average physically fit soldiers launched on the heels of a surprise preparatory barrage. In order to achieve its goal the latter was to be sudden, brief, but also extremely powerful and typically not to be preceded by registration fire forewarning the enemy of the offensive intentions. The artillery was to suddenly initiate a bombardment that would gradually intensify in the span of 10 or 20 minutes. The first aim of the barrage would be to fire large quantities of explosive rounds to pound frontline defenses and make gaps in the wire. Then it would switch to gas shells in order to nullify any counter-battery fire by enemy artillery and force artillery men and frontline defenders into their dugouts. Finally, the barrage would be moved forward returning to a mixture of gas and explosive shells aimed primarily at rear defenses including the command centers, artillery posts and reserve unit dugouts. This novel use of the artillery was in contrast to the customary, protracted barrages of the Italian Army that gave the defenders time to bring up reserves and evacuate forward trenches, while wrecking havoc on the battlefield making it difficult

26 Ufficio Storico, Rep. E-1, Raccolta 113: Comando 2. Armata, 'Impiego dei reparti d'assalto', n. 5229, 21 September 1917.

for attackers to advance. While the *arditi* quickly advanced following the rolling barrage, additional protection for the assault units was provided by the unit's own mountain and machine guns whose role was to further pin down the enemy in the dugouts. The *arditi* would then rush ahead throwing hundreds of smoke bombs and hand grenades, to keep the defenders in their shelters. The key to their success was the speed with which they crossed no man's land and the time it took them to reach the enemy's dugouts and block him before he could react. The hand grenades and the smoke bombs were instrumental in the *arditi* tactic of surging forward because hundreds of them would be thrown into the enemy's defenses leading him to think that the barrage was still unfolding. Then suddenly has the *arditi* rushed to seal the doors and openings of the enemy defenses, both hand grenades and flamethrowers were instrumental in forcing the enemy to surrender. Often the psychological impact of the flamethrower alone, with hot burning fire and oil penetrating into enemy fortifications through doors and embrasures was sufficient to dissuade the enemy from fighting any longer. The tactical instructions for the use of flamethrowers in the attack were very detailed and the Italian Army heavily relied upon them to breach enemy defenses:

> They are made to be used primarily to attack isolated enemy nuclei as well as units that persist on resisting to the end. Flamethrowers represent a most effective means of assault often allowing for the complete mop-up of conquered trenches and are also extremely useful for ambushing machine gun strong points by directing jets of flammable liquid into the embrasures. ... They can also work well in unison with machine gun squads to pursue the flanks of the enemy deployment and especially to cut down enemy units that are seeking to retreat. Flamethrowers can also be paired with teams of hand grenade throwers while advancing into enemy trenches or while attacking the enemy from the flanks.[27]

"One of the tactical innovations of the *Arditi* was the close co-operation between artillery, machine guns and assault troops, so each *reparto* received a mule carried section of two 66/17 mountain guns, which were more mobile than similar weapons (in particular the old Bettica) in use at the time."[28] The guns could be carried forward in support of infantry attacks to deal primarily with pillboxes, machine gun bunkers and other similar obstacles. In mid 1918 mortars replaced the mountain guns as each *reparto* was furnished with a section of four Stokes mortars. Weighing only 80 lbs, the mortar was much easier to carry than the much heavier mountain gun at 1,000 lbs. It therefore facilitated the *arditi* when they lunged forward into the attack providing swift artillery barrages at close range to enemy positions. Its contribution to the successful *arditi* counter-attacks on the Piave River was duly noted in the post-battle report issued by *Comando Supremo*.

27 Ufficio Storico, Comando Supremo, Ufficio Tecnico: 'Istruzione provvisoria sugli apparecchi per il lancio dei liquidi infiammabili', 1917.

28 Angelo Pirocchi, *Italian Arditi*, pp. 32–41.

Italian flamethrower training. The Italians were originally using French manufactured *Schilt* flamethrowers which were developed in 1915. Later in the conflict the Italians used a domestic-manufactured model. (Ufficio Storico – official archive, Italian military, Rome)

Arditi alpini of the XXIX *Reparto d'assalto* hand grenade training somewhere near their base in Avio, Trentino. (Ufficio Storico – official archive, Italian military, Rome)

Austro-Hungarian Stormtrooper's badge. (Kriegsarchiv Vienna)

Arditi posing for group photo with daggers, mountain cannon and Italian flag. (Ufficio Storico – official archive, Italian military, Rome)

Giovanni Messe, Commander of the IX *Reparto d'assalto* who led his unit in the important counter-attack against the Austro-Hungarian stormtroops on the Col Moschin during the Solstice Offensive of 1918. (Ufficio Storico – official archive, Italian military, Rome)

Major Giuseppe Bassi, the 'father' of the *arditi*. He was the founder of the special assault units and the creator of the *arditi* rigorous training program. (Ufficio Storico – official archive, Italian military, Rome)

Photo 64: *Arditi* of the XXIX *Reparto d'assalto* training in the Trentino. It appears that they are carrying an injured soldier. The *arditi* conducted live fire practices and often these training sessions could lead to serious wounds for some of the soldiers.

Arditi training with flamethrowers. (Ufficio Storico – official archive, Italian military, Rome)

An Italian *ardito* of the XXIX *Reparto d'assalto* is firing his *Fiat-Revelli* model 1914 machine gun. The gun was usually operated by a three-man squad consisting of an NCO, the gunner and the ammunition carrier. Certain alpine *arditi* units also had pack mules to transport the gun as well as to carry ammunition. (Ufficio Storico – official archive, Italian military, Rome)

Arditi alpini (so-called Green Flames) from the XXIX *Reparto d'assalto* with a Stokes mortar in Val Lagarina in the spring of 1918. The Stokes design was simple but highly effective. This British-manufactured weapon consisted of a smooth metal tube fixed to a base plate (to absorb recoil) with a bi-pod mount. When a bomb was dropped into the tube an impact sensitive cartridge at the base of the bomb would make contact with a firing pin, thus ejecting the bomb. (Ufficio Storico – official archive, Italian military, Rome)

Arditi training with flamethrower. (Ufficio Storico – official archive, Italian military, Rome)

Arditi unit in training. (Ufficio Storico – official archive, Italian military, Rome)

During the Solstice Offensive it was noted that the Austro-Hungarian infantry used infiltration tactics to facilitate the penetration of small but heavily armed infantry units into the rear of the Italian defenses. This tactic had relied heavily upon the stormtroopers, acting as vanguards, and largely supported by artillery and air power strikes against the enemy artillery batteries. According to *Comando Supremo* these infiltrations were met and firmly repulsed by "special *arditi* counter-attacking units supported by mortars and small mountain cannons deployed to neutralize machine gun nests."[29] Thus, similarly to the Austrian stormtroopers the *reparti d'assalto* were also used as tactical reserves to conduct counter-attacks.

Arditi tactics involved several assault platoons collaborating during the execution of an attack. Special machine guns and mountain guns units were to position their weapons in advanced positions and pin down the enemy as the assault units advanced. Assault squads, armed primarily with daggers and hand grenades, were tasked with eliminating enemy sentries and irrupt with force into the enemy's first line of defense. They were to be followed by the mop-up squads, which were more heavily armed with flamethrowers, machine guns and rifles, whose role was to eliminate pockets of enemy resistance and clear the trenches. A third squad, composed of the mountain gun and heavy machine gun sections, was to provide close cover to the infantry assault squads by destroying concrete blockhouses, enemy strong points and machine gun nests that stood in the way of a further advance by the assault units.

These types of infantry assaults required the close collaboration amongst artillery, special light artillery platoons and the assault infantry itself. A well-thought-out plan of attack was crucial to ensure success and it was to be based on extensive surveillance of enemy defenses. Even with proper intelligence the assault units could easily stumble upon undamaged barbed wire or defiladed machine guns strong points whose deadly fire could derail the operation.

The Evolution of *Arditi* Units to 1918

The *arditi*'s baptism by fire occurred during the Eleventh Battle of the Isonzo (18–19 August 1917), during which they were successfully employed in a planned attack. They then took part in probably one of their most famous battles, another planned attack, that resulted in the capture of Mount San Gabriele in September 1917.

Following the battle of the San Gabriele, where I *Reparto d'assalto* of 2nd Army fought with distinction, *Comando Supremo* encouraged other army units to constitute these special assault units. Two months later, just before the Caporetto offensive the Italian Army had already 26 *arditi* units. The 2nd Army led the way with 12 *Reparti d'assalto:* I, II, III, IV, V, VI, X, XI, XII, XIII, XIV, XV. It was followed by the 4th Army with: IV, V, VI, VIII *Reparti d'assalto*, the 3rd Army with XIX, XX, XXI, XXII *Reparti d'assalto*, and 1st Army with IV, IX, and XXIV. While the alpine 3rd

29 Ufficio Storico, Comando Supremo, Ufficio Segreteria: 'Metodi tattici del nemico', n. 25, 23 June 1918.

Army Corps (XVII), *Comando Zona Carnia* (XVIII) and *Comando Truppe Altipiani* (XVI) had one *reparto* respectively.

Following the Central Powers breakout at Caporetto, the *reparti d'assalto* were utilized in defensive and rearguard actions to stem the enemy advance and as a result were for the most part either destroyed or vastly debilitated in the bloody fighting that ensured. For example, I *Reparto d'assalto* was assigned the rearguard task of defending the city of Udine, that until October 1917 had been *Comando Supremo's* headquarters. In three days of battle, I *Reparto* suffered the loss of six officers and 385 men, while the remaining 70 soldiers were taken prisoner after having run out of ammunition.

This debacle prompted a vast reorganization of the *arditi* in the winter of 1918 with some units being disbanded and others being merged into other *reparti*. By January 1918 the Italian Army could count on 20 *reparti d'assalto*, but many initially had only one or at best two infantry companies. The *I* and *II* were some of the first units to be brought up to full rank and along with two other *reparti* participated to the Battle of the Three Mountains in January 1918. In the spring some *reparti d'assalto* remained independent while others were merged into the *Corpo d'Armata d'Assalto* (Assault Army Corps) comprising the *I* and *II Divisioni d'assalto* (Assault Divisions). These were placed under the command of Tenente General Grazioli to form a reserve force at the disposal of *Comando Supremo* and tasked with leading planned attacks and counter-attacks. Grazioli had previously written a detailed report on the need for a tactical reserve force following the example set by General Petain. The French had used to good effect special infantry forces to plug holes in the defensive system, to rotate troops in the front lines, as well as to conduct forceful counter-attacks against dangerous enemy infiltrations during the Battle of Verdun.[30] Grazioli maintained that this force, augmented by French Renault tanks and by cavalry units, could ultimately effectuate a combined arms offensive along the Piave and thus achieve the much desired breakthrough. As historian Giorgio Rochat asserts, however, the intent behind the creation of the Assault Army Corps was also likely influenced by the German example that in the spring of 1918 had used many battalions of highly trained stormtroopers to effectuate a deep penetration of the French and British front lines. *Comando Supremo* likely hoped that with the "formation of a large mass of *arditi* a major breach of the enemy line could be achieved."[31]

The formation of the two assault divisions prompted the removal and transfer of Major Bassi to a standard infantry regiment since he was fiercely opposed to the formation of the Assault Army Corps maintaining that the *arditi* were at their best when integrated into small but agile infantry battalions.

The baptism of fire of the Assault Army Corps took place during the Solstice Offensive in June 1918, where it was deployed in counter-attacks against the Austro-Hungarians. Although, its units were able to push back the enemy penetrations in the lower Piave, their battlefield performance was mixed, mainly due to the large

30 Francesco Saverio Grazioli, 'Riserva Mobile Strategica', in *Relazione Ufficiale, vol. 5, tomo 2 bis* (Rome: Ufficio Storico, 1989), pp. 491–513.

31 Giorgio Rochat, *Gli Arditi della Grande Guerra* (Udine: LEG, 1990), p. 98.

casualties sustained. The remaining *Reparti d'assalto* that were not part of the assault divisions also played an important role during the offensive that saw the Austro-Hungarian Army repulsed with heavy losses (118,000 against 86,000 Italians). While much of the success of the operation was the result of skillful counter-preparations by the artillery that caused huge casualties even before enemy infantry could join battle, the *arditi* also contributed to this success with forceful counter-attacks. The individual *Reparti d'assalto* such as the *IX* fought particularly well in Mount Grappa and Piave sectors regaining lost ground during local counter-attacks which resulted in the capture of several thousand Austro-Hungarian soldiers. This defeat marked a turning point on the Italian Front.

The Assault Army Corps then took part in the last offensive of the campaign during the Battle of Vittorio Veneto where it attacked in two different directions along the Piave River beginning on 26 October. The 1st Division attacked to the north of the Montello, while the 2nd Division to the south of it. While the former fought in the plain of Sernaglia and was able to infiltrate the Austro-Hungarian lines capturing several field guns, the latter was initially halted by the flooding of the Piave. By 29 October the river subsided and 2nd Division crossed it and then outflanked the resisting Austro-Hungarian units. The next day the Italian units captured the vital communication hub of Vittorio Veneto forcing a general retreat of the enemy infantry.

According to historian Filippo Cappellano the creation of the Assault Army Corps was one of the most important innovations introduced by the Italian army during the Great War.

> In the final battle of Vittorio Veneto, an important role was played by the Assault Army Corps, which constituted the main Italian tactical-systematic innovation of the conflict. Based on two divisions of assault infantrymen (*arditi*) and a rifle regiment (*bersaglieri*), they lacked a logistic component and were equipped with small pieces of light artillery, transportable by pack animals. They were reinforced by cavalry regiments, motorcycle units, autocannon groups and light-armored car squadrons, which played a major part in the pursuit of the routed Austro-Hungarian units. Extensively equipped with mechanical means for transporting troops, the Assault Army Corps was conceived for both rapid, wide-ranging maneuvers, and for break-through operations with the support of medium and heavy artillery.[32]

By the end of September 1918 the Italian Army could boast of having 40 *Reparti d'assalto* which were organized as follows:

32 Cappellano, Filippo: 'Warfare 1914–1918 (Italy)', in: *1914-1918-online. International Encyclopedia of the First World War*, ed. by Ute Daniel, Peter Gatrell, Oliver Janz, Heather Jones, Jennifer Keene, Alan Kramer, and Bill Nasson, issued by Freie Universität Berlin, Berlin 2014–10–08. DOI:http://dx.doi.org/10.15463/ie1418.10484 <accessed 25 November 2015>. Translated by: Mazhar, Noor Giovanni.

1st Army: XXIX, XXXI, and I *Reparto d'assalto di Marcia*
3rd Army; XI, XXVI, XXVIII, and III *Reparto d'assalto di Marcia*
4th Army: III, IX, XVIII, XXIII, LV, and IV *Reparto d'assalto di Marcia*
6th Army: LII, LXX, and VI *Reparto d'assalto di Marcia*
7th Army: VII *Reparto d'assalto di Marcia*
8th Army: XXVII LXXII, and II *Reparto d'assalto di Marcia*
1st Assault Division: VIII, X, XII, XIII, XX, XXII, X *Reparto d'assalto di Marcia*
2nd Assault Division: II, V, VI, XIV, XXX, XI *Reparto d'assalto di Marcia.*

In addition II, XVI, XXXII, XXXV, and LI fought outside Italy.

Following the Italian victory at Vittorio Veneto the *arditi* units were disbanded. The decision was prompted by the increasing involvement of the *arditi* in post-war politics especially in support of the far right parties. Hence, as soon as the war was over, *Comando Supremo* decided to dissolve the assault units.

In the following section we will attempt to answer the same questions that were raised with regards to the Austro-Hungarian stormtroopers: How successful were the *arditi* and their tactics? Did they contribute to breaking the impasse of trench warfare? Did they improve morale of the army as a whole?

Reparto d'Assalto Training Program*

Preamble: The reparto d'assalto is to be deployed in raids against enemy positions.

Given that raids are usually conducted at night or during the early dawn hours or just after dawn when the enemy's nerves and defensive attentiveness diminishes after an entire night on the alert, it is recommended that the below training exercises be conducted at night, or early dawn and preferably during cloudy days.

Individual drills:

Gymnastics, weight lifting, running through obstacles, and wrestling.

Hand grenade throwing (explosive, incendiary and smoke bombs):

- Against specific targets positioned in front, below and above the hand grenade thrower
- Throwing by standing up, kneeling down, by running or by laying close to the ground
- Throwing from the trenches and the deep walkways
- Throwing to block the enemy in the caverns and in the passageways.

Dagger:

- Dagger training using a manikin filled with straws.

Trench busting:

- Use of steel cuirass
- Use of steel shields
- Use of wire cutters to create breaches in the wire
- Use of explosive charges
- Use of small mortar bombs 58B
- Use of Bettica grenade launchers.

Surveillance and reconnaissance of enemy positions, layout, consistency, etc.

Rifle shooting
Machine gun training (light and medium guns, enemy guns, machine gun pistols, and grenade throwers)
Flamethrower training
Turning enemy positions around.

Team exercises:

Gymnastics, obstacle course
Reconnaissance, communication, signaling, use of telephone
Swift exit out of the trenches with various weapons and equipment
Ways in which to shield oneself from an enemy bombardment
Drills aimed at overcoming enemy defenses and obstacles
Advancing directly and on the flanks by special hand grenade throwing squads
Advancing directly and on the flanks by special assault, machine pistol, and machine gun squads under the protective fire of the hand grenade squads.

*From: Ufficio Storico: Appendix n.5 to Folio n. 29447, 18 July 1917.

Organization of the standard Compagnia d'assalto (Assault Company) in August 1918

	Officers	Soldiers	Weapons	Other
Riflemen and Grenade Group	4	208	4 light machine guns	2 bicycles
Machine Gun section	3	135	8 machine guns	16 bicycles and 8 mules
Flamethrower section	1	15	6 flamethrowers	2 mules
Stokes Mortar section	1	27	4	1 cart and 2 mules

Bainsizza: The Baptism of Fire of the *Arditi*

Bassi's *arditi* had their baptism of fire on the night of 19 August 1917 when I *Reparto d'assalto* charged enemy positions on the Bainsizza Plateau during the opening day of the massive Eleventh Isonzo Battle. The planned attack was to be the opening round of a large-scale offensive operation by General Capello's 2nd Army aimed at further chipping away at Austrian defenses on the Isonzo front in order to ultimately threaten Trieste and Ljubljana. The attack was launched on a large section of the Isonzo front-line, the troops in fact operated over a stretch of territory spanning from Tolmino all the way to the Adriatic Sea. Italian infantry units crossed the river at several points on makeshift bridges, but the main effort was concentrated on the Bainsizza Plateau whose conquest was intended to break the Austro-Hungarian line in two, isolating its strongholds of Mount San Gabriele and Mount Hermada. The Bainsizza was an impervious, exceedingly high, natural fortresses overlooking the Isonzo River making a frontal assault against Austrian fortified positions a truly suicidal mission. Since such an attack was out of the question, it was decided that the plateau positions would be assaulted from the north at a section where the terrain was fully covered by trees and shrubs and less steep for the assault troops to negotiate.

The *arditi*'s objective was to occupy two enemy fortified positions: Mounts Fratta and Belpoggio in order to prepare the way for a broad infantry advance on behalf of the 22nd Infantry Division. In order to fulfill their assigned task, the *arditi* were to force the crossing of the Isonzo near the foot of the plateau and were then expected to clear the base of the mountain by taking out machine gun nests situated on the enemy's first line of defense. Subsequently, they were to storm the two successive lines of defense and capture the main enemy artillery and machine gun units. Finally, they were expected to defend the two bridgeheads from likely enemy counter-attacks while protecting the Italian infantry has it landed on shore. The weapons of the assault troops consisted primarily of rifles, daggers, hand grenades, flamethrowers and small mountain guns.

The Fratta was a formidable fortress as the Austrians had established three defensive lines: the first overlooked the Isonzo River, the second was situated at the base of the mountain and the third on its peak. There were entrenched gun emplacements on the summit and on both flanks and several machine gun bunkers covering every angle at the midway point and at the base of the mountain protected by three and in some cases four rounds of barbed wire works. The mountain, occupied by troops of the 21st and 24th Austro-Hungarian Divisions, ominously overlooked the Isonzo River and its menacing defenses stood in the way of this most potent offensive.

The intense artillery barrage in support of the planned attack reversed for three days (16–18 August) thousands of shells concentrated primarily on strong points on the northern side of the Isonzo mainly Mount Fratta, Mount Semmer and Mount Kuk. At the end of the third day of shelling, Italian observers assessing the situation confirmed to their commanders that the artillery had had a devastating effect on the Austrian frontline positions including the destruction of large sections of the wire and the obliteration of several machine gun nests. Although the barrage had been impressive, the Italian artillery units had failed to execute novel tactics and the barrage's excessive length once again pre-warned the Austrians that the infantry attack was imminent. Nevertheless, the *arditi* were able to achieve a tactical surprise by attacking during the night, which was a novel tactic at least for the Italian infantry.

During the early hours of 19 August under the cover of darkness several boats transported the 250-men strong 1st Company led by Captain Radicati across the Isonzo River near Loga. The *arditi* were to be followed closely by sappers responsible for installing a number of temporary bridges to aid the infantry assault. During the early stages of the battle, the unit's mountain and machine guns were to perform key tasks in support of the infantry attack. They would not only effectuate a potent barrage to force the enemy to seek shelter in the dugouts, but would also be expected to neutralize enemy machine guns with pinpoint accuracy. In support of light artillery operations a huge electric projector had also been installed on the opposite side of the river by I *Reparto d'assalto's* special engineering section. This device, positioned on a hilltop to illuminate the battlefield, would aid with the identification of the enemy machine gun nests.

At 0400 *arditi* units disembarked from their boats and since it was still dark the sentries manning the forward outposts did not see them so they could initially carry out their work unhindered. While the guns, positioned on small hilltops near the river, began to fire, the first platoons of *arditi* silently cut down with daggers many of the forward positioned sentries.

After the Austrians had sounded the alarm, I *Reparto* platoons began to quickly advance under the arc of fire of the mountain guns. While the Italian artillery effectively neutralized the vast majority of the enemy machine guns, it was unable to destroy a well-concealed, defiladed gun unit. The latter kept up a lively and protracted fire wounding several infantrymen and forcing the bulk of the attackers to the ground. Thus, almost as soon as it had started, the attack had bogged down, as the units of I *Reparto* were impeded to advance any further by the enemy's alert reaction. But as the enemy machine gun kept clattering in the dark it eventually allowed the assailants to locate it by the muzzle flash of the weapon. While the mountain guns kept up the pressure on the enemy post by firing several shells, a small platoon outflanked and lay upon it from behind capturing the gun and 30 enemy soldiers barricaded inside a nearby dugout. Thus, by early dawn the *arditi* had cleared the first line of defense and some of their patrol units had began to pursue groups of Austrian soldiers that had evaded capture and were now precipitously descending the mountain. Shortly thereafter, the assault units proceeded to comb the trenches situated along the edge of the river rounding up numerous other groups of soldiers and four machine guns.

The *arditi* soon afterwards regrouped and stormed the peak of the mountain:

> Enemy positions, defended mainly by several dug in machine gun nests, were stormed with flanking maneuvers, whereas the entrances of the dugouts were sealed and covered with grenades. The men barricaded inside were immobilized and taken prisoner. Hand to hand combat later ensued as the unit was counter-attacked by Austrian infantry in an attempt to push us back into the river. The

> Reparto repulsed the counter-attack and then gave way to chase enemy soldiers toward the Auzzana River.[33]

The end result of 1st Company action had been the establishment of a large bridgehead at the base of Mount Fratta and the capture of 150 enemy soldiers, five machine guns and 90 guns.

At the same time, 2nd Company led by Captain Italo Porcari was tasked with forcing the second bridgehead north of the town of Auzza as well as capture the Na Ramunich height (Hill 511) on the reverse slope of the Fratta. Since this unit initially experienced delays in embarking the boats, when it finally entered into action the Austro-Hungarian units on the opposite side of the river were already on the alert along the Isonzo frontline and opened fire immediately as the infantry attack began to unfold. With their boats riddled with bullets and rendered unusable, the *arditi* were initially forced to head back to the opposite side of the river. In addition to retreating back to their lines, much of the unit's firepower was not effective in targeting the enemy's frontline defenses given the low to zero visibility. In the darkness and without any illuminating devices, the unit's own mountain guns were unable to support the fledgling attack as they could not locate and destroy the enemy machine guns despite multiple attempts. As a result, 2nd Company was forced to a standstill for a few hours until dawn. By that time, a temporary bridge had been established and the first assault platoons, despite aggressive enemy machine gun fire, managed to finally cross the river. Once on the other side, the assault company regrouped and waited until the artillery support had eliminated the menacing machine gun fire. With improved visibility as the enemy machine gun units eventually showed their location because they kept firing repeatedly, the guns were able to put them out of action after multiple attempts. After the guns had been eliminated what stood in the *arditi*'s way was one remaining advanced Austrian infantry strongpoint that kept on showering the attackers with rifle fire. Eventually this last bastion of enemy resistance was also dealt with as several assault platoons circumvented it and placed all of its occupants out of action by covering the trenches with grenades. After the first line of defense had been penetrated the fight grew in intensity as it evolved inside the enemy's main trenches, passageways and caverns. Within these confined spaces close combat conditions prevailed as daggers, hand grenades and bayonets were more useful than rifles or machine guns. Although heavy losses were sustained by both sides, the *arditi* were able to penetrate deeply into the Austrian trenches, already shattered by artillery shells and machine gun fire, and occupy them after a protracted hand-to-hand combat struggle. Once the main position had fallen, the assault units fanned out into the enemy rear to capture the main prize, the artillery guns. As a result, a desperate fight developed between the *arditi* and a small group of valiant Austrian servers of the gun batteries that were eventually overwhelmed by the attackers' superior numbers. After having smashed through the frontline defenses

33 Ufficio Storico, 2. Armata: I Reparto d'Assalto, Rapporto del comandandante della I Compagnia Primeglio Radicati, 'Rapporto sull'azione del Monte Fratta', 23 August 1917.

and seized the main position, the assault unit captured several infantrymen, three machine guns, a grenade thrower, a small cannon 37 mm and a medium gun battery of 77 mm, including their respective crews.

Without much respite, the *arditi* then proceeded to attack the second enemy line as each soldier fought his way through several sets of trenches using rifle fire, bursts of flames and hand grenades to take the objectives. They then repelled an Austrian counter-attack attempt with the aid of hand grenades. Finally, the *arditi* proceeded to storm the final objective of Na Ramunich height by assailing the Austrian contingent there deployed with hand grenades capturing two machine guns, one light machine gun and a grenade thrower. With a large bridgehead secured on the opposite side of the river 2nd Company had also achieved its objective and at 1800 it was relieved by line infantry. Its operation had been a success having captured 150 enemy soldiers and several enemy weapons as well as seized the Na Ramunich height.

The Austrian official history states that: "On the heels of a strong preparatory barrage, the Italians managed to cross the Isonzo river. After having swept aside numerous observation posts, the Italian units penetrated the Austro-Hungarian defensive deployment."[34]

Meanwhile on the same day, 3rd Company, led by Captain Pedercini, had been transferred to Gorizia to carry out an operation against the Austrian fortified hill of Belpoggio at the base of Mount San Marco. At 0440 on 19 August the *arditi* charged the first line of defense hurling hundreds of hand grenades and overran it in less than 10 minutes. They then targeted the second enemy line which was taken with a flanking maneuver mostly by working the trenches with hand grenades and daggers. Without any pause 3rd Company then charged against the third line of defense striking again the flank of the enemy deployment and afterwards clearing out several trenches. After brief but very violent close combat, the unit seized the peak of Belpoggio. At this point the Austrian artillery responded by launching heavy interdiction fire blocking Italian support infantry from advancing on Belpoggio. Alone on the hill, the *arditi* were counter-attacked but barely managed to repulse several waves of Austrian infantry units. After more than a day of fighting and after the last wave of Austrian infantry had been pushed back, Belpoggio finally fell in Italian hands. At that point the *arditi* were then relieved by line infantry. They left on the battlefield several dead soldiers but had captured 300 Austrian soldiers and several machine guns.

Thus 1st and 2nd Company had successfully forced the crossing of the Isonzo River leading to the capture of Mount Fratta, while 3rd Company had occupied Belpoggio expanding the Italian frontline positions east of Gorizia. They had in effect opened up the way for the XXIV, XXVII Army Corps and the 48th Division respectively enabling the ultimate capture of the Bainsizza plateau. Although the plateau was later captured by the deployment of masses of standard infantry units and after several more days of fighting, the *arditi* had been instrumental in favoring such an outcome.

34 Edmund Glaise-Horstenau (ed.), *Österreich-Ungarns letzter Krieg 1914–1918, vol. 6*, p. 440.

Mount San Gabriele

Given that the Eleventh Offensive had stalled and further progress beyond the Bainsizza was unlikely, Cadorna ordered the infantry units deployed along the Isonzo to dig in on 28 August 1917. The only exception to this order was the authorization given to 2nd Army to execute another attempt to seize the high ground located northeast of Gorizia and mainly Mount San Gabriele, occupied by the Austrian 57th Infantry Division.

The San Gabriele was the main protective barrier still standing in the Isonzo front blocking access to the Austrian rear. Its defenses were so extensive that they had allowed the Austro-Hungarians to repulse multiple Italian offensive attempts to the point that for the latter it had become known as 'the mountain of death'. Part of the problem for the attackers was that its defenses were based on effective concealment and were dug into the mountain. The caverns on the hilltop, protected by three rounds of barbed wire, were so deep and its steel walls so thick that they could not be destroyed even by the largest Italian field guns. Behind the wire there were numerous machine gun bunkers and several artillery emplacements connected by deep walkways. At the midway point of the mountain the Austrians had built two main advanced strongholds, the Dol on the left and the San Caterina on the right. These concrete blockhouses were built to withstand heavy barrages and they each concealed four machine guns. The blockhouses, surrounded by rounds of barbed wire and steel walls, were connected to each other and to the hilltop defenses by deep tunnels with exits on both flanks of the mountain in order to swiftly shift defensive units to the section most under enemy attack. In short, the San Gabriele had a defensive system that appeared almost impenetrable overlooking a rocky, rugged, terrain consistently swept by machine gun fire. After the standard infantry had been rebuffed numerous times, the responsibility of seizing the Austrian position was handed over to I *Reparto d'assalto* whose units were to storm its defenses and seize its hilltop. The plan of attack was prepared with much care and due diligence by Major Bassi who reconnoitered the San Gabriele on 3 September. Bassi's plan resembled the template of the Austro-Hungarian planned attack against Mount Ortigara: a swift but very intense artillery preparation to neutralize enemy defenses followed by infantry attacking under the arc of fire of the creeping barrage and of the flanking fire of the machine guns. To paralyze the enemy in its caverns over 700 guns of all sizes, one of the largest concentrations of Italian artillery ever achieved during the course of the war, were assembled for the operation.

The plan of attack was based on the *arditi* charging up the mountain on the heels of the swift artillery barrage. They were to storm enemy defenses with speed and decision in order to disarm enemy infantry while it was still taking cover inside the San Gabriele's deep caverns.

General Capello's final orders to the 11th infantry Division were as follows:

> The three assault companies must utilize both ordinary and smoke grenades to open up their way into the enemy positions. They will lead the infantry units,

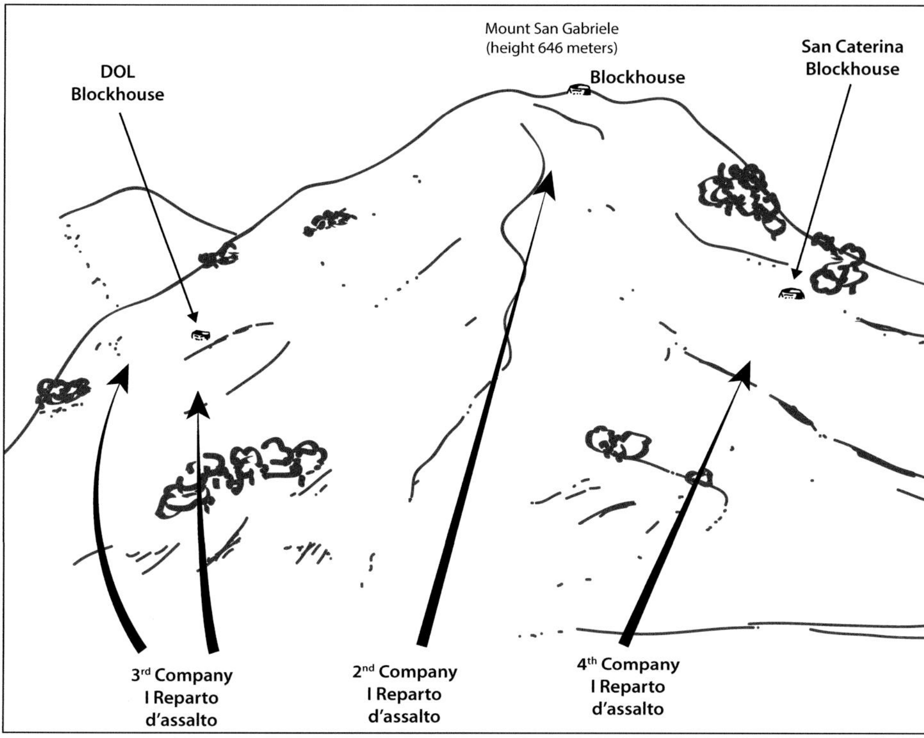

Map 5 The map shows the directions of attack of the *arditi* of I *Reparto d'assalto* which seized the Austrian position on Mount San Gabriele. The operation was one of the most successful *arditi* operations of the war with the capture of a large number of enemy soldiers and weapons.

> which in turn must follow them closely. Since the assault companies are used to advancing under an arc of artillery fire, their main tactical strength should be exploited to the fullest during the operation.[35]

The 3rd Company was to take the Dol blockhouse and then outflank the hilltop defenses on the left flank of the mountain. In order to overcome enemy resistance concentrated in the mountain's caverns and deep trenches the unit was to rely primarily upon its grenade squads and its five flamethrowers platoons.

A second assault column, composed by 2nd Company and 10 flamethrower platoons, was to charge the peak of the San Gabriele directly, while 4th Company was to attack the San Caterina blockhouse on the right flank of the mountain. Once the *arditi* had seized the hilltop, the *Arno* Infantry Brigade was required to relieve them and take control of the San Gabriele defenses. To this end, four of its infantry battalions were to be dispatched as soon as the *arditi* had thrown off the Austrians from the peak of the mountain.

35 Cited in: Filippo Cappellano and Basilio di Martino, *I Reparti d'Assalto*, p. 146.

At 0515 on 4 September 1917 the Italian artillery promptly opened fire. Hundreds of shells soon rained down on the Austro-Hungarian defenses, causing havoc amongst machine gun posts, infantry strong points, mortar and artillery emplacements, and command centers. After just 15 minutes of tremendous fire the creeping barrage was moved forward and closely behind came the assault troops concealed by the smoke and the explosive screen provided by the *Thevenots*. This fire ensured that the defenders still kept their heads down while the Italian units attacked the first line of Austro-Hungarian defenses.

2nd Company overcame enemy defenses on Hill 552 and then swiftly outflanked the western edge of the San Gabriele in order to reach its pinnacle. It was soon joined in battle by 4th Company which reached the peak five minutes later. In less than 20 minutes the assault units had reached the entrances of the enemy dugouts and had began to clash with the enemy. Surprised by the vehemence of the assault, the Austro-Hungarians defenders emerged with considerable haste from their dugouts to parry with the enemy assault detachments, but were met by brute force.

Lieutenant Paolo Giudici recalls that the battle soon fragmented in a series of hand-to-hand clashes as the *arditi* began to clear out the many bunkers and underground tunnels of the San Gabriele:

> It was a fierce struggle. All trench defenders were slaughtered ... the battle fragmented into a hundred smaller ones, and broke out around the rocks, in the midst of the barbed-wire entanglements, in the bunkers and in the tunnels ... The passages had been blocked with Thevenots, the entrances torched with flamethrowers ... The bowels of the mountain were full of enemy ... We fought in the dark, in the never-ending labyrinth, with hand grenades, dagger thrusts, shovel hits, punches, kicks and bites.[36]

After the bulk of the troops were put out of action or disarmed, the last remaining pockets of resistance were overcome while mopping-up the trenches. During this stage of the battle the psychological effect of the flamethrowers often proved instrumental in forcing the enemy to desist from fighting. As the special platoons launched jets of flammable liquid into the openings of the caverns, the smoke and the flames were enough to force the few remaining Austrian units to run out of their defensive posts and surrender. In some cases, the flammable liquid also caused explosions in the ammunition depots causing some of the roofs of the caves to fall in or sending splinters of hand grenades and debris flying everywhere and killing the enemy units inside them instantly.

As the battle raged on the pinnacle, the left wing column led by 3rd Company was initially held up by strong enemy resistance centered in the Dol blockhouse. At first it suffered losses mainly from defiladed machine gun fire while in proximity of the blockhouse. Eventually it was able to storm the blockhouse once an opening had been made in the enemy wire with hand grenades, mortars and explosives. By penetrating

36 Cited in Angelo Pirocchi, *Italian Arditi* (Oxford: Osprey, 2007), p. 48.

the breached wire the *arditi* were able to surround the position and force the enemy to surrender mainly by lobbing hand grenades into its embrasures. But once the Dol blockhouse had been captured, 3rd Company was again prevented from advancing by strong enemy reserves that suddenly emerged from defiladed positions well out of reach of the preparatory artillery fire. Attacked from the flanks and from behind by numerous enemy infantry units, the *arditi* suffered casualties and were unable to proceed any further.

Meanwhile by then on the pinnacle the fighting had subsided and scores of captured enemy soldiers were being escorted to the Italian rear defenses.

Once the San Gabriele had fallen into Italian hands the *arditi* showed all their rumbustious character when officer Salvatore Farina hoisted an Italian flag on the mountain peak. Unfortunately this brazen act of defiance of proper military protocols and procedures alerted the enemy that the mountain position was lost. As a result, the Austrian commander quickly ordered his artillery to implement aggressive counter-preparation fire. Under a heavy bombardment, the Italians were immobilized on the top of the mountain while the reserve troops of the *Arno* Brigade were prevented from reaching them by this most formidable Austrian ring of fire. The latter attempted several times to overcome the artillery siege and reach the peak of the San Gabriele but were rebuffed each time with several casualties. "Enemy interdiction fire pounded the assembly points of the Arno battalions. These areas became horrendous killing zones. As a result, Arno units were targeted and for the most part gunned down even before they had a chance to scale the San Gabriele. The *Arditi* were all alone."[37]

The Austrians, sensing that the pendulum had shifted, then put forth five consecutive attempts to retake the San Gabriele. These determined thrusts were all fought off by the *arditi* who had turned the trenches around and were armed primarily by one heavy machine gun, rifles and hand grenades to repulse the attacks. Despite the massive concentration of fire and the numerous attempts to dislodge the *arditi* from the top of the mountain, Italian defenses on the San Gabriele held. By 1900 the fighting had subsided and the *Arno* units finally took control of the heavily contested position.

Although the attack represented an important success for the Italian Army with 3,100 prisoners taken (including one general) along with 55 machine guns and 26 artillery pieces, losses amongst I *Reparto* were heavy. The assault unit began the battle with 550 soldiers and a few days later, on 6 September, it had been reduced to 180 soldiers. Given the huge losses, Major Bassi argued that the operation had ultimately been a failure. In Bassi's view, standard infantry lacked resoluteness and its action had been too disjointed from that of the *arditi*.

"For the first time," wrote Bassi, "the *Arditi* were assigned the task of opening up the enemy defenses on behalf of the infantry, which in turn had to advance in their footsteps. During the course of the battle the infantry of the Arno Brigade began to advance when it was already too late. In essence, this unit lacked pace and resoluteness. The experiment has therefore produced unsatisfactory results.[38]

37 Paolo Giudici, *Reparti d'assalto* (Milan: Alpes, 1928), p. 99.
38 Salvatore Farina, *Le Truppe d'Assalto Italiane* (Milan: Libreria Militare, 2007), p. 250.

Bassi went on to recommend that future operations involving the *arditi* should be either conducted only by the *arditi* battalions or they should be preceded by full rehearsals in the rear between the latter and the infantry units designated in support of the objectives. This would allow the infantry units to familiarize themselves with the *arditi* and their tactics.

He admonished that it was critical that the infantry and the *arditi* coordinate their movements during an offensive operation and this could only be achieved through joint rehearsals.

Historian Salvatore Farina argues that the *arditi* defending the San Gabriele had only one large machine gun at their disposal to fight off enemy counter-attacks. While the Italian large machine guns were rather bulky and could only be transported with some difficulty across no man's land, the light guns were unreliable since they jammed frequently. This probably explains the lack of an adequate number of guns during the San Gabriele operation. Most likely, the *arditi* were relying on the troops of the *Arno* Brigade to dispatch and transport the heavy machine guns to face the expected counter-attack.

Although the Eleventh Battle of the Isonzo was not decisive, the Italian Army for the first time achieved a significant breakthrough of enemy lines on the Bainsizza plateau. The retreating Austro-Hungarian troops were pushed back by several miles and the total losses on both sides were very heavy. Over 240,000 men, a third of whom were Austro-Hungarians, lost their life in this battle. Both sides also lost large quantities of weapons and depleted valuable stocks of ammunition. Both Italian and Austrian material losses were considerable especially with regards to artillery guns.[39] By the fourth year of the war, however, the Italians could replace infantry and artillery losses more quickly than the Austro-Hungarians. Moreover by mid 1917 Italian artillery production had pushed ahead of Austria-Hungary. This was witnessed by the fact that during the battle an exceedingly high volume of Italian artillery shells (about 5.5 million rounds) were fired.

Madoni

In the aftermath of the large scale Isonzo offensive in the summer of 1917, 2nd Army's General Capello directed his troops to keep the pressure on the Austro-Hungarians with planned attacks and small scale raids.

As a result, on 29 September 1917 II *Reparto d'assalto* was deployed for the first time against enemy strong points, consisting mainly of high altitude machine gun emplacements, located on Madoni mountain (800 meters high), near the Bainsizza plateau. To prevent the recurrence of the tactical deployment issues experienced on the San Gabriele, which were due primarily to a lack of coordination between infantry and assault units, General Capello laid out the following attack guidelines: "The assault units of II *Reparto d'assalto* must be readily reinforced by infantry units whose

39 Mario Silvestri, Isonzo, *1917* (Milan: RCS Libri, 2001), pp. 281–82.

primary task is to consolidate and possibly expand the territorial gains, obtained by the *Arditi*. These support units must advance on the heels of the *Arditi* and follow their trail of destruction in order to speedily take possession of their objective."[40]

The directive was meant to ensure the proper deployment of the assault units by the Italian 44th infantry Division, which was responsible for this sector of the Isonzo frontline and would also provide the necessary infantry and artillery support for the operation. The assault was to begin with a short lived but very intense artillery barrage meant to force the enemy to seek shelter in the dugouts. The *arditi* would then begin their advance toward the first-line trench while the artillery barrage was still unfolding. As the artillery moved its fire forward, the *arditi* would begin to neutralize the enemy defenses by throwing grenades ahead of them into the trench in an effort to fool the enemy into believing that the artillery barrage was still in course. Support infantry was then to be dispatched to take control of the trenches and turn around the position with its heavier weapons such as mortars and machine guns. Once the enemy trenches had been taken, the assault units would expand the scope of the offensive by taking successive rows of enemy trenches.

The success of the operation hinged upon the assault units timing their surge forward with the lifting of the artillery fire. Based on the distance separating the Italian positions from the Austrian trenches it was envisioned that it would take the assault units approximately twenty minutes to reach the Austro-Hungarian forward line on Madoni. Thus, if everything went according to plan, the assault detachments would leave their trenches 15 minutes before the artillery shifted its focus to a box barrage.

The primary role of the operation had been given to the two flanking columns which were to lead the attack, destroy the machine gun nests that had survived the preparatory barrage and finally reach the reserves' dugouts before the enemy had the chance to react.

At 0630 44th Infantry Division artillery, comprised of 200 medium and heavy guns, 200 light guns and 60 bombards began to pummel the Austrian position. The barrage, reported to be comprised of "very violent and continuous fire," catapulted on the enemy trenches a record number of explosive and gas shells. At 0745 the 89th Mountain Battery Unit completed the neutralization of Austrian defenses by firing at point blank range numerous rounds of 65 mm explosive shells. This accurate fire paved the way for the *arditi* by obliterating the few remaining machine gun emplacements dug deep into the rock that stood in the way of the attack. Most importantly the preparatory bombardment kept the enemy heads down while the assault units scaled the mountain. Accordingly, while the artillery was still pounding away, 5th Company of II *Reparto d'assalto,* led by Captain Carlo Signorelli, exited the trenches and began to cross no man's land unencumbered by enemy fire. Its left wing column, comprised of three *arditi* platoons supported by one flamethrower section, two sections of light machine gun pistols, one section of Stokes mortars, one grenade

40 Ufficio Storico, Rep. E-1, Raccolta 79: Comando 2. Armata, Comunicazione urgente, n.5293 op., 23 September 1917.

launcher section and one support infantry company, surged forward and ahead of the other columns being tasked with crossing the most exposed and longest section of no man's land. It was followed by a middle column, comprised of an *arditi* platoon, one flamethrower section, two light machine pistol sections and one support infantry company, whose task was to link up with the flanking columns on the hilltop. On the right, the 250 soldier strong assault company of the *Venezia* Infantry Brigade, which was to storm the opposite flank of the enemy deployment, also surged forward.

In a well-planned operation, the left wing column was the first unit to pounce upon the enemy arriving virtually unopposed on the mountain top. Its elements broke into the enemy trenches, bombing and bayoneting their way past three enemy strong points, killing a number of Austro-Hungarian soldiers and seizing three machine guns and several enemy soldiers. By 0835 the unit had also reached the enemy's command center on Madoni, where it captured a number of its senior officers. By that time, the other assault columns had also made their way to the pinnacle and had managed to secure a number of enemy caverns and dugouts by blocking their entrances and disarming its defenders. Once all sources of opposition had been dealt with on Madoni, the three columns then fanned out in small groups to mop up caverns and trenches situated on the reverse slope of the mountain. As the enemy was still barricaded inside deep caverns to avoid what by then had become a box barrage, the assault units once again faced little opposition. The openings of the caverns were in fact blocked by the assault platoons before the enemy had the chance to organize any sort of coordinated reaction. Grenades were lobbed into them and against the machine gun emplacements, while the embrasures were torched with flamethrowers forcing the enemy to surrender.

Lieutenant Armando Bonanni of II *Reparto d'assalto* provided the following testimony:

> On the morning of the 29th, a few minutes before the start of the operation, I was compelled to give the order to attack unable to restrain the impetuosity of my men. We lunged forward, while covered by the barrage provided by a multitude of guns, against small enemy emplacements that stood between us and the top of the mountain. We continued on toward our objective by overrunning three rows of enemy trenches that were conquered after fierce hand-to-hand combat.
>
> Once on the peak, we threw ourselves onto the reverse slope of the mountain to mop up a number of caverns where the enemy had barricaded himself. Three caverns were cleared immediately as a result of furious close combat that consumed all our stocks of hand grenades and bullets … From one of those caverns emerged a Major, seven officers and eighty Austrian soldiers, that were disarmed and then marched into captivity along with the other prisoners.[41]

41 Autori Vari, *Dizionario delle Battaglie* (Milan: Gulliver Libri, 1996), p. 132.

In less than two hours of fighting the Madoni position had been captured and the assault units began to turn it around. Sandbags were laid along the parapets of the trenches, the captured machine guns were relocated, and the heavy weapons brought up by the infantry support waves were also repositioned having been secured in position. The Austrians, however, were unwilling to concede defeat and began to shell the mountain peak with strong retaliatory artillery fire. Then at 1400 their first counter-attack was repulsed with heavy losses on both sides. During the afternoon the Austrians continued to press the Italians by putting forth several more attempts to retake possession of the position which failed with great losses.

At the end of the day, the Italians kept possession of the mountain post and also captured 2,400 soldiers, 49 officers, 25 machine guns, two mountain guns, and six grenade throwers.

The operation proved again that small assault infantry detachments dispatched on the heels of a properly executed creeping barrage could infiltrate and then overwhelm artillery and machine gun posts largely thanks to their special training and their attacking weapons. Standard infantry units could also sometimes achieve the same results but typically with many more casualties due to their large, densely packed attacking columns moving much more slowly than the *arditi*. The special assault units' success was due to detailed preparation of the planned assault, the proper handling of offensive weapons such as flamethrowers, hand grenades and machine-pistols in close combat conditions and most importantly the speed with which they executed the assault on the heels of the barrage. This last element was the vital tactical achievement of the special assault units demonstrating that a company of *arditi* could do much better in overcoming high altitude machine gun posts due to its special training than an entire infantry brigade.

The artillery fire support this time was adequate. It was not lifted too early, and nor too late resulting in few casualties by friendly fire. Finally, it appears that given the weak enemy reaction the appropriate number of shells was used to successfully pin down enemy defenses.

Conclusion

The special assault units were wiped out in late 1917 when "the *arditi* found themselves struggling to stave off defeat as 2nd Army streamed back from Caporetto."[42] This defeat led to a widespread reorganization of the *Reparti d'assalto* which took place during the winter of 1917–18. Yet we can draw some preliminary conclusions on their effectiveness from their initial experimental phase in the summer of 1917 until November 1917. From the first set of *arditi* operations General Capello drew the following lesson: "The *Arditi* are a very precious element which at all costs must not be subjected to exhaustion or depression. They should therefore be employed in offensive operations that although risky contain all the elements for certain success."[43]

42 John Gooch, *The Italian Army*, p. 203.
43 Cited in: Filippo Cappellano and Basilio di Martino, *I Reparti d'Assalto*, p. 78.

In his view the *arditi* had fought well but at times had not been properly supported or deployed by standard infantry officers.

Similarly, Italian historian Giorgio Rochat has argued that:

> 2nd Army *arditi* units demonstrated through their numerous operations that by mid 1917 a higher level of efficiency within the Italian army had been achieved ... The extensive training at Sdricca proved to be a successful undertaking. It allowed the *arditi* to generally achieve tactical surprise when attacking the enemy, to prevail during hand-to-hand combat within enemy trenches, to achieve a deep penetration of the enemy's defensive deployment and finally the execution of successful counter-attacks to repulse the enemy with flanking thrusts aided primarily by daggers and hand grenades.[44]

Successful offensive operations required complete surprise which the slow-moving standard infantry had achieved only a few times. The *arditi* on the other hand, achieved greater success because they were able to implement better planned surprise attacks. If the territorial gains of the special assault unit operations were impressive, the material gains were equally advantageous. The results of the first set of *arditi* operations were rather positive with thousands of captured enemy prisoners, many machine guns and artillery units and several other pieces of equipment had also fallen in Italian hands.

Given the results achieved and the fact that a few hundred special infantrymen had gained what up to then much larger infantry units had achieved only thanks to great sacrifice and cost, Italian tactical thinking began to change. Many infantry operations had shown that standard troops were poor at maneuvering given their lack of training and their slow-moving attack columns. To overcome ineffective infantry action, more agile, better-equipped and trained *arditi* units in the lead of the infantry attack held the promise of improved results.

By the fall of 1917 *Comando Supremo*'s main objective was to reorganize and replenish the infantry units of the 2nd and 3rd Army, including its *reparti d'assalto*, as well to begin planning a renewed offensive operation against the Isonzo sector before the winter. On the heels of the success on the Bainsizza it was estimated that given increased artillery units and shells production together with better trained and equipped assault unit detachments, the Italian Army could actually obtain the much desired breakthrough and seize Trieste.

Although the *arditi* had proved their worth in the field of battle, there were aspects of their tactical deployment that were still subject to improvement. The post-battle reports stressed that what appeared not to be working and therefore subject to reform during these early operations, was the cooperation, or the lack of, between *arditi* and infantry. On Mount San Gabriele, for instance, infantry reserves destined to relieve the *arditi* were not able to reach the peak of the mountain given that the Austrian artillery had encircled it by a ring of fire. In addition, it appeared that standard

44 Giorgio Rochat, *Gli Arditi*, p. 49.

infantry units could not keep pace with the much faster *arditi*. As a result, I *Reparto d'assalto*, armed almost completely with offensive weapons, had lost many men to enemy counter-attacks while awaiting to be relieved by the heavier equipped and therefore, slower moving infantry units. While the Austro-Hungarian stormtroopers had initially suffered from a lack of coordination with their artillery, the Italian *arditi*, during these first operations, had faced an altogether different problem. As a special force, the *arditi* had never trained or conducted full rehearsals with standard infantry units. As a result, their tactics and their conduct on the battlefield were something the standard infantry units were not accustomed to. Both Bassi and Capello maintained that *arditi*–infantry coordination could be improved only through careful planning and preparation of planned attacks and a more timely deployment of the infantry. The Austrian stormtroopers, on the other hand, had overcome this problem because once they had completed training they were returned to their infantry division. Hence, the Austrian stormtroopers were for the most part always deployed in battle along with their divisional infantry comrades. As a result, full rehearsals were conducted on a regular basis.

Infantry and artillery collaboration was also another area subject to further improvement as the length of the preparatory bombardment tended on average to last longer than the swift barrages in support of *sturmtruppen* prepared attacks. The San Gabriele bombardment, for instance, lasted three days giving ample warning to the enemy that an infantry attack was imminent. On the San Gabriele the *arditi* did experience additional issues related to infantry–artillery collaboration as some of the attackers were killed by Italian shells because they rushed ahead too quickly to the wire. In the words of *arditi* officer Paolo Giudici: "The first *arditi* fell, hit by our artillery, impatient to reach the enemy."[45]

Another issue identified in the post-battle reports was the bulkiness of the flame-throwers that limited the maneuverability of the *arditi* units within the confined spaces of enemy trenches and caverns. Although the weapon was difficult to operate, it was nevertheless recognized for its powerful shock-effect against enemy infantry and for its usefulness during mop-up operations. The machine guns supplied to the Italian Army were also another issue that was underlined in the post battle reports. The large units were bulky and were not easy to carry to support the *arditi* with flanking fire, while the light guns were not reliable and often, by not working properly, exposed the *arditi* to vehement enemy counter-attacks. This led the special assault units to rely more on the small mountain cannons and later on the Stokes mortars for direct fire support. Finally, the overall weaponry of the *arditi* was considered to be too light when turning over enemy defenses and therefore the special troops were often vulnerable to counter-attacks while waiting to be relieved by the heavier equipped and therefore, slower moving infantry units.

The Austro-Hungarian AOK by October 1917 had already gathered from several intelligence reports that the Italians had also began to deploy with consistency their own shock troops.

45 Paolo Giudici, *I Reparti d'assalto*, p. 47.

Accordingly, the official history states that: "Signs of an imminent new battle included continuing intelligence about the enemy as well as their increasing activity on the Isonzo during July. This included the deployment of new batteries, frequent air patrols, and local thrusts by detachments of stormtroops."[46] By that stage in the war the AOK recognized that the Italians had also made some progress in the development of more effective offensive infantry tactics for a long-term campaign of trench warfare. One of these changes had been the creation of special assault detachments whose potential was recognized by the AOK and could ultimately erode the tactical advantage that the Austro-Hungarian Army had enjoyed over its primary enemy.

The response of the AOK to the new threat posed by improved Italian infantry tactics was twofold. First, prior to the launch of the Caporetto offensive the AOK published a directive that called for further training for the special assault units in order to maintain the lead over the Italians that had recently formed their own special assault units. "Since the Italians have already imitated our *Sturmtruppen* model and have therefore created their own assault detachments, in the foreseeable future it is of uttermost importance to raise the overall quality of our assault troops."[47]

A second response to the rise of the *arditi* on the part of the AOK was the further bolstering of the heavy artillery: "In fact the troops did not want to do without heavy guns while themselves on the defensive, so that the enemy's artillery could be suppressed and their infantry storm tactics checked."[48]

Even through the Italians were beginning to pull away with shell and gun production, it is estimated that by the fall of 1917 the Austro-Hungarian Army was still able to deploy an exceedingly high number of artillery guns of all sizes including approximately 30 batteries of 30.5 cm howitzers.

46 Edmund Glaise-Horstenau (ed.), *Österreich-Ungarns letzter Krieg, vol. 6*, p. 432.

47 Kriegsarchiv: K.u.K., AOK, Op. Nr. 2046/10, 'Neuorganisation der *Sturmtruppen*', 17 October 1917.

48 Ibid.

6

Recovery and Final Victory

During the winter of 1917–18 the Italian Army for the most part stood on the defensive in order to recover from the great defeat at Caporetto. This stasis in operations was implemented to allow the army to rearm following the catastrophe as well as call up new classes of recruits to replenish the depleted ranks of the army corps. Another factor that prevented offensive operations was the extremely cold weather combined with large quantities of ice and snow. One of the few exceptions to a mostly defensive posture was the planned raid by XXIX *Reparto d'assalto* against the enemy strong point of Sano situated between Mount Altissimo and Rovereto. The unit was comprised primarily by soldiers coming from the *alpini* corps and they wore the characteristic *alpino/ardito* green patches. XXIX *Reparto d'assalto* had been formed by the Trentino's 1st Army to overcome the highly fortified sectors of the front such as Mount Pasubio. Given the fact that the unit was to see deployment primarily in a high mountain environment its soldiers received extensive combat as well as mountain climbing training. The unit also received specific training in long range mountain patrols with and without skis to perform not only the surveillance and intelligence gathering functions but also carry out sabotage behind enemy lines. With this type of preparation its elements were supposed to carry out special missions such as combat, reconnaissance, mountain guiding and wire cutting.[1] At Sano the Austrians had built a few fortifications with machine gun emplacements that were protected by three rounds of barbed wire, the last of which was electrified. The objective of the raid was to spring a surprise assault on the enemy in order to capture the garrison in its entirety including its commander. Since the garrison was heavily protected by obstacles of all kinds, the biggest challenge for the raiding party was how to swiftly overcome undetected the electrified wire and without causing a reaction from the enemy. Since this was the first operation of the XXIX *Reparto d'assalto* it was carefully prepared in all its details. For several days a small unit of officers and soldiers from the *arditi* unit began a thorough surveillance of the enemy position in order to determine the numerical consistency of the garrison as well as the major weapons at its disposal. After exhaustive reconnaissance it was determined that the garrison was comprised of roughly 40

1 Ufficio Storico, Rep. F-4, Raccolta 199: Comando 1. Armata, telegramma n. 35946, 12 May 1918.

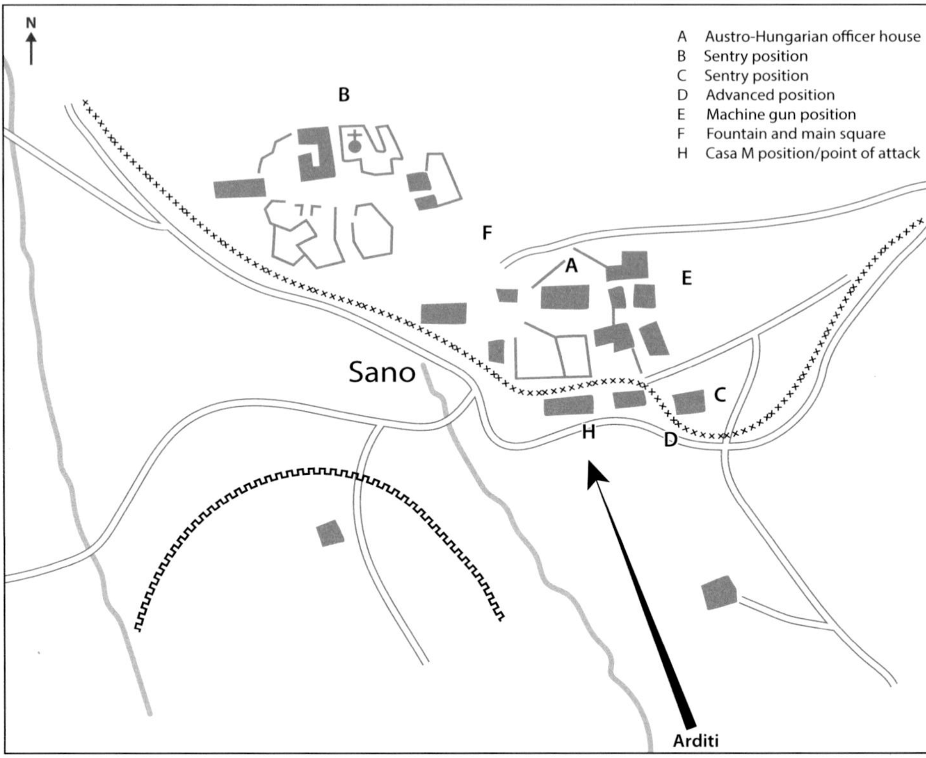

Map 6 This is the original sketch made by the commander of the XXIX *Reparto d'assalto* during the planning phase for the raid against Sano. It indicates the location of all the major Austro-Hungarian positions such as Casa M, the machine gun and sentry emplacements and the barbed wire works.

soldiers, the majority of which were stationed at the so-called 'Casa M' house in the middle of town and within a few meters of the barbed wire. The remaining soldiers of the garrison were scattered in a few smaller homes also located in the center of town; while the commander and his headquarters staff where stationed in another home nearby. The number and positioning of the sentries, machine guns and other strong points were also identified as a result of the detailed surveillance.

The reconnaissance in depth allowed the commander of the *arditi* unit to draw up a small sketch representing Sano's main enemy positions that was used to fully plan out the attack.

In order to achieve complete surprise it was determined that the raid would initially proceed without the aid of the artillery preparatory fire. The artillery would only in fact intervene toward the end of the raid in a bid to tie down the enemy while the raiding party retreated. Moreover, it was also envisioned that the unit would deploy ahead of time a sapper specialist with wire cutters to breach the enemy wire thus allowing the troops to penetrate swiftly and by surprise into Sano. The raid would

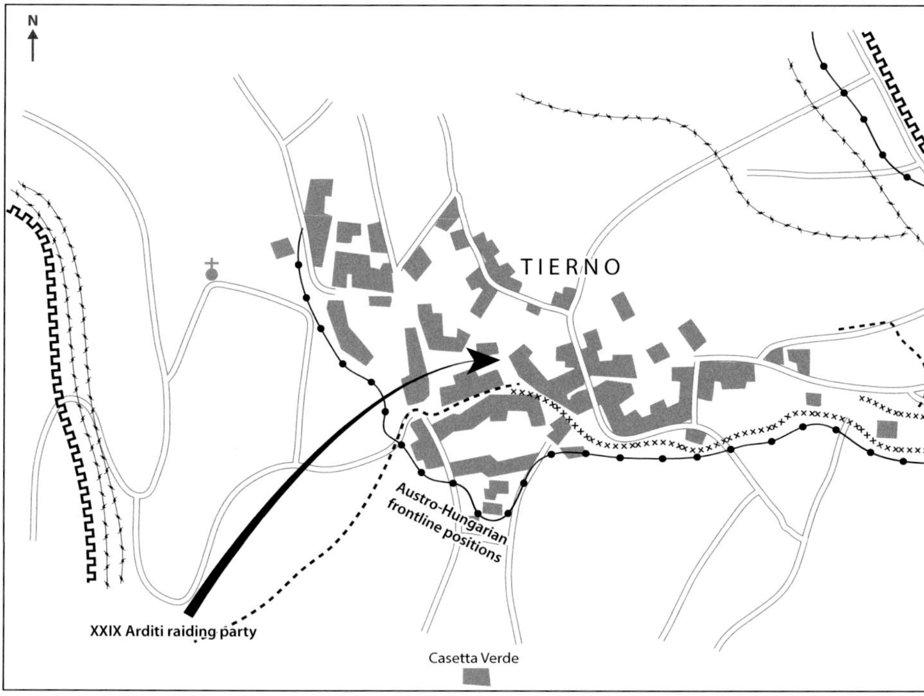

Map 7 This is a reproduction of the original sketch made by the commander of the XXIX *Reparto d'assalto* during the planning phase for the raid against Tierno. It indicates the direction and the route that the *arditi* had to follow in order to overcome the wire and attack the enemy.

be conducted primarily by two *arditi* platoons. The first platoon was expected to storm Casa M and then continue to mop up the enemy positions in the town before retreating, while the second platoon was to deploy in the outer town limits to block the main road leading into Sano thus preventing potential sallies by enemy reinforcements from interfering with the operation.

At 0815 on 19 January 1918 the two *arditi* platoons dressed in white camouflage overcoats and armed primarily with rifles and hand grenades, began their careful approach march toward Sano. Blending in very well with the snow and ice, they advanced undetected in their ghost-like overcoats without experiencing any major difficulties toward the small township. In the meantime the sapper had already started to work by carefully cutting the enemy wire and decommissioning the electrified defenses without arousing any suspicion from the enemy. Once the wire was breached, the *arditi* were waived forward and once they had passed it they began to launch several hand grenades and smoke bombs in the direction of Casa M. The enemy, completely surprised by the attack, was caught totally unprepared and was initially unable to put forth a reaction. Then after having reached the proximity of the enemy position a fierce hand-to-hand fight developed in which the *arditi* prevailed by killing 15 enemy soldiers while only losing one of their own. Shortly thereafter,

Casa M was stormed and several Austrian soldiers were captured. The building was then torched and the *arditi* began to retreat toward their lines carrying with them several prisoners including the unit's commander while the Austrian artillery fired a few retaliatory shots. Most of these landed in a nearby area in the vicinity of Sano indicating that the raid had achieved full surprise and that the bulk of the Austro-Hungarian defenders still did not know where the Italians had struck. As the unit was pulling back, the second platoon that was charged with covering the retreat was also engaged with the enemy as it ran into an enemy patrol unit. Soon fighting broke out between the two platoons and in the melee that ensued the *arditi* prevailed by killing eight and capturing two Austro-Hungarian soldiers. This platoon then also quickly retreated toward the trenches.

Meticulously prepared and well executed according to the original plan of attack, the raid achieved all of its objectives. Most importantly it had caused several enemy casualties, while the raiders had lost only one man and two injured. On 5 March the same unit raided the nearby town of Tierno but the attackers were repelled by the prompt response of the Austrian machine guns.

The Battle of the Three Mountains

On 23 December 1917 Army Group Conrad put forth the last offensive push before the winter break in order to throw off the Italians from the Asiago Altopiano. Although the Austro-Hungarian troops were unable to take the massive enemy fortifications on the Altopiano, they seized Mount Valbella, Col d'Echele, Col del Rosso, and the so-called Three Mountains, which consisted of a number of strong points bulging into the Italian defensive line. While the 21st *Schützen* Division occupied Mount Valbella, the 106th Division held Col del Rosso and Col d'Echele and the 52nd Brigade occupied Sasso Rosso. According to the Austrian official history these infantry units in January 1918 were under strength as a result of the numerous attacks that they had sustained against Mount Grappa's enemy positions and the Three Mountains in December 1917. These forces would be the target on 28 January 1918 of the Italian Army's attempt to retake possession of key terrain with a limited offensive. This operation became the first sizeable Italian offensive after Caporetto involving a large-scale artillery and infantry deployment. Prior to this offensive the Italian position on the Asiago Altopiano was rather precarious because it lacked depth being relegated to the southern edge of the massif. The conquest of the Three Mountains would have allowed the Italians to gain some breathing room and also take control of the strategic Frenzela Valley.

The operation, led by General Sanna of the 33rd Infantry Division, was carried out by the following units: I, II, IV and XVI *Reparti d'assalto*, five *alpini* battalions, the *Sassari*, *Bisagno* and *Liguria* Infantry Brigades and four *bersaglieri* regiments. The artillery support was comprised of 244 batteries well supplied by ample stocks of ammunition including 400,000 light and 500,000 medium and heavy shells, a vast number of which were of French origin with greater explosive effect than standard Italian shells. With over 900 guns, including 28 heavy field guns of 305 mm, the artillery was in a strong position to cover every angle of the enemy's defensive deployment and to implement multiple preparation barrages.

The plan of attack included a two-hour artillery barrage over a relatively narrow two mile section, of the Altopiano front line in order to rupture multiple sections of the enemy wire. A preliminary barrage concentrated on nearby enemy positions on the day prior to the start of operations was also envisioned to keep the enemy from guessing the infantry's direction of attack. The preliminary actions aimed at confusing the enemy as to the real focus of the operation also included two diversionary attacks to be put forth by the *alpini* on nearby Mount Cornone and Sasso Rosso which were to precede the main assault on the Three Mountains. The plan, which included precise instructions, "stressed the need for a rapid and sudden rupture of the enemy positions. The infantry assault shall begin as soon as the destructive fire has terminated. The assault units are to outflank the enemy from both sides and infiltrate their positions with several small teams of *arditi* and infantry. A frontal attack is to be avoided at all costs."[2] The *arditi* were to lead the infantry attack deployed as follows: II *Reparto d'assalto*, followed by the *bersaglieri* units of the 5th Brigade, was to leapfrog from the dorsal of Costalunga and Col Echar into the peak of Mount Valbella at 1,376 meters. Once this assault unit had reached the wire it would split up into three assault groups to exploit the main gaps made by the artillery. At the same time, I *Reparto d'assalto* was to open up enemy defenses on the Col del Rosso and Col d'Echele on behalf of the *Sassari* Brigade. Its 2nd Company was to lead II Battalion/151st Regiment in scaling the western edge of Col del Rosso, while its 3rd Company, supported by III Battalion/151st Regiment was to attack the same position from the opposite flank. Finally, 1st Company and III Battalion/152nd Regiment were expected to outflank enemy positions on the Col d'Echele. All three columns of attack were to be supported by mobile flanking fire provided by the heavy machine gun sections, while the light machine gun sections were to fight alongside the first infantry waves in order to immobilize the enemy as the assault developed. Both sections had been instructed to move forward in close collaboration with the assaulting units.

The artillery began operations on the afternoon of 27 January to soften up enemy defenses with violent preparatory fire. At 0730 on 28 January the artillery shifted its focus in order to concentrate on destructive fire aimed at making gaps on the enemy wire. During this second phase of the artillery barrage, the Italian Army made vast recourse to mustard gas shells for the first time during the campaign. It is reported that the poison gas shells not only had the desired effect of completely taking by surprise the enemy forces deployed on the Three Mountains, but it also initially suppressed the enemy artillery. Finally, as the troops were getting ready to leave the trenches, the artillery initiated interdiction fire to provide coverage to the infantry's advance. By this time, the *alpini* units had already proceeded to assail enemy forces on the Cornone in their bid of carrying out the diversionary attack. The latter was conquered

2 Ufficio Storico, Rep. E-5, Raccolta 110, XX Corpo d'Armata: Comando Brigata Sassari, 'Ordine di operazione, n. 247', R.P. 22 January 1918.

after fierce fighting. The mountain units then moved on to the Sasso Rosso but there were counter-attacked by strong Austrian infantry squads and eventually driven off the Cornone as well. The battle intensified during the afternoon with various reversals of fortune for both Austrians and Italians, but by 1900 both the Cornone and Sasso Rosso had fallen again into Italian hands.

Thus with the Austro-Hungarian defenders initially focused upon the Cornone sector, at 0930 II *Reparto d'assalto* and the *bersaglieri* units, subdivided into three columns, charged up the western flank of Mount Valbella on the heels of the preparatory barrage and began penetrating in small groups through the ruptured wire. Soon after they overran two sets of enemy trenches and captured 100 enemy soldiers. Up to that point everything had seemed to be working according to the original plan of attack. But when the Austrians fired a number of red flares which were mistakenly understood by the Italian artillery to be a request by their own assault units for a lengthening of the artillery fire, the situation quickly turned. As a result of this misunderstanding, the artillery stopped firing against the enemy positions altogether and the Austrian defenders, now unopposed by enemy fire, emerged from their dugouts to shower the attacking columns with machine gun and light artillery fire. Under heavy fire, the infantry units were pinned to the ground, while the *arditi,* who had pushed ahead of everybody else, risked being captured by a strong enemy counter-attack after having advanced too deeply past the wire. Caught in no man's land with no artillery support, the Italian assault infantry detachments had no other option but to speedily retreat toward the base of the mountain where a thick forest provided them with greater protection from enemy fire. Meanwhile, this general retreat placed further pressure upon the support units of *bersaglieri* of 14th and 20th Regiments, that after having had advanced on the right flank of the main two assault columns, were in turn counter-attacked by special Austrian assaults units and severely tested by the surprise enemy coup.

At the same time I *Reparto d'assalto* led infantry units of the *Sassari* Brigade against the Col del Rosso. The attackers, deployed into two columns, initially overran some of the enemy's advanced positions and then continued to make progress toward the peak of the mountain by storming several machine gun strong points. However, once having reached the halfway point of the mountain both columns were subjected to heavy fire from defilated machine guns and as a result were no longer able to proceed further. The column on the western flank, in particular, due to the heavy fire, was also forced to retreat toward the forest at the base of the mountain. For several hours this unit remained immobilized under tremendous machine gun and artillery fire without any possibility of extricating itself from its rather precarious situation. Unable to retreat any further, the unit was subjected also to a strong Austrian counter-attack that inflicted grave losses especially upon the troops of the 151st infantry, that during the fighting not only lost its commander but also the majority of its officers.

To break the deadlock, the Italian artillery was called into action in a bid to further soften up the enemy positions with mortar fire and open the way for a successive attempt by the infantry. As a result of a 30-minute destructive barrage, Col del Rosso's defenses were eventually stormed by troops from I *Reparto d'assalto* and

Sassari Brigade. Hand grenade and flamethrower platoons from these units then proceeded to eliminate the last pockets of energy resistance and rounded up 100 prisoners. Shortly after, the infantry assault continued on the Col d'Echele. Here too, on the heels of the powerful artillery barrage, *arditi* and infantry units assailed the position with both hand and smoke grenades. With frontline defenses breached, the Austro-Hungarian contingent was unable to withstand the infantry assault and was forced to capitulate.

Thus by 1600 the line consisting of Col del Rosso, Col d'Echele and Pizzo Razea had fallen into Italian hands, while the Mount Valbella was the only position on this advanced line that was still held firmly by Austro-Hungarian infantry.

By evening Italian line infantry was feverishly working to turn around the seized positions by digging trenches and by installing the barbed wire in anticipation of a likely counter-attack. The expected counter-thrust came shortly after 0400 on 29 January. Austrian artillery began to concentrate heavy fire on the lost positions which was soon followed by a massive infantry counter-attack. Intense hand-to-hand combat ensued on the Col del Rosso and Col d'Echele as the Austrians put forth a series of infantry assaults with bayonets and hand grenades to take back possession of the mountain positions. But as the sun began to protrude out from the clouds, the Italian defenders thanks to improved visibility were able to repulse the attacks but with heavy losses.

At the same time the Italian artillery was also hard at work to degrade enemy defenses on the last bastion of the Mount Valbella. At 0700 on 29 January the artillery switched to interdiction fire targeting enemy reserve elements that had amassed near Mount Valbella in anticipation of a renewed Italian offensive attempt by its infantry. The artillery fire dispersed several of these platoons forcing them to retreat from the mountain. Shortly thereafter the artillery shifted its focus again by pounding once more the last remaining enemy held position on the Three Mountains. With all guns concentrated on one target, the widespread destruction of the enemy's defenses was achieved and at 0830 the attack against the much-contested mountain top was renewed. On the left flank, 2nd Company of IV *Reparto d'assalto*, XIV *bersaglieri* Battalion/5th Regiment and LXI *bersaglieri* Battalion/14th Regiment were to attack the enemy position with the hand grenade and flamethrower units leading the way. In the middle, XVI *Reparto d'assalto*, LVI *bersaglieri* Battalion/5th Regiment and one company of XL *bersaglieri* Battalion/5th Regiment were tasked to infiltrate the enemy position from the shortest distance toward to the top of the mountain. While on the right, 1st Company IV *Reparto d'assalto*, XLIV *bersaglieri* Battalion/14th Regiment, XXIV *bersaglieri* Battalion/5th Regiment and LXXII/20th Regiment were tasked with attempting to outflank the enemy from the rear.

Due to heavy enemy fire and frequent counter-attacks the progress of each attacking column was painstakingly slow as the troops were forced to advance in small groups hopping into shell holes or behind large boulders in order to avoid the enemy's furious fire. At 1030 the left wing column managed to penetrate the walkway that lead to the peak of the mountain and began to make considerable inroads into the enemy defenses mainly with rifle fire and hand grenades.

The other two columns, however, were not able to keep pace being consistently targeted by heavy enemy artillery shelling and unable to overcome strong pockets of enemy resistance. Sensing that the battle had once again reached a standstill, the commander of the 33rd Infantry Division reinforced each assault column with fresh reserve units. The precious support provided by the reserve units (XL *bersaglieri* Battalion/14th Regiment and one battalion of the *Bisagno* Infantry Brigade) had the desired effect as the two main columns were pushed further up toward the peak of the mountain. Reinforced by fresh troops, the assault columns renewed their attack on the peak of the Valbella once again at 1300. Enemy strong points were subjected to concentrated machine gun and hand grenade fire as the noose was tightening with every passing minute. Finally, the right wing column managed to bomb its way through the enemy trenches closely followed by flamethrower units investing the enemy with burning liquid and smoke. Thanks to these multiple efforts at 0100 the Valbella position had been breached.

As the Austro-Hungarian retaliatory fire began to diminish considerably, the other two remaining columns were also able to climb to the peak of the mountain to begin the mopping up process of the enemy dugouts and trenches.

The successful operation yielded a total of 100 officers, 2,500 soldiers, six guns and 100 machine guns. Italian losses were also severe including 45 dead officers, 158 injured and 38 missing, 534 dead soldiers, 3,162 wounded and 1,286 missing. IV *Reparto d'Assalto* lost 300 soldiers and nine officers, while II *Reparto* lost 140 soldiers. Two factors were the primary drivers in the Battle of the Three Mountains: effective use of artillery support and the attempt, albeit flawed and not completely successful, of the adoption of infiltration tactics by the assault detachments. As Gooch asserts, "Although by no means an unvarnished success, the battle marked progress in the use of artillery."[3]

According to the post-battle report of the 33rd Infantry Division several factors had contributed to the success of the operation. First, "detailed analysis of the strength and layout of the enemy strong points, based on aerial photographs, sketches and most importantly, extensive on-site reconnaissance by both artillery and infantry officers, laid the groundwork for the infantry assault."[4]

Second, the good mobility of the machine gun squads, that provided accurate and close support in different stages of the battle, greatly aided the assaulting units. Most machine gun platoons were able to advance in close collaboration with the infantry and supported it with flanking fire at several critical stages when the enemy needed to be pinned down. Third, the close cooperation between artillery and infantry and the strong effort put forth by the former in following the infantry advance in all its stages, including its reliance on aerial reconnaissance to identify enemy targets. The artillery operation was further bolstered by the availability and use of French artillery shells which proved to have a more devastating effect than Italian shells.

3 John Gooch, *The Italian Army*, p. 262.
4 Ufficio Storico: Comando della 33. Divisione di Fanteria, 'Relazione sulle operazioni per la riconquista dei Tre Monti', 2 February 1918.

Fourth, "the breakout role assigned to the Reparti d'Assalto was carried out accordingly. By fighting in the lead of the multiple infantry columns, the *Arditi* were able to create gaps in the enemy defenses by taking advantage of their specific training and weapons. They were then the first units to come to blows with the enemy."[5]

Raid Against Marco Railway Crossing

Thanks to thorough and continuous reconnaissance of the enemy positions, the *arditi* of the Valbella *Reparto d'assalto* identified another important target of opportunity at the Marco railway crossing station (Trentino sector) that was occupied by a small enemy garrison. After careful preparations it was observed that the enemy systematically reduced the number of sentries on duty during the early morning hours in order to allow the vast majority of the garrison to take breakfast. Accordingly, the 1st Company of the Valbella *Reparto* led by Captain Bramante decided to attack it on a cloudy day and to further increase its chances of success to do so during the early hours of the morning. The plan was risky, given the enemy's fixed defenses and ample barbed wire works, but it was sound in concept. On 2 April 1918 at 0200 the two platoons approached Marco and then lay low in a wooded area for several hours where they awaited for the order to attack. According to the attack plans, the Italian artillery began to blast a nearby enemy post at 0400 in order to distract the enemy into believing that an infantry attack against it was imminent.

At 0700, after having carefully cut the wire, the *arditi* broke through the enemy's defenses. After having quickly surrounded the objective they began to submerge it with several hand grenades. Several enemy soldiers that survived the attack attempted to escape from the back of the building but the majority were apprehended, while a few others were cut down by machine gun fire. The building at the railway crossing was destroyed, 11 soldiers were killed and 15 were captured at a cost of four wounded *arditi*. Following the brilliant raid, General Pecori Giraldi of 1st Army issued the following communiqué: "The great feat carried out by the *reparto d'assalto* of this Army Corps should serve as an example for other units to carry out similar daring operations. These types of operations are the essential tasks of the *arditi* and should be carried out on a regular basis by all the units of this Army Corps."[6]

The Capture of Mount Corno (Later renamed Corno Cesare Battisti)

Between 10–13 May 1918 in the Mount Pasubio sector the Italian Army was able to score a significant victory when a handful of *arditi* captured the highly fortified Mount Corno stronghold after three days of hard fighting. The possession of this mountain peak, which at the time was defended by units of the 1st *Kaiserjäger*

5 Filippo Cappellano and Basilio Di Martino, *I Reparti d'Assalto*, p. 509.
6 Pompilio Schiarini, *L'armata del Trentino* (Milan: Mondadori, 1925), p. 112.

Regiment, not only gave the Austrians an excellent position from which to control the Vallarsa Valley but also the ability to block any offensive attempt against the second largest town in Trentino, Rovereto. During the war the Italians called Mount Corno 'the spy of the Vallarsa Valley' because from its height the enemy was able to observe large swathe of land spanning all the way to the Italian rear defenses. For the Italians Mount Corno was also a site that held significant symbolic importance being the location where on 10 July 1916 the Austrians had captured Cesare Battisti and Fabio Filzi, the two Trentino volunteers and Austrian citizens who subsequently faced a court martial and were hanged at the Buonconsiglio Castle in Trento for high treason.

Initially, the Italians had opted to take the mountain by detonating a mine under the enemy position. During the winter of 1917–18 several Italian sapper units bored through the rock in order to construct a tunnel that reached the Austrian defenses. But in the spring of 1918, when the tunnel had almost been completed, an Austrian officer who had deserted from the Mount Corno garrison furnished valuable intelligence that altered the plan of attack. The officer not only furnished information on an Austrian attempt to dig a counter-tunnel to pre-empt the Italian plan, but also ample intelligence on the mountain's intricate system of defense. This information alerted the commander of the *Murge* Brigade Colonel Eugenio Lombardi who decided to postpone the work on the tunnel and prepare for a surprise coup against the enemy position before the latter had the opportunity to detonate the mine. The intelligence provided by the Austrian officer was found to be very useful as it furnished a comprehensive description of the enemy's defenses as well as invaluable information on the timing and frequency of the rotation of the troops that made up the post's defensive garrison. Most importantly, very valuable information on several openings in the wire that were used to regularly rotate troops in and out of the position was also provided and this last piece of information gave rise to a plan of attack that comprised a surprise coup without artillery preparation. The plan issued by the commander of the *Murge* Brigade stated that: "the aim is to spring a surprise attack against the enemy positions on Mount Corno and on Peak 1,801 in order to capture the enemy garrison and hold the position."[7] The attack was to begin on 10 May and its goal was to seize the peak at 1,801 meters above sea level. In order to surprise the enemy the operation, which was to be undertaken by the 2nd Company of V *Reparto d'assalto* and by a company from the *Murge* Brigade, was to be implemented at night and by penetrating into the openings in the wire. The troops of the V *Reparto d'assalto* were thought to be highly suited for this type of operation since its core was comprised by very young volunteers coming from the *alpini*, *bersaglieri* and infantry units with less to lose than the standard infantry soldier. The vast majority of these volunteers were not married, had no children, were all under 23 years of age and had good athletic abilities.

During the night on the 9–10 May 1918 two infantry columns, one attacking the right flank of Mount Corno and the other on the left flank, attempted to circumvent

7 Ufficio Storico, Rep. B-1, Raccolta 114S, 251E, V Corpo d'Armata: Comando Brigata Murge, 'Azione offensiva su Monte Corno e quota 1,801', n. 439, 8 May 1918.

the enemy positions on Peak 1,801. In order to reach them they had to cross steep mountain gullies in the darkness in order to finally assemble at the designated point which they did eventually reach albeit with some delay. At 0500 the *arditi* column on the right stormed the so-called Seletta Battisti, which was situated under the main peak position, and swiftly penetrated into the enemy's intricate cavern and trench system. The first line defenders and the sentries were quickly overwhelmed but the noise produced by the explosion of the hand grenades alerted the rest of the enemy garrison that an enemy attack was underway. As a result, the Austro-Hungarians occupying the peak position opened up great machine gun fire that prevented the *arditi* from advancing any further. Given the density of the enemy's barbed wire works combined with the determined enemy response, the assault units were forced to seek shelter in the cavern system on the Seletta Battisti under the peak of the mountain where they dug in along with 35 prisoners. Thus, after the first day of battle it appeared that an impasse had been reached as the Austrians still firmly controlled the peak of the mountain, while the Italians were stationed right under it at the entrance of the caverns. In all likelihood the few Italians on the Seletta could not have held out for much longer without the aid of reinforcements and given the lack of food, water and ammunition. Determined not to lose the hold on the advanced platform of the Seletta Battisti position, the commander of the *Murge* tasked one of the Brigade's platoons to try to reach the caverns where the *arditi* had dug in. Accordingly, at 0800 on 10 May a platoon of 36 soldiers attempted to break the siege and penetrate into the Seletta. During its advance on open ground over 25 soldiers were wounded by the enemy machine gun fire and one soldier died, but a lieutenant and 10 of his men managed to reach it and make contact with the *arditi*.

The Austro-Hungarians had by then realized that the Italians were strengthening their positions on the Seletta in an attempt to hold it for the long term. In order to block this attempt at 1600 several Austro-Hungarian platoons armed with light machine guns began descending from the peak in order to reach the Seletta and clear it of the enemy presence. But the alert action of the dug-in Italians along with the interdiction fire of their artillery forced the *Kaiserjägers* to retreat. Later on, in the cover of darkness, the same troops attempted to reach the position again, but they were repelled again by the alert response of the defenders.

The next day the Austrians renewed the attempt to break the stalemate with a determined counter-attack aimed at clearing the Seletta Battisti which was preceded by a pinpoint barrage. On the night of 11 May the Austro-Hungarian artillery fire grew in intensity and soon after several platoons armed with light machine guns and rifles counter-attacked the Italians barricaded inside the mountain's cavern system. The enemy thrust while forceful was initially repressed by a combination of hand grenades and machine gun fire. Shortly thereafter several platoons of the *Murge* Brigade intervened in the fight by enveloping the Austrian alpine troops and trapping them nearby the caverns. As a result of this outflanking maneuver a dozen Austrians were killed, while 20 were captured. Thus, on the morning of 12 May, two days after the battle had begun, the situation was once again at a standstill with both contenders locked into what appeared to be an intractable situation. The

Italians were still determined in capturing the mountain peak but faced the same conundrum of the Austro-Hungarian assault columns. Given that a frontal attack entailed advancing toward the peak on open ground and under the watchful eye of the enemy's machine guns, it was thought that it was too much of a risk to attempt it. After much consideration an alternative route that led into the peak position was identified by the Italian commander that involved storming the mountain peak from the rear. This entailed climbing a wall of rock for approximately 175 feet in silence and without causing any alarm such as a misstep or a rock fall. In essence, the plan called for a great feat of alpine warfare to be carried out by specifically selected troops. Thus, on 13 May the impasse was finally broken by this daring operation conducted by a handful of *arditi*. The latter, led by Lieutenant Carlo Sabatini of 3rd Company V *Reparto d'assalto*, were able to silently scale the mountain wall with ropes and rock axes and then suddenly erupt into the enemy trenches and saturate them with hand grenades. At the time, the position was occupied by 26 enemy soldiers but there was only one sentry on duty and a team of three soldiers that were manning the machine gun position, while the remaining members of the garrison were inside the dugouts.

> The ascent to the top of the mountain was extremely difficult for the five soldiers involved as they had to climb the steep wall with the aid of a rope and picks facing the precipice on one side and the potential threat of the enemy's machine guns on the other. The enemy garrison appeared on that afternoon to have been less vigilant than usual, but one misstep could have derailed the entire operation. The lack of oversight gave the men the opportunity to advance all the way under the steel shield of the enemy's position. Suddenly, the five *arditi* stormed the position by taking out the sentry with daggers and then by killing the remaining soldiers with hand grenades.[8]

In a few minutes, after the remaining soldiers of the enemy garrison that had survived the grenade attack had been overcome in a wild melee, the *arditi* were able to take control of the enemy position. The brilliant *coup de main* had led to the capture of one officer and five soldiers, two machine guns and one mountain cannon. Most importantly, the peak position had been seized from the enemy.

The White Battle

During the Great War the Western sector of the Italian Front passed through the two main mountain ranges of the Ortles-Cevedale and the Adamello-Presanella, which constitute Italy's largest glacier, and the Tonale Pass, the vital height from which one could control the main route leading from the Trentino to Lombardy. Needless to say fighting or simply surviving in such high altitude positions and especially within

8 Ufficio Storico, Rep. B-1, Raccolta 13D Brigata Murge: Comando Brigata Murge, 'Relazione riassuntiva dei fatti d'arme e dei lavori eseguiti sul Corno Battisti', 31 May 1918.

a 10-mile wide glacier was extremely difficult and presented enormous difficulties of all kinds to the military authorities on both sides. Prior to the war, for instance, the troops had conducted field exercises on the glacier but had never stationed troops on it overnight or for long periods of time. The Italian official history, for example, states that: "No one during the pre-war period would have thought that war could be waged on the highest peaks as the physical environment of the mountains is truly challenging to humans. The rarefaction of the air is an obstacle to proper breathing, the low temperatures cause frostbites and even more potentially harmful ailments, the fury of nature causes great violence and disruption and every human activity is destined to cease during the winter."[9] The greatest danger was the constant threat of avalanches, while the issue of how to supply the troops guarding the highest peaks on a daily basis also provided numerous ongoing challenges. Supplies had to be dragged by hand or by pack mules, and with drifting snow often the supply columns necessitated skis and sleds, which were always in short supply. Supply routes were often in poor condition due to heavy snow, ice and rain or were not in existence so that the soldiers in the supply columns had to improvise. In some cases the supply columns were dispatched during the night forced to march in difficult terrain with no visibility. Troop shelter, for instance, at the beginning of the war was another huge issue since troops stationed in the mountains had little or no protection from the elements. In winter, for instance, the soldiers faced temperatures as low as minus 35 degrees Celsius and the snowfall often isolated their positions from the main barracks located in the valley floors. In such a harsh environment basic soldiering duties became almost impossible. The sentries, for instance, even though fully covered by several layers of clothing could only stay in their post for maximum 20 minutes. If they stayed longer they risked frostbite or more serious ailments so a constant rotation of the sentries had to be implemented on a daily basis. Shoveling the snow from the entrances and roofs of dugouts, wooden huts and caverns in the rock had also to be done daily and placed incredible burdens on the soldiers. Both tasks placed the high mountain garrisons under severe strain and the troops also had to be fed. Thus, pure survival in positions that were 3,000 meters or higher was quite a feat in itself and probably presented more challenges than combating the enemy, at least during the long winters. During offensive operations, the troops had to content not only with the enemy but also with the harsh conditions of the mountains. The assault units often were forced to clear a path through ice and snow and avoid calamitous slips and falls which often proved deadly. The artillery support teams were especially challenged by the high mountain environment as the troops had to transport the guns and the ammunition through deep snow or under inclement weather conditions that considerably slowed down their movement. The special mountain groups faced even more difficult challenges since often they were tasked with scaling a mountain peak in order to arrive at the enemy position by using ice picks, ropes and other special climbing equipment.

Early on in the conflict both armies decided to maintain fortified positions on the Tonale Pass and up on the mountain crests on either side all year round, which

9 Emilio Battisti, *La Guerra sul ghiacciaio: Parte 2* (Rome: Ufficio Storico, 1933), p. 17.

increased the supply difficulties and the strain on the troops deployed there. In 1915 the Austro-Hungarians held particularly strong positions on the Adamello, Corno di Cavento, Cima Presena and the Monticelli with multiple dug-in artillery units well concealed inside caverns and numerous machine gun firing points strategically located to dominate the view over key passes and access routes. Particularly strong were the positions on the Monticelli, a true mountain fortress, that were comprised of artillery emplaced in bomb-proof caves and of several hidden machine gun nests. The strategically placed machine guns, in particular, were very hard to locate being positioned on the flanks to enfilade enemy units and thus were very difficult to overcome. An Italian intelligence report stated that: "The crests of the Monticelli have been transformed into highly fortified blockhouses while numerous machine gun strong points keep constant watch over our positions."[10]

The Austrians at the beginning of the war had also managed to occupy the Paradiso Pass, an excellent observation point and a natural barrier from which a handful of well-armed soldiers could block any enemy attempt to reach the Trentino. From this position they could also prevent enemy troops from crossing the glacier during the day. Near the Presena Pass the Austrians had also built a deep cavern that served the purpose of shielding reserve units from enemy artillery fire. From this central position called La Sgualdrina, the Austro-Hungarian command could easily dispatch troops for timely counter-attacks. Thus, given the enemy's extensive defenses, the operation presented numerous challenges that required adequate planning and a detailed and precise attack plan. A day prior to the *alpini* attack, the Austro-Hungarian positions were defended by the following units: a half Regiment of the 170th and 173rd *Kaiserjäger*, k.k. *Landsturm* Battalions, four high mountain companies, three independent machine gun companies, seven mountain batteries (six cannons and one howitzer) and two trench mortar batteries.

Since 1915 the Italian *alpini* units had been given the almost impossible task of advancing in this extremely difficult high altitude environment along the route of the Tonale Pass and against the well-fortified positions. The most important actions prior to the so-called 'White Battle' in the spring of 1918 had taken place in stages or as soon as the snow and winter conditions had relented. In the spring of 1916 with a bold stroke the *alpini* units had seized Lobbia Pass and Mount Adamello including the capture of its glacier. However, they were eventually checked by the major Austro-Hungarian offensive of May 1916. In the spring of 1917 the Italians had achieved further success by seizing the observation and artillery strongpoint of the Corno di Cavento with a bold stroke. In 1918 they were determined to finish the job by capturing the route over the crest of Cima Presena (3,059 meters high) and the Monticelli and to penetrate the Sole Valley. The offensive thrust was to be a two-pronged initiative. On the first day of operation the assault units were to capture the three high peaks of Mount Presena, Zigolon and Maroccaro, while on the second day they were to advance on the Paradiso Pass and finally capture the Monticelli peaks.

10 Ufficio Storico, *L'Esercito Italiano nella Grande Guerra 1915–18: Le Operazioni del 1918, vol. 5, tomo 1* (Rome: Ufficio Storico, 1988), p. 265.

Since the Austrian defenses were centered on two parallel lines of trenches located on two parallel set of mountain ranges and thus dominating the high ground, a frontal assault was out of the question. Moreover, given the high altitude location of the enemy positions, the presence of snow and ice all year round, and the consequent difficulty in bringing up artillery and support weapons and equipment of all kinds, made the operation both challenging and extremely risky. "Therefore, it required meticulous planning, training and careful selection of the troops destined to take part in the attack. Given the great challenges that it presented, the operation was assigned to General Quintino Rocchi, an expert of mountain warfare and a commander of both *alpini* and mountain artillery units. The latter spent several months creating selected *arditi* units that were to be assigned to the vanguard of the first assault wave."[11] The advance had to be made during the night to conceal the infantry columns as they marched forward, while the attacks themselves were to be made simultaneously and from the flanks of the enemy positions. It was hoped that by attacking in small, well-camouflaged groups that were advancing on the more impervious but less visible routes leading to the mountain peaks that the enemy would have less time to react or to harass them as they marched forward.

The operation was planned with careful preparations that included the construction of a tunnel through the mountain ridge leading up to Cima Presena, one of the key objectives of the initiative. This secret tunnel would allow the attackers to infiltrate the enemy lines and ultimately deploy troops and equipment in an area from which they could take the defenders by surprise. Despite the bad weather conditions for several months the troops worked on digging the tunnel, in clearing and enlarging the main roads, and laying out paths for the pack mule columns for the transportation of the artillery pieces, the shells, food and water. A diversionary attack with troops with skies against the opposite flank of the Tonale Pass was also part of the intricate deception plan and it was to precede the main attack. It was envisioned that such action would divert the enemy's attention and perhaps some of its units from the main sector to be seized. The artillery support was carefully assembled so as not to alarm the enemy as each artillery piece to be deployed in the operation was transported at night. The guns were carefully positioned on the mountain peaks surrounding the enemy positions so that the latter could be encircled by a ring of fire during the attacks. On the Cavento, for example, the *alpini* had strategically positioned a 149 mm mountain howitzer with a full stock of explosive shells, each of which had been carried manually.

Along with 188 guns and several trench mortars, the III Army Corps also made available high numbers of special poison gas shells to create a "special poison gas zone to block any potential reinforcements from reaching the peaks under attack."[12]

The offensive thrust would not only involve subterfuge and heavy artillery but was also to be carried out in strength with the deployment of over 2,000 soldiers and

11 Gianni Pieropan, *Storia della Grande Guerra sul Fronte Italiano* (Milan: Mursia, 2000), p. 631.

12 Ufficio Storico, *L'Esercito Italiano nella Grande Guerra 1915–18: Le Operazioni del 1918, vol. 5, tomo 1* (Rome: Ufficio Storico, 1988), p. 265.

involving special skiing patrol units, *alpini* special high mountain companies, five *alpini* battalions (*Monte Mandrone, Pallanza, Edolo, Monte Cavento* and *Monte Granero*) with their respective *arditi* assault platoons, three additional *arditi* assault platoons of the *Monte Rosa, Val Brenta* and *Tolmezzo* Battalions, and last but not least the troops of the III *Reparto d'assalto*. This unit was the first *arditi* battalion comprised overwhelmingly by *alpini* soldiers. It had been founded on 1 October 1917 by soldiers coming from the III Army Corps including three infantry platoons, three *alpini* platoons, two *alpini* machine gun sections and even its commander, Captain Arturo Barbieri came from the *alpini*. "For several months the unit was furnished with a highly specialized training regimen and its core was comprised by highly skilled *arditi* mountain climbers able to scale rocky cliffs even under the threat of machine gun fire."[13]

Given that the *arditi* were expected to reach enemy positions located on hard to get to gullies, rocky slopes and peaks, special mountain companies were formed whose core was comprised of experienced mountain climbers. These platoons were to form the first wave of the assault force that with their bold leadership and decisiveness would lead the standard infantry. The *arditi* were trained to advance along broken and obstacle rich terrain, and to climb mountains with the aid of only ropes and picks and while launching grenades. They practiced endurance training by conducting exercises by running quickly uphill and downhill. Finally, they harnessed the ability to advance under the arc of fire of the machine guns.

The end result of the extensive training was that the unit not only possessed some of the most able high mountain platoons of the entire Italian Army but also that it would be able to attack with small but fast and agile teams on skis heavily armed with machine guns, grenades and smoke bombs.

The *arditi*, in particular, were to play a key role during the operation as it entailed a prolonged approach march during the night as it was impossible to advance in the daytime under the alert view of enemy artillery and machine gun positions, as well as scale walls of rock during the last stage of the assault.

During the night of 24–25 May a powerful artillery preparatory fire was unleashed by nine heavy, 117 medium and 62 light guns along a front that spanned from the frontline glacier positions all the way to the Austrian rear of Pizzano and Santa Caterina. The largest guns deployed were eight 240 mm bombards whose specific task was to destroy the machine gun and artillery emplacements located on the mountain crests. The first phase of the barrage involved the shelling of the observation posts, command centers and the artillery posts located in the rear to impede the enemy's ability to react to the infantry assault. Phase two involved the creation of a cloud of poison gas over the defenders' routes leading to the area in order to isolate the front-line positions and prevent the reserves from reaching the targeted areas. Finally, phase three of the barrage involved destructive fire over the main frontline outposts to wear down the defenses and inflict casualties. This last phase of the preparatory fire was

13 Francesco Fattuta, 'Contributo ad una storia delle truppe d'assalto', in *Studi Storico-Militari* (Rome: Ufficio Storico, 2002), p. 530.

The entrance of the cavern of the Doss Alto di Zurez where the *arditi* penetrated into the Austro-Hungarian position to storm the enemy garrison in the summer of 1918. (Ufficio Storico – official archive, Italian military, Rome)

Arditi strong point during the Solstice Offensive, Summer of 1918. (Ufficio Storico – official archive, Italian military, Rome)

Arditi crossing the Piave River in the Fall offensive of 1918. (Ufficio Storico – official archive, Italian military, Rome)

Arditi unit advancing against the enemy. (Ufficio Storico – official archive, Italian military, Rome)

Arditi of the III *Reparto d'assalto* in a trench in the Tonale sector in 1918. (Ufficio Storico – official archive, Italian military, Rome)

Arditi of the I *Reparto d'assalto* storming Mount Fratta during the massive Eleventh Battle of the Isonzo in 1917.(Ufficio Storico – official archive, Italian military, Rome)

Arditi post in the vicinity of Monte San Michele in 1918. (Ufficio Storico – official archive, Italian military, Rome)

Arditi strong point fighting to stop the Austro-Hungarian advance during the Battle of the Solstice in June 1918. (Ufficio Storico – official archive, Italian military, Rome)

The photo shows the exits of the caverns from which the *arditi* emerged from to attack Mount Pertica on 26 October 1918. (Ufficio Storico – official archive, Italian military, Rome)

Italian machine gun strong point. *Fiat-Revelli* machine gun model 1914 squad in position during the 1918 Battle of the Solstice. The machine gun weighted only 37 lbs making it one of the lighter machine guns of the war. It operated through a 400 round per minute rate of fire. (Ufficio Storico – official archive, Italian military, Rome)

Arditi of the XXIII *Reparto d'assalto* celebrate after the victorious Battle of the Solstice. (Ufficio Storico)

Arditi of XXIX *Reparto d'assalto* attacking a high altitude mountain position. (Ufficio Storico – official archive, Italian military, Rome)

Austro-Hungarian mountain unit grenade launcher position. (Ufficio Storico – official archive, Italian military, Rome)

Austro-Hungarian mountain artillery unit. (Ufficio Storico – official archive, Italian military, Rome)

Austro-Hungarian small howitzer. (Ufficio Storico – official archive, Italian military, Rome)

Ardito being awarded a gold medal of military valor in the Tonale Pass rear lines. (Ufficio Storico – official archive, Italian military, Rome)

Austro-Hungarian high mountain position. (Ufficio Storico – official archive, Italian military, Rome)

Arditi attacking enemy with hand grenades in Nervesa della Battaglia in October 1918.

also to be aided by bomber planes that despite the strong winds and the snow would play a vital role in targeting enemy positions on the morning of 25 May.

As the artillery preparation began to unfold, during the night marching in a straight line hundreds of *alpini* of Operation 'White Battle' began their approach toward the Austro-Hungarian positions. Since on the night of the operation a heavy snowstorm was blanketing the icy mountains of the Adamello-Presanella the troops were almost invisible as they drudged forward dressed in the white camouflage snow suits. Some were advancing by foot, others by skies, while some units were transporting heavier equipment such as mountain cannons with packed mules. While the *arditi* were in the lead, they were closely followed by the standard *alpini* units and finally by the slower moving artillery and mortar support units.

Given the grave weather conditions these soldiers experienced an extremely dangerous journey as the snowstorm greatly hindered their visibility. In addition to the problems presented by poor visibility there was a great danger related to avalanches. Even before clashing with the enemy, the Italians in fact suffered their first casualties when an entire unit of the *Monte Pallanza* Battalion was overcome by an avalanche while negotiating the ascent in order to reach a steep mountain pass. The avalanche resulted in the death of three officers and 106 *alpini* who were were buried alive under several feet of ice and snow.

Although in the darkness of the night the Austrian positions were barely visible, the enemy from its defensively advantageous positions was in full alert and ready to fire upon any Italian troops that came within its shooting range. The positions, that were all located on mountain peaks 3,000 meters above sea level, had been reinforced with barbed wire fences, steel cages and shields, machine gun nests, artillery strong-points and deep trenches. Although they had been heavily targeted during the night by the artillery, the majority of the posts were still fully garrisoned and still remained a formidable barrier for the Italians to overcome.

At 1130 on 25 May 1918 the troops had finally reached the outer perimeter of the enemy positions and shortly thereafter began their assault as soon as the artillery fire was moved forward. The *arditi* platoon of the *Monte Mandrone* was the first unit to swing into action by negotiating an exposed cliff and then by storming the enemy garrison stationed on the Maroccaro. The latter, having been surrounded and then forced to engage in harsh hand-to-hand combat was ultimately forced to surrender. The Italian official history recalls that: "Our assault units reached the Maroccaro so swiftly that the enemy did not have a chance to activate its machine guns. From the distance one could recognize the *arditi* with their white camouflage over-suits surround enemy positions, storm them with hand grenades and then force out of the dugouts and caverns groups of Austrian soldiers."[14]

After 10 minutes of fighting the peak Austro-Hungarian positions had been overrun. At that point some of the men sought refuge in the caverns while others

14 Ufficio Storico, *L'Esercito Italiano nella Grande Guerra 1915–18: Le Operazioni del 1918, vol. 5, tomo 1* (Rome: Ufficio Storico, 1988), p. 265.

sought to flee into the icy tunnels of the mountain. While the former were captured the latter were for the most part cut down by machine and rifle fire.

In a similar fashion the *Monte Cavento* Battalion was able to storm Mount Zigolon with a bold stroke that entailed scaling the mountain from the rear and taking the enemy position from behind. At the same time the *Val Baltea* and *Pallanza* Battalions were able to capture the garrison defending Presena Pass but were unable to proceed upon Cima Presena after numerous attempts that were all thwarted by strong enemy fire. It was the combination of heavy criss-crossing fire coming from both the Squaldrina and Presena positions that forced the assailants to pull back.

Emboldened by the fact that the *alpini* were retreating, in the afternoon at approximately 1500 the Austro-Hungarian units put forth a determined counter-attack aimed at retaking possession of the Presena Pass. However, after having advanced midway toward the pass, the gallant effort was itself halted by heavy counter artillery fire.

Soon afterwards, the Italians retook the initiative with a renewed attempt to seize Cima Presena with some of the *arditi* platoons of the *Monte Mandrone* managing to gain a foothold on the peak of the mountain. However, they were then immediately pushed back by a fierce Austrian counter-thrust that overwhelmed them under an avalanche of rocks, machine gun and rifle fire.

The second failed attempt to take the peak forced the Italians to go back to basics with a renewed focus upon artillery preparation. The pinpoint artillery barrage that resulted, had the desired effect as it wounded or buried alive under piles of rocks many members of the enemy garrison. As a result of the devastating fire that brought down trenches and the roofs of several caverns, at 2000 *Monte Cavento and Mandrone arditi* platoons were finally able to scale the mountain from three directions unencumbered by enemy fire and ultimately overcome any remaining enemy opposition.

The result was the loss of the mountain summit, the capture of several soldiers as well as two mountain cannons. With the conquest of the Presena all the objectives of the first day of operation had been achieved, while the Paradiso Pass and the Monticelli remained the two main objectives of day two.

The Austro-Hungarian official history summarizes operations on the Presena line as follows: "The main blow was struck by five *Alpini* battalions, reinforced by many storm detachments and followed by five more battalions. In the affected sector on 25 May the *Alpini* did take the defenders completely by surprise; after bitter hand-to-hand combat that lasted all day they defeated the Austrians and captured the Cima Presena."[15]

During the early hours on 26 May the Italian artillery kick-started the operations by effectuating a pinpoint barrage to further soften up the targeted enemy positions, while the *arditi* began their approach march to surround the Paradiso Pass. As the enemy was subjected to thunderous fire, the assault units slowly made their way down from the mountain gullies of the Castelaccio-Lagoscuro crests and marched into the glacier plateau of the Presena by walking on the snow that had been hardened by the

15 Edmund Glaise-Horstenau (ed.), *Österreich-Ungarns letzter Krieg 1914–1918, vol. 7*, p. 209.

freezing night temperature. The hard snow and the lack of light allowed the unit to arrive undetected under the enemy position. At 0200 the *arditi* of III *Reparto d'assalto* stormed the Paradiso Pass taking the enemy completely by surprise with hand grenades and smoke bombs. Immediately as the smoke enveloped the trenches, the Austro-Hungarians opened heavy machine gun fire that although it depleted some of the ranks of the first assault wave "was not able to halt the dash of the attackers that continued to advance swiftly and decisively to the target."[16] After climbing over slopes and walls of rock the *arditi* broke through the enemy wire and proceeded to assail the enemy machine gun posts with bayonets and hand grenades. Soon after having penetrated the enemy position, they were aided by the assault platoons of the *Monte Granero* and *Edolo alpini* battalions that charged the enemy from a south-easterly direction. The combined thrust of the *alpini* and the *arditi* finally overcame all enemy opposition leading to the capture of over 100 soldiers and three officers.

In the meantime, the *alpini* units of the *Monte Cavento* Battalion had surrounded the Squaldrina position managing to block the entrances of the enemy caverns and forcing the enemy to surrender there as well. Several dozens of enemy soldiers were escorted into captivity.

The next and final objective were the rocky spires of the Monticelli that despite the destructive artillery fire were still heavily defended by Austrian troops dug into high altitude machine gun emplacements. Initially, III *Reparto d'assalto* was able to surround one of its multiple peaks (Peak 2,863) but was unable to capture the enemy contingent that promptly pushed it back by opening up a hellish machine gun fire. In fact after heavy hand-to-hand combat the unit was thrown out of the trenches by the alert action of the brave enemy garrison. It then attempted to circumvent the enemy position on Peak 2,582 but even here it was unable to reach the pinnacle as the Austro-Hungarian defenders were able to repel the attacks while inflicting heavy losses on the attackers. Unable to proceed, the unit had no other option but to dig in under the crest of the enemy position where it was subjected to a constant barrage of machine gun fire throughout the night. The operation against the Monticelli demonstrated once again how difficult it was to advance in treacherous terrain of the high mountains under harsh weather conditions and against a well dug-in enemy.

The attack was resumed the next morning and it began with a clash of artillery fire as the Austro-Hungarian artillery was especially effective in counter-battery fire, while the Italians were able to inflict casualties with their pinpoint barrages concentrated upon the peaks of the Monticelli. The Italians continued to pour their artillery fire into the mountain fortress, gradually reducing it to a rubble of rock and steel and little by little had the better of the artillery duel by overpowering the Austrian retaliatory fire. On the heels of a two-hour long barrage, the *Reparto d'assalto* climbed up the glacier by openly disregarding heavy enemy fire to then resolutely attack Peak 2,582. By penetrating through openings in the wire, the assault unit then engaged the enemy in hand-to-hand combat. Initially, the Austrians put forth strong resistance but after their officers had fallen and as the fighting intensified, their infantry

16 Emilio Battisti, *La Guerra sul ghiacciaio*, p. 53.

troops were finally overrun. As the Italian troops were now getting closer to the key position of Peak 2,545, the Austrian artillery intervened very heavily into the fighting by putting forth a massive interdiction fire aimed at stopping their advance. The artillery fire was so fierce that both the troops of the III *Reparto d'Assalto* and the *Edolo* Battalion, advancing from two opposite flanks were forced to retreat and seek shelter. This prompted the Italians assault units to request the intervention of their own artillery which began to mercilessly target Peak 2,545 and the Austrian batteries positions. At 1100 while the *arditi* were attacking from the left flank, the *Edolo* Battalion advanced from the right along the crests of the Monticelli in order to put forth the double envelopment of the main enemy position. At first the *arditi* stormed Peak 2,863 after having softened up the enemy position by launching against it hundreds of hand grenades. Despite strong enemy machine gun fire, from this position they continued to climb in a bold maneuver over walls of rock and ice and in rapid succession forced the Austrians to evacuate Peak 2,609 and eventually their stronghold on Peak 2,545. As the Italian official history states:

> The attack, which was conducted by small units of assault infantry, proceeded to systematically wrest possession of every peak of the Monticelli. In full cooperation with the artillery fire, by 1530 all enemy positions had been seized.[17]

The operation led to the capture of 870 Austrian soldiers plus 12 guns, 14 trench mortars and 25 machine guns. Italian losses were 14 officers (2 dead, 12 wounded) and 214 soldiers (58 dead, 153 wounded and three missing). The loss of the Presena summit in itself was very significant, since it provided the Italians with a vantage point from which they could not only view the Vermigliana Valley but that represented a jump-off platform to ultimately conquer a vast section of the Trentino.

The operation, a masterpiece of alpine combat, demonstrated how *arditi* tactics could be effectively deployed in a high altitude environment. At first the diversionary assault mounted by troops with skis north of the Pass attracted considerable enemy fire. At the same time the *arditi* platoons of *Monte Mandrone* Battalion were quick in scaling the rocks and to reach the enemy held crest thus taking full advantage of the enemy's state of confusion regarding the true objectives of the operation. The first assault set the pace for the rest of the operation as the artillery first intervened to degrade the enemy positions and was quickly there after followed by the *arditi* units surrounding the peak positions and storming them by force. It is noteworthy to point out that most attacks were carried out by troops that had to climb high peaks covered by strong rifle and machine gun fire. Their only chance of success, and which they took full advantage of, resided upon pressing the attack on the heels of the artillery barrage and against the flanks of the position. The successful storming of the enemy positions was conducted as soon as the last artillery bomb exploded in the trenches giving the defenders no time to organize the defenses or to parry the blow.

17 Emilio Battisti, *La Guerra sul ghiacciaio*, p. 55.

The Seizure of the Capo Sile Defenses

In the most eastern section of the Italo-Austrian front, at Capo Sile near where the Sile River flows into the Adriatic Sea, the Italian 3rd Army had managed to maintain a bridgehead, despite repetitive enemy infantry attacks, on the Austrian held side of the river. This position served mainly as an advanced observation post as well as a position from which to launch attacks. In order to widen the bridgehead and to use it as a jump-off platform for a major offensive operation, the XXIII *Reparto d'assalto*, a unit comprised exclusively by soldiers from the *bersaglieri* arm including its flame-thrower, mortar and machine gun sections, was ordered to spring a surprise attack upon the Austro-Hungarian units holding the northern bank of the river.[18] The latter position was held by the 12th *Honvéd* Division, whose forces were deployed behind several rounds of barbed wire in numerous machine gun strongpoints and scattered along three parallel trenches. Not only were the well fortified enemy defenses an obstacle but the thick vegetation of the lower Piave also made a rapid advance by the attackers more troublesome.

The XXIII *Reparto d'assalto* was particularly suited to lead such an operation given its extensive training in close combat and in rehearsing and implementing raiding techniques and tactics. The unit was formed in September of 1917 and its initial force was of 26 officers, and 770 soldiers. "Its main assigned goal was to open up the enemy defenses in order to precipitate a large-scale infantry advance ... but it was also expected that it would carry out raids on a regular basis to capture enemy soldiers, to conquer terrain and to keep the enemy on the alert at all times."[19]

In order not to arouse the enemy's suspicion, the reconnaissance of the positions situated on the northern bank of the river was done mostly at night, while the *arditi* unit destined to take part in the operation was transported by small boats to the designated assembly area on the same night of the attack. To further avoid any potential intelligence problems, the communication of the plan of attack was given to the local commander by word of mouth, while it was also forbidden to talk about the plan of attack over the phone.

In order to further confuse the enemy, two days prior to the day in which the attack was to take place, the Italian artillery began to pummel a vast enemy area around Capo Sile, including the area destined to be attacked. It was hoped that a barrage covering a fairly wide section of the front line would keep the enemy from guessing the direction and the ultimate objective of the infantry attack. A diversionary action against a nearby target sector was also implemented followed by a targeted barrage into the same location to further confuse the enemy. It was hoped that all of these diversionary actions would confuse the enemy as to the real objective of the attack and favor a surprise raid against its positions at Capo Sile.

18 Ufficio Storico, Rep. E-5, Raccolta 31: Comando 3. Armata, 'Reparti d'assalto', n. 32755, 28 September 1917.

19 Filippo Cappellano and Basilio di Martino, *I Reparti d'assalto*, p.543.

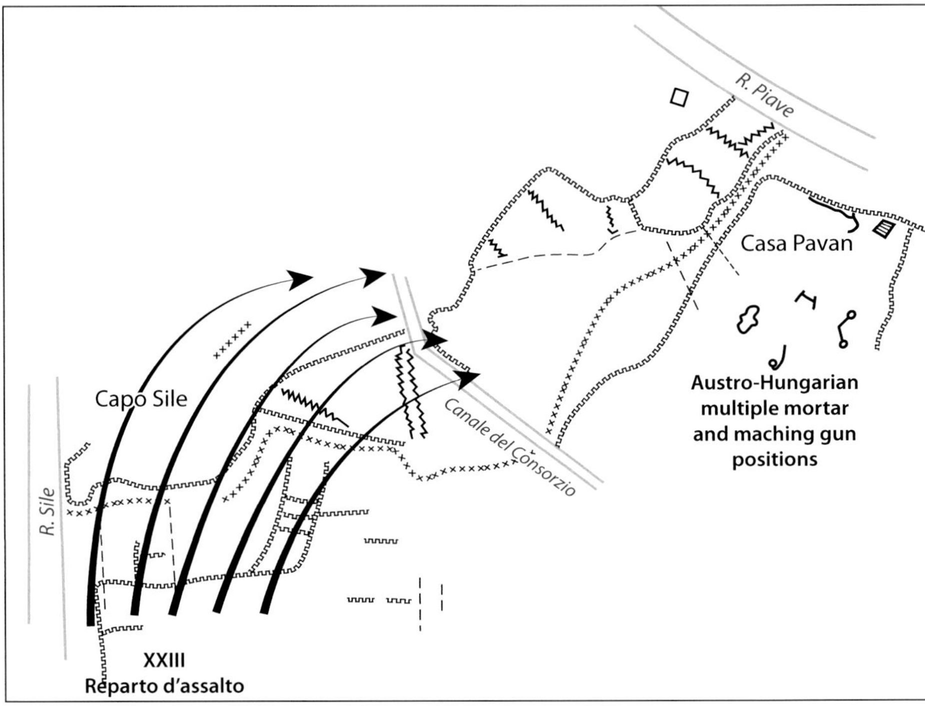

Map 8 This is a reproduction of the original sketch made by the commander of the XXIII *Reparto d'assalto* during the planning phase for the storming of the Capo Sile bridgehead. It indicates the location of all the major Austro-Hungarian positions and all of the barbed wire defenses.

On the day of the attack (26 May 1918) the Italian artillery opened up the hostilities by laying down a diversionary barrage by concentrating fire on a nearby area to Capo Sile that had already been the target of a raid two days in advance. At 2130 the Italian artillery blasted the Capo Sile defenses, while several machine guns located on the flanks of the Austro-Hungarian positions also began to target the enemy to ensure that the latter, submerged by a hail of bullets, was in no position to oppose the raid. Then approximately 20 minutes later the artillery prolonged its fire beyond the enemy's first line of defense and the *arditi*, subdivided into five assault columns began to rush the enemy's defenses. Preceded by the fire of 12 flamethrowers that had invested the enemy positions with huge flames and plenty of smoke, the *arditi* irrupted with force into the first line of defense without facing any opposition as the majority of the garrison had fled from the powerful artillery barrage and the subsequent flame attack. As a result, the remaining enemy troops were easily rounded up and captured.

This is how one of the *arditi* officers remembers the impact of the flamethrowers during the early stages of the battle:

> Our flamethrowers have hit the enemy trenches from the flanks and head on. They have caused horrendous casualties as some enemy troops were trapped

> in the trenches and were burned to death. The flamethrowers then began to shift their attention upon the machine guns. The latter had opened up fire and had caused our first casualties of the night. ... On our left flank I then saw the flamethrowers unit advancing once again and lighting up the dark night sky with huge bursts of flames.[20]

Ten minutes later, as the artillery once again switched and lengthened fire toward the rear enemy defenses, a second *arditi* column broke through the intermediate line of defense, which was bolstered mainly by machine guns, and captured its main strongpoints. After this line had been seized, a third *arditi* column quickly irrupted into the enemy's third line of defense capturing several soldiers. Then on the heels of the retreating Austro-Hungarian infantry, the *arditi* and the support troops in their wake rushed to occupy the trenches. Shortly thereafter, the trenches were 'turned around' by infantry and by sappers while the *arditi* pushed forward again by clearing the two locations of Casa Senza Nome and Casa Pavan where several pillboxes were neutralized. By midnight, as the *arditi* had reached all of their objectives, they were returned to the rear. At approximately the same time, the enemy began its counter-battery fire upon the bridgehead which caused only a few casualties since the two companies of the LIX *bersaglieri* that had previously occupied it had already dug themselves into position. Shortly thereafter, the enemy counter-attacked, but this assault was repelled mainly by the newly installed machine guns in position. Two days later the Austro-Hungarians attacked again in order to seize the expanded bridgehead, but were once more repelled.

> At Capo Sile on the night between 26–27 May our *bersaglieri* and *arditi* units, aided by the effective use of flamethrowers and precise accompanying artillery fire, stormed the enemy positions on the northern bank of the bridgehead and advanced 750 meters deep into the enemy's deployment. Despite a strong enemy reaction, the position was held by our troops. The enemy suffered several casualties including the capture of seven officers, 433 soldiers, four mortars and 10 machine guns.[21]

In turn, the Italians had suffered 19 dead, 130 wounded and 10 missing.

The operation demonstrated that along with the 'White Battle' and the seizing of Mount Corno, that the Italian military had recovered from the blow at Caporetto and that it was resuming, after a prolonged period of stasis, a more offensive-minded strategy. Even General Foch, the military head of the inter-Allied command, congratulated General Diaz for the brilliant operation conducted by his troops at Capo Sile.

20 Ludovico Lommi, *Da Bersagliere ad ardito* (Bassano del Grappa: Itinera Progetti, 2003), p. 91.
21 Filippo Cappellano and Basilio di Martino, *I Reparti d'assalto*, p.544.

The Italian Army of 1918

The revitalization of the Italian Army took place during the winter 1918 imposed an interlude which forced both military instruments to halt major operations. The first step taken by the military and the political authorities was to provide all types of support to industry in order to quickly replace the weapons and equipment that had been seized by the Austro-Hungarians at Caporetto. Accordingly, the major industrial concerns throughout 1918 worked feverishly to manufacture high volumes of weapons and supplies to replace what had been lost and to re-arm the front line troops. After having lost 3,152 artillery weapons between October 1917 and December 1918, by April 1918 the Army was supported by 5,871 pieces of artillery, or approximately 80 percent of the total weapons it possessed prior to the debacle. The Army grew further in terms of its weaponry just a few months later. In the beginning of June 1918 the army could count upon 6,294 pieces of artillery, of which 135 heavy, 2,922 medium and 3,237 light guns. In addition, a very large number of trucks were manufactured, so that some of the originally horse-drawn batteries were now motorized.

Infantry units were re-armed with heavy machine guns so that by June 1918 each division had 120 heavy and 72 light machine guns.[22] This was made possible by the record amount of ammunition and equipment manufactured at an exceptionally rapid pace by Italian manufacturers but also with key supply contributions from both France and Great Britain especially with regards to artillery shells and the supply of Stokes mortars respectively. Small- to mid-size mortars were one of the few areas where the Italian Army held a numerical as well as an efficiency edge throughout the war against its rival. Mortar batteries were quickly assembled to support infantry operations. Although the batteries operated at shorter ranges than most Austro-Hungarian weapons, the Italian Army was often able to outgun the enemy by deploying them in large numbers. Another step that was taken was to call up the young recruits of the classes of 1899 and 1900 who reinvigorated the depleted field armies that had been overwhelmed at Caporetto. Third, the Italians also gave greater prominence to training the standard infantry soldiers than they had done at the beginning of the war in order to deploy better-prepared troops on the battlefield. In particular, General Diaz insisted on a policy aimed at preserving the soldiers' life as much as possible especially by avoiding fruitless offensive operations that had prevailed during Cadorna's reign. Fortifications, pillboxes, trenches, barbed wire works and other defensive positions were strengthened to provide further protection for the frontline troops.

These reforms went hand-in-hand with selected changes to infantry and artillery units and tactics. As far as infantry units were concerned the Italian *Comando Supremo* expanded the number of *arditi* units so that every corps was assigned an *arditi* battalion and a special assault division was also formed. This unit would in essence become a general reserve at the disposal of the High Command to be deployed

22 Cesare Manzoni and Alessandro Ricagno, *Evoluzione organica dell'esercito italiano prima e durante la grande guerra* (Turin: Einaudi, 1920), pp. 209–233.

as a mass counter-offensive force to halt and then push back an enemy breakthrough of the forward trenches.[23]

To instill and promote aggressive action, General Diaz instructed his subordinates to provide medals and other types of recognition for soldiers who distinguished themselves when their units carried out raids and planned attacks. Moreover, it was established that soldiers who managed to capture prisoners during raids should receive a prize of 100 Lire per soldier captured and a leave of absence of 10 days.

In addition, like the Austro-Hungarian Army General Diaz revitalized the standard infantry divisions. "On the organizational level, Diaz sanctioned the indivisibility of the division, whose components of infantry, artillery, and corps of engineers and services always had to operate in concert and were not to be mixed with other large units, which, had been the norm at the time of Cadorna. This was done in order to improve the cohesion and harmony among the various elements of the various corps, and therefore the combat performance of the division itself."[24] Similarly to the Austro-Hungarians the Italians assigned one artillery regiment to each infantry division in order to increase cooperation between the gun batteries and the infantry troops during the offensive. In order to improve the mobility of the *arditi*, the assault divisions were furnished with mountain rather than field artillery batteries.

The artillery also changed or refined tactics adopting many reforms already implemented by the French at Verdun. Under the command of General Roberto Segre, for example, the artillery was trained to respond more quickly and energetically to the Austro-Hungarian artillery preparatory fire. Segre's guidelines included the provision for laying down destructive counter-fire whenever the enemy attacked by not only responding to the enemy's guns but also by targeting the assembly points of enemy troops, thus weakening their offensive thrust from the start. These tactical guidelines were further cemented in General Diaz's 'Use of Large Units in Attack and Defense' directive that stressed "that it was artillery fire in preparing an offensive, rather than in completing the work of destruction, that was supposed to intensify its neutralizing action and to seek surprise."[25] Thus the Italian artillery by 1918 had adopted some of the same tactics that the Austrian artillery had deployed to support the *sturmtruppen* attacks. Sudden barrages to paralyze enemy activity and facilitate an infantry advance had become almost as important as the destructive fire lasting many hours that was more common in the Allied side.

Pinpoint artillery was not only critical during the preparation of attacks, but also to stifle enemy attacks with counter barrage fire aimed at both enemy infantry and artillery. Due to the losses in equipment sustained at Caporetto the total number of batteries went up very little in 1918. What did change, however, was the quality of

23 Filippo Cappellano and Basilio Di Martino, *Un esercito forgiato nelle trincee. L'evoluzione tattica dell'esercito italiano nella grande guerra* (Udine, Gaspari Editore, 2008), pp. 174–182.

24 Filippo Cappellano, Warfare 1914–1918 (Italy), in: *1914–1918-online. International Encyclopedia of the First World War*, Freie Universität Berlin, Berlin 2014–10–08. DOI:http://dx.doi.org/10.15463/ie1418.10484 <Accessed 15 June 2016>. Translated by: Mazhar, Noor Giovanni.

25 Filippo Cappellano, 'The Italian Artillery in World War One', p. 214.

the equipment with the almost complete substitution of obsolete guns with modern ones. By mid 1918 it is estimated that the Italian Army possessed 7,000 guns, slightly more than the Austro-Hungarians. Similarly, to the enemy the Italians had greater numbers of indirect fire weapons vis-à-vis the beginning of the war, more fully staffed observation teams that could also count upon aerial reconnaissance and greater numbers of tractors and trucks to tow the large guns.

Finally, infantry defensive tactics also were subjected to a vast overhaul. On the Piave, in particular, the Italian Army assumed a zonal defense in depth rather than a linear defensive system comprised of four main lines of defense. The two most advanced lines were set approximately three miles deep consisting of trenches, numerous barbed wire barriers and multiple machine gun nests. Two more defensive lines were studded with multiple firing and strongpoints the first of which was full of machine guns emplacements, while the last line was comprised of artillery gun batteries of all sizes. On the mountainous sector such as on the summit of Mount Grappa, the front was turned into an extensive system of fortifications of all kinds, the majority of which were dug deep into the rock complete with artillery batteries that could fire in multiple directions. A vast underground, bomb-proof cavern was built to host multiple artillery batteries and machine guns. The Asiago Altopiano had also been transformed into a mountain fortress with several lines of parallel trenches dug within a difficult to penetrate and see forest and interspersed with hidden machine gun nests.

It was these new fortifications and a new tactic of meeting the enemy assault units in an encounter battle after they had passed through the zonal defensive system and the killing zone that the Italian Army would rely upon to face the coming blow of the Austro-Hungarians. This new defensive deployment relied upon a first line that was thinly held and that was charged with slowing down the enemy's offensive thrust. The second more robust line would engage the enemy as it entered the killing zone that was characterized by the depth of the defensive positions between the second and third line forcing the enemy to cover much ground under the constant threat of artillery and machine gun fire. The third and fourth line also maintained several reserve dugouts where the *arditi* and other attacking forces would emerge from after the barrage had subsided in order to fight off the enemy encroachments.

Solstice Offensive

In mid June 1918 the Austro-Hungarian Army launched its greatest offensive in the Italian front. According to the AOK this was to be a two-pronged offensive against the Italian positions on the Asiago Altopiano and the Piave River. The aim of the offensive was to breach the Italian positions and reach the plains and ultimately Italy's industrial heartland with a massive artillery barrage and a large scale deployment of infantry.

The Italians however had learned from past mistakes. At Caporetto they had buttressed frontline defenses with advanced artillery emplacements and machine gun posts. The vulnerability of the troops had been further increased by deploying the vast majority of the infantry on one major line of defense with few reserves at the back to prop up any sector under attack. For this offensive the Italians had deployed their infantry, especially on the Piave, on four major lines of defense, thus moving from a linear to a zonal defensive deployment. The first line was thinly held mainly by sentries and advanced infantry groups. The second and third line were held by the vast majority of the infantry troops and buttressed by numerous machine guns, mortars and small cannons and their aim was to break up the infantry attacks. Finally, all along the fourth line the Italians had placed the majority of their artillery batteries and the large sized mortars and howitzers. The aim of these units was to proactively attack the infantry columns as they assembled for the attack and to respond aggressively with counter-battery fire to the Austrian artillery. By this time, the Italian High Command had also constituted numerous reserve units, many of them comprised of *arditi* units, which were held in the rear and were tasked with counter-attacking the enemy.

Asiago Altopiano

The Austro-Hungarian operation began on 15 June, was opened with a powerful barrage that was then followed by the infantry attack. Following heavy fighting in the Asiago Altopiano sector, after the Austrian 18th Division had wrested control of the vital Costalunga position from the hands of the *Padova* Brigade, General Sani of XIII Army Corps had received the following order from his superior:

> This command has placed at your disposal the reserves of the Army Corps (242nd infantry and 3rd *bersaglieri*), in addition to the *Regina* Brigade and the *LII arditi* Battalion. This last unit must be deployed accordingly to its proper offensive role rather than be used for trenchline duties. I reiterate that Costalunga must be recaptured by special assault units that shall effectuate a slow but progressive infiltration of the enemy lines and without losing too many casualties.[26]

During the afternoon of 17 June two infantry columns were assigned the task of retaking the position. The first column, comprised by the 1st Company of LII *Reparto d'assalto*, with six flamethrowers and two machine gun pistols, a *bersaglieri* unit and a machine gun unit, was tasked with attacking the enemy from the south. While a second column, comprised of the 2nd Company of LII *Reparto d'assalto* and *bersaglieri* units was charged with taking Costalunga's eastern flank. The *arditi* assault unit had been constituted in May 1918 from *alpini* from the 52nd Division, the vast majority of which were battle hardened having taken part to the Mount Ortigara battle. The unit was also comprised by a light machine gun company, a standard machine gun unit, a Stokes mortar unit and a flamethrower unit.[27]

26 Ufficio Storico, Rep. E-1, Raccolta 92: 6. Armata, 'Cima Echar', n. 877, 17 June 1918.
27 Ufficio Storico, Rep. F.4, Raccolta 199: Comando 6. Armata, 'Costituzione *reparto* d'assalto alpino', n. 22411, 1 May 1918.

At 1545 the assault units began to advance but given the enemy's presence all around the Costalunga position they were forced to proceed very slowly as the snipers began to take their toll on both infantry columns. After two hours of fighting they were forced to stop their advance altogether having depleted all their stocks of hand grenades. After a brief pause, where they were resupplied with additional hand grenades, they resumed the advance toward the main position.

At 1730, largely thanks to the support provided by fresh reinforcements, an advanced position of the Costalunga, Hill 1,236, was seized from the enemy with a quick sally. From this advanced platform both *arditi* and *bersaglieri* were able to launch successive attacks against the enemy positions and slowly penetrate into the post's intricate cavern and trench system to engage the enemy in close combat fights. Fighting in such close quarters mainly within pillboxes, stone sandars and caverns that had been for the most part damaged by the artillery barrage was very dangerous as the enemy could emerge and spring to attack from anywhere. In such a threatening environment the flamethrower squads played a key part in flushing out the enemy from advanced positions as dense clouds of smoke and jets of burning fuel were enough to force several enemy occupied strongpoints to capitulate. The gruesome weapon was used during assaults on pillboxes, caves and trenches and other enclosed spaces. Dedicated flamethrower teams were deployed in close coordination with infantry when suitable targets were identified. Flanked by light machine gun and rifle platoons, the flamethrower two-man teams advanced against enemy units to smoke them out of their defenses.

> The infantry attack, which was preceded by violent artillery preparatory fire, had first encountered a strong enemy reaction centered on multiple machine guns and several artillery batteries. But eventually, the troops had been able to overcome it and to enter into Costalunga, seizing several sections of it but without fully occupying it.[28]

By 1900 much of the fighting died down as the Italian command of XIII Army Corps opted to consolidate its hold on the captured positions rather than continuing the mop-up operation of the entire enemy held post in the darkness of the night which would have intensified the potential for heavy losses.

The next day there was continued protracted heavy fighting around the Costalunga salient, but by night time both contenders had fought themselves to a standstill.

Then on 19 June at dawn the Italian units sprang a surprise attack that liberated the entire Costalunga position. "At dawn on the 19 the adversary, worn down by four days of heavy fighting and subjected to an endless run of attacks by our infantry, finally was forced to evacuate the position. A surprise attack without the aid of a preparatory barrage caught the enemy by surprise and forced him from the position."[29]

28 Ufficio Storico, *Relazione V*, n. 1, narrazione, p. 444.
29 Ibid., p. 444.

The Italians had thus managed to recapture this very vital position that constituted one of the main defensive bastions of the Asiago Altopiano and had also captured 80 soldiers, of whom two were officers, and eight machine guns. This operation stopped any major advance on the part of the Austro-Hungarians along the Altopiano sector.

Mount Grappa

On the Mount Grappa sector the troops of the 23rd Austro-Hungarian Infantry Division had advanced all the way to Peak 1,503 of Mount Coston in order to surround from the flanks the Grappa massif where some of the lead elements were expected to reach the Italian artillery positions. After having overwhelmed several Italian strongpoints these troops were halted after much tough fighting originally by elements of VI *Reparto d'assalto,* and a few infantry units. According to the Italian official history: "Supported by the flanking fire of the mountain guns of the 69th Mountain Battery and the 3rd Battery/50th Artillery Regiment, units of 239th Infantry and VI Reparto d'assalto stopped the enemy advance in its tracks."[30] Then, later in the afternoon the same troops with the aid of a battalion from the *Bari* Brigade counter-attacked the enemy on the Coston and after a wild fight managed to push him off Peak 1,503. Moreover, strong patrols from the same units were dispatched to the Danoro Valley to completely clear it of the enemy's presence. Austrian stormtroopers had managed to infiltrate the Italian rear but were captured after a protracted shooting match. As a result of the counter-thrust, the Italian 15th Division successively retained its hold on the trenches between Mount Rivon, Mount Coston, Peak 1,503, Peak 1,490 and Osteria Cibara preventing an envelopment of the Grappa massif.

Still on the Mount Grappa sector the Austro-Hungarian 67th and 85th Battalions of the 56th Infantry Brigade had achieved deep penetrations by overrunning three consecutive defensive lines. The furthest position that they had managed to occupy was the Col Moschin which comprised the Italian third line. The advance had caused considerable consternation especially because the Italian command did not know at that point whether the Austro-Hungarians were planning to attack the fourth and final line of defense before the plains. It was therefore decided to deploy the sector's tactical reserve, the IX *Reparto d'assalto.* Even though the *arditi* were required to hastily conduct a long drawn out approach march in order to reach the basin of their first objective (Col Fagheron), they were deployed almost immediately because of the gravity of the situation. Another reason for their quick deployment was determined by the belief of the Italian commanders that the Austrians had not been able to turn around the captured positions. After the *arditi* battalion had regrouped, its 1st Company was charged with retaking possession of the advanced position of Palazzo Negri, while its 2nd Company was tasked with seizing the Fagheron. At 1400 the *arditi* struck Palazzo Negri where the Austro-Hungarians had deployed several units armed with machine guns. Notwithstanding strong defensive fire, the assault units

30 Ibid., p. 481.

were able to surround the position and reduce it with the aid of hand grenades. At the same time, the 2nd Company charged the Fagheron defenses where it encountered a small unit of Italian soldiers comprised by an officer from the *Genio* (Captain Rossone) and a few infantrymen that had valiantly resisted the enemy onslaught by maintaining a foothold on the position. Once having broken through the enemy encirclement and freeing up of the small unit, the *arditi* were tasked with retaking possession of the main peak of the mountain. After the position was subjected to heavy artillery fire, the storm units began to run toward the peak of the mountain where the Austrians had barricaded themselves by launching toward the enemy positions several smoke and hand grenades that concealed their advance. The explosions and the smoke caused by the special grenades not only greatly hindered the enemy's defensive effort but they also fooled him into thinking that the Italian preparatory fire was still in full swing. As a result, the *arditi* were able to arrive at the entrances of the caverns almost unhindered by enemy fire and surprise the bulk of the Austro-Hungarian troops that were caught while still trapped inside the dugouts. As the latter began to filter out of their shelters they were met by the *arditi* armed primarily with knives, hand grenades and flametrowers to torch the entrances. The hand-to-hand fighting for control of the mountain peak that ensued was very fierce and it was witnessed by the fact that only 16 enemy soldiers were taken prisoner out a force of 500 soldiers, who were either wounded or killed.[31] Some units of the company then launched a fierce attack against the nearby Chiesa San Giovanni position and after having overwhelmed its garrison they were able to re-establish communications with the flanking units of the *Calabria* Brigade. At the same time, two platoons also stormed the small forest near the San Giovanni church where they were able to block the entrances of the enemy caverns killing some of them while capturing others (1 officer and 15 soldiers).

Without respite, at 2030 the commander of the *Basilicata* Brigade issued the order to the IX *Reparto d'assalto* to get ready to take the next objective, the Col Fenilon. Shortly thereafter the Italian artillery enacted repressive fire against the Fenilon in order to soften up enemy defenses and pave the way for the infantry attack which was scheduled to start at 2200. When the artillery lengthened its fire the *arditi* charged up the mountain enveloping the enemy positions with a ring of fire.

The following is an extract from the post-battle report of Major Giovanni Messe, commander of the IX *Reparto d'Assalto:*

> At 2200 hours the artillery started to lengthen its fire and the assault units began to run toward the Fenilon. The *Arditi* submerged the peak of the mountain with tremendous fire battering it with grenades and jets of flammable liquids. The enemy could not see us as the peak was covered by a thick fog and the darkness of the night further reduced visibility. Even the flames and the explosions caused by the hand grenades did little to improve it. The enemy fought with determination and desperation but was quickly overrun: whomever

31 Ibid., p. 372.

> put up resistance was killed in the trenches. At 2300 the enemy unit had been completely destroyed and the Fenilon was occupied by our troops. Five officers 80 soldiers, four machine guns and other important material fell in our hands.[32]

This is how *ardito* Lieutenant Alberto Businelli recalls the battle on Col Fenilon:

> We approach the enemy line, as shells land like drumbeats. Suddenly we yell a formidable A noi! The artillery stops at once and hundreds of Thevenots, after one or two seconds, fall on the enemy trenches. There is a tremendous blast, soon followed by machine gun bursts. Some *arditi* fall but the others pass over the wire and spread out on the mountain top, searching out the enemy in every recess, in every trench in every bunker, shouting Messe a Noi. They are like Devils, passing over from one target to another: a Thevenot, a jet flamethrower and away! To the next one! And after a while everything is broken up, destroyed. The Austrian soldiers see the *arditi* ahead, on the left, on the right, behind them … we stop only when we do not find any more of the enemy.[33]

The *arditi* had been able to recapture two mountain tops occupied by the Austro-Hungarians during the offensive. But at 0400 on 16 June the commander of the *Basilicata* Brigade issued a further order committing the *arditi* to recapture Col Moschin at all costs along with an infantry battalion of the 92nd Division.

At 0700 the *arditi* assembled at the base of the mountain ready to go into action from their jump off positions, while the artillery targeted the peak with great force.

> Even before the artillery had lengthened its fire, the troops of the Reparto went to the attack. With great enthusiasm the 'Black Flames' ran to the top of the mountain and there clashed with the enemy. Some enemy were killed while others taken prisoner. Ten minutes after the attack had begun the enemy position had been encircled and overwhelmed. Soon after 26 officers and 250 soldiers were marched into captivity, while 17 machine guns and a small cannon had also been seized.[34]

The Austrian official history reports that "In the morning of 16 June a reinforced enemy storm battalion, after powerful artillery preparation, attacked the Col Moschin where at 0700 they overwhelmed the remnants of the 85th Infantry Division. About 25 officers and 225 men were taken prisoner."[35]

32 IX *Reparto d'Assalto*, 'Relazione sui combattimenti del 15–16 giugno per la riconquista della quota 1318 e della linea marginale Col Moschin-Col Fenilon', Cited in Alberto Businelli, *Gli arditi del IX* (Milan: Edizione Militare, 2007), p. 166.

33 Alberto Businelli, *Gli arditi del IX* (Milan Libreria Militare 2007), p. 50.

34 IX *Reparto d'Assalto*, 'Relazione sui combattimenti', p. 166.

35 Edmund Glaise-Horstenau (ed.), *Österreich-Ungarns letzter Krieg 1914–1918, vol. 7,* p. 301.

Austrian mountain artillery unit located at Rifugio Bosi on Monte Piana. (Author's photo)

Austro-Hungarian position on the Alpe Mattina. (Author's photo)

Italian infantry position in 1918. (Ufficio Storico – official archive, Italian military, Rome)

Arditi unit with Stokes mortars, daggers and *Moschetto* TS rifles celebrate victory after the June 1918 counter-attack in the lower Piave. (Ufficio Storico – official archive, Italian military, Rome)

Italian infantry charging the enemy in the summer of 1916. The photo clearly shows how infantry attacked in successive waves before the more refined infiltration tactics were implemented in 1917–18. (Ufficio Storico – official archive, Italian military, Rome)

Italian infantry troops attacking an enemy position on Kuk Mountain during the Tenth Battle of the Isonzo in May 1917. The troops were the Adrian helmet and are armed primarily with the model 91 rifle. (Ufficio Storico – official archive, Italian military, Rome)

The First World War cavern on Mount Paterno. (Fondazione Berti)

Italian trench on Mount Paterno. (Author's photo)

Engraved badge of an Italian sapper/engineer battalion on Mount Paterno. (Author's photo)

Austro-Hungarian trench position near the Torre di Toblin facing the Tre Cime di Lavaredo. (Author's photo)

Austro-Hungarian cavern in the Alpe Mattina position near the Torre di Toblin. (Author's photo)

Italian trench position near Oppacchiasella on the Carso in 1917. Note how sandbags were placed on top of the defensive wall to increase its height and make the trench deeper.

Italian machine gun position. (Ufficio Storico – official archive, Italian military, Rome)

Alpini during the 'White Battle'. (Ufficio Storico – official archive, Italian military, Rome)

Alpini ski patrol unit. (Ufficio Storico – official archive, Italian military, Rome)

Corno di Cavento under the Italian artillery bombardment in July 1918. (Ufficio Storico – official archive, Italian military, Rome)

Thus, the prompt response of the IX *Reparto d'assalto* supported by standard infantry and along with effective artillery fire was able to check and then push back this most promising enemy advance. As a result of this operation the Austro-Hungarian Army sustained heavy casualties amongst its best-equipped and trained stormtrooper units.

Lower Piave

Given that the defensive position of the Italians along the lower Piave was worsening by the minute due to dangerous enemy infiltrations, the 3rd Army commander decided to deploy the I *Divisione d'Assalto* in order to counter-attack in the sector (Fossalta di Piave, Pralongo-Losson) where the enemy had advanced the furthest.

The objective of its deployment was to halt the enemy infiltrations effectuated by troops of the 9th Cavalry Division and the 57th Infantry Division that had managed to create several large bridgeheads, some a few miles deep, into the Italian defenses. The goals were first to seal the breaches and then to forcefully counter-attack the enemy and push him back over the Piave.

Given that the enemy penetrations were fairly deep, the *Comando Supremo* had authorized the immediate deployment of the I *Divisione d'assalto* but given the hastiness with which the latter was deployed on the battlefield its counter-attack was poorly planned and no provision was made for a preparatory barrage to be put down prior to the *arditi* lunging at the enemy. As a result, much of the fighting took the form of very chaotic skirmishes, between *arditi* and Austrian stormtroopers and infantry as the fulcrum of the assault division's activity took place in and around Fossalta di Piave.

The XXX *Reparto d'assalto*, an *arditi* battalion comprised in large part by *alpini*, fought within the I *Divisione d'assalto* between 17–20 June and the dynamics of its deployment were very similar to those experienced by other units of the assault division. This unit had been rebuilt after the Caporetto debacle and it was mostly comprised by soldiers coming from the *alpini* corps hence its soldiers wore the green patch *ardito* badge that distinguished mountain troops from the standard infantry soldiers who wore a black badge. The unit had trained for over three months and it had 850 soldiers, a light machine gun company, a standard machine gun company and a mortar unit.

On 17 June 1918 the XXX *Reparto d'Assalto* was deployed in the Pralongo-Losson sector to shore up the defenses of the XXIII and XXVIII Army Corps that in some sections of the line had been overwhelmed and pushed back by Austrian stormtroopers while a secondary objective was to reestablish communications with the flanking units. The *arditi* had been trusted with halting the enemy attack as well as regroup the standard infantry units that had been dispersed and thrown into disorder by the speed and firepower with which the enemy stormtroopers had seized their positions. In order to carry out its goals the unit was hastily transported by lorries to the affected area after the local commander of the 231st Infantry Regiment had pleaded with 3rd Army headquarters for reinforcements. At 1720 as soon as the entire unit had dismounted from the lorries and had had barely the time to assemble in battle formation at Casa Sernaiotto it was thrown into combat. Immediately, its 2nd Company began to clash with the Austrians who had managed to infiltrate the main road and were about to envelop an entire infantry strongpoint. The fighting between the assault groups soon broke out into a series of small, uncoordinated melees. According to the commander of the *Reparto*:

> The *arditi* company launched a counter-attack mainly with bayonets that pushed the enemy back beyond the main road between Casa Gasparinetti and Casa Levi. Given that the company had lost several men, at 1830 I dispatched as reinforcements two rifle platoons, and a machine gun section belonging to 1st Company. While the former was to back up 2nd Company, the latter was to position itself on the left side of main road and fire upon the enemy from the flank.[36]

But as soon as the situation had seemed to have been restored, at 1900 the Austro-Hungarian infantry units put forth a second attempt to breach and overrun the line held by the *arditi*. For two hours, one Austrian-Hungarian attack after another was fought off with a combination of machine gun fire and local counter-attacks with hand grenades to re-establish a cohesive defensive line. Given the strong pressure exerted by the enemy on the advanced trenchline, the *arditi* were buttressed with further support as the 3rd Company was also dispatched to take part in a planned counter-attack to relieve some of the advanced positions. Shortly thereafter the counter-attack involving two *arditi* companies struck the assault columns of the Austro-Hungarians with hand grenades and flamethrowers while the machine guns fired upon them from the flanks. The combination of heavy machine gun fire and hand grenades had the desired effect as the Austrians were once again forced to pull back. Once again the line held with the crew-served weapons repelling the dense attacking enemy formations, while the assault patrols were checked and the attackers were finally fought off with casualties.

By 2100 while the XXX *Reparto d'Assalto* had successfully fought off with this counter-assault the second Austrian attempt to breach the defenses, the unit had not yet achieved its second objective. In fact it had not been able to reestablish communications with the Italian troops positioned on both its flanks and it was still unknown whether those positions had been breached or not.

During the night there was no let-up in the fighting as some Austro-Hungarian assault patrols attempted several times to circumvent the *arditi* positions by infiltrating past them under the cover of darkness. However, the prompt response of the unit's machine gun units was instrumental in stopping the infiltrations.

The next day *arditi* platoons were ordered to retake possession of several forward trenches past the main road along the Scolo Palombo that had not yet been fully evacuated by the enemy. "Once inside the trenches, the *arditi* were able to free some

36 Ufficio Storico, Cartella B-4, 3020 bis: XXX Reparto d'Assalto, Maggiore Luigi Marotta, 'Relazione sull'impiego del battaglione nei giorni 1–20 giugno 1918', 23 June 1918.

Italian soldiers that had been wounded the prior day as well as kill several Austrians that despite being wounded themselves were not willing to surrender."[37]

Then all of a sudden the enemy counter-attacked again in mass and as a result the unit was again deployed to fend off the Austro-Hungarian attack that sought to rupture the Italian positions between Casa Sernaiotto and Scolo Palombo. Here the Austrians were pressing forward their attack with multiple infantry and stormtrooper platoons. As the *arditi* were quickly deployed on the line they encountered several stragglers that were retreating from the battlefield. These soldiers were regrouped and redeployed as line infantry. The 2nd Company was deployed on the frontline along with the machine guns while the 1st and 3rd Company were initially held back in order to be used for the counter-attack.

For four hours the enemy attacked repeatedly but all assault waves were repelled and pushed back with grave losses.

> The enemy kept on advancing against our positions but as they ran toward our defenses with full assault gear including their rucksacks and ammunition they were mowed down by a combination of machine guns and rifle fire. Throughout the battle seven platoons of *arditi* (each consisting of an officer and 30 soldiers) were deployed for quick counter-attacks that yielded some prisoners and some machine guns.[38]

By night-time on day two of the deployment, after having sustained heavy losses, the enemy appeared to be resigned to the fact that it was not possible to proceed any further. Then when all of a sudden the battle had seemed to have died down in the middle of the night some Austrian assault patrols attacked again. The enemy was apparently doing all that it could to attempt to break through and advance toward the plains but the prompt response of the defenders repelled them with heavy losses.

On the morning of 19 June while the bulk of XXX *Reparto d'Assalto* was deployed at Casa Sernaiotto, several of its platoons patrolled the advanced Italian lines but although they found the trenches full of cadavers they did not come into contact with any Austrians. At 1930 one of the platoons made a reconnaissance at Casa Levi where they found several Italian soldiers dispersed in the trenches and that had retreated to that position following the Austrian attack. The entire *Reparto* was therefore deployed to reestablish order and a new defensive line. By overcoming some resistance on the part of some infantry units, the *arditi* were able to redeploy the 26th, 70th and 231st Infantry Battalions and they did not forego "more coercive means when some soldiers resisted and our men were forced to injure them to reestablish order."[39]

Total XXX *Reparto d'assalto* losses were as follows: three dead, five wounded amongst the officers, 50 dead, 121 injured and seven missing amongst the soldiers.

37 Ibid.
38 Ibid.
39 Ibid.

After the *arditi* and the infantry had conducted their counter-attacks in the Asiago and Piave sectors, the Royal Air Force gave chase to the retreating Austro-Hungarian troops. For two days the fighter squadrons targeted the troops that were making their way back to the Austrian lines. It is estimated that "eighty percent of Austrian bridging across the Piave was destroyed by Allied air and artillery bombardments."[40]

The deployment of the *arditi* in the massive Solstice Offensive proved to be for the most part effective but especially when they were deployed as a tactical reserve to seal the breaches and then to forcefully counter-attack the enemy and push him back over the Piave. In some cases their deployment, even in the counter-attacking mode, was successful but also highly costly. The I *Divisione d'assalto*, which fought in the lower Piave sector, for instance, repelled the enemy attack, but also lost several of its soldiers. Its losses were largely the result of the timing of its deployment and because it was ordered to go into action without the aid of a proper artillery barrage: "The intervention of thousands of *arditi*, even though deployed in a chaotic fashion, had strengthened our defenses and had worn down the enemy. But the assault division could have been employed much more effectively if it had been deployed the day after and after a prolonged artillery preparatory barrage."[41] Unlike IX *Reparto d'assalto*'s deployment in the Grappa sector, the assault division, too hastily and without the support of a proper artillery barrage, was not put in a position to inflict the maximum damage on the enemy. The unit was able to still inflict casualities and push back the enemy but the gains came at considerable cost.

Tenente General Grazioli published a post-battle report that summarized the combat effectiveness of the unit. Grazioli argued that given the hastiness with which the unit had been thrown into the fighting it was not able to fully deploy from a tactical perspective the principles of fire and movement. Grazioli went on to argue that its soldiers lacked an adequate number of hand and smoke grenades, which in his view were the most important tactical weapons of the *arditi*. He praised the work of the crew-served weapons sections such as the mortar, machine gun and small cannon groups and argued that furnishing the division with additional machine guns, as many others had argued, would have been a mistake since it would have it slowed down and limited its ability to maneuver.[42]

General Diaz as the supreme commander also issued a post-battle report reflecting on the elements of the defensive system that worked well versus those that worked less well or not at all. On the Asiago/Grappa sector, Diaz stated that the artillery batteries had successfully "surprised the enemy and had smothered the attack in the early stages," while on the Piave sector it had not produced similar results. Rather in this sector of the front line the "immediate, converging and repetitive counter-attacks"[43] by infantry and *arditi* had led to the successful outcome.

40 John Schindler, *Isonzo: The Forgotten Sacrifice of the Great War* (Westport: Greenwood Press, 2001), p. 285.

41 Ottavio Zoppi, *Due volte con gli arditi sul Piave* (Bologna: Zanichelli, 1938), p. 31.

42 Ibid.

43 Basilio di Martino, *Trincee-Reticolati e colpi di mano* (Valdagno: Gino Rossato, 2000), p. 37.

Diaz also commented on the enemy's tactics especially the ways in which the Austro-Hungarian Army deployed its stormtroopers and the infantry battalions. "The stormtroop battalions, equipped with plenty of machine guns and flamethrowers, were deployed on all sectors of the frontline as the vanguard of the attack … After they broke through the main positions they were relieved by standard infantry battalions and the stormtroopers continued to advance on the flanks."[44] According to the report the best way to stop the stormtroopers and stymie their offensive impetus was through the counter-preparatory fire by the artillery deployed quickly and early.

Raids, Small Scale Operations and Planned Attacks

Still bruised from the outcome of the Solstice Offensive, for many months after June 1918 the Austro-Hungarian Army stood on the defensive. Its main hope for victory relied on a major offensive on the Western front by the Germans that could conclude the war there and that could then lead to a concentration of Central Power forces along the Italian front. As the AOK took a 'wait and see' approach, the Italians began to aggressively attack their enemy with a host of small operations. The aims of these small-scale actions were to capture prisoners and weapons, improve frontline positions, inflict casualties and generally to conquer key positions that would represent future jumping-off platforms for an Italian mass offensive. Outlined below are some of the most important of the 50 or so small raid operations carried out by the Italians after the Solstice Offensive.

One of the first operations of this kind was the attempt to recover the advanced positions surrounding the Grappa massif (mainly the Solaroli peaks, the Roccolo di Ca' Tasson Ridge and Mount Pertica) which were of crucial importance to the Italians in order to rectify the frontline following the Solstice Offensive. On 9 July the commanders of VI and XVIII Corps drafted a plan of attack that was later approved by the Army Corps commander General Gaetano Giardino.

As part of this operation XXX *Reparto d'assalto* took part in an operation aimed at retaking possession of Peaks 1,672 and 1,676 of the Solaroli mountains, which the Austrians had conquered during the Solstice Offensive, while VI *Reparto d'assalto* fought near Mount Grappa.

Subsequently to the great offensive units of the 48th Austro-Hungarian Infantry Division had built extensive fortifications on the peaks of the Solaroli with the addition of several machine gun and artillery posts. The Austro-Hungarians were determined to offer prolonged resistance and maintain the advanced bridgehead in the Grappa massif sector at all costs.

The offensive thrust was led by the 3rd Company of XXX *Reparto d'assalto* and by the II Battalion/37th Infantry. The plan of attack envisioned that the assault units would charge against the enemy following a poison gas attack, consisting in the simultaneous

44 Ufficio Storico, Comando Supremo, Ufficio Segreteria: "Metodi tattici del nemico," n. 25, 23 June 1918.

opening of 400 mustard gas canisters. Accordingly, at 0130 on 14 July a cloud of deadly gas was released. Two hours later the Italian artillery effectuated a 10 minute pinpoint barrage against the Solaroli positions followed by the charge of the assault units. As the assailants began to run across no man's land they were targeted from the onset by strong enemy fire. Soon after the assault bogged down and the *arditi* were able to only capture an advanced frontline position near Peak 1,672 but failed in the ultimate capture of the main Solaroli peaks. This action was not successful largely because of the delay that incurred between the release of the gas and the infantry attack.

On the same day a small assault unit comprised by the 2nd Company of VI *Reparto d'assalto*, *arditi* assault platoons of the *Modena* and *Marche* Brigades, the 208th flame-thrower platoon, and three infantry battalions (II and III/ 41st Infantry, III/252nd Infantry), took Peak 1,503 of the Roccolo di Ca' Tasson Ridge, north-east of Mount Pertica. The ridge was of strategic importance in the Grappa massif sector and gave the Austrians the ability to control Italian movements all the way to the rear in the Malga Valpore di Fondo. The latter had already attempted on 6/7 July to take possession of the Roccolo, but the operation had not succeeded given the prompt response of the Austro-Hungarian troops of the 48th Division.

As planned, at 0430 on 15 July 1918 a rain of shells of unprecedented intensity and weight suddenly fell upon all positions between Mount Pertica, Roccolo di Ca' Tasson and the nearby Calcino valley. Immediately afterward the Italian infantry stormed forward. They penetrated the defenders' trenches on Peak 1,503 and with the aid of hand grenades and daggers the position was captured in less than 10 minutes. The *arditi* then attempted to move against Peak 1,440 but were rebuffed by a strong enemy reaction. On the same day at 2300 the Austrian stormtrooper assault patrol units of the 48th Division attacked Peak 1,503 under cover of darkness and managed to enter into its defenses where heavy fighting ensured. As a result, the *arditi* of VI *Reparto d'assalto* where called back from the rear in order to drive into and clear the positions taken by the Austro-Hungarians. By 0200 on 16 July the fighting died down and the Italians had retained possession of Peak 1,503.

On the night of 24 June 1918 a platoon of the 3rd Company/XXIX *Reparto d'assalto* raided an enemy position near Sano, in the Trentino. The *arditi* first cut the wire and then attacked the enemy position without the aid of the artillery. The results of the sally were the capture of four Austrians and no losses were sustained.

Further Offensive Progress in the Western Glacier

In order to achieve a further penetration into the enemy's defensive deployment on the westernmost section of the front, the commander of the Italian 7th Army instructed his subordinates to take possession of the mountain crests beyond the Presena and Monticelli summits, mainly Mount Stablel, and the Menecigolo as well as recapture the Corno di Cavento.

The plan of attack was similar to the one adopted during the 'White Battle' with the artillery creating a ring of fire around the enemy peak positions while the assault units surrounded them and then attacked them with hand grenades. This time, however, it was decided not to deploy the diversionary attack by the ski assault companies.

In the morning of 19 July the Italian artillery opened a heavy bombardment on both sides of the Tonale Pass and south of the upper Val di Genova to paralyze the enemy's rear. It was later directed against the positions on the Monticelli and on the crest of the Presena. Soon after, in preparation of the infantry attack, the sector held by troops of the 49th Infantry Division on the Stablel, the Crozzon di Lares and Corno di Cavento was heavily targeted by explosive shells. At 0900 Italian assault units attacked the enemy positions. III *Reparto d'assalto* quickly outflanked the enemy outpost on the Stablel by scaling the most impervious flank of the mountain which was under constant machine gun fire. Once outflanked the enemy outpost was pinned down by a flurry of hand and smoke grenades and subsequently attacked by the *arditi*. As of mid morning all enemy resistance had crumbled.

The Corno di Cavento positions were also subjected to very heavy artillery fire by 43 pieces ranging from light 65 mm mountain cannons to one large 149 mm cannon. The artillery preparation was so massive that the Austro-Hungarian main cavern on the peak was damaged by trench mortars. The collapse of this cavern left the garrison (29th High Mountain Company) without any protection from the ongoing bombardment and as a result it suffered heavy casualties. Shortly thereafter at 0930 the *arditi* assault platoons of the *Monte Mandrone* and *Val d'Intelvi alpini* Battalions, followed by the *Val Baltea* Battalion and a machine gun company attacked the peak from two sides. Despite their weakened position the garrison held out in stubborn fighting and the first assault was repulsed by concentrated machine gun fire. After the Italian artillery further poured shells into the peak position, the *alpini* assault units continued to advance toward the peak from the west and north. On the peak of the Cavento the *alpini* thrusts led to bitter infantry combat. Led by the commander of the *Monte Mandrone* assault platoon (Lieutenant Luca degli Albizzi) the *alpini* threw themselves at the enemy garrison launching several hand grenades. "The commander was the first to reach the area just below the peak where a horrendous scene presented itself. Several heaps of dead Austrians soldiers lay motionless on the ground. Their mangled bodies had been the victims of the pinpoint barrage and the covering machine gun fire coming from Punta Calvi."[45]

Shortly thereafter the peak position was surrounded and the Austrian soldiers were forced from their caverns and dugouts. A total of 61 prisoners (including three officers), five machine guns, and one mountain cannon were seized.

Seizure of Doss Alto

The Italian Army achieved a significant victory with the recapture with a bold stroke of the Doss Alto di Zurez (703 meters), situated to the north of Mount Altissimo. The position had been seized by the Austro-Hungarians in June 1918 and a few days later

45 Vittorio Martinelli, *Corno di Cavento* (Pinzolo: Povinelli, 2000), p. 225.

the Italians had implemented a failed attempt to retake it. Following the first attempt the Austrians had taken additional defensive measures by building a concrete fortification on the peak which was connected to a 500-feet long tunnel that snaked inside the mountain. From its numerous embrasures the Austro-Hungarian troops, 24th High Mountain Company, not only controlled a vast area below including the main road to the mountain as well as the railroad line beneath it near the San Giovanni Pass, but also the Italian positions of Mount Altissimo.

In contrast to the first attempt to take the height, the second operation was carefully prepared by the commander of the XXIX *Reparto d'assalto* Captain Gastone Gambara. The surveillance of the enemy position had determined that:

> The enemy occupies only the Doss Alto but not its immediate surroundings which are not fortified. Moreover, enemy patrols are less active during the daytime, while they are much more active at night. The enemy appears to be on high alert during the night with several patrols and numerous sentries on duty. During the day the eastern flank of the mountain is not patrolled at all and the flank appears to be unoccupied as several of our units made noises during the daytime to elicit an enemy reaction that never materialized. The south-east and southern flank however, are heavily patrolled by numerous sentries. On those flanks the enemy keeps numerous snipers which keep a constant watch. Our frontline troops believe that the enemy has there emplaced several machine guns.[46]

On the basis of the information collected Captain Gambara determined that the Doss Alto should be attacked during the daytime on a sunny day when many of the defenders typically rested in the trenches while the sentry patrols, given the good visibility, tended to be less active. In addition, the attack was to take place along the eastern flank of the mountain which was much less occupied and patrolled by the enemy. The operation was to be undertaken by one assault company (2nd Company of XXIX *Reparto d'assalto*), one machine gun company, one flamethrower section and units from the *alpini Exilles* Battalion.

The assault company was to lie in wait hidden under tall grass and trees during the night in a nearby forest that distanced approximately 400 feet from the Doss Alto positions. The assault unit was supposed to go in first followed by the flamethrower section whose objective was to seal the entrances of the caverns, while the machine gun section was to fire with great continuity on the embrasures and block any potential reaction from the enemy's own eight machine gun units.

Strong fire from several trench mortars began early in the morning of 3 August; it was reinforced after 1100 "by fire from artillery of all calibers, which blanketed all positions in the area. During this preparatory bombardment the Italian stormtroops penetrated the main position on the summit of the Doss Alto. The garrison had

46 Ufficio Storico, Comando XXIX Reparto d'assalto, Rep. E-5, Raccolta 210: 'Relazione su ricognizione eseguita in regione Dosso Alto', n. 546, 27 July 1918.

taken shelter from the firestorm in a cavern and did not realize that the Italians had entered the defenses and then pushed past the summit to the northern edge of the mountain."[47]

A small *arditi* platoon that had reached the pinnacle and had penetrated into the enemy's defenses managed to then descend by stealth into the tunnel and assail the main position with hand grenades. This unit, armed also with a flamethrower, after causing the initial shock with the hand grenades, was able to force the capture of a large number of soldiers that were sheltering in a cavern. As the flamethrower began to spew smoke and flames into the entrance of the cavern, the Austrian soldiers were forced to surrender. After the position had been stormed by the small unit the Italians proceeded to mop up the remaining troops who were captured after four hours of heavy fighting. For their part the Austro-Hungarians recovered from the initial shock and hurried the Riva *Sturmbaon* to the scene in order to recover the Doss Alto with repeated counter-attacks. The newly positioned Italian garrison was able to repeal these determined counter-attacks also with the aid of the artillery that at 1500 began to seal off the perimeter of the main area thus preventing any enemy reinforcements from reaching the Doss Alto position.

At the end of the day when the fighting subsided the Austro-Hungarians had suffered the loss of 30 dead soldiers including the commander of the garrison and 163 soldiers (including four officers) were captured. In turn, the Italians suffered 14 dead and 27 wounded amongst the *arditi* and eight dead and 10 wounded amongst the *alpini*.

The operation was well conducted with good cooperation between infantry and artillery.

The key to its success was how accurately the assault units had followed the lead of the artillery barrage by arriving at the entrances of the caverns as soon as the barrage was moved forward. "The key contribution made by the artillery arm was effective and swift both during the counter-battery fire phase and as well as during the tail end of the operation when it sealed off the enemy position."[48]

With the capture of the Doss Alto the Italians had managed to recover the last of the high ground which they had lost in this sector of the front line during the Solstice Offensive.

On 11 September near the town of Sano in the same sector (Trentino) as the Doss Alto the *arditi* conducted another raid. At 0700 a few patrol units from XXIX *Reparto d'assalto* reinforced by volunteers from the 34th Czech Regiment, having diverted the electrical current of the wire attacked an enemy outpost with hand grenades. They killed six enemy soldiers and captured 12. The enemy fought back with determination and the *arditi* suffered casualties.

47 Edmund Glaise-Horstenau (ed.), *Österreich-Ungarns letzter Krieg 1914–1918, vol. 7*, p. 458.
48 Ufficio Storico, *Relazione V*, n. 2, narrazione, p. 230.

Raid in the Val Brenta

During the Solstice Offensive the Italians had been forced to evacuate the Grotella position located in the Brenta Valley. As part of the plan to recapture lost ground and inflict casualties upon the enemy, four platoons of LXX *Reparto d'assalto* and six platoons of the *Livorno* Infantry Brigade supported by one flamethrower, one machine gun and three Stokes mortar sections were tasked to attack it on 14 September 1918. The operation was conceived as a small-scale raid following a pinpoint 10 minute hurricane barrage that aimed to stun the enemy into submission. In order to achieve surprise it was determined that there would be no prior artillery registration and that the troops involved would only be briefed on the plan of attack only two hours prior to the start of the operation. The troops were assembled on the night between 13/14 September and lay in wait near the exit of the trenches. At 0530 a pinpoint destructive fire by gun batteries of all sizes began to target the enemy's machine gun nests as well as the infantry dugouts. This was followed by a powerful barrage to silence the enemy's artillery. Through the intensity of the barrage the objective of complete surprise was achieved as the Austro-Hungarian artillery initially failed to respond. At 0600 the artillery lengthened the fire and the attacking columns emerged from their trenches. "The *arditi* on the right flank and the infantry on the left irrupted into the enemy's trenches without facing any resistance whatsoever even when they reached the entrances of the caverns where the enemy had assembled and from which it had not yet emerged. In front of the caverns the fight grew in intensity especially because the enemy had no intention to surrender and fought with extreme decision in order to lift the siege and avoid capture."[49] Notwithstanding the strong opposition encountered the assault units were able to succeed and to hold on to the position. The Austro-Hungarians had suffered a severe blow with 346 soldiers captured (including 13 officers), several dozens of dead soldiers, five mortars, and 13 machine guns were also seized. In turn, the Italians suffered the following losses: one dead, three wounded amongst the officers and 24 dead, 134 wounded amongst the soldiers.

The operation was successful because the officers who led it had worked very hard in identifying the position of the enemy's machine guns and this allowed the artillery to knock them out during the preparatory barrage. The pinpoint barrage not only eliminated the most egregious threat to the advance of the attacking columns, but it also stunned the defenders given the intense artillery bombardment, which made up for its short duration by the vast number of batteries deployed. Lastly, the attacking columns had been given clear objectives and throughout the operation they managed to maintain the initiative especially when fighting the enemy in close combat with hand grenades, bayonets and daggers. Once again the powerful barrage was complemented by the speed of the attacking columns which reached the enemy's caverns before the latter had any opportunity to organize its defenses.

49 Filippo Cappellano and Basilio di Martino, *I Reparti d'assalto*, p. 750.

Mount Grappa

Very bitter fighting flared up again on the Roccolo di Ca' Tasson Ridge when VI *Reparto d'assalto* stormed Peak 1,443 on 16 September 1918. Here the Italians drove into the positions held by the 48th Infantry Division and captured two machine gun outposts. The nearby positions on the Val dei Pez, the frontline sector south-west of the Col dell'Orso, were also attacked on the day. According to the Italian post-battle report the assault units "having blinded the enemy machine guns with hand grenades and flamethrowers, irrupted with force into the enemy's outposts on the Malga Val dei Pez and Malga Fossa di Confin. The enemy garrison, which was still in large part hiding in the caverns, was paralyzed by our hand grenades and pistol machine fire. It was quickly overwhelmed and then captured in its entirety."[50]

The war booty consisted of 200 enemy soldiers, one 75 mm Skoda mountain cannon and several hand grenades. While the Val dei Pez position remained in Italian hands on the night of 16–17 September a most valiant counter-attack by troops of 48th Infantry Division was able to wrest back the parts of the trenches that had been lost on the Roccolo ridge.

In the spring of 1918 General Diaz had enacted the following directive:

> I have ordered the Army Corps commanders to instruct their troops to execute along various sectors of the frontline raids and small scale offensive thrusts that should not only help to maintain the high fighting spirit of our soldiers but should also serve to capture prisoners and useful intelligence. These actions should be repeated with regularity so that the enemy will be kept on constant high alert.[51]

It was meant to spur more offensive trench raiding across all sectors of the frontline taking advantage of the debilitated condition of the Austro-Hungarian Army especially after the failed Solstice Offensive. As a result, the phase of the war that ran between the Solstice Offensive and the final Battle of Vittorio Veneto witnessed the emergence of a more aggressive Italian Army which often gained the upper hand against the Austro-Hungarians. Thus, while the latter had enjoyed the upper hand for most of 1917 with the probing stormtrooper patrols, the quick raids and the powerful counter-attacks which had yielded large amounts of prisoners and the capture or recapture of important frontline positions, in mid 1918 it was the Italian Army, led by its assault units, that was winning the battle of attrition. Not only was the Italian Army more active with raids and small scale offensive operations, but it was also gaining the upper hand in the artillery duel.

With regards to this phase of the war, the Austro-Hungarian official history states that:

50 Ufficio Storico, Comando VI Reparto d'Assalto, 'Rapporto del comandante Ettore Viola', 28 September 1918.
51 Ufficio Storico, Comando Supremo Circolare n. 9465

> Nevertheless, here also there were fights against probing Italian patrols; the roar of Italian artillery could be heard almost every day in the mountains east of the Brenta, just as on the Asiago plateau. That the enemy batteries had much more ammunition available than did the Austro-Hungarian artillery was clearly evident from a report by 11th Army. They estimated that on the Asiago plateau alone the allies were firing 14,615 rounds a day against our 5,730; between the Brenta and the Army's eastern flank.[52]

Despite the fact that some Italian raids and offensive thrusts failed, several did succeed and they contributed to further demoralize the enemy after his failed offensive. The *Comando Supremo* tracked the number of prisoners captured by both armies during July–October 1918 and the results clearly showed that the Italians had gained the upper hand. It can be argued that finally after many months of trailing the Austro-Hungarians, the Italians were now on even footing with them tactically. Moreover, they now enjoyed a more powerful war machine supported by a national economic system that was quickly outpacing Austro-Hungary's declining economic base. The stage had been set for the final confrontation. Lastly, the local successes gave the Italian Army a morale-boosting tonic that was badly needed after the great reversal of fortune of 1917.

Table 6.1 Prisoners Captured by the Italian and Austro-Hungarian army between the Battle of the Solstice and the Battle of Vittorio Veneto

Prisoners Captured by Month	Austro-Hungarian Prisoners	Italian Prisoners
July 1918	468	55
August 1918	1,519	100
September 1918	1,324	0
October 1918	813	176
Totals	4,124	331

Source: Ufficio Storico

Vittorio Veneto: The Final Battle

In October 1918 the Central Powers were in disarray because the German large-scale offences in the Western Front had failed and also because the Austro-Hungarian Piave Offensive had been repelled with heavy casualties. The weakest component of that alliance, the Austro-Hungarian Army, was under considerable strain mainly due to a host of internal and external factors such as the food and raw material shortages and the domestic workers' unrest. The most important factor that debilitated the fighting conditions of the Habsburg Army was the economic decline of its military-industrial

52 Edmund Glaise-Horstenau (ed.), *Österreich-Ungarns letzter Krieg 1914–1918, vol. 7,* p. 564.

complex which ultimately impacted the productivity of the workers. As a result, industry was not able to surpass the record number of weapons and shells produced in 1917. Artillery production is one prime example of Austria-Hungary's economic decline in 1918. For the first six months of 1917 the domestic industry had manufactured 2,225 artillery pieces, while during the same time in 1918 it had managed to manufacture only 1,296 pieces. During the same period shell and cartridge production also fell precipitously.[53] In contrast, the Italian adversary was producing record numbers of weapons and ammunition and by then had decisively pulled ahead of its rival.

Knowing that the Italian mass attack was imminent, the Austro-Hungarian Army was committed to offer prolonged resistance along the Piave and Mount Grappa sectors. The Austrians held on the frontline 63 infantry divisions (many of which were understrength), while the Italians fielded 57 infantry divisions but by then they had greater numbers of artillery batteries, mortars and machine guns. On the Grappa, the Austrian defenses were formidable with three rounds of barbed wire and mutually supportive strongholds centered on machine gun and mortar emplacements. To the rear of the defenses several artillery batteries formed the fourth and final line of defense.

Along the Piave, the Austrians built an elastic defense structure based on a zonal defensive approach. The first line, the so-called *Kaiserstellung*, was centered upon machine gun nests and infantry strongholds. Approximately three kilometers behind the first line there was a much deeper and staggered second line called *Königstellung*. This was comprised of deflilated machine gun nests interspersed with infantry strongpoints, sniper positions, mortar, grenade thrower and small artillery emplacements. To the rear of this line stood the heavy artillery batteries and the reserve units positions.

Despite the rise of nationalist tendencies within the various ethnic/national components of the Habsburg Monarchy and the food scarcity forced by the Allied embargo, the Austro-Hungarian Army resisted to the bitter end. As Cruttwell asserts, "much as the Austrians fell behind their great ally in technical efficiency, it remains to the everlasting credit of their kindly and hard-working officers that this array of scarecrows and skeletons maintained for three days a strong and often desperate resistance to the utmost efforts of the whole Italian power."[54] Resistance in fact stiffened as the *arditi* and the infantry advanced both on the Grappa and Piave sectors and the ultimate collapse only came about after the troops from some of the nationalities of the Dual Monarchy refused to fight.

The Italian plan of attack entailed a main thrust against the Piave River line in order to split in two the Austro-Hungarians there deployed (Belluno Army) by taking the key logistic and weapon hub of Vittorio Veneto. At the same time, a secondary offensive against enemy forces deployed in the region of Mount Grappa was also to be executed in order to keep the Austrians from redeploying troops to the Piave.

53 John R. Schindler, 'Austria-Hungary in the First World War', p. 153.
54 C.R.M.F. Cruttwell, *A History of the Great War*, p. 602.

The battle began on the night of 23/24 October under grave conditions as torrential downpours caused the Piave River to overflow. As a result, the offensive against the Piave sector had to be postponed due to the inability to lay the temporary bridges, while the offensive in the Grappa region went ahead as scheduled.

Over 600 Italian aircraft were expected to execute saturation bombing of the Austro-Hungarian frontline positions both in the Piave and Grappa sectors, but the planes could not take off due to the poor weather and visibility. Thus, the planned bombardment could only be executed by the artillery arm. The latter collaborated extensively with the infantry attack by laying down a strong barrage on the opponents front and rear defenses, but the effort was hampered by the poor visibility. The barrage began during the night but since aerial reconnaissance could not be carried out it was impossible to determine the accuracy of the artillery fire as well as correct the range of the batteries. At 0500 on 24 October the artillery laid down the proper preparatory barrage but due to the heavy fog many of the enemy dugouts, most of which were positioned on the reverse slope of the mountains, were not hit by the shells, while many sections of the wire were also not targeted and were fully functioning on the morning of the attack.

The Italian 4th Army led by General Gaetano Giardino then stormed ahead. The offensive in the Mount Grappa sector was to be a multi-pronged initiative with the IX Army Corps units set to take Mount Asolone (40th and 41st *Honvéd* Divisions), the VI Army Corps against Mount Pertica (48th Infantry Division and 13th *Schützen*), the XXX Army Corps against the mountain positions directly in front of Mount Grappa (50th Infantry Division) and the 50th Division against Mount Valderoa (43rd Infantry Division). The Austro-Hungarian infantry was dug in on the mountain tops surrounding the Grappa massif and their primary defensive strategy was to activate the deadly machine guns as the enemy advanced. The guns were strategically dug in into caverns that were for the most part impervious to enemy artillery fire.

The infantry attacks were launched on the morning but, as expected, they were for the most part met and eventually rebuffed by the destructive enemy machine gun and artillery fire. The only two successes of the day were the capture of Mount Valderoa by the troops of the *Aosta* Brigade, which overcame two parallel trenchlines and captured 150 enemy soldiers, and the capture of Mount Forcelletta by the I Battalion/40th Infantry led by its *arditi* assault platoon. But apart from these two local successes, all other units involved in the morning attacks suffered high casualties and the enemy appeared determined to offer prolonged resistance all along the Grappa massif. As the Austro-Hungarian official history asserts: "Thus the attack by Giardino's Army had been completely shattered along the still-solid front of the *Belluno Armeegruppe* by evening of the first day of the battle in the Grappa mountains."[55]

The orders for the following day, however, were still to attack against all enemy positions in a further bid to tie down the enemy infantry on the Grappa.

55 Edmund Glaise-Horstenau (ed.), *Österreich-Ungarns letzter Krieg 1914–1918*, vol. 7, p. 635.

The next day the artillery once again kick-started operations with the preparatory fire which was also aided by Italian air squadrons this time which bombed the Austro-Hungarian positions.

The major thrust on the 25 October was to be provided by the troops of the 18th Infantry Division against the bulwark of Mount Asolone. IX *Reparto d'assalto* with the II and III Battalions/139th Infantry Regiment were to storm the mountain from several directions and seize the vital position of Hill 1,486. The following is an extract from the post-battle report written by the commander of the IX *Reparto d'assalto* detailing the hard fight on the Asolone:

> At 0828, before the artillery had lengthened its fire, the *reparto d'assalto* charged the enemy with a surprise attack. The 3rd Company charged against Peak 1,486, while both 1st and 2nd Company where directed against the slope between Peaks 1,520 and 1,486. On every section of the frontline the enemy was overwhelmed, while the 3rd Company continued to advance by mopping up the reverse slope on Costone di Casera Pra' della Falla and then by advancing toward the valley floor (Valle delle Saline) where it was able to block the entrances to the enemy dugouts and shortly thereafter kill several soldiers belonging to the enemy's reserve units. In the meantime, the 1st Company, closely shadowed by 2nd Company, had already reached Peak 1,486 having dispatched two of its platoons to mop up enemy defenses in the Valle delle Saline. Shortly thereafter while 3rd Company repulsed several counter-attacks from enemy units emerging from the Valle delle Saline, the 1st and 2nd Companies, after having taken Peaks 1,472, 1,471 and 1,476 stormed with great force Col della Beretta, which they seized after a wild fight. On the peak they captured several enemy soldiers and machine guns …
>
> The enemy's artillery, which up to that point had been almost non-existent, began to fire with noticeable power on our positions. A short while later we were also subjected to mortar fire. Then the enemy's machine guns also joined the fight and their criss-crossing fire caused several casualties in our midst. Shortly thereafter 10 enemy columns moved against Col della Beretta but they were first subjected to heavy rifle fire and then finally repulsed by a cascade of hand grenades.
>
> The enemy then attempted for a second time to storm our positions but was once again fought off by a combination of rifle fire and hand grenades.[56]

Ultimately after continuous attempts to retake possession of Col della Beretta, the enemy was finally able to clear it out, while its advances on Mount Asolone were initially repulsed by the *arditi*'s firm defensive stance on the mountain summit. At 0915 the Austro-Hungarians, led by the stormtroopers of the 99th Moravian Infantry Regiment attacked again, and the troops were forced to evacuate the Mount Asolone as well. "IX *Reparto d'assalto* had to also retreat and was forced to open up a path by

56 Cited in Alberto Businelli, *Gli arditi del IX*, p. 169.

engaging the enemy in close combat to break the encirclement. Therefore, despite a strenuous effort put forth by our troops, our adversary had been able to retake the frontline of Mount Asolone, Hill 1,486, and Hill 1,440."[57]

The battle led to the capture of 600 Austro-Hungarian soldiers, several machine guns and artillery pieces and other material of all kinds, while grave losses in the ranks of IX *Reparto d'assalto* with five dead and eight wounded amongst the officers and 30 dead, 140 wounded and six missing amongst the soldiers, were also sustained.[58]

Once again the operation demonstrated the persistent problem plaguing the large scale *arditi* operations, mainly the inability of the standard infantry units to keep the pace of the *arditi* leaving the latter isolated on the mountain top to face the enemy counter-thrust. Armed primarily with offensive weapons, the *arditi* of IX *Reparto d'assalto* suffered casualties from the enemy to counter-attacks while waiting to be relieved by the heavier-equipped, but slower moving infantry units. In fact, the latter never made it to the Col della Beretta being prevented from moving forward by the enemy's artillery interdiction fire. This largely explains why the mountain top had ultimately to be evacuated.

On the same day XVIII *Reparto d'assalto* supported by troops of the 240th Infantry Regiment and two machine gun companies stormed the Mount Pertica defenses. The plan entailed a two-pronged attack: a central column set to take the peak position while a second column was to take possession of the flanking machine gun position of Hill 1,451. At 0700 the artillery, facilitated in its attempt by a bright blue sky, began its pinpoint preparatory fire mainly with the aid of medium and light guns. At 0830 the artillery lengthened its fire to the second line as the *arditi* exited the caverns on Mount Grappa and began to run toward the peak of the mountain. The central column led by the XVIII *Reparto d'assalto* irrupted with force in the enemy trenches and engaged the enemy in strong hand-to-hand combat.

> We slowly made our way by crawling on the terrain that had been shattered by the fire from our artillery. We kept our heads down as the splinters from the shells were flying everywhere. All of a sudden our artillery stopped firing. This was then followed by a loud shout of 'A Noi!' We immediately got up and started to run toward the mountaintop. As we inched closer to the objective we began to hurl hand grenades at the enemy. The vast majority of the enemy troops were still trapped in the dugouts and bunkers while the few that had managed to man their defensive positions were engaged in hand-to-hand combat. After much fighting these troops were finally overcome.[59]

However, unfortunately for the attackers the infantry column of the 240th was unable to take the flanking position of Hill 1,451 which consisted of several dug-in

57 Ufficio Storico, *Relazione V*, n. 2, narrazione, p. 464.

58 Ufficio Storico, IX Reparto d'assalto: 'Relazione sull'azione spiegata dal IX Reparto d'assalto nel combattimento di Monte Asolone il 29 Ottobre 1918.'

59 Ermes Rosa, *Arditi sul Grappa* (Bassano del Grappa: Itinera Progetti, 2003), p. 163.

machine gun nests. The latter not only repulsed the standard infantry but also began to hit from the flank the *arditi*, causing severe casualties in their ranks and halting their attack. At the same time, strong enemy reserve units had reached the peak of the mountain and begun to hurl hand grenades at the attackers forcing them to retreat. Shortly thereafter, troops from the 73rd Infantry Regiment and a battalion of the 120th Infantry Regiment pushed the *arditi* off the peak and recovered the mountain position with a counter-thrust.

Thus, as the infantry attack had bogged down, the Italian artillery was called into action again and one by one, as the machine gun teams showed their positions, they were blasted away by the mountain guns. As a result, Hill 1,451 was seized shortly thereafter. Once the machine guns were made inoperative, the central column was able to resume its advance. It quickly made its way back to the top of the mountain and cleared it of any enemy presence and the Austro-Hungarian defenders were forced back to the Osteria del Forcelletto. The storming of Mount Pertica yielded the capture of 250 soldiers and 40 machine guns.

After two days of fighting the results were for mostly negative. The *arditi*, following insufficient and predictable artillery preparations, charged up against fortified enemy positions of Mount Asolone and Mount Pertica and were repelled several times with huge losses. The fully functioning machine gun nests tore through the first assault waves causing huge casualties. At the end of the second day of battle only the Pertica was occupied after much hard fighting.

On 26 October the infantry attacks resumed once again across the Grappa sector, but the only hard-won victory for the Italians was the capture of Col del Cuc, after three days of combat and huge losses. At dawn the Italian artillery began to pound the Col del Cuc with both explosive and gas shells, but the guns were not able to penetrate the enemy's defenses and especially the machine gun positions located deep inside the mountain.

After the artillery lengthened its fire, two infantry columns began to assail the enemy positions. In the middle one company from the *Monte Pelmo alpini* Battalion and three infantry companies from the 40th Infantry were able to outflank and overtake Hill 1,186 just below the main enemy position. Meanwhile on the left flank, the *arditi* of III *Reparto d'assalto* and III Battalion/39th Infantry, put forth two consecutive attacks at 0300 and 0500 that were both repulsed with losses by the machine guns.

Having conquered the jumping-off platform of Hill 1,186, the Italian units were determined not to let the chance to take the whole mountain slip away. As a result, the artillery began another preparatory fire at 1515. The first assault wave, comprised by the assault platoon of the 39th Infantry Regiment, III *Reparto d'assalto* and the assault platoon of the *Monte Pelmo* then surrounded the peak of the mountain. After much heavy close combat fighting, the enemy position held by troops of the 14th *Schützen* Regiment was finally occupied with the capture of 427 prisoners, 16 machine guns and 130 rifles. Against this flank of the Grappa, the Italians had lost 600 soldiers and had achieved only one local success on the third day of fighting.

All other offensive attempts aimed at taking the Mount Asolone, Col della Berretta Solaroli, Ca' Tasson and Mount Spinoncia were thwarted by strong enemy fire.

The Austro-Hungarian official history states that:

> With these fruitless attacks on 26 October the 4th Italian Army had fully exhausted their strength. The seizure of Mount Pertica, the forward positions at Col del Cuc and Mount Forcelletta (on the western slope of the Col dell'Orso) and of the Valderoa Heights east of Mount Solarolo had cost the Italians almost 35,000 men dead, wounded or missing. When General Giardino compared the ground gained with the heavy casualties, he recognized that the failed attack in the Grappa mountains was a defeat. The outcome of these three days of combat clearly indicated that the strength and cohesion of the Austro-Hungarian divisions guarding the positions in Armeegruppe Belluno's sector had not declined as much as had been hoped on the Italian side.[60]

Piave River

On the Piave front, General Cavan's 7th English Division had already landed on Papadopoli Island, upstream from Ponte di Piave, in the evening of 23 October and had secured a bridgehead on the enemy side of the river. On 26 October the water level of the Piave finally subsided after the rains had stopped and the Italian military was able to start the work of establishing the temporary bridges to allow the bulk of the troops to cross the river. During the day Italian artillery fire increased considerably targeting primarily the frontline positions held by the 6th Army; toward evening the trench mortars intervened to destroy the enemy's command centers, while at 1900 gas shells were also fired. By 2300 several bridges had been established and the Italian Army was preparing to attack the Austro-Hungarian positions on the left bank of the Piave. The three main areas on the left bank of the Piave which were to be assailed were: the Allied 10th Army was to expand the bridgehead at Grave di Papadopoli, the 12th Army troops were to cross the river at Priula and were then to head to Valdobbiadene and the 8th Army was to take Sernaglia.

The task of storming the Austrian frontline strongholds on the opposite side of the river was given to the two Assault Divisions. The I *Divisione d'assalto* was responsible for forcing the crossing of the Piave at Piana di Sernaglia on behalf of 8th Army and then reach the so-called Linea dei Mulini and ultimately the area of the five villages (Mosnigo, Moriago, Fontigo, Sernaglia and Falze') were the bulk of the Austrian defenses were concentrated, while II *Divisione* was supposed to cross the river at Priula and lead the way on behalf of the 12th Army infantry forces. Once they had managed to cross the river and eliminate the first line of enemy defense, the two divisions were to link up and converge on Vittorio Veneto, the logistics and supply hub of the Austro-Hungarian Army, and pave the way for a broad infantry advance by 8th and 12th Army. The operation was conceived as pincer movement against the Austro-Hungarian 6th Army that held the bulk of the defensive positions on the lower Piave.

60 Edmund Glaise-Horstenau (ed.), *Österreich-Ungarns letzter Krieg 1914–1918*, vol. 7, p. 672.

In the plans of the *Comando Supremo* the I *Divisione d'assalto* was tasked with a key role in the offensive which consisted in storming the frontline defenses and creating a large bridgehead on the left side of the Piave River. This would have allowed the bulk of the infantry to land safely on the Austrian held side of the river and then advance en masse against the enemy positions. The assault division had been formed in the spring of 1918 and it was comprised by the following units:

First Assault Group consisting of X, XX *Reparti d'assalto*, I *Bersaglieri* Battalion, 390th Machine Gun Company.
Second Assault Group consisting of XII, XIII *Reparti d'assalto*, VII *Bersaglieri* Battalion and 392nd Machine Gun Company.
Third Assault Group consisting VIII, XXII *Reparti d'assalto*, IX *Bersaglieri* Battalion and 393rd Machine Gun Company.
Two mountain artillery groups (IX and XXIX *Gruppi Artiglieria di Montagna*) with 65 mm guns.
Three machine gun companies.
One small cannon group (37 mm guns).
One cavalry unit.
One sapper battalion.
One group of support services.

The action by the I *Divisione d'assalto* began with strong preparatory fire by the Italian artillery which shelled the left bank of the Piave. Under the cover of the artillery barrage, the XII *Reparto d'assalto* crossed the river first with small boats to establish three temporary bridgeheads near where the three bridges were to be established to let the I *Divisione d'assalto* cross the river. While several boats were overturned by the strong and overpowering currents of the river and their crews were swept away, several *arditi* platoons managed to land on the opposite side and under cover of darkness and fog, they surprised and penetrated the thinly held outpost line.

Shortly after 2300 the Austrian artillery began to interfere with the landings by firing numerous artillery shells which wreaked havoc on both friends and enemy alike located near the banks of the river. This effort combined with the return of the heavy rains slowed down the advance considerably. Finally at 0230 the *arditi* platoons of the division crossed the river and began to clash with the enemy. As a result of these preliminary rounds of fighting approximately 50 soldiers were captured along with several machine guns. While the Italian artillery lengthened its fire, the bulk of the division took some time to regroup once on the left flank and then continued its advance. As they marched in small groups toward the five villages the fighting became more intense as the Austro-Hungarian Army had built stronger defenses on the second and third line. These defenses were very well concealed and were centered on abandoned houses, bushes, ditches and small hills. Small groups of Austrian snipers and machine gun teams had been scattered throughout these positions and the fighting took the form of close quarters hand-to-hand combat where each position had to be taken by pinning it down with small mountain artillery, mortars or machine guns and then by circumventing and overtaking it with the aid of hand grenades.

The Austro-Hungarian official history states that by early morning many of the Austrian positions had been seized:

> General Edler von Karapancza's 12th *Schützen* Division, driven out of their positions on the river bank, were still fighting desperately in the morning around their guns on the right wing near Sernaglia. But the Division's left wing was also soon in extreme danger. Here the 1st Italian Assault Division broke into the trenches near Chiesola and Falzé; moreover, they pushed the right wing of Field Marshal Lieutenant von Schamschula's 41st *Honvéd* Infantry Division back over the Soligo Brook in wild and very costly fighting.[61]

At 0830 the *arditi* were finally able to storm Sernaglia after heavy fighting as several rearguard Austro-Hungarian troops had put up firm resistance and many of them had to be killed or captured after having refused to surrender. With the capture of Sernaglia the Italians had reached two of their objectives: the capture of Austrian guns including 20 artillery pieces, four mortars and 50 machine guns and had secured a three-mile bridgehead into the enemy positions.

The Italian official history states that:

> At dawn the units of the 11th Hussar Division, which were tasked with defending the five villages, were overwhelmed. Mosnigo was conquered while Sernaglia was bypassed. In full adherence to the directives given by General Caviglia, our assault units penetrated deeply into the enemy deployment by assailing the enemy artillery batteries. This allowed the capture of 20 artillery pieces.[62]

Their next objectives were the hills surrounding Sernaglia and to bypass the Soligo River were the Austrians had placed the majority of their heavy guns.

But as the troops moved forward in order to take the next objective, in the afternoon of 27 October the Austro-Hungarian infantry launched a series of counter-attacks, some led by stormtroopers, in order to stop the enemy advance and re-establish their defensive positions. These localized thrusts were undertaken by small teams comprised of 50 to 100 soldiers that used infiltration tactics to penetrate and sow confusion in the Italian ranks. All these attempts were repulsed with great difficulty and heavy losses were had by both sides.

But due to the lack of reinforcements given that the rains had again caused an overflow of the river, on the night on 27 October I *Divisione* was counter-attacked in force again by Austro-Hungarian infantry forces in a bid to throw it back into the Piave River. As a result, the *arditi* were forced to pull back on to the Sernaglia-Villamatta line, which represented a more narrow and easier to defend line of the defense, while

61 Edmund Glaise-Horstenau (ed.), *Österreich-Ungarns letzter Krieg 1914–1918*, vol. 7, p. 618.
62 Ufficio Storico, *Relazione V*, n. 2, narrazione, p. 519.

the Austrian guns smashed the bridges behind them. The Austro-Hungarian official history states that:

> At this critical moment the gallant and often distinguished Lower Austrian 84th Infantry Regiment forces threw themselves into the gap from the west. The Regiment struck with elan, pushing the enemy back at some points; but in front of Sernaglia and near Mosnigo they encountered much larger Italian forces and had to entrench upon the open and rain-soaked battlefield, under destructive fire from the enemy artillery.[63]

For two nights the *arditi* were forced on the defensive as reinforcements could not be transported across the Piave due to bad weather and enemy fire. During those two nights of 27–28 October the *arditi* fought back numerous attempts by the Austrians to surround and capture them mainly by using their small mountain cannons, the Stokes mortars and the machine guns. The enemy would advance in small groups using infiltration tactics. On the other hand, the Italians would let the enemy initially advance and would then attempt to attack it from behind and from the flanks. These skirmishes continued to take a toll on both sides, but however the major problem faced by the I *Divisione d'assalto* was that it was cut off from the bulk of the Italian troops and as a result it was quickly running out of ammunition. Since the Piave could not be crossed because of the high water level, the troops were resupplied primarily by aircraft dropping boxes of food and ammunition while the sappers tried to establish new bridges.

Finally on the morning of 29 October the water levels subsidized as the rain stopped and the Italian XXVII Army Corps and the II *Divisione* were able to cross the Piave and engage the enemy at Susegana and San Salvatore. Its maneuver in fact encircled the enemy forces positioned against the I *Divisione d'assalto* and eventually caused a rout of the front line defenses. By then Austrian forces facing encirclement pulled back from the banks of the Piave as the *arditi* and infantry units began to chase the retreating units past Falze' and Col Capriolo. The I *Divisione* did face limited opposition while fighting for control of Falze' but it was mostly from rearguard troops that were covering the retreat of the bulk of the Austro-Hungarian troops. On the same day, the English infantry forces had also captured Austro-Hungarian positions manned by the 26th Infantry Division and after a very powerful artillery barrage had successfully crossed the Monticano River. It was at that point that the Isonzo Army Command gave the general retreat order. As the Austro-Hungarian official history asserts:

> On 29 October the lines of Field Marshal Boroevic's Army Group had been broken again at two points (near Soligno and southeast of Conegliano on the Monticano), and the rear areas were in an uproar due to the mutiny of the reserves. Frankly, the situation was hopeless.[64]

63 Edmund Glaise-Horstenau (ed.), Österreich-Ungarns letzter Krieg 1914–1918, vol. 7, p.
64 Ibid., p. 621.

As the Austro-Hungarians retreated they were chased by the infantry travelling on foot and by the cavalry and some armored cars. The air force continued to pound the retreating troops from above forcing them to disperse and slowing down their retreat. During the final stages of the battle entire battalions were captured en masse, several junior and senior officers were also captured including a handful of generals.

Between 26 and 29 October the final tally of the Battle of Sernaglia was 293 dead, 823 wounded and 56 missing (the missing were troops that were swept away during the early crossing of the Piave on the 26th) amongst the I *Divisione d'assalto*. In turn, they had killed or wounded up to 1,500 enemy soldiers, had captured 3,500 prisoners, 36 artillery pieces (mostly medium to light caliber guns) 168 machine guns, 1,516 rifles, six mortars, and five grenade throwers.

II *Divisione* had captured 4500 prisoners, 30 artillery pieces, 50 machine guns. Its losses were 38 dead and 128 wounded.

The Battle of Vittorio Veneto was a hard fought encounter that demonstrated the pitfalls as well as the merits of the Italian Army. The major pitfall was the going back to the old way of attacking the enemy with the breakthrough battle tactics dominated by frontal assaults and by an insufficient artillery preparation. The lack of super heavy artillery and shells was keenly felt has the dug in Austrian defenses where not sensibly degraded. In addition, the length of the preparatory barrage (i.e., more than a half day) alerted the defenders of an impending attack and gave them time to bring up some reserves on the Grappa massif to parry the offensive. Most of the old tactics were displayed primarily on the Mount Grappa sector, while on the Piave the *reparti d'assalto*, the artillery and the artillery furnished a more positive account of themselves displaying a combination of old and new tactics.

One of the bright spots of the offensive was the hard work carried out by the air force arm both during the preparation of the offensive as well as during the battle itself. "During the Battle of Vittorio Veneto, Italian pilots flew everything from mass bombing missions to artillery spotting and photo reconnaissance, the latter needing only thirty seven minutes to deliver a photo to the local command."[65]

A few days prior to the battle the air force completed numerous reconnaissance missions aimed at counting enemy guns and identifying their position mainly taking inventory of the flashes of the guns. During the battle the air force conducted over 1,000 sorties to bomb enemy positions. This effort was attested by the fact that the air force lost 84 pilots in 1918, a majority of whom fell during the final battle.[66]

Another bright spot was the relentlessness of the *arditi* assault units especially in the Mount Grappa sector where in many instances they reached and cleared out enemy positions despite hellish machine gun fire that caused many casualties.

Even though these troops achieved few of their overall objectives, mainly due to staunch defensive thrusts by the Austro-Hungarian troops, their ultimate sacrifice hastened the collapse of the Dual Monarchy. Similarly on the Piave the assault division fought valiantly despite being outnumbered and surrounded by the enemy after

65 Spencer C. Tucker, *The European Powers in the First World War: An Encyclopedia*, p. 373.
66 Ibid., p. 301.

the Austro-Hungarian artillery destroyed the temporary bridges. After 29 October the assault division displayed its ability for advancing quickly with its combined arms units, although this success is not easy to measure since by then sections of the Austro-Hungarian Army were already collapsing.

Conclusion

The last year of the war saw the assault units, *reparti d'assalto*, at the forefront of most offensive operations. A comparison between the initial Battle of the Three Mountains and the attack against the Capo Sile defenses in the summer demonstrates the vast improvements made by the Italian Army during that year. The first battle was fought by an exceedingly high number of battalions, it was waged for two days and the artillery preparation was long-winded. The summer attack was initiated by a dawn pinpoint barrage followed by the storming forward of a few infantry and assault companies. While both achieved the ultimate objective, the second operation was less costly and it was conducted much more expeditiously. The so-called 'White Battle' also achieved similar results with the use of few, well trained, crack mountain *arditi* units that achieved considerable territorial conquest with the aid of a preparatory barrage that although brief was able to pave the way for the assault units. Both operations differed from the Battle of the Three Mountains in terms of the much more limited use of infantry units and the much more preponderant role played by the artillery in stunning into submission the enemy forces. Such an operation demonstrates the improvements that had been made by the Army as a whole and its adoption of the more advanced integration tactics of the Western Front.

The *arditi* and other like-minded offensive troops achieved considerable local successes and prevailed against the Austro-Hungarian stormtroopers in the realm of small-scale raiding. By adopting similar tactics, such as fighting at night or by forming special hand grenade squads, the Italians had by 1918 breached the gap with the more tactically advanced units of the Austro-Hungarian Army.

Conclusion

In 1915 both the Austro-Hungarian and the Italian Army were still heavily imbued with the pre-1914 offensive spirit and their standard infantryman was still primarily armed with the weapons suited for earlier wars such as the rifle and bayonet. In addition, the same infantryman lacked a steel helmet and his non-camouflaged uniform was not very practical when charging against an entrenched machine gun defense in a mountainous environment.

During 1915 both armies also fought similarly by charging against the enemy either in packed infantry columns or in separate waves, although by 1916 the Austro-Hungarians were better deployed defensively with respect to the beginning of the war and were starting to adopt new, and more innovative offensive tactics. Both armies also lacked the heavy field guns, howitzers and adequate numbers of shells necessary to destroy concrete defenses or deep trenches and their infantry battalions lacked adequate numbers of machine guns. In short, in 1915 both armies were unprepared for fighting a long-term war of attrition where victory necessitated outlasting and outfighting the enemy.[1] As a result of the huge losses sustained by both armies (the Austro-Hungarians on the Eastern Front in 1914–15 and the Italians on the Isonzo in 1915–16) changes to adopt new tactics and more suitable weapons were slowly introduced. Both armies could look at the Western front for viable examples of adaptation to trench warfare. Initially, the Italians looked to the French Army as an example, in particular given the extensive collaboration between the two high commands, while the Austro-Hungarians had as example the more powerful and professional German Army. By the end of the war both armies had been particularly influenced by the infiltration tactics adopted by the Germans.

Strategic and tactical innovation first began on the Western front. By the first Battle of Ypres the entrenched trench warfare fossilized and became the dominant feature of the war. Both the Allies and the Central Powers were forced to adapt to the new environment but at the same time they never gave up in looking for ways to overcome the stalemate. The British, for example, developed special teams of bombing raiders that carried bags of hand grenades to mop up captured enemy trenches and were the first to use light Lewis machine guns in the attack. In 1917 the Royal Artillery's combination of creeping barrages in support of infantry attacks, and accurate predicted fire for preparatory barrages and counter-battery fire, gave their operations a major

1 William Philpott, *War of Attrition: Fighting the First World War* (New York: The Overlook Press, 2015).

edge over their opponents. Lastly, the British were the first to combine the tank with infantry making the former an integral part of the attack. The infantry attacking enemy trenches and machine gun strong points could by 1917 advance through no man's land behind the tanks, which not only provided cover and support but also acted as a mobile artillery arm.[2] As the battle of Cambrai demonstrated, the value of the tank as an offensive weapon was immeasurable even though the British Army's inability to fully exploit the deep penetration achieved by tanks and infantry forces on the first day of battle did not lead to a definitive victory.

The French also innovated with the adoption of German best practices such as the defense in depth principle that jettisoned the established practice of defending with one continuous trenchline. General Petain was also responsible for the introduction of new offensive tactics based on the so-called methodical battle. Petain maintained that a vast increase in artillery firepower laid the foundation for successful infantry attacks. Prolonged barrages against the first line of enemy defense would be followed by determined infantry attacks. Soon after the process was repeated against the second enemy line of defense as the artillery was moved up to confront the next challenge. As Doughty correctly argued Petain "insisted on careful preparation of all attacks and refused to rely on anything other than firepower to blast the enemy back."[3] The Allied offensive in the Second Battle of the Marne on 18 July 1918, which included a combination of elements that both the French and British armies had struggled to fully integrate for most of the war, represented the culmination of maneuver warfare and technology. "Using the method of artillery support evolved since the Battle of Cambrai, a brief preparation followed by a violent rolling barrage, the French forces moved forward, heavily dependent upon a mass of 346 tanks to provide direct fire support and crush the defensive wire."[4] Although the Allies, especially the British, still relied on more prolonged barrages than the Central Powers, by then they had perfected the art of the rolling barrage thanks to superior mapping and artillery registration procedures. But it was the new weapons, tank squads in close cooperation with infantry, that achieved a near tactical breakthrough at Second Marne by penetrating deeply into the German defensive deployment.

Another feature of the Allied attack was the massive reliance on air power for both reconnaissance and for the bombing of enemy defenses. As the battle unfolded, both French and British airplanes flew countless missions in support of the infantry attack. By then the Allies enjoyed almost complete control of the air space above the field of battle thanks to the great French industrial transformation and expansion which by 1918 had decisively pushed ahead of the Central Powers in new aircraft production.

Thus air power, tanks and armored vehicles on the Allied side and German stormtrooper tactics were the three most innovative elements that reintroduced a

2 Paddy Griffith, Battle *Tactics on the Western Front 1916–18* (Yale: Yale University Press, 1994).

3 Robert A. Doughty, *Pyrrhic Victory: French Strategy and Operations in the Great War* (Harvard: Harvard University Press, 2008), p. 468.

4 William R. Griffiths, *The Great War*, p. 153

degree of mobility in a war that up to 1916 had been totally dominated by entrenched positional warfare.[5]

Beginning in 1916 both the Austro-Hungarian and the Italian Army sought to introduce elements of the German and Allied tactical systems of warfare, mainly the introduction of infiltration tactics at the expense of the breakthrough battle and the elements of defense in depth approach. Like all other combatants, the Italian and the Austro-Hungarian armies achieved most of their tactical improvements during the last two years of the war. But how did their tactical evolution measure up to the demands of trench warfare and to an industrial-type war? According to military historians Allen Millett and Williamson Murray one of the main features of military effectiveness is tactical effectiveness. Its key components include:

1. The army's approach to training
2. Troop morale and unit cohesion
3. Having the proper weapons for offensive operations
4. Consistency in the application of battle tactics
5. A high degree of combined arms integration
6. The degree to which tactical solutions favor the swift, unexpected and overpowering use of offensive force.

How did the Italian and the Austro-Hungarian Army measure up to the six variables of tactical effectiveness and how did their offensive operations compare to the more advanced tactics and weapons used by the Germans and the Allies in the Western Front?

Training

The Austro-Hungarian Army had already integrated most of the key points of modern stormtroop tactics by early 1917. The first innovation was a change in the way the special assault battalions were trained by assimilating the training techniques and curricula of the German stormtroopers. In late 1916 the AOK introduced the stormtroops training manual which became the basis of assault patrols and battalions training within the Habsburg Army. This consisted in specific hand grenade, rifle and wire demolition training and was widely used to train successive waves of assault troops. To achieve a degree of uniformity amongst the assault patrols and the storm battalions of the Army, the AOK then issued a directive aimed at establishing a common structure amongst the *sturmtruppen* units. This was followed by specific guidelines for rewarding highly skillful and audacious stormtroopers that had distinguished themselves in combat. In 1918 the Army was fully reorganized and the stormtrooper battalions became the spearhead of the newly constituted infantry divisions. These units by then not only had their own special assault detachments but

5 Ibid., p. 129.

also their own expanded artillery regiments and even their own air force unit which was used for advanced reconnaissance of the enemy's positions. The artillery itself was bolstered with more modern, more effective guns and its tactics evolved in support of the infantry advance in its various stages. The 1918 structure of the infantry division of the Austro-Hungarian Army thus reflected all the lessons learned of four years of fighting in the trenches and within the confines of a war of attrition dominated by tremendous firepower.

The Italian Army initially lagged the enemy in terms of the establishment of formal training camps and curricula for the assault troops. Although the Italian Army had experimented with special trench busting units as early as 1915, it was finally forced to constitute the *arditi* units to emulate the success achieved by the Austrian *sturmtruppen* in early 1917. Thus, in June of 1917 the Sdricca training camp was established where the *arditi* of 2nd Army began to train and from which the first two *arditi* battalions would emerge from in the summer of 1917. By that time, a uniform organization for the *arditi* was also established that consisted in increasing infantry specialization and by arming the special units with new weapons to breach entrenched defenses. The high level and comprehensive training received by the *arditi* became the bedrock of their successes in 1917–18 and it was also responsible, together with their offensive weaponry, for the great changes in the offensive tactics of the Italian Army.

Morale

Troop morale increased considerably within the Austro-Hungarian Army as a result of the rise of the stormtrooper battalions. The latter in fact imbued the Army with the new offensive spirit and their battlefield successes buoyed standard infantry forces that had shown considerable fatigue after three years of constant frontline fighting. In addition to the stormtroopers, the morale of the Austro-Hungarian soldiers deployed on the Italian front was always higher than of those deployed in Eastern Europe. Presumably this had to do with the fact that the majority of the soldiers considered Italy as the 'hereditary enemy' of the Dual Monarchy. In addition, the troops on the Italian front did not witness the huge reversals of fortune suffered by the 2nd and 3rd Austro-Hungarian armies deployed in the Eastern front such as the capitulation of Fortress Przemysl and the Carpathian Mountains campaign of 1915. This likely greatly diminished the morale of these troops.

The *arditi*, on the other hand, also positively influenced the standard infantry soldiers has their initial successes produced and coincided with some of the first major territorial breakthroughs achieved by the Italian Army in the conflict. Unfortunately, the *arditi* units were almost wiped out by the Central Powers' Caporetto Offensive, which caused a grave crisis within the Italian Army and destroyed the morale of the frontline troops of the 2nd Army. In 1918, after the Italians had successfully defeated Austro-Hungarian attempts to invade the Piave and Mount Grappa, the Army has a whole recovered and morale and a rise in national sentiment flourished within the standard infantry and artillery battalions. The *arditi* did much to improve morale in

1918 by carrying out dozens of swift raids against the enemy that often yielded a high number of prisoners and captured war booty. Their success together with General Diaz's more measured approach revitalized the Italian infantry divisions. Moreover, the *arditi* were instrumental in fighting off the major Solstice Offensive with spirited counter-attacks to repulse the enemy back to its original lines. This further improved the morale of the army.

Weapons

The great challenge faced by both armies was how to quickly arm the infantry with weapons to penetrate the wire and overtake fortified defenses and expeditiously fulfill the demand for a great increase in the number of guns capable of high trajectory fire to destroy fortified positions. In the field of battle the Austro-Hungarians led the way on the Italo-Austrian front by developing special infantry bombing sections to be used in planned attacks and small raids against enemy lines. Pioneer and special mountain units were also expanded and strengthened and armed with new weapons such as flamethrowers, *minenwerfer* and small grenade launchers which had become essential to breach the enemy wire. Each infantry division also could count upon expanded machine gun sections with more and better technologically advanced machine guns. Most importantly, by 1916 the Austro-Hungarian Army initiated a major reorganization of its artillery arm by initially shifting resources from the obsolete fortress artillery to mountain and field artillery. It also began to replace obsolete units mainly with modern 30.5 cm siege mortars, 150 mm, 100 mm and 75 mm mountain guns and by revamping its artillery batteries. By mid 1916 the Austro-Hungarian Army had practically replaced all if its obsolete weapons and its total number of artillery pieces had increased by 50 percent since the beginning of the war. This upward trend continued until 1918 when the Austro-Hungarian Army could count upon record levels of artillery batteries. In fact, three numbers stand out for the immense progress made by the Austro-Hungarian Army of 1918. First, the total number of artillery guns had risen from the 3,000 pieces of 1914 to 6,916. Second, the artillery battery mix had been profoundly changed with the introduction by 1916 of large numbers of high-trajectory, indirect fire guns necessary for trench warfare. Field howitzers, mortars and mine-throwers increased almost sixfold from the 120 of 1914 to 679 of 1918.[6] Third, in 1915 the Austro-Hungarian artillery was often outgunned by the enemy due to the fact that many of its models were obsolete. Tunstall points out that during the Carpathian offensive the "Second Army field howitzer batteries required repair. The lengthy turnaround time for such service signified that many guns remained out of action for long periods."[7] By 1918 the 5th Army, for example, could count upon over 85 percent of its guns during the Piave Offensive, while the repair time for artillery batteries had been cut down considerably. All of these reforms made the rise of the

6 http://www.austro-hungarian-army.co.uk/artyorg.html <Accessed 2 January 2017>
7 Tunstall, *Blood on the Snow*, p. 196.

special assault units of stormtroopers possible. In fact, these units might never have been successful, for instance, if the Austro-Hungarian Army did not have by 1917 modern artillery guns and tactics which were integral to the success of well-executed stormtrooper operations. In addition, the stormtroopers might never have been able to breach the enemy wire if unable to count upon their expanded special sections armed with large quantities of flamethrowers, small mortars and light artillery pieces. Some of this equipment was furnished by the Germans, while the majority was produced by the domestic industry which greatly aided the emergence of the Austrian stormtroopers. Even though by 1918 Austria-Hungary economic base had begun to decline, its army had been vastly modernized and its troops were deploying advanced tactics. In addition, by mid 1918 the army could count upon 65 stormtrooper battalions, 10 half battalions for a total of approximately 70,000 stormtroopers and many hundreds of storm assault patrols within the standard infantry battalions.

The Italian military leadership, although benefiting from a year of neutrality from which it could observe weapon and tactical developments on the Western Front, lagged behind the Austro-Hungarians in the race to re-arm itself for a long term campaign of trench warfare. In the beginning it lacked almost everything including heavy guns and machine guns for the infantry. By 1918 thanks to increased industrial output and greater collaboration with the Allies, the Italian Army had the necessary quantities of weapons and ammunition to fight off the last enemy offensive. For example, by then the artillery arm not only had record numbers of 240 mm mortars "that played a key role in preparatory fire and in destroying the enemy's secondary defenses"[8] but it also could count upon numerous batteries of heavy artillery guns. It is estimated that by 1818 the Italian artillery had over 7,000 guns. Trench mortar formations were one of the distinctive advantages of the Italian Army. Already by the end of 1916 there were 2,062 mortars varying in caliber between 58 to 240 mm, while the Austro-Hungarians had fewer of these weapons. By 1918 the Army could count upon 2,400 trench mortars. In terms of machine guns the standard Italian infantry regiment had only two or four guns in 1915, while by 1918 each battalion had 14 guns.

One of the most important innovations for the Italian Army was the formation of the *arditi* units which was the result of experiments within 2nd Army as well as the adaptation of tactics and reforms already implemented by the Austro-Hungarians. As John Gooch has correctly argued, the Austro-Hungarian army's *sturmtruppen* "provided both a model and a stimulus"[9] for the Italian Army. In 1917 line infantry was also changing in a way that it was becoming more adept in fighting a prolonged war of attrition with the addition within its rifle companies of special rifle-grenade and hand grenade squads. The *arditi* enjoyed the use of large quantities of advanced weapons such Stokes mortars, 65 mm mountain guns, flamethrowers and the highly versatile *Thevenot* smoke and explosive grenades. By 1918 the only Italian weapon that continued to truly lag behind that of Austria-Hungary was the light machine

8 Filippo Cappellano, 'The Italian Artillery', p. 206.
9 John Gooch, *The Italian Army* , p. 201.

gun whose performance never even came close to the German Maxim light gun. But the Italians made up for this deficiency by using large amounts of other offensive weapons such as mortars and small mountain cannons. In 1918 the Italians had 40 *reparti d'assalto* battalions and two *arditi* assault divisions with approximately 50,000 *arditi* soldiers. In addition, by then lower level assault units named the "*Plotoni di arditi reggimentali*" or Regimental *arditi* platoons had been formed within many infantry regiments. Initially created in 1917 these platoons assumed the tasks of everyday patrols and small close combat actions by adopting the tactics and weapons of the *arditi*. Their objective was to filter down to the standard infantry the successful tactics of the *arditi*.

Consistency

Consistency in the application of stormtrooper tactics was one of the factors that enabled the *sturmtruppen* to achieve important successes in 1917. Despite the fact that the stormtroopers experienced some difficulties during their first deployments such as suffering losses due to uncoordinated artillery fire and their erroneous deployment as frontline defensive troops, their commanders continued to adhere to German-inspired assault tactics. By late 1917 the early experimentation finally paid off as the Austro-Hungarian Army properly deployed its stormtrooper battalions in well-planned and tactically astute operations that yielded the massive success at Caporetto. As a result, the latter were deployed properly in several large-scale attacks that were well coordinated and where the infantry and the artillery arm worked well together in a harmonious fashion to reach the designated goal. The consistency in launching swift and precise artillery bombardments followed by the sudden surge forward of the stormtroopers equipped with new tactical weapons such as light machine guns, mortars and flamethrowers, allowed the Austro-Hungarian Army to achieve success on the battlefield, especially during the Mount Ortigara and the Caporetto offensives. These operations were aided by the fact that the mountainous terrain and the difficult operating conditions necessitated experienced assault, high mountain, troops supported by equally experienced mountain artillery batteries. The Austro-Hungarian Army by the spring of 1917 had adequate numbers of such trained troops. Another factor that was fairly consistent in Austro-Hungarian tactics was the way in which the standard infantry followed the lead of the stormtroopers and put forth its attack as a second wave that surged forward in close coordination with the special forces. This was the result of the close collaboration between the two entities and also because the stormtroopers were not a separate combat arm. The Italians on the other hand took longer to incorporate the proper storm tactics and the *arditi* would largely be wiped out during the winter battle of 1917 where they were erroneously deployed as line infantry troops. In fact, initial difficulties were experienced when the *arditi* were used for defensive purposes for which they were neither trained nor equipped such as during the defense of Udine in late 1917. These were new, experimental units and sometimes commanders simply did not understand how to use them properly or given the grave crisis faced by the Italian Army as a result of the Caporetto Offensive, commanders inappropriately used them to prop up infantry in the defensive. Another initial difficulty that characterized the Italian Army was the lack of coordination between the *arditi* and the standard infantry with the latter often unable to keep pace with the speed of the assault units. Often this meant that infantry was not able to reach the positions taken by the *arditi* who were left to fend for themselves in advanced positions and face repetitive enemy counter-attacks. In 1918, however, several operations that saw the combined effort of *arditi* and infantry did much to achieve a more harmonious and coordinated advance tactics between the two branches. A problem that persisted for most of the war was the artillery's persistence in using very long-winded preparatory fire that often pre-warned the enemy as to the direction of an impending attack. In 1918, however, in some operations the artillery did improve its performance with more accurate, surprise pinpoint barrages that opened the way for the infantry/*arditi* advance. As a result of good artillery preparation and extensive reconnaissance many *arditi* operations were successful in achieving tactical surprise and capturing enemy strongpoints. The 'White Battle' or the raid at Capo Sile are a testament to how much the cooperation between artillery and infantry had improved by the fourth year of the war.

Combined Arms

Finally both armies demonstrated considerable talent in integrating the combined arms approach that was being perfected on the Western Front. During the Solstice Offensive, for example, German and Austrian air forces preceded the main infantry attack by providing both aerial reconnaissance of the enemy's guns as well as saturation bombing of the enemy's defenses. The air force was then followed by the artillery barrage and finally by the storming forward of the infantry and the special units. Similarly, the Italians were able to implement this combined arms approach to good effect during the Battle of Vittorio Veneto. The Italians by then also could deploy a greater number of aircraft thanks to a greatly expanded industrial base in support of the war which surpassed Austria-Hungary in 1918 in the production of airplanes and heavy artillery. Unlike the Western Front, both the Italians and the Austro-Hungarians, however, failed to introduce the tank in the offensive. This was the result of several factors but mainly due to a weaker industrial economic base which forced both countries to deploy their resources for artillery and machine guns production rather than diverge funds into armored vehicles. This failure was also due to the mountainous terrain of battle which made the use of tanks in the offensive much less viable than on the flatter surface of the Western Front. Overall however, despite the lack of armored vehicles these 'lesser powers' successfully adopted into their offensive plans several elements of the so-called combined arms tactics that would then be perfected by the German Army in the Second World War. Both the stormtroopers and the *reparti d'assalto* were integrated well within the newly developed combined arms approach. The former, for instance, worked very cohesively with the artillery arm, while the latter operated in conjunction with the cavalry, armored cars squads and airplanes during the last phase of the Battle of Vittorio Veneto.

Both military units were able to react to the changes imposed by industrial warfare and were also able to introduce a degree of innovation despite having weaker economic bases than the main protagonists on the Western front and generally more conservative military leaderships. With regards to the Austro-Hungarian Army military historian John Schindler has correctly argued that by the Caporetto Offensive it had evolved into a very capable fighting force grounded upon a vast increase in artillery firepower. The vast expanse in firepower that had been made possible by the advanced technological know how and the increased production base by such entities as the Skoda Works factory together with a much more effective use of artillery in the battle, enabled the Austro-Hungarian Army to reap enormous benefits. By the end of 1917 the standard infantry division had not only enormous artillery firepower but also considerable infantry attacking thrust provided by the stormtroopers that combined to inflict a major defeat against the enemy. With regards to the progress made by the Austro-Hungarian Army in 1917–18, the official history states that:

> The Army had been substantially enlarged, reorganized and modernized; it was better equipped with artillery and technical resources than ever before. From a purely organizational and tactical standpoint, it was a respectable instrument of force. Overall it was a worthy representative of a large and important state, and it seemed determined to fight for an honorable peace and, afterwards, to protect the rebirth of the fatherland.[10]

By late 1918, however, all the offensive efforts made in 1917 were nullified by the weakening of the war industry. The vast shortages of key components such as steel, the loss of worker productivity and the growing problems with overtaxed railways and other sectors of the transportation industry meant that the war effort by the fall of 1918 began to lag and that the Austro-Hungarian Army lost the initiative.

The Italians on the other hand, by 1918 had made a considerable recovery. The domestic industry had grown exponentially and had overcome the Habsburg industry in terms of output and efficiency. By 1918 the army could count on over 7,000 artillery guns, vast amounts of mortars, machine guns and small mountain cannons. Moreover, the infantry that was deployed on the battlefield was better trained and was deployed, for the most part, in offensive operations that were more adequately planned and that did not cause needless loss of life. Most importantly, through the *arditi* and other offensive troops, the army was able to return to maneuver warfare to disjoint enemy defenses with the former's advanced training and weaponry.

As military historians Cappellano and di Martino assert:

> The army, thanks to the constant effort by the High Command to innovate and mobilize the nation behind the war effort, had become by 1918 a redoubtable

10 Edmund Glaise-Horstenau (ed.), *Österreich-Ungarns letzter Krieg* , Vol. 7, p. 541.

> instrument, well armed and equipped and sufficiently trained and motivated. Tempered by four years of warfare, the army did not cut a poor figure when compared to other armies of the Great War or when it faced the Habsburg Army or when some of its units were requested to fight in France or Macedonia ...[11]

Differences/Similarities

The *arditi* and the stormtroopers had similar combat roles such as executing raids against the enemy lines to capture prisoners and weapons and pave the way for the standard infantry during major operations. At the center of their tactics were similar operating procedures such as the careful selection of the objectives, the collection of in depth intelligence on the enemy's deployment, full rehearsals before the offensive action, followed by swift and surprise attacks preceded by pinpoint barrages.

Another similarity was the military capacity of both armies. In fact while both by 1917–18 wanted to fully transition to the more rewarding infiltration tactics they lacked some of the most important means to achieve the purpose. Both, for instance, lacked adequate numbers of NCOs to drive such tactics as well as the firepower that was available to infantry on the Western Front. The Italian Army of the First World War was renowned for having lost the majority of its junior career officers in 1915 and it never had comparable light machine guns for maneuver warfare such as the British Lewis gun or the German Maxim gun. By 1917 the stock of junior officers and NCOs was also dwindling in the Austro-Hungarian Army. The official history, for instance, in regards to the Solstice Offensive asserts that: "The attack here very quickly broke down into numerous isolated actions; to succeed in fighting at this level an army needs many non-commissioned officers well-trained in tactics, and such was no longer the situation of the Austro-Hungarian Army in 1918."[12] Moreover, although the Army was furnished with German light machine guns and trench mortars in 1917–18, its divisions never had comparable numbers of these weapons as the standard German infantry division of 1918. Both the leaders of the Austro-Hungarian and the Italian Army also envied the massive amounts of heavy artillery guns available to both the Allies and the Germans in the Western Front. The armies on the Italian front had grown their artillery arm both in terms of the deployment of the number of guns and shells, but they were never able to match the firepower of the British or the German artillery, for example. The opening barrage by the British XIV Army Corps during the Battle of Vittorio Veneto on 24 October 1918, for instance, took completely by surprise the Austrian 29th Division forces because it commenced without prior fire registration and its unprecedented intensity killed many frontline troops. Both Italians and Austrians could never match such intensity or the lethality of French or British shells.

11 Filippo Cappellano and Basilio Di Martino, *Un Esercito Forgiato nelle Trincee,* p. 200.
12 Edmund Glaise-Horstenau (ed.), *Österreich-Ungarns letzter Krieg,* Vol. 7, p. 404.

The limitations mentioned above, along with several other organizational and economic factors, largely explain why their transition toward the full adaptation of the German infantry model was not fully completed by 1918. It also explains why stormtroop tactics were expanded only to certain sections of the infantry, whereas within the German Army it was expanded in 1918 to the infantry as a whole.

On the other hand, some of the differences were in how the special troops fought alongside the standard infantry and in the choice of their weapons.

While the stormtroopers were considered by the AOK as standard infantry units that had received better training and hence could be deployed for special operations, the *arditi* were considered from the onset as a separate combat arm from the standard infantry. Thus, while the stormtroopers were often deployed alongside the standard infantry units from their own division, the *arditi* were exempt from frontline trench duty and were deployed only for specific combat missions. In 1918 the Italian High Command made the *arditi* into a truly elite force by constituting two assault divisions that were in essence a separate and unique combat arm. While the *arditi* remained under the command of the Army Corps commander, the stormtroopers battalions in 1918 were placed under the command of the divisional commander to further integrate them into the standard infantry. This reflected the long term view of the Austro-Hungarian High Command whose aspiration, following the German example, was to train the whole infantry to storm tactics. The Italian High Command, on the other hand, perceived the *arditi* as something different from the infantry and although the latter by 1918 was also better equipped and trained it never received the extensive training or reached the degree of specialization of the *arditi*. The *arditi* were meant to substitute the standard infantry in select assault operations, while the *sturmtruppen* were to supplement and increase the combat effectiveness of the infantry. This can be witnessed by the fact that the *arditi* fought better when deployed independently from the infantry, while the stormtroopers had achieved a higher degree of integration with the standard infantry and with the artillery arm. As Knox asserts in reference to the Italians: "Coordination between infantry and supporting arms by 1918 was far inferior to that of the Austro-Hungarians, whose stretched defense depended on it."[13]

Moreover, the stormtroopers simply by belonging to a standard infantry division, they trained extensively with the standard infantry carrying out joint rehearsals or by simply training the standard infantry to the storm tactics. Hence their tactics were more familiar to the infantry and on the battlefield the two entities fought much more harmoniously than the *arditi* and the Italian infantry. Many operations of the *reparti d'assalto* enjoyed great successes throughout 1917 and 1918. However, some failed because the *reparti d'assalto*, armed almost completely with offensive weapons, were often vulnerable to counter-attacks while waiting to be relieved by the heavier equipped and therefore, slower moving infantry units.

The choice and availability of weapons also distinguished the two armies. Although for the most part they fought with similar tactics and weapons there were a few salient

13 MacGregor Knox, *To the Threshold of Power, 1922–33* (Cambridge: Cambridge University Press, 2010), p. 206.

differences between the *arditi* and the stormtroopers. The former used daggers extensively in close combat situations and in 1918 they were equipped with excellent Stokes mortars that could be brought up close to the frontline to cripple enemy defenses. The stormtroopers, on the other hand, rarely used knives or daggers and preferred the use of steel clubs during hand-to-hand combat. They lacked comparable mortars but in turn had excellent, more effective, light and large machine guns than the Italians. In terms of tactical weapon innovation what is also very interesting when looking at the Italian front is the peculiarity of the widespread adoption of the flamethrower by both sides. The Germans can in fact be credited with the creation of the first flamethrower platoons in support of infantry attacks during the war. The German Army took the lead in the introduction and refinement of this weapon, while the Allies remained less enthusiastic about the flamethrower. In contrast, beginning in 1917 the two combatants on the Italian front frequently used flamethrowers during attacks and succeeded in winning battles as a result. The Italians used the French *Schilt* flamethrower to good effect in several *arditi* operations such as the seize of Mount San Gabriele, while the Austro-Hungarians attached flamethrower sections to the stormtrooper units and later constituted a dedicated flamethrower battalion. Austro-Hungarian flamethrower platoons were particularly successful during the last six months of 1917 where the weapon was widely used and proved highly effective in several key battles.

In conclusion what was the impact of these special units upon the final outcome of the war? The stormtroopers were one of the factors, alongside the greater experience of the Austro-Hungarian infantry with fighting in the trenches of the First World War, the strong, high mountain defensive positions and the greater efficiency of its artillery, that gave the Austro-Hungarian Army a tactical edge over the Italians for many months. Although the former were not the determining factor of Caporetto, the stormtroopers played a key role in the advance as well as the capture of key high mountain positions. The second role of the stormtroopers was the revitalization of the Austro-Hungarian infantry after it had fought continuously for over three years and as a result by 1917 was showing significant signs of fatigue. The stormtroopers also enabled the Austro-Hungarian Army to win the majority of trench raiding duels throughout 1917 by capturing more prisoners and weapons.

The *arditi* contributed similarly to their Army. In 1917–18 the Italian High Command deployed the *Reparti d'assalto* to introduce a degree of movement to what had previously been a war of attrition and frontline stasis. At a non-strategic and at a much more localized, tactical level, the *reparti d'assalto* provided the Italian Army with an effective way of breaking the stalemate of trench warfare and gaining some specific territorial conquests. Thirdly, their tactics contributed to bridging the gap with Austro-Hungarian offensive tactics and then in late 1918 in winning the trench duels between opposite raiding parties.

Both the Italians and the Austro-Hungarians adopted innovation by following the lead of greater powers. The Italians where strongly influenced doctrinally and tactically by the French Army, while the Austro-Hungarians followed their more powerful ally, the German Army. The Austro-Hungarians were the first to introduce new tactics on the Italian front, which were the result of the close collaboration that existed between the former and the German High Command and which was the impetus for extensive tactical and weapon knowledge sharing.

During 1916 and 1917 the Austro-Hungarians held the upper hand in terms of tactics and weapons on the Italian front, even though the Italians enjoyed numerical superiority. Already in 1916 the Austrian infantry and mountain units experimented with infiltration tactics during the Asiago Offensive. Then in the spring of 1917 the *sturmtruppen* began conducting counter-attacks by adopting the same tactical procedures of their German counterparts. These consisted mainly in close artillery-infantry coordination, creeping barrages by mortar and artillery batteries of different caliber as well as well timed infantry assaults conducted by specially trained units. The Austrians were also the first army on the Italian front to use flamethrowers and poison gas shells. Their tactics worked well throughout 1917 allowing its army to achieve a few local tactical successes as well as a major breakthrough at Caporetto.

The end of the 1917 campaign during the siege of Monte Grappa signaled the end of the success for the *sturmtruppen*. In 1918 the Italian defensive system changed as the army took the necessary counter measures to confront the special assault units and their storm tactics. Instead of deploying the troops on a forward trench, combat zones and autonomous infantry strongpoints were established. Line infantry was staggered in depth and concentrated with the bulk of its heavy weapons on the second and third line of defense. The combat zone became four miles deep and each defensive line was constituted by wire and other obstacles, bunkers, camouflaged machine gun and hidden mortar emplacements. This fortified zone was also supported by reserve line infantry and by *arditi* units which were summoned for counter-attacks. This meant that during the attack phase of the Solstice Offensive the *sturmtruppen* had to not only take the forward lines but also break through the other three defensive lines in order to win the battle. Despite the large number of available assault companies, they were simply not enough to breakthrough the combat zone. This was one of the causes, why the Solstice Offensive failed. Other factors that contributed to the defeat of the stormtroopers was a more effective deployment of machine guns from the Italians as well as the use of artillery to aggressively shell assault infantry assembly areas from the onset of the battle.

The Austrian artillery also followed the same historical trajectory. After the rebuilding of 1916 the Austro-Hungarians had more heavier weapons than the Italians. The Austrian artillery, in particular, had two areas of strength: it had hundreds of excellent mountain guns and it had several batteries of heavy caliber guns which even the better equipped German ally envied. But like its infantry units, the Austrian artillery ultimately declined this time as a result of weakness in the Habsburg economic system which was not able to keep pace with the needs of its army both in terms of production rates of new weapons and ammunition. Another great weakness of the Austrian Army was its lack of vehicles and armored cars to move the troops and the artillery forward during the battles of Caporetto and Piave. The huge tactical success achieved in both battles could not be further exploited because the artillery and the standard infantry units could not keep pace with the much faster *sturmtruppen* assault units.[14]

Tactical effectiveness is determined by the interaction between the two armies locked in conflict. The stormtrooper tactics were winning in 1917 because they were new, they were innovative and the Italian enemy could not properly confront them. In 1918, however, the situation turned precipitously.

In 1916–17 the Italians initially trailed the Austro-Hungarians both tactically and in terms of firepower, and frequently the Austro-Hungarians would gain the upper hand and negate with swift counter-thrusts what the Italians had conquered after much heavy fighting. However, starting with the Battle of Mount Grappa and then during the Solstice Offensive the Italians deployed better defensive tactics to fight off the enemy's spirited attacks. These new ways of deploying the infantry and artillery defensively and the *arditi* for counter-attacks eventually checked the stormtrooper tactics. This effort was the result of considerable transformation. First, the Italian High Command disseminated the new stormtrooper tactics to lower-level commanders so that they could properly study them and ultimately check them on the battlefield. Second, the defensive network was strengthened and the artillery was utilized to intervene early to break up enemy attacks with counter-battery fire. Third, the infantry was better trained and the new offensive tactics were developed which mirrored the infiltration tactics adopted on the Western front. Fourth, the Army was reorganized with its infantry regiments rebuilt, the artillery and the air forces were expanded and a renewed focus was placed on the formation of new *arditi* units. Then between June and September 1918 the Italians gained the upper hand in the realm of trench raiding where the *reparti d'assalto* were responsible for the majority of the offensive actions that yielded a high number of captured materials and prisoners. The 1918 reformation of the army, the great expansion of the artillery and of the *arditi* battalions laid the groundwork for the final offensive that allowed the Italian Army to win the war. Although, the Italians did not deploy tanks in 1918, its army had incorporated some of the successful tactics adopted by the Allies such as saturation bombing by the air force prior to the commencement of the infantry attack, better-timed infantry assaults especially with regards to the cooperation with the artillery arm. It was this impetus for a renewed offensive maneuver spearheaded by the *arditi* that brought the war to a final conclusion.

14 See Holger H. Herwig, 'The German Victories: 1917–18,' in Hew Strachan (ed.), *The Oxford Illustrated History of the First World War* (Oxford: Oxford University Press, 2011), p. 258.

Appendix

Visiting the Sites of Austrian-Italian Front

Introduction

In the mountains along the Austrian/Italian border the scars of the First World War are still very visible. Trenches, caverns, tunnels, and artillery positions can still be visited today, while conducting breathtaking excursions in the Italian Alps. In certain cases these war relics have been restored and preserved in open-air museums such as on Mount Piana. For those interested in visiting these battlefield sights I outline below a few itineraries/day trips centered in the Sesto Dolomites between the provinces of Bolzano and Belluno.

Few of the thousands of tourists that every day visit the Tre Cime di Lavaredo (Three Peaks of Lavaredo) realizes that they are walking on mountain paths that are surrounded by the remains of the Great War. These remains can be found pretty much all around. The peaks include: Cima Piccola di Lavaredo (Small Peak 2,857 m), Cima Grande di Lavaredo (Big Peak 2,998 m) and Cima Ovest di Lavaredo (West Peak 2,973 m).

The point of departure to reach the Tre Cime is the Rifugio Auronzo (Mountain Lodge Auronzo) located behind the three mountains and easily reachable by bus from Cortina or Dobbiaco. From the mountain lodge after a half-hour of brisk walk one reaches a small church built by the *alpini* and dedicated to Maria Ausiliatrice and the Rifugio Lavaredo (Lodge Lavaredo).

Shortly thereafter after having negotiated a steep mountain pass one reaches Forcella Lavaredo with the three peaks visible on the left. At the base of the Cima Piccola, the shortest of the three located immediately on the left, there are visible remains of Italian fortifications and trenches that can easily be visited and that offer an excellent observation point for the valley and the mountains that face the three peaks. On the middle peak, the Italians had placed into position a very big light that was used to spot enemy patrol units approaching the Tre Cime during the night. Fortifications abound at the base of the mountain.

Mount Paterno is to the right of the Forcella. This mountain was made famous by the incident that occurred in 1915 when the Austrian mountain guide and

Standschützen Sepp Innerkofler fell to his death while climbing its peak at night. The Austrian master climber had almost reached the top:

> Ten steps below the top Innerkofler crosses himself and with a wide arc hurls a grenade over the wall of the summit outpost. He then throws a second and a third. Suddenly, an *Alpini* soldier appears, his face bleeding from the effects of the first grenade. Shouting "So! You won't go away?" [meaning, "I am going to get you."] Standing above the wall, he holds a rock high over his head. He throws it, and Sepp is fatally hit. Raising his arms toward the sky, he falls backward and plummets [50 meters] into a narrow mountain chimney, dead. The Alpino who hurled the rock is Pietro de Luca, an engineer of the Pieve di Cadore Battalion.
>
> Source: http://www.worldwar1.com/itafront/sepp_ink.htm

The Paterno is also famous for its long tunnel built by the Italian troops during the war. The tunnel was used as an observation point, as a dug in machine gun position and as a way to bring up supplies to the troops stationed in the high altitude positions. The entrance is easily reachable from the Forcella Lavaredo at the midway point of the mountain. At the left on the entrance there is an emblem sculptured into the rock which was engraved by the Italian sapper unit that constructed the tunnel in 1915. The tunnel itself can be visited with the aid of a flashlight, helmet and a pickaxe or walking stick. It was restored in the 1970s by the *alpini* of the Cadore battalion and by the Berti Foundation. The walk inside the tunnel lasts approximately 30 minutes and it leads into the right flank of the Paterno in the proximity of the Rifugio Locatelli. While walking through the tunnel one can stop and look out of several machine gun and rifle embrasures for beautiful views of the valley below.

An easier route that does not necessitate the use of special equipment is found at the base of the Paterno. This leads to the Rifugio Locatelli which was built on the site of the old *Dreizinnhutte* that was owned by Sepp Innerkofler, and used as a small lodge to house the tourists that came from Vienna or Venice in the early 1900s.

Mount Paterno and its tunnel dug by the *Alpini* troops during the war. The tunnel was used as an observation point, as a dug-in machine gun position and as a way to bring up supplies to the troops stationed in the high altitude positions. (Belluno Tourist Agency)

A view of Rifugio Locatelli (Locatelli Mountain Lodge) in the 1970s which was built on the site of the old *Dreizinnhutte* that was owned by Sepp Innerkofler, the famous mountain climber and guide. The building was used as a small lodge to house the tourists that came from Vienna or Venice in the early 1900s. (Walther Schaumann)

The mountain hut was destroyed by Italian artillery shells on the first day of the war, but today it is the site of the Rifugio Locatelli, one of the most visited mountain lodges in the Alps. Next to the lodge there is a small church that can also be visited.

From Rifugio Locatelli one can take the path n. 101 that leads to the Rifugio Pian di Cengia after a one hour brisk walk. The site of the lodge was an important artillery position between 1915–17. From the Rifugio one can take a high mountain path that after a 45-minute brisk uphill walk leads to Punta Fiscalina which was not only a key observation point during the war but also an impenetrable machine gun position. All around the peak there are remains of trenches and caverns. Outside of one of these caverns one can still see the chopped wood that the *alpini* had assembled in anticipation of the winter on 1917.

A photo taken in the 1970s from the inside of a cavern dug by the *alpini* during the war and overlooking the Tre Cime di Lavaredo (Three Peaks of Lavaredo). (Ghedina)

Remains of Italian positions at the base of the Three Peaks. (Author's collection)

Italian cavern on Mount Paterno. (Author's collection)

Commemorative plaque remembering Sepp Innerkofler. (Author's collection)

Itinerary 1: Scaling the Austrian stronghold of Toblin Tower

- Starting point: Rifugio Antonio Locatelli (Locatelli Lodge) Mt. 2405
- Arrival Point: Cima della Torre di Toblin (Toblin Tower) Mt. 2617
- Estimated time for the trip: 1.5 hours for the entire journey
- Trail signs marked with red triangles

This excursion requires extensive mountaineering experience with ropes, pickaxe, and helmet. Hiring a mountain guide is highly recommended for those that do not have such experience.

Toblin Tower was held by the Austrians during the First World War and it was one of their key observation and artillery strong points in the Tre Cime di Lavaredo sector. It was a true eagle's nest, allowing the Austrians to control large swathes of territory and to barrage from above enemy positions. The itinerary begins at the Rifugio Locatelli where behind the church a small mountain path leads first to the Sasso di Sesto and then to the base of Toblin Tower. On the Sasso di Sesto there are several caverns and trenches built by the Italians in 1915 that can be observed on the left while walking toward Toblin Tower. Once arrived at the base of the Tower one can observe the remains of Austrian trenches on both sides. By continuing to walk under the western wall of the mountain you will eventually reach the ledge and the first section of steel and wood climbing ladders to scale the mountain. The main path toward the peak must be tackled with the help of the special climbing equipment such as ropes with metallic hooks. The path is fairly easy to follow as there are numerous signs as well as numerous steel ladders and hooks fixed to the rock which help to reach the top. During the climb numerous Austrian positions can be observed. Near the peak there are numerous remains of slit trenches and caverns that had been dug by the Austrians between 1915–17. From the peak one can observe a magnificent panorama of the Three Peaks.

The ascent takes about 45 minutes. The descent and the return to the lodge are via the same path.

Itinerary 2: Locatelli Mountain Lodge/Three Peaks of Lavaredo

- Starting Point: Rifugio Tre Scarperi (Three Peaks Lodge) Mt. 1626
- Arrival Point: Rifugio Antonio Locatelli (Locatelli Lodge) Mt. 2405
- Estimated time: 3.5 / 4.00 hrs.
- Path Trail No. 105 (Part of the High Mountain Way No. 4)

One of the most interesting hiking paths of the Dolomites where one can enjoy beautiful views of the forests, mountain brooks and rivers as well explore numerous First World War positions and strongholds.

The excursion begins at the Rifugio Tre Scarperi (Three Peaks Refuge) in the beautiful and wild Val Campo di Dentro Valley. From the mountain lodge we take the main path no. 105 which leads from the valley up to the Alpe Mattina. After approximately one hour and half of steady walking uphill, we arrive at the Mountain Pass of the Alpe Mattina. Here one can enjoy not only a great view of the Three Peaks of Lavaredo but also explore on the left side of the path a large Austro-Hungarian cavern and several slit trenches. These were used by the soldiers to keep a watchful eye on the Italians on the Three Peaks and on the Sasso di Sesto. As we climb up the beautiful peak of the Scarperi Tower we can turn back and have a clear view of the Pusteria Valley, one of the main logistical hubs of the Austrians during the war.

After having passed the Alpe Mattina we first can see the Toblin Tower on the right (which was held by the Austrians) and then the Sasso di Sesto. On this peak we can observe numerous remains of military positions, such as caverns, slit trenches, deep walkways, barbed wire etc. which were manned by the Italian *alpini* until 1917. After having walked on the Sasso di Sesto with a short descent we arrive at the chapel and then at the nearby Antonio Locatelli Refuge. From this central position we can enjoy one of the most captivating scenery in the Alps such as the beautiful and vertical northern walls of the Three Peaks of Lavaredo and Mount Paterno on the left. In the background you can see Mount Cristallo and its perennial glacier. On the way back to the Val Campo di Dentro Valley one can take the time to explore the Austrian trenches with great detail and that also offer beautiful views of the surrounding mountains.

Austro-Hungarian cavern on Alpe Mattina which during the war was used to house a kitchen and soldiers' dugouts. (Author's collection)

Austrian trenches overlooking the Three Peaks. (Author's collection)

Remains of Austrian trenches overlooking the Three Peaks. (Author's collection)

Itinerary 3: Mount Piana Military Museum

- Starting Point: Misurina
- End Point: Mount Piana, 2400 meters
- Estimated time: 2.5 / 3.00 hrs.
- Path Trail No. 122

Monte Piana was a key defensive stronghold for both the Austrian-Hungarians and the Italians during the Great War. Due to its extensive fortifications the Friends of the Dolomites association along with the *alpini* of the *Bassano* battalion decided in the 1980s to turn it into an open-air war museum.

The peak of the mountain can be reached in two ways. First, one can take a shuttle jeep for approximately 10 Euro from the Ristorante Grazianella near the town of Misurina and reach the peak in less than 10 minutes.

Second, one can hike for approximately 90 minutes on a broad and smooth road which had originally been built by the *alpini* during the war to bring up supplies.

This second option is highly recommended since the hike is not particularly difficult and it allows the visitor to travel through a dense forest bypassing along the way a brook and an alpine pasture with cows with their characteristic mountain bells.

Once on the southern peak of Monte Piana the point of departure is Rifugio Bosi, named after Major Angelo Bosi who fell on Mount Piana. The lodge was built on the same site where the Italian troops were based during the war. Nowadays the Rifugio has a small museum with several interesting artifacts from the war and a small Austrian mountain cannon.

From the Piana we can begin to walk north toward the old front line where both Italian *Arditi* and Austro-Hungarian stormtroopers dueled to the death in October of 1917. The southern side of the mountain has many Italian trenches, caverns and strong points each of which has been excavated, numbered and identified by tables that detail their historical significance. The highlights include the assault company headquarters, the compressed air mortar position, the sentry observatory position and the strong point that once hosted the Bettica grenade launchers. Having visited the southern side of the mountain we can head to the northern peak, the Mount Piano, which was held by the Austrians. The highlights here include the tunnel of the *Kaiserjägers*, which is located on a reverse slope and various artillery and machine gun positions. On a ledge under the Austrian position one can also visit the Guardia Napoleone position, a tunnel built by the Italians to take by surprise their enemy.

Mount Piana should be visited on a clear sunny day since when it rains the mountain is usually submerged by a dense fog which can significantly impair visibility. The last thing one wants to do is fall into a crevice or lose their way and sense of direction while on the mountain top.

Once having headed back to Rifugio Bosi the return trip can be made by walking back to Misurina or by taking the shuttle.

Remains of trenches and observation posts on Mount Piana. (Author's collection)

First World War Commemorative Cross on Mount Piana remembering those who died in the conflict. (Author's collection)

Austrian mountain gun on Mount Piana (Author's collection)

Commemorative monument to the memory of *ardito* Lieutenant Ruggero de Simoni, Gold medal awardee, while fighting on Mount Piana in October 1917. (Author's collection)

Italian cavern and concrete position on the Punta Fiscalina.

Austrian concrete fortifications on Mount Piana. (Author's collection)

Austrian machine gun embrasures on Mount Piana. (Author's collection)

Austrian concrete pillbox on Mount Piana. (Author's collection)

Commemorative First World War monument, Innsbruck. (Author's collection)

Austrian light grenade launcher, Innsbruck museum. (Author's collection)

Painting of decorated WWI Austro-Hungarian veteran Innsbruck museum. (Author's collection)

Austro-Hungarian High Mountain stormtrooper Innsbruck museum. (Author's collection)

Below is a list of highly recommended museums:

Military Museum of the Austro-Hungarian Mountain Troops in Innsbruck: http://www.tiroler-landesmuseen.at/page.cfm?vpath=haeuser/das-tirol-panorama-mit-kjm-/haus
National Museum of the *Alpini* in Trento: http://www.museonazionale*alpini*.it/
Marmolada Glacier Museum of the Great War: http://www.museomarmoladagrandeguerra.com/en/
Great War Museum Cortina: https://www.cortinamuseoguerra.it/index.php/en
Lagazuoi Museum: http://lagazuoi5torri.dolomiti.org/dengl/Cortina/laga5torri/musei/index.html
Sasso di Stria Museum: http://lagazuoi5torri.dolomiti.org/dengl/Cortina/laga5torri/musei/sassostria.html
White War Museum: http://www.museoguerrabianca.it/

Bibliography

Austrian Archive Sources

Austrian State Archives, Kriegsarchiv, Vienna.

Kriegsarchiv: K.u.K. 12. FABrigade Kommando, Op. Nr. 26/833, 7 July 1916.

Kriegsarchiv: K.u.K. AOK, Op. Nr. 30662, 25 September 1916.

Kriegsarchiv: K.u.K. AOK, Op. Nr. 34435, 24 November 1916.

Kriegsarchiv: K.u.K. AOK, Op. Nr. 36/300, '*Anleitung für die Ausbildung der Sturmtruppen*', 2 December 1916.

Kriegsarchiv: 26. Gebrige Brigade, Op. Nr. 217/5, '*Direktiven fur den uberfallsartigen angriff durch Sturmpatrouillen*', 12 June 1917.

Kriegsarchiv: K.u.K. Abschnittskommando Karnischer Kamm Nr. 239, '*Wahrnehumgen uber der gagner*', 28 January 1917.

Kriegsarchiv: K.u.K. AOK Op. Nr. 29/021, 12 October 1917.

Kriegsarchiv: K.u.K. 11. Armee oberKommando, Op. Nr. 3678, 11 January 1918.

Kriegsarchiv: K.u.K. 73. Infanterie Regiment, Op. Nr. 643, 16 February, 1917.

Kriegsarchiv: K.u.K. 11. Armee Kommando Op. Nr. 669, 24 February 1917.

Kriegsarchiv: AOK Op. Nr. 34/61, K.u.K. Abschnittskommando 27. Infanterie Regiment, 'Überfall der Sturmpatrouillen', 17 March 1917.

Kriegsarchiv: K.u.K. 11. Armee Kommando, Op. Nr. 317/67, 'Hochjalpine Sturmhalbkompagnie', 4 June 1917.

Kriegsarchiv: K.u.K. 11. Armee Kommando, Op. Nr. 1456, 22 May 1917.

Kriegsarchiv: K.u.K. 5. Armee Kommando, Op. Nr. 2454/30, 24 April 1917.

Kriegsarchiv: K.u.K. Abschnittskommando III, 'Tatigkeit der *Sturmkompagnie*n vom 28. 5', Op. Nr. 24/50, 6 May 1917.

Kriegsarchiv: K.u.K., 5. Armee Kommando, Op. Nr. 24/52, June 10, 1917.

Kriegsarchiv: K.u.K. 11. Armee Kommando, Op. Nr. 256/2345, 30 June, 1917.

Kriegsarchiv: Franz Conrad von Hoetzendorf, 'Juni-Schlacht auf der Hochflache der Sieben Gemeinden', 29 June 1917.

Kriegsarchiv: K.u.K. 21. Gebirge Brigade Kommando Op. Nr. 526, 18 August 1917.

Kriegsarchiv: K.u.K. Sturmabteilung d. 21. Gebirge Brigade Kommando 'Malga di Londo', 20 August 1917.

Kriegsarchiv: K.u.K. 11. Amree Kommando, Op. Nr. 2046, 'Eingehende Vorbereitung von *sturmtruppen*-unternehmungen', 6 October 1917.

Kriegsarchiv: K.u.K. XX Korps Kommando, Op. Nr. 3904/24, '*Sturmtruppen* für Monte Piana', 5 October, 1917.

Kriegsarchiv: K.u.K. Rayons Kommando V, Op. Nr. 1504/11, 10 October, 1917.
Kriegsarchiv: K.u.K. 56. Gebirge Brigade Kommando, Op. Nr. 367/90, 18 October, 1917.
Kriegsarchiv: K.u.K. 49. InfDionskmdo, Op. Nr. 1600/16, 'Monte Piana/ Unternehmen', 24 October 1917.
Kriegsarchiv: K.u.K. 38. Infanterie Brigade Kommando, Op. Nr. 521, 1 November 1917.
Kriegsarchiv: K.u.K. 11. Armee Kommando, Op. Nr. 321/3435, 21 December 1917.
Kriegsarchiv: K.u.K. AOK, Op. Nr. 42/363, 11 January 1918.
Kriegsarchiv: Anton Pitreich, 'Piave-front', unpublished manuscript.
Kriegsarchiv, K.u.K. 27. Infanterie Kommando, Op. Nr. 3416/92, 19 June, 1918.
Kriegsarchiv: AOK, MKSN 69–6–14, 'Junischlacht in Venetien', 14 July 1918.
Kriegsarchiv: K.u.K. AOK, Op. Nr. 2046/10, 'Neuorganisation der *Sturmtruppen*', 17 October 1917

Italian archive sources

Ufficio Storico dello Stato Maggiore dell'esercito, Rome.
Diario Storico della 3. Armata, vol. 1 (Padova: Museo storico 3. Armata, 1915).
Ufficio Storico, Comando Supremo: Ufficio Operazioni, Ufficio Affari Vari e Segreteria 'I nostri metodi di attacco nel giudizio degli ufficiali dell'esercito nemico', n. 14250, Relazione del 31 Luglio 1916.
Ufficio Storico: Comando Supremo, Ufficio Operazioni, 'Impressioni di un ufficiale austriaco sull'azione delle truppe italiane,' n. 1973, Relazione del 25 Luglio, 1915.
Ufficio Storico, Raccolta F.1–13: Diari Storici.
Ufficio Storico, Carteggio Divisioni di Fanteria, BA 9196–91917: 'Relazione del Ten. Gen. Ruggeri sulla sorpresa nemica in regione Bocche', 30 April 1917.
Ufficio Storico: Riassunti storici dei corpi e comandi nella guerra 1915–1918: Val Tanaro.
Ufficio Storico: Riassunti storici dei corpi e comandi nella guerra 1915–1918 Brigate di Fanteria (Rome: AUSSME, 1927).
Ufficio Storico, E1, Raccolta 17: XXIX Corpo d'Armata, n. 9655, 22 May 1917.
Ufficio Storico, *L'esercito Italiano nella grande guerra, vol. 4* (Rome: Ufficio Storico, 1954).
Ufficio Storico: E-1, Raccolta 17, Comando 1. Armata, 'Contegno delle truppe', n. 49917, 4 September 1917.
Ufficio Storico, Raccolta F. 11, b. 12: Reparti d'assalto, n. 4799.
Ufficio Storico, E-1, raccolta 17: Relazione del Comando Supremo, 'Difesa della regione Melette', 14 December 1917, n. 74192.
Ufficio Storico: 'Cenni descrittivi di alcuni apparecchi lanciafiamme germanici', Comando supremo Ufficio Tecnico.
Ufficio Storico, Raccolta E5–34: Comando 17. Divisione, Generale Leoncini, 'Relazione sulle operazioni svolte dalla 17. Divisione di fanteria nei giorni 15–16–17 giugno 1918', 28 June, 1918.

Ufficio Storico, Rep. E-2, Racc. 88 1. Armata: Comando V Corpo d'armata, 'Fatto d'arme del 30 Agosto 1918 su M. Majo', n. 7143, 5 September 1918.
Ufficio Storico, Rep. E-2, Racc. 88 1. Armata: Comando V Corpo d'armata, 'Fatto d'arme del 30 Agosto 1918 su M. Majo', n. 7143, 5 September 1918.
Ufficio Storico: Promemoria del Reparto Operazioni del Comando Supremo alla segreteria del capo di stato maggiore dell'esercito, 'Reparti d'assalto nell'esercito Austro-ungarico', 23 January 1917.
Ufficio Storico: Promemoria di servizio n.9 del Centro Informazioni del comando XX corpo d'armata, 'Corso d'istruzione per truppe d'assalto (da due prigionieri austriaci del 73. reggimento di fanteria', 23 February 1917.
Ufficio Storico, Circolare n. 3024: Comando Supremo, Ufficio Segreteria del Capo di Stato Maggiore, 'Ammaestramenti tattici', 9 July 1917.
Ufficio Storico, Raccolta E-5,17, IV Corpo d'Armata: Comando 11. Divisione Fanteria, 'Squadre per operazioni offensive e per ricognizioni ardite', n. 6367, 17 May 1916.
Ufficio Storico, Rep. B-1, Raccolta 137D, 1407d: Comando Brigata Lambro, 'Constituzione nuclei speciali nella Brigata', n. 1277, 7 March 1917, Diario storico 206 Reggimento Fanteria, 1–15 March 1917.
Ufficio Storico: Comando 48. Divisione, Ufficio Stato Maggiore, "Memoria del capitano Bassi Sig. Giuseppe sulle pistole mitragliatrici", n. 1949, op. 6 April, 1917.
Ufficio Storico, IX Reparto d'Assalto: 'Istruzione dei reparti d'assalto', 14 October 1918.
Ufficio Storico, Rep. E-1, Raccolta 113: Comando 2. Armata, 'Impiego dei reparti d'assalto', n. 5229, 21 September 1917.
Ufficio Storico, Comando Supremo, Ufficio Segreteria: 'Metodi tattici del nemico', n. 25, 23 June 1918.
Francesco Saverio Grazioli, 'Riserva Mobile Strategica', in Relazione Ufficiale, vol. 5, tomo 2 bis (Rome: Ufficio Storico, 1989), pp. 491–513.
Ufficio Storico, 2. Armata: I Reparto d'Assalto, Rapporto del comandandante della I Compagnia Primeglio Radicati, 'Rapporto sull'azione del Monte Fratta', 23 August 1917.
Ufficio Storico, Rep. E-1, Raccolta 79: Comando 2. Armata, Comunicazione urgente, n.5293 op., 23 September 1917.
Ufficio Storico, Rep. F-4, Raccolta 199: Comando 1. Armata, telegramma n. 35946, 12 May 1918.
Ufficio Storico, Rep. E-5, Raccolta 110, XX Corpo d'Armata: Comando Brigata Sassari, 'Ordine di operazione, n. 247', R.P. 22 January 1918.
Ufficio Storico: Comando della 33. Divisione di Fanteria, 'Relazione sulle operazioni per la riconquista dei Tre Monti', 2 February 1918.
Ufficio Storico, Rep. B-1, Raccolta 114S, 251E, V Corpo d'Armata: Comando Brigata Murge, 'Azione offensive su Monte Corno e quota 1,801', n. 439, 8 May 1918.
Ufficio Storico, Rep. B-1, Raccolta 13D Brigata Murge: Comando Brigata Murge, 'Relazione riassuntiva dei fatti d'arme e dei lavori eseguiti sul Corno Battisti', 31 May 1918.

Ufficio Storico, Rep. E-5, Raccolta 31: Comando 3. Armata, 'Reparti d'assalto', n. 32755, 28 September 1917.

Ufficio Storico, Rep. E-1, Raccolta 92: 6. Armata, 'Cima Echar', n. 877, 17 June 1918.

Ufficio Storico, Rep. F.4, Raccolta 199: Comando 6. Armata, 'Costituzione *reparto* d'assalto alpino', n. 22411, 1 May 1918.

Ufficio Storico, Cartella B-4, 3020 bis: XXX Reparto d'Assalto, Maggiore Luigi Marotta, 'Relazione sull'impiego del battaglione nei giorni 1–20 giugno 1918', 23 June 1918.

Ufficio Storico, Comando XXIX Reparto d'assalto, Rep E-5, Raccolta 210: 'Relazione su ricognizione eseguita in regione Dosso Alto', n. 546, 27 July 1918.

Ufficio Storico, Comando VI Reparto d'Assalto, 'Rapporto del comandante Ettore Viola', 28 September 1918.

Ufficio Storico, IX Reparto d'assalto: 'Relazione sull'azione spiegata dal IX Reparto d'assalto nel combattimento di Monte Asolone il 29 Ottobre 1918.'

Books and journal articles

Enrico Acerbi, *Strafexpedition* (Valdagno: Edizioni Rossato, 2003).

Robert Asprey, *The German High Command at War: Hindenburg and Ludendorff and the First World War* (New York: W. Morrow, 1991).

Antonio Berti, *Guerra in Ampezzo e Cadore* (Milan: Mursia Editore, 1985).

Autori Vari, *Dizionario delle battaglie* (Milan: Gulliver Libri, 1996).

Stephen Biddle, *Military Power: Explaining Victory and Defeat in Modern Battle* (Princeton: Princeton University Press, 2004).

Adone Bettega, *Grande Guerra in Val di Fiemme, Fassa e Biois: Cima Bocche, Passo San Pellegrino, Passo Valles, Pale di San Martino, Passo Rolle, Val Travignolo* (Valdagno: Rossato Editore, 2010).

Stephen Bull, *British Infantryman Versus German Infantryman* (Oxford: Osprey, 2014).

Alberto Businelli, *Gli arditi del IX* (Milan: Libreria Militare, 2007).

Filippo Cappellano, *L'artiglieria austro-ungarica nella grande guerra* (Novale: Rossato, 2001).

Filippo Cappellano and di Martino Basilio, *I reparti d'assalto italiani nella grande guerra (1915–1918)* (Rome: Ufficio Storico, 2007).

Filippo Cappellano and Basilio Di Martino, *Un esercito forgiato nelle trincee* (Udine: Gasperi Editore, 2008).

Filippo Cappellano and Marco Montagnani, *L' inferno nelle trincee. I lanciafiamme italiani nella grande Guerra* (Udine: Gaspari, 2015).

Filippo Cappellano, 'Italian Artillery during the First World War', in Sanders Marble (ed.), *King of Battle: Artillery in World War One* (Boston: Brill, 2016).

Franz Conrad, *Gefechtsausbildung der Infanterie* (Vienna: L.W. Seidel and Sons, 1900).

Robert Crowley (ed.), *The Great War* (New York: Random House, 2003).

C.R.M.F. Cruttwell, *A History of the Great War, 1914–18* (Oxford: Oxford University Press, 1936).

Die Minenwerfer, *Abschnitte aus der Gefechtslehre* (Vienna: Teil VII, 1918).

Basilio di Martino, *Trincee, reticolati, e colpi di mano* (Valdagno: Rossato, 2000).

Robert A. Doughty, *Pyrrhic Victory: French Strategy and Operations in the Great War* (Harvard: Harvard University Press, 2008).

Timothy C. Dowling, *The Brusilov Offensive* (Bloomington: Indiana University Press, 2008.

Exerzierreglement fur die K.U.K. Fubtruppen (Vienna: Seidel and Sons, 1911).

Salvatore Farina, *Le truppe d'assalto italiane* (Milan: Libreria Militare, 2007).

Theo Farrell, 'Improving in War', *Journal of Strategic Studies*, n.33, vol.4, 2010, pp. 567–594.

Francesco Fattuta, 'Contributo ad una storia delle truppe d'assalto', in *Studi Storico-Militari* (Rome: Ufficio Storico, 2002).

Peter Fiala, *Die letzte Offensive Altösterreichs. Führungsprobleme und Führerverantwortlichkeit bei der öst.-ung. Offensive in Venetien, Juni 1918* (Boppard a. Rh.: Boldt, 1967).

Robert Thomas Foley, 'A Case Study in Horizontal Military Innovation: The German Army, 1916–1918', *Journal of Strategic Studies*, vol. 35, n.6, 2012, pp. 1–29.

B.H. Liddell Hart, *History of the First World War* (London: Pan Books, 1972).

B.H. Liddell Hart, *The Real War* (Boston: Little, Brown and Company, 1930).

Peter Hart, *The Great War: A Combat History of the First World War* (Oxford: Oxford University Press, 2013).

Maximillian von Hoen, *Geschichte des Salzburgisch-oberösterreichischen K.u.k. Infanterie-Regiments Erzherzog Rainer Nr. 59 für den Zeitraum des Weltkrieges 1914–1918* (Salzburg: Rainerbund, 1931).

Holger H. Herwig, *The First World War: Germany and Austria-Hungary 1914–1918* (London: Arnold, 1997).

Otto Gallian, *Monte Asolone 1918* (Graz: Leykam, 1933).

Otto Gallian, 'Ufgaben des *Sturmtruppen*fuhers', *Militar*, n. 21, June 1921, p. 33.

Paolo Giudici, *Reparti d'assalto* (Milan: Alpes, 1928).

Edmund Glaise-Horstenau (ed.), *Österreich-Ungarns letzter Krieg 1914–1918* (Vienna: Verlag der Militärwissenschaftlichen Mitteilungen, 1936), Vol. 1 through 7.

John Gooch, *Army, State and Society in Italy, 1870–1915* (New York: St. Martin's Press, 1989).

John Gooch, 'Italy During the First World War', in Allen Millett and Williamson Murray (eds.), Military Effectiveness Volume I: First World War (Boston: Unwin Hyman Inc., 1988), pp. 171–192.

John Gooch, *The Italian Army and the First World War* (Cambridge: Cambridge University Press, 2014).

Paddy Griffith, *Battle Tactics of the Western Front: The British, Army's Art of Attack 1916–18* (New Haven: Yale University Press, 1996).

William R. Griffiths, *The Great War: Strategies and Tactics of the First World War* (Garden City Park, Square One Publishers, 2003).

Helmuth Gruss, *Die deutschen Sturmbataillone im Weltkrieg* (Berlin: Aufbrau und Verwendung, 1939).

Bruce I. Gudmundsson, *Stormtroop Tactics: Innovation in the German Army, 1914–1918* (New York: Praeger, 1998).

Irene Guerrini and Marco Pluviano, *Le fucilazioni sommarie della prima guerra mondiale* (Udine: LEG, 2004).

Peter Jung, *The Austro-Hungarian Forces in World War I (1): 1914–16* (Oxford: Osprey, 2003).

Peter Jung, *The Austro-Hungarian Forces in World War I (2): 1916–18* (Oxford: Osprey, 2003).

Ernst Jünger, *Storm of Steel* (New York: Penguin, 2014).

Alfred Krauss, *Die Ursachen unserer Niederlage; Erinnerungen und Urteile aus dem Weltkrieg* (Munich: J.F. Lehmann, 1920).

Heinz von Lichem, *La Guerra in Montagna, Vol. 2* (Bolzano: Athesia, 2007).

Ludovico Lommi, *Da Bersagliere ad ardito* (Bassano del Grappa: Itinera Progetti, 2003).

Erich Ludendorff, *Ludendorff's own story, Vol. 2* (New York: Harpers and Brothers, 1919).

Timothy Lupfer, 'The Dynamics of Doctrine: The Changes in German Tactical Doctrine During the First World War', *Leavenworth Papers*, 1981.

Cesare Manzoni and Alessandro Ricagno, *Evoluzione Organica dell'Esercito Italiano prima e durante la grande guerra* (Turin: Einaudi, 1920).

Vittorio Martinelli, *Corno di Cavento* (Pinzolo: Povinelli, 2000).

Alessandro Massignani, *Le truppe d'assalto austro-ungariche nella grande guerra* (Valdagno: Rossato Editore, 1996).

Chris McNabb, *The Flamethrower* (Oxford: Osprey, 2015).

Militargeschichtliches Forschungsamt, *Handbuch zur deutschen Militargeschichte 1648–1939, vol. 3* (Munich: Bernard & Graefe, 1979).

Allen Millett and Williamson Murray (eds.) *Military Effectiveness Volume I First World War* (Boston: Unwin Hyman Inc., 1988).

Christoph Neumayer, and Erwin A. Schmidl (eds.), *Des Kaisers Bosniaken. Die bosnisch-herzegowinischen Truppen in der K.u.K. Armee* (Vienna: Verlag, 2008).

David Nicolle, *The Italian Army of World War I* (Oxford: Osprey, 2003).

Christian Ortner, Stefan Rest (eds.), *Sturmtruppen. Österreichisch-ungarische Sturmformationen und Jagdkommandos im Ersten Weltkrieg* (Vienna: Verlag Militaria, 2005).

Christian Ortner, *Die Österreichisch-ungariche Artillerie von 1867–1918* (Vienna: Verlag Militaria, 2007).

Christian Ortner, *Storm Troops* (Vienna: Verlag Militaria, 2014).

Christian Ortner, *The Austro-Hungarian Artillery from 1867 to 1918: Technology, Organization and Tactics* (Vienna: Verlag Militaria, 2007).

Leopold Othmar, *Das III Baon (I.R.74) an der Dolomitenfront auf Bocche-Lusia, Riesengebirgler im Weltkrieg* (Vienna: Reichenberg, 1935).

William Philpott, *Three Armies on the Somme: The First Battle of the Twentieth Century* (New York: Random House, 2009).

Gianni Pieropan, *Storia della grande guerra, 1915–18* (Milan: Mursia, 2004).

Angelo Pirocchi, *Italian Arditi: Elite Assault Troops, 1917–20* (Oxford: Osprey, 2007).

Maggiorino Radicati, *I Reparti d'assalto nella guerra 1915–18* (Turin: Sezione *Bersaglieri* A. Lamarmora, 1957).

Manfried Rauchensteiner, *Der Tod des Doppeladlers: Österreich-Ungarn und der Erste Weltkrieg* (Graz: Styria Verlag, 1993).

Manfried Rauchensteiner, *The First World War and the End of the Habsburg Monarchy, 1914–1918* (Vienna: Boehlau Verlag GmbH & Co., 2014).

Eugen Redl, *La battaglia del Monte Ragogna* (Udine: Gaspari Editore, 2006).

Giorgio Rochat, *Gli arditi della grande guerra* (Udine: LEG, 1990).

Giorgio Rochat, 'The Italian Front', in John Horne (ed.), *A Companion to World War I* (New York: Wiley & Sons, 2012), pp. 82–97.

Erwin Rommel, *Infantry Attacks* (London: Greenhill Books, 2006).

Ermes Rosa, *Arditi sul grappa* (Bassano del Grappa: Itinera Progetti, 2003).

Gunther E. Rothenberg, *The Army of Francis Joseph* (West Lafayette: Purdue University Press, 1998).

Pompilio Schiarini, *L'armata del Trentino* (Milan: Mondadori, 1925).

Walther Schaumann, 'Der österreichische Gegennagriff auf die Punta San Matteo (3692 m ü. m.) am 3 September 1918', Allgemeine Schweizerische Militärzeitschrift, n. 10, 1968, pp. 576–589.

Walther Schaumann & Peter Schubert, *Isonzo, 1915–1917: Krieg ohne Wiederkehr* (Bassano del Grappa: Ghedina & Tassotti, 1993).

John Richard Schindler, *A Hopeless Struggle: The Austro-Hungarian Army and Total War 1914–18*, Unpublished Thesis, McMaster University, 1995.

John R. Schindler, 'Austria-Hungary in the First World War', in Sanders Marble (ed.), *King of Battle Artillery in World War I* (Boston: Brill, 2016).

John R. Schindler, *Isonzo: The Forgotten Sacrifice of the Great War* (Westport: Greenwood Press, 2001).

Viktor Schemfil, *Das K.u.K. 3. Regiment der Tiroler Kaiserjäger im Weltkritg 1914–1918* (Bregenz: J.N. Teutsch, 1926).

Viktor Schemfil, *Die Pasubio-Kämpfe 1916–1918: Das Ringen um den Eckpfeiler der Tiroler Front* (Bregenz: Z.A. Teutsch, 1937).

Viktor Schemfil, *Die Kämpfe am Monte Piana und im Cristallo-Gebiet. Südtiroler Dolomiten: 1915–1917* (Innsbruck: Universitätsverlag Wagner, 1984).

Mario Silvestri, *Isonzo, 1917* (Milan: RCS Libri, 2001).

Robert Skorpil, *Pasubio* (Bolzano: Athesia, 1974).

Adolf Sloninka von Holodow, *Die Kampfe um die Ortigara-Lepozze Stellung im Juni 1917* (Hall: Verlag Der Kaiserschützen Regimenter, 1927).

Lawrence Sondhaus, *Franz Conrad Von Hötzendorf: Architect of the Apocalypse* (Boston: Humanities Press, 2000).

Hew Strachan (ed.), *The Oxford Illustrated History of the First World War* (Oxford: Oxford University Press, 2011).

Hans Strohschneider, *Das Schutzenregiment Graz Nr. 3 und der steirische Landsturm im Weltkrieg 1914–18* (Graz: Verlag, 1932).

Roberto Tessari, *Il Montello nella grande guerra* (Udine: Gaspari Editore, 2004), p. 34.

Charles Theune, *Flammenwerfer und Sturmtruppen* (Berlin: Landes Verlag, 1921).

Mark Thompson, *The White War: Life and Death on the Italian Front, 1915–18* (New York: Basic Books, 2008).

Spencer C. Tucker, *The European Powers in the First World War: An Encyclopedia* (London: Taylor & Francis, 1999).

Pasi Tuunnainen, *Finnish Military Effectiveness in the Winter War, 1939–1940* (London: Palgrave Macmillan UK, 2016).

Ufficio Storico, *L'Esercito Italiano nella Grande Guerra 1915–18: Le Operazioni del 1918, vol. 4, tomo 1* (Rome: Ufficio Storico, 1988).

Ufficio Storico, *L'Esercito Italiano nella Grande Guerra 1915–18: Le Operazioni del 1918, vol. 5, tomo 1* (Rome: Ufficio Storico, 1988).

Ufficio Storico, Emilio Battisti, *La Guerra sul ghiacciaio: Parte 2* (Rome: Ufficio Storico, 1933).

Ufficio Storico, *Le Istruzioni tattiche del capo di stato maggiore dell'esercito negli anni 1917–18* (Rome: Ufficio Storico, 1980).

Ernst von Verdross, 'Kriegserlebnisse eines Österreichischen Sturmzugskommandanten', *Schwizerische Monatschrift für Offiziere aller Waffen*, 1929, pp. 51–76.

Luciano Viazzi, *Guerra d'aquile* (Milan: Mursia, 1996).

Fritz Weber, *Tappe della disfatta* (Milan: Mursia, 1977).

Hermann Wendt, *Verdun 1916* (Berlin: E.S. Mittler & Sohn, 1941).

Wanda Wilcox, 'Training, Morale and Battlefield Performance in the Italian Army, 1914–1917', in Jonathan Krause (ed.), *The Greater War* (London: Palgrave, 2002).

Ernst Wisshaupt, *Die Tiroler Kaiserjäger im Weltkriege 1914–1918: vol. 2* (Vienna: Simon Franz Goth, 1936).

David T. Zabecki (ed.), *Germany at War: 400 Years of Military History* (Santa Barbara: ABC-CLIO, 2014).

Ottavio Zoppi, *Due Volte con gli Arditi sul Piave* (Bologna: Zanichelli, 1938).

Internet

Filippo Cappellano, 'Warfare Italy 1915–18', can be found at: http://encyclopedia.1914-1918-online.net/article/warfare_1914-1918_italy. <accessed 6 June 2015>

http://www.frontedolomitico.it/Uomini/protagonisti/DeSimoneRuggero.html <accessed June 25, 2016>

www.austro-hungarian-army.co.uk<Accessed 7 October 2016>

http://news.bbc.co.uk/2/hi/europe/3592268.stm <Accessed 25 August 2016>

Index

INDEX OF PEOPLE

INDEX OF PLACES

INDEX OF MILITARY UNITS & FORMATIONS

INDEX OF WEAPONRY & EQUIPMENT:

INDEX OF GENERAL & MISCELLANEOUS TERMS